Mutual Intercultural Relations

D1525574

In culturally diverse societies, one of the biggest questions on our minds is 'how shall we all live together?' *Mutual Intercultural Relations* offers an answer to this fundamental and topical issue. By exploring intercultural relationships between dominant/national and non-dominant/ethnic populations in seventeen societies around the world, the authors are each able to chart the respective views of those populations and to generate 'general' principles of intercultural relations. The research reported in this book is guided by three psychological hypotheses which are evaluated by empirical research: multiculturalism, contact and integration. It was also carried out comparatively in order to gain knowledge about intercultural relations that may be general and not limited to a few social and political contexts. Understanding these general principles will help in the development of public policies and programmes designed to improve the quality of intercultural relations in culturally diverse societies around the world.

John W. Berry is an emeritus professor at Queen's University and a chief research fellow at the National Research University Higher School of Economics in Moscow. He has received honorary doctorates from the University of Athens, and the University of Geneva and has published over thirty books in the areas of cross-cultural and intercultural psychology with various colleagues. He is a fellow of the Canadian Psychological Association, the Netherlands Institute for Advanced Study, the International Association for Cross-Cultural Psychology and the International Academy for Intercultural Research. His main research interests are in the role of culture in human development and in acculturation and intercultural relations, with an emphasis on applications to immigration, multiculturalism, educational and health policy.

Culture and Psychology

Series Editor
David Matsumoto, *San Francisco State University*

As an increasing number of social scientists come to recognize the pervasive influence of culture on individual human behaviour, it has become imperative for culture to be included as an important variable in all aspects of psychological research, theory and practice. Culture and Psychology is an evolving series of works that brings the study of culture and psychology into a single, unified concept. The series includes:

Mutual Intercultural Relations

Edited by

John W. Berry

*Queen's University, Canada, and National Research
University Higher School of Economics,
Russian Federation*

CAMBRIDGE
UNIVERSITY PRESS

University Printing House, Cambridge CB2 8BS, United Kingdom

One Liberty Plaza, 20th Floor, New York, NY 10006, USA

477 Williamstown Road, Port Melbourne, VIC 3207, Australia

314-321, 3rd Floor, Plot 3, Splendor Forum, Jasola District Centre, New Delhi - 110025, India

79 Anson Road, #06-04/06, Singapore 079906

Cambridge University Press is part of the University of Cambridge.

It furthers the University's mission by disseminating knowledge in the pursuit of
education, learning and research at the highest international levels of excellence.

www.cambridge.org
Information on this title: www.cambridge.org/9781316635230
DOI: 10.1017/9781316875032

First published 2017
First paperback edition 2019

A catalogue record for this publication is available from the British Library

ISBN 978-1-107-18395-7 Hardback
ISBN 978-1-316-63523-0 Paperback

Contents

Figures

Tables

Contributors

ANNIS, R.C., Brandon University, Canada.

AU, A.K.Y., Hong Kong Polytechnic University, Hong Kong.

BANO, S., Banaras Hindu University, Varanasi, India.

BERRY, J.W., Queen's University, Canada, and National Research University Higher School of Economics, Russian Federation.

BOEHNKE, K., Jacobs University Bremen, Germany, and National Research University Higher School of Economics, Russian Federation.

BRYLKA, A., University of Northampton, UK.

BUHOLZER, A., University of Teacher Education, Lucerne, Switzerland.

CHEN, S.X., Hong Kong Polytechnic University, Hong Kong.

DANDY, J., Edith Cowan University, Australia.

DUNN, K., Western Sydney University, Australia.

EGMOND, MARIEKE VAN, University of Hagen, Germany.

GALYAPINA, V., National Research University Higher School of Economics, Russian Federation.

GIBSON, R., University of Guelph, Canada.

GRAD, H., Universidad Autonoma de Madrid, Spain.

GUI, Y., Henan University of Economics and Law, China.

HAENNI HOTI, A., University of Teacher Education, Lucerne, Switzerland.

HANKE, K., GESIS-Leibniz Institute for the Social Sciences, and Jacobs University Bremen, Germany.

HEINZMANN, S., University of Teacher Education, St. Gallen, Switzerland.

HUI, B.P.H., University of Cambridge, UK.

INGUGLIA, C., Università degli Studi di Palermo, Italy.

JASINSKAJA-LAHTI, I., University of Helsinki, Finland.

JETTEN, J., University of Queensland, Australia.

KRUUSVALL, J., Tallinn University, Estonia.

KÜNZLE, R., University of Teacher Education, Lucerne, Switzerland.

KUS-HARBORD, L., Tallinn University, Estonia.

LAURI, M.A., University of Malta, Malta.

LEBEDEVA, N., National Research University Higher School of Economics, Russian Federation.

LEPSHOKOVA, Z., National Research University Higher School of Economics, Russian Federation.

LO COCO, A., Università degli Studi di Palermo, Italy.

MAKAROVA, M., Tallinn University, Estonia.

MISHRA, R.C., Banaras Hindu University, Varanasi, India.

MOTTI-STEFANIDI, F., National and Kapodistrian University of Athens, Greece.

MÜLLER, M., University of Teacher Education, Lucerne, Switzerland.

MUSSO, P., Università degli Studi di Palermo, Italy.

NETO, F., Universidade do Porto, Portugal.

NETO, J., Universidade do Porto, Portugal.

PARADIES, Y., Deakin University, Australia.

PAVLOPOULOS, V., National and Kapodistrian University of Athens, Greece.

RAUDSEPP, M., Tallinn University, Estonia.

RENVIK, T.A., University of Helsinki, Finland.

ROBINSON, L., Central Queensland University, Australia.

ROHMANN, A., University of Hagen, Germany.

RYABICHENKO, T., National Research University Higher School of Economics, Russian Federation.

SAFDAR, S., University of Guelph, Canada.

SAM, D. L., University of Bergen, Norway.

SAMMUT, G., University of Malta, Malta.

TATARKO, A., National Research University Higher School of Economics, Russian Federation.

TRIPATHI, RAMA CHARAN, University of Allahabad, India.

VALK, A., Tallinn University, Estonia.

VETIK, R., Tallinn University, Estonia.

ZIAIAN, T., University of South Australia, Australia.

Contributor Biographies

ROBERT C. ANNIS is the former director of the Rural Development Institute at Brandon University, Canada. He has served as a professor in the Departments of Native Studies, Psychology, and Rural Development. He received his Masters degree from Queen's University, Canada, and his PhD from Strathclyde University, Scotland. He has published numerous academic articles and reports concerning demographic, social, cultural, and community development issues facing rural Canadians, and is co-author of *On the Edge of the Forest: Cultural Adaptation and Cognitive Development in Central Africa.* (1986). Dr. Annis has served on the editorial advisory board for the *Journal of Rural and Community Development,* as book review editor for the *Journal of Cross-Cultural Psychology,* and as editor of the *Bulletin of Cross-Cultural Psychology.* He is interested in the interface of policy, research, and practice, and has volunteered his time and expertise to numerous organizations. He has served as a president of the Canadian Rural Restructuring Foundation and as a member of the International Comparative Rural Policy Studies Consortium. He currently serves as chair of the Board for Community Futures, British Columbia.

ALGAE K. Y. AU is a PhD candidate in the Department of Applied Social Sciences at the Hong Kong Polytechnic University. During her undergraduate studies, she received various awards including the Scholarship for Outstanding Students, and the Outstanding Thesis Award in Psychology, and was placed on the Dean's Honours List. Her main research interests include neurocognitive, social, and cross-cultural psychology. She has published several articles in these areas. In her doctoral thesis, she investigates the interaction effect of social axioms on academic achievement among adolescents in Hong Kong.

SHABANA BANO is Assistant Professor of Psychology at Banaras Hindu University, India. She received her PhD at Banaras Hindu University.

She has been a Shastri Fellow at the University of Guelph (Canada). Her research interests are focused on issues of social identity, acculturation, mutual attitudes, and intercultural relations of Hindu and Muslim groups in India. Different forms of schooling, such as Sanskrit and Quranic, and their influence on social-psychological development of children and adolescents have been a central theme of her research. She has widely published in scientific journals and edited books in these areas. She is the co-author of a textbook, *Industrial and Organizational Psychology*, which has been published in Hindi. She seeks to apply her research findings for the promotion of harmonious intercultural relationships in the multicultural society of India.

JOHN W. BERRY is Professor Emeritus of Psychology at Queen's University, Canada, and a research professor, National Research University Higher School of Economics, Moscow, Russia. He received his PhD from the University of Edinburgh, and honorary doctorates from the University of Athens, and the University of Geneva. He has published over 30 books in the areas of cross-cultural, intercultural, social and cognitive psychology with various colleagues. These include *Cross-Cultural Psychology: Research and Applications*, third edition (Cambridge University Press, 2011); *Handbook of Acculturation Psychology*, second edition (Cambridge University Press, 2016); and *Immigrant Youth in Cultural Transition* (2006). He is a fellow of the Canadian Psychological Association, the Netherlands Institute for Advanced Study, the International Association for Cross-Cultural Psychology, and the International Academy for Intercultural Research. From CPA, he received the Hebb Award for Contributions to Psychology as a Science, and the award for Contributions to the Advancement of International Psychology, the Interamerican Psychology Prize from the Sociedad Interamericana de Psicologia, and the Lifetime Contribution Award from IAIR. His main research interests are in the areas of acculturation and intercultural relations, with an emphasis on applications to immigration, multiculturalism, and educational and health policy.

KLAUS BOEHNKE is vice dean of the Bremen International Graduate School of Social Sciences Jacobs University Bremen and Deputy Head of the International Laboratory for Sociocultural Research at the National Research University Higher School of Economics in Moscow. He received his PhD in Psychology from Berlin University of Technology (1985). After assistant and associate professorships at the Free University of Berlin, he became a professor in the Department of Sociology of Chemnitz University of Technology in 1993, moving to Jacobs University Bremen in 2002. He has published some 400 academic pieces, including publications in *Science*, the *American Journal of Sociology*, and the *Journal of Personality*. He is president-elect of the International Association for Cross-Cultural Psychology. His research interests cover diverse topics of political socialization.

ASTERIA BRYLKA is a researcher in the Institute for Social Innovation and Impact (ISII) at the University of Northampton, United Kingdom. She completed her PhD in Social Psychology at the University of Helsinki, Finland, in 2016. Her doctoral dissertation examined identity, and contact-related determinants of reciprocal intergroup relations in ethno-culturally diverse societies. Asteria has presented in various international conferences and published on topics such as intergroup relations and contact, national and ethnic identity, labour market discrimination and acculturation. Her research interest also includes social impact and well-being. Besides social psychology of intergroup relations, Asteria has a strong background in clinical and health psychology, and quantitative research methods.

ALOIS BUHOLZER is Professor of Educational and Social Sciences at the University of Teacher Education, Lucerne, Switzerland. He received his doctorate in educational sciences from the University of Zurich, Switzerland. He founded the Research Institute for Diversity Education, Lucerne. He now directs numerous research projects, including the evaluation of the national program on "Promotion of Integration" on behalf of the Federal Office of Migration. His research interest teaching-and-learning research with a principal focus on diversity and inclusion, as well as on the activities of teachers in inclusive schools. His current research deals with the formative assessment of teachers in inclusive school classes

SYLVIA XIAOHUA CHEN is a professor in the Department of Applied Social Sciences at the Hong Kong Polytechnic University, and also a Registered Psychologist and an associate fellow at the Hong Kong Psychological Society. She received her PhD in Psychology from the Chinese University of Hong Kong and her MA in counselling psychology from Santa Clara University, USA. Her research focuses on the social psychology of bilingualism and biculturalism, globalization and multiculturalism, personality and social behavior in cultural contexts, and cultural diversity and mental health. To this end, she has published over 60 journal articles and book chapters. She was a recipient of the

Early Career Award (from the International Association for Cross-Cultural Psychology), the Michael Harris Bond Award for Early Career Research Contributions, and the Jung-heun Park Young Scholar Award (both from the Asian Association of Social Psychology). She also received several academic awards from the American Psychological Association Division 52 (International Psychology), the Gallup Positive Psychology Institute, the Hong Kong Psychological Society, and the Hong Kong Association of University Women during 2004–2007. Currently, she serves as an associate editor of the *Journal of Cross-Cultural Psychology* and the *Asian Journal of Social Psychology*.

JUSTINE DANDY is a senior lecturer in the School of Arts and Humanities at Edith Cowan University. She was awarded her PhD from the University of Adelaide in 2000 and has held teaching and research positions at Flinders University and the University of Western Australia. Her research interests are in social and cross-cultural psychology, specifically cultural identity, intergroup relations, and attitudes to immigration, multiculturalism, and diversity. Her current research is focused on intercultural attitudes and relations in Australia and other culturally diverse communities. In 2011, she conducted a national study on drivers for social cohesion in multicultural Australian communities for the Ministerial Council for Multicultural Affairs. She has published extensively on attitudes to immigration and multiculturalism and is the Australian team leader for MIRIPS. She is a member of the board of the International Academy for Intercultural Research (2017–2021) and a member of the International Association for Cross-Cultural Psychology.

KEVIN DUNN is Professor of Geography and Urban Studies, Dean of Social Sciences and Psychology, Western Sydney University, Sydney, Australia. He received his PhD from the University of Newcastle (Australia). Professor Dunn's areas of research include the geographies of racism, immigration and settlement, Islam in Australia, and local government and multiculturalism. His books include *Landscapes: Ways of Imagining the World* (2003), and his recent articles are published in *Analyses of Social Issues and Public Policy, Race and Class, Ethnicities, The Australian Geographer, Studia Islamika,* the *Journal of Intercultural Studies.* and the *Australian Journal of Social Issues.* He is a fellow of the New South Wales Geographical Society and is its vice president. His Everyday Racism app received second prize in the UN competition for best community relations initiative in 2014 (from 600+ entrants).

The Everyday Racism app was also the 2014 Co-Winner of the UN global #peaceapp competition: http://alltogethernow.org.au/news/eve ryday-racism-project-wins-prestigious-award/. His co-authored *Introducing Human Geography: Globalisation, Difference and Inequality* (2000) was awarded first prize in the tertiary category for wholly Australian texts (the Australian Awards for Excellence in Educational Publishing).

MARIEKE VAN EGMOND is a scientific researcher at the University of Hagen, Germany. She obtained her Master of Sciences degree from the Radboud University, the Netherlands, and her PhD from the Bremen International Graduate School of Social Sciences at Jacobs University Bremen, in Germany, with special distinction. Upon completion of her doctoral research, she continued to work in the field of cross-cultural psychology on topics such as the strength of social norms across cultures, processes of acculturation and radicalization, and beliefs about learning and motivation from a cross-cultural perspective.

VICTORIA GALYAPINA is a leading researcher of the International Laboratory for Socio-Cultural Research and associate professor in the Department of Psychology at The National Research University Higher School of Economics, Moscow, Russia. She received her PhD in Social Psychology from the Institute of Psychology, Russian Academy of Sciences. She is a member of the International Association for Cross-Cultural Psychology. She has published more than 70 journal articles and book chapters in Russian and English. She has extensive practical experience in improving intercultural relations. She implemented scientific and practical projects on the psychological support of victims of armed conflicts and terrorist attacks in the North Caucasus. Her research interests focus on problems of intercultural relationships, mutual acculturation of ethnic minorities and majorities, and intergenerational transmission of values and social identity.

RYAN GIBSON is Libro Professor of Regional Economic Development in the School of Environmental Design and Rural Planning at the University of Guelph, Canada. He holds research and adjunct appointments with the Rural Development Institute at Brandon University, the International Centre for Northern Governance and Development at the University of Saskatchewan, and Saint Mary's University. He received his PhD from the Department of Geography at Memorial University of Newfoundland. Dr. Gibson's main research interests focus on rural development, governance, immigration and mobility, and public policy. Recent book publications include *Place Peripheral: Place-based Development in Rural, Island, and Remote Communities* (2015) and *Building Community Resilience* (forthcoming in 2017). Dr. Gibson is the current president of the Canadian Community Economic Development Network, past-president of the Canadian Rural Revitalization Foundation, and chair of the Institute of Island Studies Advisory Board.

HECTOR GRAD is an associate professor in the Department of Social Anthropology of the Universidad Autónoma de Madrid, Spain. He received his PhD in Social Psychology at the Universidad Complutense de Madrid. His main research focuses on interdisciplinary national and international projects, studying how personal values and different constructions of nationalism affect the compatibility between national, regional, and supranational identities, and the intercultural relations in metropolitan societies. This research was published in the Spanish *Journal of Social Psychology and Journal of Language and Politics*, as well as in *Analysing Identities in Discourse* (2008) and *Families across Cultures: A 30-Nation Psychological Study* (Cambridge University Press, 2006). He is a fellow of the Institute of Migrations, Ethnicity and Social Development at the Universidad Autónoma de Madrid, and was Spanish Deputy Representative in the Rapid Response and Evaluation Network of the European Monitoring Centre on Racism and Xenophobia.

YONGXIA GUI is a lecturer in the School of Marxism at Henan University of Economics and Law in China, and teaches a general education psychology course. She received her PhD from Southwest University in Chongqing, China. She was awarded a scholarship from the China Scholarship Council to spend a year in Canada as a visiting graduate student at the University of Guelph, where she carried out research on Chinese international students. She has also carried out research on the adaptation of rural-to-urban migrant workers in China. Her current research deals with gender issues, especially the relationship between unmitigated communion (over-involvement with the problems of others) and psychological health.

ANDREA U. HAENNI HOTI is Professor of Educational and Social Sciences at the University of Teacher Education, Lucerne, Switzerland. She received her doctorate in educational sciences at the University of Fribourg, Switzerland. She has been a visiting scholar at Columbia University in New York (USA) and at the University of Hamburg

(Germany) with two grants from the Swiss National Science Foundation. She has also held a guest professorship at the University of Toronto (Canada) and at the University of Augsburg (Germany). She has carried out research projects on nationalism and xenophobia among Swiss youth and transcultural educational sciences. Her main research focus is on cultural diversity, acculturation, multilingualism, and equity in schools. Her latest research project examines the acculturation orientations of primary school students and their class teachers and how the perceived match or mismatch regarding these affects the quality of the teacher-student relationship and the psychosocial adaptation and educational success of the students.

KATJA HANKE is a senior researcher at GESIS-Leibniz Institute for the Social Sciences in Mannheim, Germany. She received her PhD from Victoria University of Wellington, New Zealand. After completing post-doctoral fellowships in Taiwan, and at the Bremen International Graduate School of Social Sciences in Germany, she was a University Lecturer and Marie Curie Fellow at Jacobs University Bremen, Germany. Her work focuses on cross-cultural and intercultural research methods. Her current research interests include intercultural relations, acculturation, applied social psychology, and measurement invariance testing.

SYBILLE HEINZMANN is a research collaborator and lecturer in foreign language didactics at the University of Teacher Education, St. Gallen, Switzerland. She received her doctorate in English Applied Linguistics from the University of Fribourg, Switzerland. Her research focuses on multilingualism and diversity in the school setting. Her main research topics are mobility, language-learning motivation, language attitudes, and intercultural skills. She has been a visiting scholar at the Department of Second Language Studies at the University of Hawai'i. Her current research examines the linguistic, motivational, and intercultural effects of exchange activities between primary school classes in German- and French-speaking Switzerland.

BRYANT P. H. HUI is a PhD student in Psychology and research associate at the University of Cambridge, England. He obtained his Masters degree in Social Sciences at the Hong Kong Polytechnic University, Hong Kong, where he developed a passion for research on cross-cultural, social, and health psychology. His Masters thesis examined the role of bicultural integration and multicultural ideology in facilitating psychological adaptation and intercultural contact, which has been published in the *International Journal of Intercultural Relations*. His current research interests are centred on the interplay among individual, situational, and cultural factors in prosociality and well-being. He is also very keen on analysing multicultural (i.e., multi-town/state/nation) data sets using multilevel modelling and machine-learning algorithms.

CRISTIANO INGUGLIA is Assistant Professor of Developmental and Educational Psychology in Università degli Studi di Palermo, Italy. He received his PhD in Public Relations. He is involved in several international research projects in EU and non-EU countries. His research interests focus on the field of developmental psychology, as related to the social development of children, adolescents, and emerging adults, especially with regard to their positive development, acculturation processes, and socio-psychological adaptation, and the development of mutual intercultural relations.

INGA JASINSKAJA-LAHTI is Professor of Social Psychology at the Faculty of Social Sciences of the University of Helsinki, Finland. She has done extensive research on intergroup relations and immigrant integration in Finland and has published widely in international scholarly journals. Her most recent research interests concern the reciprocity of intergroup relations and identity negotiations in an immigration context with a focus on both majority-minority and minority-minority relations. Currently, she is leading the project focussing on inter-ethnic and inter-religious relations in Finland, Estonia, and Norway (SOPU; Kone Foundation), which is a multidisciplinary study on the building blocks of secure neighbourhood. She is also an associate editor of the *International Journal of Intercultural Relations*.

JOLANDA JETTEN is Professor of Social Psychology at the University of Queensland. She received her PhD from the University of Amsterdam. She received an ARC Future Fellowship and took up a three-year UQ Development Fellowship in 2017. Her research is concerned with group processes, social identity and intergroup relations, as represented by her most recent books: *The Wealth Paradox* and *The Social Cure*. She has published over 140 peer-reviewed articles, over 35 chapters and four books. Jolanda is the former co-chief editor of the *British Journal of Social Psychology (BJSP)* and currently serves as co-chief editor of *Social Issues and Policy Review*. She has also served as an associate editor for the *BJSP*, and is currently an associate editor with *Comprehensive Results in Social Psychology*. She was awarded the British

Psychological Society Spearman Medal in 2004 and the Kurt Lewin Medal from the European Association of Social Psychology in 2014. Jolanda is the former president of the Society of Australasian Social Psychology and served on the Australian Research Council College of Experts. She was elected as fellow of the Association of Social Sciences in Australia in 2015.

JÜRI KRUUSVALL is a researcher and lecturer at the School of Governance, Law and Society, Tallinn University. He received his PhD from Tartu University in Psychology. His main research interests include sociology of interethnic relations, sociology of youth and education, and environmental sociology.

ROLAND KÜNZLE is Lecturer in Educational and Social Sciences at the University of Teacher Education, Lucerne, Switzerland. He has taught at the secondary-school-level for some years after studying mathematics and natural sciences at the University of Fribourg, Switzerland. His work consists in training teachers of kindergarten, primary, and secondary schools. As a research associate in the Department of Research and Development, he has been involved in various research projects in the following research areas: didactics of geography, dealing with acculturation and intercultural education, integrative promotion, career starts of teachers, new media, and school social work. His current research project examines the issue of the expectations held by different actors in school social work, being carried out at the University of Teacher Education, Lucerne, in cooperation with the Lucerne School of Social Work.

LARISSA KUS-HARBORD is a research advisor in the New Zealand Police Department (Response and Operations Research and Evaluation group). She received her PhD in Psychology from Victoria University of Wellington, New Zealand. She recently completed a Mobilitas postdoctoral research project "The Impact of Power Reversal, Social Changes, and Division between Ethnic Groups on Intergroup Relations and Subjective Well-Being" at the Institute of International Social Studies in Tallinn University. Her research interests and publications focus on acculturation, intergroup relations, subjective well-being, and social representations of history.

MARY ANNE LAURI is Professor of Social Psychology at the University of Malta and a visiting fellow at the London School of Economics and Political Science, UK. She received her PhD from the London School of Economics. She is past president of the Maltese Psychological Association. Between 2006 and 2016, she served as pro-rector at the University of Malta. She has co-authored several publications and published in both local and international journals. She sits on various boards both within and outside the University of Malta. Her areas of research include media psychology, social marketing, social representations, and well-being. She remains actively involved in political, media and voluntary organisations.

NADEZHDA LEBEDEVA is a professor in the Department of Psychology and is the head of the International Laboratory for Socio-Cultural Research at The National Research University Higher School of Economics in Moscow, Russia. She received her PhD from the Institute of Psychology, Russian Academy of Sciences. She is academic director of the Masters Program on Applied Social Psychology of the Higher School of Economics and Tilburg University, The Netherlands. She is a member of the International Association for Cross-Cultural Psychology, and the International Academy for Intercultural Research. She is the author or editor of 26 books, and over 250 articles and book chapters on social and cross-cultural psychology. Her research interests are values, value transmission, identity, intercultural relations, acculturation, creativity and innovations, and social and cultural change.

ZARINA LEPSHOKOVA is a senior researcher in the International Laboratory for Socio-Cultural Research and associate professor in the Department of Psychology at the National Research University Higher School of Economics, Moscow, Russia. She received her PhD from the National Research University Higher School of Economics, Moscow, Russia. She is a member of the International Association for Cross-Cultural Psychology. She has published a monograph *Adaptation Strategies of Migrants and Their Psychological Well-Being (the Cases of Moscow and the North Caucasus)* and over 30 articles in the areas of acculturation, cross-cultural, intercultural and social psychology with various colleagues. Her research interests focus on problems of intercultural relationships, mutual acculturation of ethnic minorities and majorities, multiple identities and their perceived incompatibility, social disidentification, and intergenerational transmission of values and social identity.

ALIDA LO COCO is Full Professor of Developmental and Educational Psychology and coordinator of the PhD program in Psychological and Behavioral Sciences at the Department of Psychological, Educational and Training Science, Università degli Studi di Palermo, Italy. She is Rector's Delegate for Vocational Guidance. In past years, she was coordinator of the Developmental and Educational Psychology Section of the Italian Psychological Association. Her research interests are focused on such topics as social, emotional, and personality development; peer relationships and friendship, empathic responsiveness, students' academic and psychological adjustment, intercultural relations, autonomy and relatedness during adolescence, and cultural studies.

MARIANNA MAKAROVA is a PhD candidate at the School of Governance, Law and Society of Tallinn University, Estonia. Her research focus is on the relations between history, socio-economic status, and intergroup hierarchy on the one hand and identity formation, strength of identity, and identity motivation, on the other. Marianna works currently as the head of research development at the Estonian Integration and Migration Foundation, which is a state agency within the Estonian Ministry of Culture.

RAMESH C. MISHRA is Professor of Psychology at Banaras Hindu University, India. He received his DPhil from the University of Allahabad. He has been a post-doctoral research fellow and Shastri Research Fellow at Queen's University (Canada) and a visiting professor at the Universities of Konstanz (Germany) and Geneva (Switzerland). He has also been a fellow-in-residence at the Netherlands Institute of Advanced Study and a Fulbright Scholar-in-Residence at Wittenberg University (USA). He is the Fellow and a past president of the National Academy of Psychology (India). His research has focused on understanding ecological and cultural influences on human development. He is the co-author of *Ecology, Acculturation and Psychological Adaptation: A Study of Adivasis in Bihar* (1996), *Development of Geocentric Spatial Language and Cognition: An Eco-Cultural Perspective* (2010), *Ecology, Culture and Human Development: Lessons for Adivasi Education* (2017) and co-editor of *Psychology in Human and Social Development: Lessons from Diverse Cultures* (2003).

FROSSO MOTTI-STEFANIDI is Professor of Psychology at the National and Kapodistrian University of Athens, Greece. She received her PhD from the Institute of Child Development, University of Minnesota. She is a recipient of the Distinguished International Alumni Award of the

College of Education and Human Development of the University of Minnesota and a fellow of the Association for Psychological Science. She has served as president of the European Association of Developmental Psychology and as president of the European Association of Personality Psychology. She currently serves on the Governing Council of the Society for Research in Child Development. Her main research interests center on the study of immigrant youth adaptation, development, and acculturation. She has developed (together with Ann Masten, Jens Asendorpf, and Vassilis Pavlopoulos) the Athena Studies of Resilient Adaptation longitudinal project, which is framed from within a resilience developmental perspective. It includes two longitudinal studies one conducted before and the other during the Economic Recession in Greece. She is author of over 150 papers and chapters in Greek and English, two books in Greek, and is co-editor of the book *Positive Youth Development in Global Contexts of Social and Economic Change* (2017).

MARIANNE MÜLLER is Professor of Statistics at Zurich University of Applied Sciences and a Lecturer for Biostatistics at the Swiss Federal Institute of Technology, Zurich, and a statistician at the University of Teacher Education, Lucerne. She received her doctorate in mathematics at the University of Zurich, Switzerland. Within the framework of a postdoctoral fellowship of the Swiss National Fund, she then worked for two years at Queen Mary & Westfield College of the University of London in the field of experimental design. As a research associate at the Institute for Social and Preventive Medicine in Berne, she was jointly responsible for the design and data analysis in social and health science studies and thus became acquainted with the practical aspects of statistics. She is an expert in the field of scale development, in particular Rasch modeling and is involved in the software development for Rasch modeling within an international team of the European Rasch Training Group. She is the author of a fundamental book on statistics for health sciences, *Statistik für die Pflege. Handbuch für die Pflegeforschung und -wissenschaft* (2011).

PASQUALE MUSSO is a research fellow at the Università degli Studi di Palermo, Italy. He obtained his Master's degree in Developmental and Educational Psychology and a PhD in Public Relations at the University of Palermo, Italy. He has ongoing participation in different research projects in European and non-European countries. His research interests focus on issues in developmental psychology, as related to the social development of adolescents and emerging adults, especially to their positive development, acculturation processes and socio-psychological adaptation, and the development of mutual intercultural relations. He is actively involved in international professional service as president-elect of the Early Researchers Union of the European Association of Developmental Psychology.

FÉLIX NETO is Professor Catedrático of Psychology in the Faculdade de Psicologia e de Ciências da Educação at the University of Porto, Portugal, and director of the Psychology Doctoral Programme at the University of Porto. He earned a PhD in Normal and Abnormal Anthropology from the École des Hautes Études en Sciences Sociales, France, and a PhD in Social Psychology from the Faculdade de Psicologia e de Ciências da Educação, Universidade do Porto, Portugal. He obtained a Habilitation in psychology at the University of Coimbra in 1990. He was previously coordinator of the Master on Cross-Cultural Relations at Universidade Aberta and director of the Center of Cognition and Emotion. His research interests focus on migration, gender stereotypes, racial attitudes, love, loneliness, forgiveness, happiness, and implicit cognitions. He is author of 18 books in the areas of social psychology and cross-cultural psychology, and over 300 papers published in Portuguese, English, French, Catalan, Spanish, and Italian.

JOANA NETO is an assistant researcher at the Universidade Católica Portuguesa, Portugal. She received her PhD in Cognitive Psychology, from the École Pratique des Hautes Études, France, and her Masters degree in Social Economics from the Universidade Católica Portuguesa, Portugal, and Masters degree in Human Resource Management and Economics from Universidade do Porto, Portugal. She has also worked as a social value analyst. Her research interests are focused on issues of cross-cultural, social and cognitive psychology and economics, social economics and international human resource management. She has published her research in these areas in scientific journals and edited books.

YIN PARADIES is Professor of Race Relations and deputy director (research) at the Alfred Deakin Research Institute for Citizenship and Globalisation, Deakin University, Australia. He received his PhD from the University of Melbourne, Australia. He has authored more than 150 publications and is an invited reviewer for over 70 journals, with his work published in the highest-ranking journals of several disciplines, including: *Social Science and Medicine, International Journal of*

Epidemiology, *Ethnic and Racial Studies*, and the *Journal of General Internal Medicine*. He conducts interdisciplinary research on the health, social, and economic effects of racism as well as anti-racism theory, policy, and practice. With a focus on Australia and Brazil, his research is undertaken across diverse settings, including workplaces, schools, universities, housing, the arts, museums and healthcare.

VASSILIS PAVLOPOULOS is Associate Professor of Cross-Cultural Psychology at the Department of Psychology, National and Kapodistrian University of Athens, Greece. He received his PhD in Social Psychology from the National and Kapodistrian University of Athens. He is associate editor of *Psychology: The Journal of the Hellenic Psychological Society*. He has been coordinator of the Social Psychology section of the Hellenic Psychological Society. He has published more than 70 papers in English and in Greek, in the form of journal articles or book chapters. Also, he is co-editor of two social psychology volumes in Greek. His research interests focus on acculturation and intercultural relations, positive adaptation of immigrant youth, perceived discrimination, beliefs about justice, cross-cultural study of personal and political values, and the cultural correlates of behavioural intentions.

MAARIS RAUDSEPP is a senior researcher at the Institute of International and Social Studies in the School of Governance, Law and Society of Tallinn University, Estonia. She received her PhD in Psychology from the University of Tartu, Estonia. Her research focus is on the forms of group identity, representations of ethnic outgroups in the media, relations between ethnic self-esteem and attitudes towards the outgroup, social representations of human rights and equal treatment, promotion of intergroup trust, processes of acculturation, and autobiographical memory and personal meaning construction.

TUULI ANNA RENVIK is University Lecturer in Social Psychology at the Open University of the University of Helsinki, Finland. She received her PhD from the University of Helsinki. Her research interests include intergroup relations, acculturation, and immigrant integration. Most recently she has worked in a research project concerned with the most pertinent pre- and post-migration factors in the long-term adaptation of immigrants from Russia to Finland. Currently, she is involved in research projects on everyday understandings of multiculturalism, subjective perceptions of changing intergroup contexts, and prejudice reduction in schools.

LENA ROBINSON is Professor of Social Work and Human Services at Central Queensland University, Australia. She received her PhD at the University of Surrey, UK. She is an international scholar, who has delivered guest/public lectures and conference papers in London, India, South Africa, Ethiopia, Singapore, Indonesia, China, Australia, Canada, Sweden, and the United States. In 2003, she was a Fulbright scholar in residence at Central Connecticut State University. She has also worked in Mozambican and British universities. Professor Robinson has published and researched widely in the field of race, ethnicity, immigration, cross-cultural psychology, and social-work practice.

ANETTE ROHMANN is Professor of Community Psychology at the University of Hagen, Germany. She obtained her DrPhil at the University of Münster. Her current research interests include acculturation, social diversity and intercultural communication, cross-group contact, and theory-practice exchange. She is a member of the Research Center for the Psychological Study of Individual and Community Change, a research center at the University of Hagen dedicated to understanding how individuals and communities manage social, demographic and/or cultural change.

TATIANA RYABICHENKO is a research fellow at the International Laboratory for Sociocultural Research and a lecturer at the Department of Psychology National Research University Higher School of Economics, Russia. She obtained her Masters degree in Psychology from the Higher School of Economics, and is involved in several research projects of the laboratory sponsored by The Higher School of Economics and the Russian Science Foundation. She is a member of International Association for Cross-Cultural Psychology. Her research interests focus on intercultural relations, adaptation of migrants and ethnic minorities, cultural continuity, value transmission in ethnic minority and ethnic majority families, and comparative studies on individual values and acculturation

SABA SAFDAR is Director of the Centre for Cross-Cultural Research at the University of Guelph, Canada. She received her PhD from York University, Canada. With her graduate students, Professor Safdar conducts research examining the wide range of factors that are relevant in understanding the adaptation processes of newcomers including immigrants, refugees, and international students. Professor Safdar is associate editor of the *International Journal of Intercultural Relations* and member of the editorial board of the *Journal of Cross-Cultural Psychology*. Professor Safdar has led and participated in large number of multidisciplinary and multicountry projects and has held academic appointments in Canada, the USA, the UK, France, Spain, India, and Kazakhstan.

DAVID LACKLAND SAM is Professor of Cross-Cultural Psychology at the University of Bergen, Norway. He obtained a BSc (Honors) degree in Psychology from the University of Ghana, before migrating to Norway as a student, where he received his PhD from the University of Bergen, Norway. He divides his position at the University of Bergen between the Department of Psychosocial Science (Faculty of Psychology) and the Centre for International Health (Faculty of Medicine and Dentistry). He teaches courses in cross-cultural psychology, medical anthropology and cultural psychiatry. His research interests include psychology of acculturation, and the role of culture in health. Sam has published extensively on young immigrants' psychological adaptation in general, and from a cross-cultural comparative perspective. Sam was co-editor of two books on acculturation (in 2006), and a co-author of the third edition of *Cross-cultural Psychology: Research and Applications* (Cambridge University Press, 2011). His latest book is the second edition of *the Cambridge Handbook of Acculturation Psychology* (2016), which he edited together with John W. Berry. Sam is a fellow of the International Academy of Intercultural Relations and is the incoming president of this Academy. He has also served as an executive board member of the International Association for Cross-Cultural Psychology.

GORDON SAMMUT is Senior Lecturer in Social Psychology at the University of Malta and a visiting fellow at the London School of Economics and Political Science. He received his PhD from the London School of Economics. His interests concern intercultural and intergroup relations, the theory of social representations, modalities of social influence, and issues relating to divergent perspectives in social relations. He is co-editor of *Papers on Social Representations* and chief-editor of *Cultural Encounters and Social Solidarity* (special issue: Papers on Social Representations, 2011), editor-in-chief of *The Cambridge Handbook of Social Representations* (2015), *Understanding Self and Others: Explorations in Intersubjectivity and Interobjectivity* (2013), and *Methods of Psychological Intervention: Yearbook of Idiographic Science*, Vol. VII.

ALEXANDER N. TATARKO is a professor and leading research fellow at the International Laboratory for Socio-Cultural Research at The National Research University Higher School of Economics, Moscow, Russia. He received his PhD from the Institute of Psychology, Russian Academy of Sciences. He has published 8 books and over 100 articles (in Russian and English) in the areas of cross-cultural and social psychology with various colleagues. He is a member of the International Association for Cross-Cultural Psychology and the International Academy of Intercultural Relations. He was the coordinator of several projects devoted to cross-cultural aspects of social capital in Russia. He participated in the implementation of the training of intercultural relations and ethnic tolerance in the North Caucasus of Russia. His main research interests are intercultural relations and social capital with an emphasis on its peculiarities in multicultural societies.

RAMA CHARAN TRIPATHI is a retired professor of psychology at the University of Allahabad, India. Till recently, he was a National Fellow of the Indian Council for Social Science Research. He received his PhD from the University of Michigan. He is a fellow of the National Academy of Psychology (India). His research has focused on understanding of intergroup relations in India involving Hindus and Muslims. Among his publications are *Norm Violation and Intergroup Relations* (1992), *Psychology, Development and Social Policy in India* (2014), *Perspectives on Violence and Othering in India* (2016). He also edits the journal *Psychology and Developing Societies*.

AUNE VALK works as the Head of the Analysis Department at the Ministry of Education and Research, Estonia. She received her PhD in Psychology from the University of Tartu. She is the member of the Estonian Psychologists' Association and International Association for Cross-Cultural Psychology. Previously she worked at the University of Tartu and was a national project manager for the OECD study of adult skills PIAAC (Programme for International Assessment of Adult Competences).

RAIVO VETIK is Professor of Comparative Politics at Tallinn University. He received his PhD in Political Science at Tampere University, Finland. During the period 1998–2008 he was director of the Institute of International and Social Studies at Tallinn University. His research interests include ethnic and national identity, immigration and multiculturalism, integration policies, and semiotics of culture and politics.

TAHEREH ZIAIAN is a professor in the School of Psychology, Social Work and Social Policy, a full member of the Sansom Institute for Health Research, the University of South Australia, and a visiting professor at the University of NSW, Faculty of Medicine. She received her PhD from the University of Adelaide. She is a Community Health Psychologist and has been engaged in transcultural psychology and public health research for more than 29 years. With over 60 publications and over 70 conference/seminar presentations at national and international conferences she has made substantial contributions to the public discourse on migrants' and refugees' mental health in Australia and internationally. Her research has also influenced national policies in relation to multicultural mental health and has achieved research impact both nationally and internationally. She is a member of several journal editorial boards and government committees, and has been awarded a number of 1st category and competitive research grants, including ARCs. She has been the recipient of many awards including a British Commonwealth Award for Excellence in Women's Health.

Acknowledgements

Most of the work by John Berry on the MIRIPS project was carried out while he was a Research Professor at the International Laboratory for Sociocultural Research, in the National Research University Higher School of Economics (HSE), Moscow, Russian Federation. This work was supported by a grant from the Russian Science Foundation (project No. 15–18-00029)}.

I would like to thank my colleagues at HSE for their collegiality and support during this period, especially Professors Nadezhda Lebedeva and Alexander Tatarko. Others who helped me in various ways while in Moscow are Anna Lipatova, Ekaterina Bushina, and Zarina Lepshokova.

Assistance in editing of the manuscript was provided by Deladem Nyamadi (Ghana), David Lackland Sam (Norway) and Lucia Bombierio and Maria Bultseva (Russia). I also thank the Centre for Applied Cross-Cultural Research at Victoria University of Wellington (New Zealand) for hosting the MIRIPS project website, and Katja Hanke (Germany) for managing the project discussion forum

John W. Berry

1 Introduction to Mutual Intercultural Relations

John W. Berry

Queen's University, Canada, and Higher School of Economics, Russian Federation

1 Introduction: Understanding Cultural Diversity and Equity

There is probably no more serious challenge to social stability and cohesion in the contemporary world than the management of intercultural relations within culturally plural societies. Successful management depends on many factors including a research-based understanding of the historical, political, economic, religious and psychological features of the groups that are in contact. The core question is: 'How shall we all live together?' (Berry, 2003a).

In the project on which this book is based, we seek to provide such research by examining three core psychological principles in seventeen culturally plural societies. This project is entitled Mutual Intercultural Relations in Plural Societies (MIRIPS). A description of the project is available on line at www.victoria.ac.nz/cacr/research/mirips.

The first goal of the project is to evaluate three hypotheses of intercultural relations (multiculturalism, contact and integration) across societies in order to identify some basic psychological principles that may underlie intercultural relations across cultural contexts. Second, in order to understand the *mutual* character of intercultural relations, these hypotheses are examined in both the dominant (national) populations and in the non-dominant (immigrant and ethnocultural) communities. These goals are pursued by repeatedly examining some features of intercultural relations in a number of societies that vary in their intercultural contexts. The third goal is to relate the pattern of findings to the contextual features of these societies, including a country's extant cultural diversity and their policies that deal with their diversity. These societies also vary in their history, political and economic characteristics with respect to the relationships among groups. These contextual factors provide background information within which to interpret the psychological findings. The fourth goal is to employ the findings and relationships to propose some policies and programmes that may improve the quality of intercultural relationships globally.

The design of the project is an exercise in replication across contexts in order to discern what may be culturally universal and what may be culturally specific in how diverse groups of peoples engage in their inter-cultural relations. If there are consistencies in the empirical findings across these contexts, then they may serve as a basis for promoting more positive intercultural relations more generally in many societies.

Many of the ideas, concepts and research instruments used in this project are derived from two earlier studies: The International Study of Attitudes Towards Immigrants and Settlement (ISATIS; see Berry, 2006) and the International Comparative Study of Ethnocultural Youth (ICSEY; see Berry, Phinney, Sam and Vedder, 2006a and b).

The core ideas are that are addressed in the MIRIPS project are:

1. *Multiculturalism hypothesis:* When individuals feel secure in their place in a society, they will be able to better accept those who are different from themselves; conversely when individuals are threatened, they will reject those who are different.
2. *Contact hypothesis:* When individuals have contact with, and engage with others who are culturally different from themselves, they will achieve mutual acceptance, under certain conditions.
3. *Integration hypothesis:* When individuals identify with, and are socially connected to, both their heritage culture and to the larger society in which they live, they will achieve higher levels of well-being than if they relate to only one or the other culture, or to neither culture.

These three hypotheses will be elaborated in section 6 of this chapter.

1.1   *Outline of the Book*

This book has three main parts. First, this chapter outlines some core ideas in the study of intercultural relations and acculturation, including an elaboration of these three hypotheses. In the second part, evidence relating to these hypotheses will be provided in reports of empirical research in 16 chapters. There are 17 societies studied, each with at least one non-dominant (ethnic/immigrant) group and a dominant (national) group sampled: Australia, Azerbaijan, Canada, Estonia, Finland, Germany, Greece, Hong Kong (China), India, Italy, Latvia, Malta, Norway, Portugal, Russia, Spain and Switzerland. These societies provide the varying contexts for the evaluation of these three hypotheses. The third part of the book provides a chapter summarising and interpreting the various empirical findings and suggesting some policy applications of the findings.

1.2   Diversity and Equity Around the World

Ethnic, cultural, religious and linguistic diversity are commonplace in most countries. This project includes societies in which many of these forms of diversity are present, but to varying degrees. These variations allow the examination of contexts for intercultural relations.

To illustrate the extent of this diversity, Alesina, Arnaud, Easterly, Kurlat and Wacziarg (2003) used data from a number of Organisation for Economic Cooperation and Development (OECD) countries. They created two indexes, called *ethnic fractionalisation* and *linguistic fractionalisation index*. These are based on the probability that two randomly selected people in a society will not belong to the same ethnic group or speak the same language. This research shows that, according to this statistic, among industrial countries, the highest scores are found for Canada, Belgium and Switzerland; in the middle are France, Sweden and the UK; lowest scores are found for Japan and Denmark. More recently, Alesina, Harnoss and Rappoport (2016) constructed an index of population diversity for 195 countries. This index has two components: proportion of foreign born and diversity of origin of immigrants. This new index largely confirms the variation in diversity found in these earlier studies. In a similar approach, Fearon (2013) examined 822 ethnic groups in 160 countries and allocated them to a place on two indexes of *ethnic fractionalisation* and *cultural diversity*. In the present study, we distil these indicators to provide a single indicator that ranks the countries in the project. We refer to this index as the *ethnic diversity index*.

However, diversity is not the only focus of this project. In addition to diversity, there is the issue of equitable participation of all groups and their individual members in the life of the larger society (Berry, 2016). If there is diversity without all groups and individuals being able to interact and share their cultures, to have an equal role in the life of the plural society, then a form of segregation may come into existence. So, while these indexes portray the actual degree of ethnic and cultural diversity across societies, there are two other approaches that deal with the issue of participation. The first is the degree of migrant integration across 37 societies; this is the Migrant Integration Policy Index (MIPEX, 2010, www.mipex.eu/countries). It includes estimates of integration of migrants in a number of domains: labour mobility, family reunion, education, political participation, long-term residence, access to nationality and anti-discrimination laws. Highest integration scores are for

Sweden, Portugal and Canada; in the middle are Germany, the UK and France; and the lowest scores are for Cyprus, Latvia and Turkey. In this study, we refer to this as the *integration index*.

A third approach is to describe and quantify the policy response to such diversity. This is done in the Multicultural Policy Index (MPI; Banting and Kymlicka, 2006–2012; www.queensu.ca/mcp/). The Multicultural Policy Index monitors the evolution of multiculturalism policies in a number of Western democracies. This index brings together both the diversity and equity issues. This policy project provides information about multiculturalism policies in a standardized format; it thus serves well as a basis for making of comparisons across societies in this project. The index includes a set of nine criteria to assess the degree of promotion of multiculturalism (by policy and practice) in plural societies. These include a government policy promoting multiculturalism; a multicultural ministry or secretariat; adoption of multiculturalism in the school curricula; ethnic representation in the media; exemptions of cultural groups from codes that are rooted in the dominant society (e.g., Sunday closing); allowing dual citizenship; funding of cultural organisations; and funding of bilingual or heritage language instruction). Highest scores for multicultural policy development in 2010 are for Australia, Canada, Belgium and Sweden; in the middle are the UK, the United States and the Netherlands; lowest are Switzerland, Japan and Denmark. In this study, we call this the *policy index*.

Related to this policy index are the reports of Bloemraad (2011; Wright and Bloemraad, 2012). Bloemraad (2011) examined the policies and practices of multiculturalism in various countries and tracked changes over the years from 1980 to 2010 using the MPI. The rankings on this index put Canada and Australia in first place, followed by Sweden, New Zealand, Belgium and the United Kingdom. Towards the middle are Spain, Portugal and the United States. Lowest placed are France, Germany, Italy, Switzerland and Denmark. Of particular interest is the Netherlands, which was rather high in 2000, but dropped to a low score in 2010. This earlier high position in the Netherlands was the result of longstanding 'pilarisation' policies (Fleras, 2009), while the drop may reflect the assertions in the Netherlands that multiculturalism has failed there (Vertovec and Wessendorf, 2010).

Why are multicultural policies good for society and individuals? There is now substantial evidence that diversity policies produce positive outcomes for a society as a whole and for both dominant and non-dominant groups. For example, Alesina et al. (2015) found that diversity relates positively to economic prosperity for the society as a whole. Multicultural policies can also benefit dominant groups in society. Kesler and Bloemraad's (2010) 19-country study showed that multicultural policies increase a sense of belongingness, defined in terms of civic participation. Yet despite these positive outcomes, multicultural policies have often been misunderstood as exclusionary and perceived as threatening by members of the dominant ethno-cultural group (Plaut, Garnett, Buffardi and Sanchez-Burks, 2011).

For non-dominant groups, there are also some positive outcomes: anti-discrimination policies in diverse societies improve economic outcomes for immigrants (Aleksynska and Algan, 2010), and immigrant-native wage gaps are lower in countries with more favourable integration policies as defined by the Migrant Integration Policy Index (Nieto, Matano and Ramos, 2013). Immigrants also experience more belongingness in terms of citizenship acquisition, have higher levels of trust and report lower levels of discrimination in countries with more multicultural policies (Koopmans, Statham Giugni and Passy, 2005; Wright and Bloemraad, 2012). Multicultural models of diversity are associated with greater inclusiveness, less racial bias and more engagement from non-dominant groups (Plaut et al., 2011; Plaut, Thomas and Goren, 2009).

Overall, multicultural approaches have been shown to promote 'positive psychological, educational and organisational outcomes for minorities and organisations' (Plaut et al., 2011, p. 2). More generally, Bloemraad and Wright (2014, p. 292) have concluded 'that multicultural policies appear to have some modest positive effects on socio-political integration for first-generation immigrants and likely little direct effect, positive or negative, on those in the second generation'.

For the present project, these findings of positive outcomes of diversity for economic, social and political indicators are important because they provide a basis for the hypotheses being evaluated in this project. As we shall see in the discussion of the three hypotheses next, we propose that when economic conditions are generally good in a society, there is more shared security for everyone; this likely means less competition and a lower sense of economic threat (see multiculturalism hypothesis). And when there are policies and practices that promote the equitable participation and inclusion of everyone, greater mutual acceptance and well-being are expected (on the basis of the contact and integration hypotheses).

These variations in cultural diversity and integration, and in a country's policy response to their diversity, provide the contextual background for the psychological examination of intercultural relations among individuals within these 17 societies. That is, we will examine the patterns of findings across the country-specific chapters to see if there are any variations in adaptation outcomes that may relate to a society's placement on these indexes. In addition to their actual placement on these indexes, we will also examine any large discrepancies between them. For example, when cultural diversity is high, but the policy response to this diversity is low, there may be poorer outcomes for the quality of intercultural relations, and the adaptations made by indivduals.

Not all the countries in the project are included in these indexes. However, we may rank the countries in the MIRIPS project on the three indicators, placing them on the three dimensions: diversity, integration and policy. In some cases, some of the countries do not appear on these published indices. In these cases, the country researchers have provided an estimate of their placement in the rank order (marked by an asterisk).

The 17 societies in the project may be classified into three levels on each of the three multiculturalism dimensions: high, medium and low. When this is done, we find for the diversity index that there are seven countries that are relatively high: Canada, Estonia, Latvia, Switzerland, India*, Australia and Spain. Five countries are medium: Russia, Germany, Greece, Azerbaijan and Finland. And five countries are relatively low: Italy, Hong Kong, Norway, Portugal and Malta. On the integration index, five countries are relatively high: Portugal, Finland, Norway Canada and Australia. Six countries are medium: Germany, Spain, Italy, India*, Switzerland and Estonia. And six countries are relatively low: Greece, Malta, Russia*, Azerbaijan* and Latvia (Hong Kong was not estimated). Finally for the policy index, seven countries are relatively high: Australia, Canada, India, Finland, Norway, Portugal and Spain. Four countries are medium: Russia*, Germany, Greece and Azerbaijan*. And five countries are relatively low: Italy, Estonia*, Latvia, Switzerland and Malta* (* Indicates that the placement of the country is estimated).

It is clear that countries on the three indicators diverge in substantial ways. For example, Italy is low on diversity and policy, but middle on integration; and Portugal is middle on diversity and policy, but high on integration. We may conjecture that when there are disjunctions in the placements of a society on these indexes, there may be problems for intercultural relations there. For example, when actual cultural diversity is high, but the policy response to this diversity is low, this may present a poorer context for the quality of intercultural relations.

Nevertheless, we can provide the general placement of these societies with respect to the overall *climate* for their intercultural relations. Australia, Canada, Finland and to a lesser extent Portugal provide a positive context for diverse cultural communities. In contrast, Greece, Estonia, Italy, Switzerland, Latvia and Malta may provide a less positive climate. In the last chapter of this book, we will examine whether these variations on the dimensions of diversity, integration and policy, and disjunctions among them, have any association with the level of support for the three hypotheses.

2 Psychological Approaches to Intercultural Relations

The Mutual Intercultural Relations in Plural Societies project is focused on the psychological aspects of intercultural relations, but it takes into account some of the social and political contextual features of the larger societies and of the interacting groups within them. It is situated within the broad field of *cross-cultural psychology*, which addresses the question: how can we account for similarities and differences in human behaviour across cultural contexts? It has two core principles (Berry, Poortinga, Breugelsmans, Chasiotis and Sam, 2011). First, individual behaviours should be understood within the cultural contexts in which they have developed and are now being displayed. And second, individual behaviours should be examined and compared across a number of cultural contexts in order to distinguish those that are specific to particular groups from those that might have more general validity. With these two principles in mind, the ultimate goal of cross-cultural psychology, and also of this project, is to eventually achieve a set of universal principles that underlie human behaviour everywhere. These universals are the common substrate of psychological functioning; they are the processes or capacities that all human beings share at birth. During the course of development, cultural experiences shape these basic qualities into competencies and performances. For example, all human beings have the capacity to acquire language; the culture in which they are socialized influences which language(s) they will acquire; and the intercultural setting will influence which language they will actually use. Knowledge of these features of human behaviour is essential if we are to understand intercultural relations as a set of pan-human, but culturally situated, phenomena. If there are some general principles to be found, then broadly applicable policies may be possible to develop on the basis of these general principles. More generally, it may eventually be possible to achieve a 'global psychology' (Berry, 2013).

The project is also situated in the field of *intercultural psychology* (Sam and Berry, 2016). This field deals with the question: 'If individual behaviours are shaped in particular cultural contexts, what happens when individuals who have developed in different cultural contexts meet and interact within a society?' There are two domains of psychological interest here: (1) ethnocultural group relations and (2) acculturation. The study of ethnocultural group relations has usually examined the views and behaviours of the dominant group(s) towards the non-dominant ones, using concepts such as *ethnic stereotypes, attitudes,*

prejudice and *discrimination*. These views have been assessed with respect
to a number of specific topics, such as attitudes towards specific ethnocultural groups, immigrants, or the value of cultural diversity for a society.
This 'one-way' view of ethnocultural relations has usually missed examining the important reciprocal or mutual views held by non-dominant
groups towards dominant group(s). However, an early study in Canada
(Berry, Kalin and Taylor, 1977) took the point of view that all groups
(including dominant and non-dominant groups) in a culturally plural
society need to be examined in order to have a comprehensive understanding of their mutual relationships. This early study set the stage for
a number of follow-up studies and further analyses, including the *reciprocal mutual attitudes* among dominant and non-dominant groups (Kalin
and Berry, 1996), and the development of scales assessing the intercultural views of a number of interacting groups (Berry and Kalin, 2000).
The ISATIS project extended research on these issues internationally
(Berry, 2006). Many of these earlier scales and specific items have continued to be used in national surveys in various countries. The MIRIPS
project continues this approach.

The second domain of psychological interest is that of acculturation,
defined as 'the process of cultural and psychological change that takes
place as a result of contact between cultural groups and their individual
members' (Berry, 2005, p. 698). Early views from anthropology about
the nature of acculturation are a useful foundation for contemporary
discussion. Two formulations in particular have been widely quoted.
The first, from Redfield, Linton and Herskovits (1936, p. 149), defines
acculturation as follows:

Acculturation comprehends those phenomena which result when groups of individuals having different cultures come into continuous first-hand contact, with
subsequent changes in the original culture patterns of either or both groups ...
Under this definition, acculturation is to be distinguished from culture change, of
which it is but one aspect, and assimilation, which is at times a phase of
acculturation.

In another formulation, the Social Science Research Council (1954, page
974) defined acculturation as:

culture change that is initiated by the conjunction of two or more autonomous cultural systems. Acculturative change may be the consequence of
direct cultural transmission; it may be derived from non-cultural causes, such
as ecological or demographic modification induced by an impinging culture; it
may be delayed, as with internal adjustments following upon the acceptance of
alien traits or patterns; or it may be a reactive adaptation of traditional modes of
life

In the first formulation, acculturation is seen as one aspect of the broader concept of culture change (that which results from intercultural contact), is considered to generate change in 'either or both groups', and is distinguished from assimilation (which may be 'at times a phase'). These are important distinctions for psychological work and are pursued later in this chapter. In the second definition, a few extra features are added, including change that is indirect (not cultural but rather 'ecological'), is delayed (internal adjustments, presumably of both a cultural and a psychological character, take place over time), and can be 'reactive' (i.e., rejecting the cultural influence and changing towards a more 'traditional'-way of life rather than inevitably towards greater similarity with the dominant culture). Much contact and change occur during colonization, military invasion, migration and sojourning (i.e., tourism, international study and overseas posting). This process continues after the initial contact in many settler societies where ethnocultural communities maintain and evolve features of their heritage cultures. Over time, groups and individuals from both sides make various adaptations, involving mutual accommodations, in order to live in the culture-contact settings. This process can occasionally be stressful, but it often results in some form of mutual accommodation that both parties have created in order to live together in relative harmony.

Following an initial period of anthropologists working with indigenous peoples, recent acculturation research has focused on how immigrants (both voluntary and involuntary) changed following their entry and settlement into receiving societies. Most recently, research has examined how ethnocultural groups and individuals (those who have become established in generations following immigration) relate to each other and change as a result of their attempts to live together in culturally plural societies (see Sam and Berry, 2016 for an overview of this literature). Nowadays, as globalization results in the growth of trade and the need for political relations, all peoples in contact play important roles in facilitating this development: Indigenous national populations (First nations, Metis and Inuit) are experiencing continuing colonization as new waves of immigrants, sojourners (especially guest workers) and refugees gather to establish large ethnocultural populations in these countries.

Graves (1967) introduced the concept of psychological acculturation. This refers to individuals who are participants in a culture-contact situation, and who undergo changes induced by both the external (usually dominant) culture and the changing culture (usually non-dominant) of which individuals are members. These psychological changes include such rather superficial domains as what food is eaten and what clothes are worn, through to more deep-rooted psychological features of individuals, such as their identities and values.

There are two reasons for keeping the cultural and psychological levels distinct. The first is that cultural settings set the stage for individual behavioural development. The psychological features brought to the acculturation process, and the psychological changes that take place following migration, can only be understood by also understanding their cultural and intercultural roots. In order to discern the links between these cultural and psychological phenomena, both levels need to be studied and understood in their own terms. The second reason for studying the two levels independently is that not every individual enters into, participates in, or changes in the same way during the acculturation of his or her group. There are vast individual differences in psychological acculturation, even among individuals who have the same cultural origin and live in the same new acculturative arena. Some individuals may conform to the way of acculturating of their community and family, but others may not. In short, there is no simple relationship between cultural and psychological features of acculturation: not every group, nor every individual, engages the process in the same way, nor evidences the same outcomes.

Although these early anthropological definitions still serve as the basis for much work on acculturation, there are some more recent dimensions that have been proposed. First, it is no longer considered necessary for acculturation to be based on 'continuous first-hand' contact. With growing use of telemedia, acculturation may take place remotely, in line with earlier work on cultural diffusion, in which aspects of culture flow across boundaries without actual intercultural contact. For example, research by Ferguson and Bornstein (2012) has shown that Jamaican youth are taking on U.S. American cultural and psychological attributes without ever having been in direct personal contact with that society. Rather, they are exposed to U.S. culture through telemedia and tourism.

The second new dimension examines acculturation that takes place over the long term. Rather than being a phenomenon that occurs within the lifetime of an individual or in a few generations, acculturation can take place over centuries or even millennia. This long-term aspect of acculturation has been examined by Gezentsvey-Lamy, Ward and Liu (2013) with Jewish, Maori and Chinese samples, all communities that have remained as ethnocultural groups over centuries following intercultural contact.

A third dimension has become prominent with the increasing cultural diversity of many migrant-receiving societies, where there is no longer one single dominant group with which migrants and ethnocultural groups can be in contact (van Oudenhoven and Ward, 2012). With multiple groups available in the larger society, the pattern of intercultural contacts becomes more complex. As a result, more ethnographic research becomes necessary in order to understand this increasingly complex network of intercultural relations. For example, Berry and Sabatier (2010) examined the acculturation of immigrant youth who had settled in Montreal, Canada. In this city, there are two dominant groups (French and English) with whom immigrants may be in contact. They sometimes select one, the other, or both dominant groups.

A fourth dimension is that of contact within plural societies that results from large-scale internal migration. These migrations involve dimensions of rural-to-urban and regional cultural differences that set the stage for their acculturation. For example, Gui, Zheng and Berry (2012) examined migrant worker acculturation with men moving from peasant villages to large metropolises in China. This phenomenon is also important within the Russian Federation (Lebedeva and Tatarko, 2013), where individuals from other regions are moving to large cities and changing the cultural complexity of these metropolises.

Finally, as for other areas of psychological study, a qualitative perspective has begun to challenge the traditional quantitative approach to acculturation research (Chirkov, 2009). A response by Berry (2009) argued that both perspectives are required for a comprehensive understanding of acculturation phenomena. This dual approach begins with using the more qualitative traditions of cultural anthropology, with its close observation of daily activity, and the interpretation of the meanings assigned by people to these activities. Based on this qualitative information, more quantitative methods can be developed that draw from psychological science, using samples, interviews, tests and statistical analyses. The framework in Figure 1.1 makes this dual approach explicit.

As for the study of ethnocultural group relations, research on acculturations has also typically been a 'one-way' research approach and has missed examining the views of members of the dominant group(s) regarding how they think that non-dominant groups and individuals *should* acculturate and live in the plural society. These views of dominant groups and of the larger society have come to be known as *acculturation expectations* (Berry, 2003b). In MIRIPS, these concepts of *acculturation* strategies and expectations are also sometimes referred to as *intercultural* strategies and expectations, and are used interchangeably with the terms acculturation strategies and expectations (see section 4).

In keeping with these global interests and goals for psychology generally, the goals of the MIRIPS project are to evaluate the validity of the three hypotheses outlined earlier in many different cultural and intercultural contexts. If they are widely supported, then some general principles of intercultural relations may become established. Where they are not supported, the specific conditions (cultural, economic, historical and political) that prevail in those contexts will need to be examined to discern why there is no support.

3   General Framework for the MIRIPS Project

The project is guided by a framework that identifies the main concepts and variables, and suggests their inter-relationships. Figure 1.1 is divided into two main parts: the cultural context on the left and the psychological processes and outcomes on the right. This framework displays and links cultural-level and psychological-level acculturation phenomena in the two (or more) groups in contact. It serves as a kind of map of those phenomena that need to be conceptualized and measured during acculturation and intercultural relations research.

In keeping with the complexity of this figure, in this MIRIPS project we attempt a comprehensive examination of many acculturation and intercultural relations phenomena: (1) the characteristics of the two or more cultural groups prior to contact; (2) the nature of the contact between them; (3) the cultural changes that are taking place in both groups; (4) the

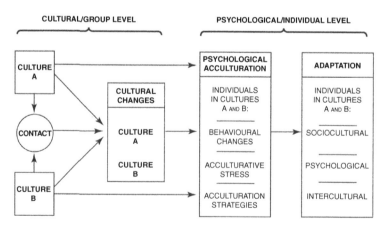

Figure 1.1. Framework for conceptualising intercultural relations and acculturation in plural societies.

psychological changes experienced by individuals in both groups in contact; and (5) the longer-term adaptations that may be achieved.

In a sense, Figure 1.1 lays out a kind of map for the complete study of acculturation and intercultural relations. Ideally, all components should be addressed in research projects, a goal that we have attempted to achieve in this project.

At the cultural level (on the left) we need to understand key features of the two (or more) original cultural groups (A, B and so on) prior to their major contact, the nature of their initial and continuing contact relationships and the resulting dynamic cultural changes in the groups as they emerge as ethnocultural groups during the process of acculturation. The gathering of this cultural-level information requires extensive archival and ethnographic community-level work. These cultural changes can range from being rather easily accomplished (such as evolving a new economic base), through to being a source of major cultural disruption (such as becoming colonized and enslaved).

At the individual level (on the right), individual changes due to acculturation are often thought of as limited to only 'cultural' changes. However, changes may take place in many domains of daily life. For example, they can be physical (e.g., setting up temporary houses and camps to accommodate refugees and asylum seekers), biological (e.g., changes in people's resistance to diseases), political (e.g., the introduction of immigration policies), economic (e.g., the economic contribution of foreign workers), social (e.g., ethnic discrimination) as well as cultural (e.g., language or religion) or a combination of all of these kinds of group-level changes.

At the individual level we need to consider the psychological acculturation that individuals in all groups in contact undergo and their eventual adaptation to their new situations. Identifying these changes requires sampling a population and studying individuals who are variably involved in the process of acculturation. There are three kinds of change that have been identified: behavioural, stress and strategies.

First, behavioural changes can be a set of rather easily accomplished *behavioural changes* (e.g., in ways of speaking, dressing and eating habits) or they can be more difficult to accomplish (e.g., changes in identities, self-concept and values)

Second are changes that are challenging, even problematic, in which *acculturative stress* becomes manifest. This concept was introduced (Berry, 1970) to reconceptualise the commonly used notion of 'culture shock' (Ward et al., 2001). This new term was developed to address two problems with the concept of culture shock. First, shock is usually a negative experience, whereas stress can either be positive (eustress) or negative (distress). During acculturation, intercultural experiences of individuals alert them to challenges, which may provide new opportunities (positive) or diminish them (negative). Second, the term 'culture' suggests that the source of the challenge is in a culture; however, the source is really in the intersection between two or more cultures that encounter each other. Hence the term 'acculturative' is preferred over the term 'culture'. In essence the negative side of acculturative stress is often manifested by uncertainty, anxiety and depression.

Third, individuals also develop and engage in *acculturation strategies* and *expectations* as their preferred way to acculturate and relate to each other (see section 4). *Acculturation strategies* and *expectations* are a major focus of current research. They have both attitudinal and behavioural components.

Finally, there are three kinds of adaptation. The first two of these were identified by Ward (1996) who distinguished between *psychological adaptation* and *sociocultural adaptation*. The first refers to adaptations that are primarily internal or psychological (e.g., sense of personal well-being and self-esteem; it is sometimes called 'feeling well'). The second are sociocultural, and are sometimes called 'doing well'. This form of adaptation is manifested by competence in carrying out the activities of daily intercultural living. A third form of adaptation has been proposed by Berry (2015). This is the concept of *intercultural adaptation*, which refers to the extent to which individuals are able to establish harmonious intercultural relations, with low levels of prejudice and discrimination. These three forms of adaptation will be elaborated in section 5.

4   Intercultural Strategies and Expectations

One concept that is central to and underlies all aspects of acculturation and intercultural relations phenomena is the way in which people seek to relate to each other. These are the *strategies* and *expectations* that all groups and their individual members have, whether explicitly or implicitly, when they engage in intercultural relations. These strategies and expectations are relevant to both the domains of intercultural relations (ethnocultural attitudes and acculturation), and can be held by both the dominant and non-dominant individuals and groups that are in contact. For example, the national policies that were described earlier may be seen as a public strategy for dealing with relationships among the diverse cultural groups in a plural society. Whether it is the colonizer or the colonized, immigrants or those already settled, it is clear that individuals and groups hold preferences with respect to the particular ways in which they wish to engage their own and the other groups with whom they are interacting. When examined among non-dominant ethnocultural groups that are in contact with a dominant group, these preferences have become known as *strategies*. These were earlier called *relational attitudes* (Berry, 1974) and *acculturation attitudes* (Berry, 1980). When examined among the dominant group, there are two aspects. The first are the views that are held about how non-dominant groups *should* acculturate; these have been called *acculturation expectations* (Berry, 2003). Second are the views held by the dominant group about how they *themselves* should change to accommodate the other groups now in their society.

There are large variations in how people seek to relate to each other; not all groups and individuals seek to engage in intercultural relations in the same way. These variations are called *strategies* and *expectations* because they consist of both attitudes and behaviours (that is, they include both the preferences and the actual outcomes) that are exhibited in day-to-day intercultural encounters. These intercultural strategies and expectations are based on the same three underlying issues: (1) the degree to which there is a desire to maintain the group's culture and identity; (2) the degree to which there is a desire to engage in daily interactions with other ethnocultural groups in the larger society (including the dominant national culture); and (3) the relative power of the groups in contact to choose their preferred way of engaging each other.

Four strategies have been derived from the first two issues facing all acculturating peoples. These issues are presented in Figure 1.2, where

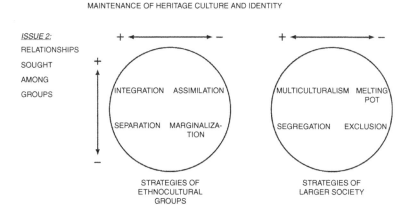

Figure 1.2. Intercultural strategies in ethnocultural groups and expectations in the larger society.

they are shown as being independent of (i.e., orthogonal to) each other. That is, preferences for cultural maintenance and for intercultural contact are not necessarily related to each other. Their independence has been empirically demonstrated in a number of studies (e.g., Ben-Shalom and Horenczyk, 2003; Berry and Sabatier, 2011; Dona and Berry, 1994; Ryder, Alden and Paulhus, 2000). On the left of Figure 1.2 are the strategies of non-dominant groups and their individual members. On the right are the expectations of dominant groups in the larger society and of their individual members. The power relations between these two sectors of the population in a plural society are present in the relationships between these strategies (on the left) and expectations (on the right). Typically the dominant group has more power than the non-dominant group to decide on the policies and practices that are operating in the plural society. This difference in power creates an 'asymmetric field' (Horenczyk et. al., 2013; Vetic, 2016).

The first two issues can be responded to on attitudinal dimensions, represented by bipolar arrows (above and to the left of the two circles). Generally, positive or negative orientations to these issues intersect to define four ways of acculturating. Preferences for these ways carry differ-ent names, depending on which groups (the non-dominant or dominant) are being considered. From the point of view of non-dominant ethnocul-tural groups (strategies, on the left of Figure 1.2), when individuals do not wish to maintain their cultural identity and seek daily interaction with other cultures, the *Assimilation* strategy is defined. In contrast, when individuals place a value on holding on to their original culture, and at the same time wish to avoid interaction with others, then the *Separation* alternative is defined. When there is an interest in both maintaining one's original culture, while in daily interactions with other groups, *Integration* is the option. In this case, there is some degree of cultural integrity maintained, while at the same time seeking, as a member of an ethnocul-tural group, to participate as an integral part of the larger society. Finally, when there is little possibility or interest in cultural maintenance (often for reasons of enforced cultural loss), and little interest in having relations with others (often for reasons of exclusion or discrimination), then *Marginalization* is defined.

Two observations are important in understanding this framework. First, the use of circles to represent the intercultural space defined by these two basic issues was intended to dissuade researchers from drawing lines between the four sectors, thereby creating discrete boxes (Ward, 2009) into which individual can be placed, or be 'boxed' into one way of engaging in intercultural relations. There is much evidence that indivi-duals explore where in this circular intercultural space they prefer to engage their own and other groups. For example, in a longitudinal study of immigrant female adolescents from Hong Kong settling in New Zealand, Ho (1995) found that they explored various strategies, eventually ending after three years with a preference for the integration strategy. Similarly, in a cross-sectional study of immigrant youth settled in 13 societies, Berry et. al. (2006) found that there was a transition from marginalization to integration as the most preferred strategy. In both studies, it appears that youth discover that it is possible to be 'both', and settle on the integrative way of living interculturally.

Second, just as these four sectors do not define fixed ways to engage in intercultural relations, they are also not bounded in the sense that a preference for one precludes a similar preference for another strategy. When preferences for the four ways of acculturating are assessed independently (as they are in many of the studies in this project), an individual can have variable preferences (from high to low) for each of the four ways. For example, individuals may most prefer integration, but also accept that assimilation may also be useful in some situations in their intercultural living.

The inclusion of the larger society and their expectations (on the right-hand side of the framework) is rooted in the original anthropological definition of acculturation, which clearly established that *both* groups in contact would become acculturated (Redfield, Linton and Herskovits, 1936). The role that the dominant group plays in the emergence of these strategies is portrayed on the right side of Figure 1.2, where different (but parallel terms) are used to refer to the four expectations. Assimilation when sought by the non-dominant acculturating group is termed the *Melting Pot*. When separation is forced by the dominant group, it is *Segregation*. Marginalization, when imposed by the dominant group, is *Exclusion*. Finally, for integration, when cultural diversity is a feature of the society as a whole, including all the various ethnocultural groups, it is called *Multiculturalism*. With the use of this framework, comparisons can be made between individuals and their ethnocultural groups, and between non-dominant peoples and the larger society within which they are acculturating. In the country-specific chapters, the terms used to describe these various ways of engaging in intercultural relations are sometimes used interchangeably. For example, when the *melting pot* expectation is being discussed, an author may sometimes refer to this expectation as a desire for non-dominant individuals to *assimilate*. The context usually makes the meaning clear.

As noted earlier, the views of the larger society have been examined for decades (e.g., by Berry, Kalin and Taylor, 1977; and Berry and Kalin, 2001). The expectations, ideologies and policies of the dominant society and the attitudes of their individual members constitute an important element of intercultural research. This approach emphasizes the reciprocal nature of acculturation and intercultural relations. The view that there is a close connection, including an interaction and mutuality, between the strategies of the non-dominant and the expectations of the dominant communities has been reinforced by the work of Bourhis and colleagues (e.g., Bourhis, Moise, Perreault and Senecal, 1997) in their presentation of an interactive acculturation model. This approach has been further developed by Navas and colleagues (Navas, Rojas, García and Pumares, 2007), Safdar and colleagues (Safdar, Lay and Struthers, 2003), and by Horenczyk and colleagues (2013).

In Figure 1.2, the two circles show the terms used for the intercultural strategies of ethnocultural groups and the expectations held by the larger society. The terms used to name these two kinds of groups now vary considerably from one society to another. In some countries, they are called 'minority' and 'mainstream'; in others they are 'non-dominant' and 'dominant'; and in yet others they are 'ethnic' and 'national'. In the country chapters in this book, authors vary in their terminology when referring to these two kinds of groups, according to their preferences. However, in each case the terms used will clearly distinguish between the dominant group in the society, and those that are non-dominant.

The discussion up till this point of the strategies of non-dominant individuals and groups should not be taken to imply that they have complete freedom to choose how they want to acculturate. This freedom, of course, is not always the case; different groups usually have different power, creating a situation of asymmetrical acculturation (Vetic, 2016). When the dominant group enforces certain forms of acculturation or intercultural relations, or constrains the choices of non-dominant groups or individuals, then the third element in Figure 1.2 becomes necessary: the power of the dominant group to influence the strategies available to, and used by, the non-dominant groups. As a result, there is a mutual, reciprocal process through which both groups arrive at strategies that will work in a particular society, and in a particular setting. For example, integration can only be chosen and successfully pursued by non-dominant groups when the dominant society is open and inclusive in its orientation towards cultural diversity. Thus a mutual accommodation is required for integration to be attained, involving the acceptance by both groups of the right of all groups to live together as culturally different peoples. This strategy requires non-dominant groups to adopt the basic values of the larger society, while at the same time the dominant group must be prepared to adapt national institutions (e.g., education, health, labor) to better meet the needs of all groups now living together in the plural society.

In recent years, there have been some variations in how these acculturation strategies are conceptualised and assessed (Berry and Sabatier, 2011). In some cases, the second dimension is conceptualized, not as preferring to have contact with and to participate with other groups in the daily life of the larger society, but as either *adoption* of the culture of the larger society, or as *identification* with the larger society (Liebkind, 2001).

The original operationalization of the second dimension as 'contact and participation' with others in the larger society is the most commonly one used in the MIRIPS project. It is important to note that the second dimension does not specify the dominant national group only, but can include members of any groups other than one's own. This is important because, as noted earlier, in most plural societies, there is not usually only one 'other' group with which to engage (Ward and van Oudenhoven, 2013).

However, the use of cultural adoption as the second dimension is also sometimes used in the MIRIPS project. This approach was first used by Dona and Berry (1994) and has become a common way to operationalise this second dimension in the research literature. The third approach, identification with the larger society is also sometimes used, but is not used in the MIRIPS project.

There are now three approaches to the assessment of intercultural strategies and expectations. All of them are used in the various chapters in the MIRIPS project. They are all based on ethnographic research in order to understand the intercultural issues that exist between the groups and individuals in contact. This is required because the issues that arise during intercultural contact, and that initiate the process of acculturation, vary from one intercultural contact situation to another. Sometimes the issues are language, religion, values, dress, food, male-female relations, parent-child relations, social activities, friendship choices, schooling, media use, prejudice, discrimination; the list is virtually endless. These are sometimes referred to as the 'domains' of acculturation.

The first method was to develop four scales, one to measure each of the four strategies (Integration, Assimilation, Marginalization and Separation) for each of the acculturation domains identified in the preliminary research. This approach was summarized by Berry, Kim, Power, Young and Bujaki (1989). Individuals respond (on a 5-point scale from strongly agree to strongly disagree) to statements that portray the strategy.

In a second method, scales were developed by creating items to portray the two underlying dimensions (cultural maintenance, participation in the larger society) for each domain (first used by Dona and Berry, 1994).

The scores of individuals on these two underlying dimensions can then be crossed (using various points of split: the theoretical midpoint of each scale; the mean; or the median). On this basis, individuals can be placed in a space where those high on both dimensions are considered to be pursuing integration. Those who are high on one and low on the other dimension are considered to be pursuing either assimilation or separation. And those low on both are treated as pursuing marginalisation.

A third method uses cluster analysis of a number of acculturation variables. These include scales to assess the four acculturation attitudes, and scales to assess the two cultural identities, the two languages and the two social networks that individuals deal with during their acculturation (for both the heritage cultural and the larger society). For example, individuals in a cluster are considered to be pursuing integration when they have a positive attitude towards the integration strategy, who identify with both their heritage culture and the larger society, who speak both their heritage and national languages, and who have social relationships with members of both groups (Berry, Phinney, Sam and Vedder, 2006).

To capture these views held by individuals in the larger society, the construct of *multicultural ideology* was introduced by Berry et al. (1977). This concept includes the views that cultural diversity is good for a society and its individual members (i.e., there is a high value placed on cultural diversity and maintenance), and that such diversity should be shared and accommodated in an equitable way (i.e., there is a high value placed on contact and equitable participation among all groups). This combination of the acceptance of both cultural diversity and equity among groups and individuals constitutes the basis of the integration and multiculturalism strategies. In addition, the notion of multicultural ideology incorporates a third element: acceptance that the dominant society and its members should be prepared, themselves, to change in order to accommodate others in the larger society (i.e., mutual accommodation).

In various studies, multicultural ideology has been assessed by a scale that loaded integration items positively, and melting pot, segregation, and exclusion items negatively. Results generally support its construct validity (e.g., Berry et al., 1977; Berry and Kalin, 1995), and others have also found that integrationist views usually contrast with the other three attitudes (e.g., van de Vijver et al., 1999). Multicultural ideology has close empirical links to the concept of intercultural adaptation, including ethnic attitudes and prejudice, but is more explicitly related to practices for managing intergroup relations in culturally diverse societies. The assertion that there is a close connection between the attitudes of the non-dominant and dominant communities has been reinforced by the work of Bourhis and colleagues (e.g., Bourhis, Moise, Perreault and

Senecal, 1997) in their presentation of an interactive acculturation model. This approach has been further developed by Navas and colleagues in Spain (Navas, Rojas, García and Pumares, 2007), and Safdar and colleagues in Canada (Safdar, Lay and Struthers, 2003).

5   Adaptation and Well-Being

The outcomes of intercultural contact are constantly changing; there are ups and downs in how well individuals manage their intercultural transitions. However, at some point, the adaptations achieved by them can be assessed in order to determine how well individuals and groups are doing in their intercultural living. These outcomes may be either positive or negative in valence; that is, the concept of adaptation does not simply imply 'well-adapted', but can also mean 'mal-adapted'. This is because adaptations may or may not improve the 'fit' between individuals and their environments. It is thus not a term that necessarily implies that individuals or groups change to become more like their environments (i.e., adjustment by way of Assimilation), but may involve resistance and attempts to change their environments, or to move away from them altogether (i.e., by Separation).

As noted above, there are usually three kinds of adaptation examined. First, adaptations can be primarily internal or *psychological* (e.g., sense of well-being, or self-esteem; 'feeling well'). Second, *sociocultural* adaptation refers to how well an individual lives in the larger society, manifested for example in competence in the activities of daily intercultural living ('doing well'). Third, they can be *intercultural*, which links individuals to other groups and individuals in the larger society by establishing harmonious intercultural relations, with low levels of prejudice and discrimination ('relating well').

Adaptation is also multifaceted. The initial distinction between psychological and sociocultural adaptation was proposed and validated by Ward (1996). While conceptually distinct, they are empirically related to some extent (often with a correlation of +.40). However, they usually have different time courses and different experiential predictors. Psychological adaptation is predicted by personality variables, social support, and life change events, while sociocultural adaptation is predicted by cultural knowledge, degree of contact and positive intergroup attitudes. Psychological problems often increase soon after contact, followed by a general (but variable) decrease over time; positive sociocultural adaptation, however, typically has a linear improvement with time (see Ward et al., 2001, for a comprehensive review).

The concept of intercultural adaptation includes the acceptance of cultural diversity as good for a society and a willingness to change oneself in order to accommodate those who are culturally different. Positive intercultural adaptation includes tolerance: the acceptance of culturally different people in general, and positive evaluations of both specific ethnic groups in a society, and immigrants to a society. This form of adaptation is also empirically related to psychological and sociocultural adaptation, while remaining conceptually distinct, and being assessed by different scales.

The most important question about adaptation is whether there is a 'best way' to acculturate that is associated with better adaptation. In an overview article, Berry (1997) asserted: 'Psychological accultura-tion is influenced by many individual-level factors. In particular, the integrationist or bi-cultural acculturation strategy appears to be a consistent predictor of more positive outcomes than the three alterna-tives of assimilation, separation or marginalisation' (Berry, 1997, p. 27). This generalisation has found support in many specific studies which have been precursors to the present study (e.g., Berry, et.al, 2006; Berry and Sabatier, 2011; Gui, Berry and Zheng, 2012).

The most comprehensive examination of, and support for, the relation-ship between acculturation strategy and adaptation was carried out by Nguyen and Benet-Martinez (2013) using meta-analysis across 83 studies with over 20,000 participants. They found that integration (biculturalism in their terms) was found to have a significant and positive relationship with both psychological adaptation (e.g., life satisfaction, positive affect, self-esteem) and sociocultural adaptation (e.g., academic achievement, career success, social skills, lack of behavioural problems).

To illustrate the positive link between acculturation strategy and adap-tation, in the study of immigrant youth (Berry et al., 2006), we asked the question: 'is it the case that *how* an adolescent acculturates relates to *how well* they adapt?' The pattern in our findings was very clear: those in the integration profile had the best psychological and sociocultural adapta-tion outcomes, while those in the marginalisation/diffuse profile had the worst; in between, those with a separation/ethnic profile had moderately good psychological adaptation but poorer sociocultural adaptation, while those with an assimilation/national profile had moderately poor psycho-logical adaptation and slightly negative sociocultural adaptation. This pattern of results was largely replicated using structural equation model-ling with the same data set. We also examined relationships between the two forms of adaptation and perceived discrimination: we found that discrimination was negatively and significantly related to both psycholo-gical and sociocultural adaptation.

6 Hypotheses Guiding the MIRIPS Project

Three hypotheses are evaluated in the project: the *multiculturalism hypothesis;* the *contact hypothesis* and the *integration hypothesis.* These hypotheses have been derived from the multiculturalism policy advanced by the Government of Canada (1971). One key paragraph of the policy identifies the goal, and some steps to be taken to achieve this goal:

A policy of multiculturalism within a bilingual framework . . . [is] the most suitable means of assuring the cultural freedom of all Canadians. Such a policy should help to break down discriminatory attitudes and cultural jealousies. National unity, if it is to mean anything in the deeply personal sense, must be founded on confidence in one's own individual identity; out of this can grow respect for that of others, and a willingness to share ideas, attitudes and assumptions (emphasis added).

A framework (Figure 1.3) for examining the Canadian multiculturalism policy was proposed by Berry (1984). The fundamental goal of the policy (upper right) is to enhance mutual acceptance and to improve the quality of intercultural relations among all cultural groups. This goal is to be approached through three main programme components: the *cultural*

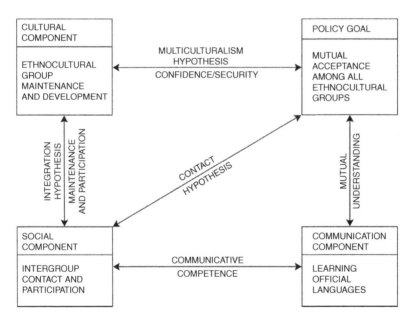

Figure 1.3. Framework for examining the Canadian multiculturalism policy (adapted from Berry, 1984).

diversity component (upper left); the *intercultural* component (lower left) and the *official language learning* component (lower right).

In addition to these components, there are three links among the components that give rise to the three hypotheses. These are the main hypotheses that are being examined in MIRIPS: the *multiculturalism hypothesis*; the *integration hypothesis* and the *contact hypothesis*, and are shown as links among the policy components in Figure 1.3.

The *multiculturalism hypothesis* is expressed in the policy statement as the belief that confidence in one's identity will lead to sharing, respect for others, and to the reduction of discriminatory attitudes. We have considered this 'confidence' to involve a sense of security, or conversely a sense of threat, to one's person or ethnocultural group. The multiculturalism hypothesis (advanced by Berry et al., 1977, p. 192) is that such a sense of security in one's identity is a psychological precondition for the acceptance of those who are culturally different. Conversely, when one's identity is threatened, people will reject others.

Three kinds of security have been conceptualized by Berry et al., (1977): cultural, economic, and personal. Cultural security refers to a sense that aspects of one's culture (such as identity and language) have a secure status in the society. Economic security refers to the sense that one's economic status (such as job security and house prices) are not going to be diminished in culturally diverse settings. Personal security refers to the sense that one is free to move around without being accosted or attacked. The MIRIPS project assess all three forms of security.

Initial findings from national surveys (Berry et al., 1977; Berry and Kalin, 1995) lend support to this link between confidence in one's identity and mutual acceptance. In those studies, measures of cultural and economic security were created with respect to extant diversity and the continuing flow of immigration. These two security scores were correlated positively with each other and with various intercultural attitudes: cultural security was negatively correlated with ethnocentrism, and positively with multicultural ideology and with perceived consequences of multiculturalism. Economic security had a similar pattern of correlations with these variables. In New Zealand, using a structural model, Ward and Masgoret (2008) found that security was positively related to multicultural ideology and with attitudes towards immigrants. In Russia, Lebedeva and Tatarko (2013) studied migrants from the Caucasus to Moscow and Muscovites. They found that cultural security predicted tolerance, integration and social equality in both groups, but to a lesser extent among Muscovites. In Estonia, a representative sample of Russian speakers was asked about their intercultural strategies, their ethnic self-esteem, their experience of discrimination and their level of cultural threat, civic engagement and economic and political satisfaction (Kruusvall, Vetik and Berry, 2009). The four usual intercultural strategies were found. Groups following the separation and marginalistion strategies had the highest levels of threat and lowest levels of self-esteem and civic engagement. In contrast, the integration and assimilation groups had the lowest threat and discrimination, and highest civic engagement and satisfaction. From this sampling of empirical studies, it is possible to conclude that security in one's own identity and place in society underlies the possibility of accepting cultural 'others'. This acceptance includes being tolerant, accepting cultural diversity in society, and accepting immigrants to, and ethnocultural groups in, that society.

Since the introduction of the multiculturalism hypothesis in 1977, the relationship has been proposed in an inverse way (called the 'integrated threat hypothesis') and colleagues (Stephan, Renfro, Esses, Stephan and Martin, 2005). They proposed that a sense of threat will undermine the possibility of engaging in positive intercultural relations. The threat hypothesis argues that a sense of threat to a person's identity will lead to rejection of the group that is the source of threat, and, in some cases, to an enhanced ethnic identity (called 'reactive identity'; Branscombe, Schmitt and Harvey, 1999).

Different types of threat have been studied, including realistic threat (e.g., due to real group conflict over resources), symbolic threat (e.g., conflicting values and beliefs) and intergroup anxiety (e.g., uncertainty about how to relate to the out-group). The experience of discrimination is one of the more frequently used indicators of threat that undermines a person's sense of security. Such discrimination has been shown to be related negatively to the pursuit of the integration strategy (Berry et al., 2006) and of well-being (Schmitt, Branscombe et al., 2014). A meta-analysis of the threat hypothesis (Reik et al., 2006) found substantial empirical support for the hypothesis. We consider that this concept of perceived threat is parallel to the earlier work on the role of security, but is phrased in the reverse direction to that of security.

In sum, the multiculturalism hypothesis proposes that a high sense of security will predict a preference for the strategies that engage in contact and participation in the larger society: Integration and Assimilation. In addition, this hypothesis proposes that secure individuals will achieve a higher level of intercultural adaptation, including high scores on Multicultural Ideology and Tolerance. The opposite is also predicted: when individuals are threatened, especially by acts of discrimination, they will prefer the Separation and Marginalization strategies, and exhibit low levels on the Multicultural Ideology and Tolerance scales.

The *contact hypothesis* is the second link in the policy framework. This hypothesis proposes that intercultural contact and sharing will promote mutual acceptance under certain conditions. The contact hypothesis asserts: 'Prejudice ... may be reduced by equal status contact between majority and minority groups in the pursuit of common goals' (Allport, 1954). Allport proposed that the hypothesis is more likely to be supported when certain conditions are present in the intercultural encounter. The effect of contact is predicted to be stronger when there is contact between groups of roughly equal social and economic status; however, in most intercultural situations, equal status is rare. A second condition is that the contact should be voluntary (sought by both groups, rather than imposed). A third condition is that contact should be supported by society, through norms and policies promoting contact and laws prohibiting discrimination.

A good deal of research has been carried out to test this hypothesis (see Hewstone and Swart, 2011). In a large meta-analysis, Pettigrew and Tropp (2011) examined hundreds of studies of the contact hypothesis, which came from many countries and many diverse settings (in schools, at work and in experiments). Their findings provide general support for the contact hypothesis: intergroup contact does generally relate negatively to prejudice in both dominant and non-dominant samples: Overall, the results from the meta-analysis reveal that greater levels of intergroup contact are typically associated with a lower level of prejudice. This effect was stronger where there were structured programs that incorporated the conditions outlined by Allport than when these conditions were not present.

In sum, the contact hypothesis proposes that under certain conditions, more intercultural contact will be associated with more mutual acceptance. Specifically, more contact will predict higher intercultural adaptation (both Multicultural Ideology and Tolerance) and should also predict a preference for the two strategies of Integration and Assimilation.

The *integration hypothesis* is the third link in the framework. This hypothesis proposes that when individuals and groups seek integration, by being doubly or multiply engaged (in both their heritage cultures and other groups in the larger society), they will be more successful in achieving a higher level of well-being, in both psychological and social domains, than if they engage only one or the other of the cultural groups. To illustrate the positive link between acculturation strategy and adaptation, a study of immigrant youth (Berry et al, 2006) found this relationship between integration and well-being (psychological and sociocultural adaptation) in a large sample of immigrant youth settled in 13 countries around the world. The general pattern in our findings was very clear: those in the integration profile had the best psychological and sociocultural adaptation outcomes, while those in the marginalization profile had the worst; in between, those with a separation profile had moderately good psychological adaptation but poorer sociocultural adaptation, while those with an assimilation profile had moderately poor psychological adaptation and slightly negative sociocultural adaptation. This pattern of results was largely replicated using structural equation modelling with the same data set. We also examined relationships between the two forms of adaptation and perceived discrimination: we found that discrimination was negatively and significantly related to both psychological and sociocultural adaptation.

This relationship between multiple cultural engagements and well-being has been extended from immigrant samples to ethnocultural groups in Europe (Koots-Ausmees and Realo, 2015). Apart from research with immigrants and ethnocultural groups, there is now clear evidence that having multiple social links and identities provides the basis for higher levels of well-being (Jetten, Branscombe, Haslam et al., 2015). A possible explanation is that those who are doubly engaged with both cultures receive support and resources from both, and are competent in dealing with both cultures. This double social capital (Putnam, 2007) included bonding to one's own cultural community and bridging to others in the larger society. The associations afforded by these multiple social and cultural engagements may well offer the route to success in plural societies.

Most recently, using a large representative sample of immigrants to Canada, Berry and Hou (2016) found that those preferring integration (assessed as having a strong sense of belonging to both heritage culture and to the larger Canadian society) had the highest scores on measures of life satisfaction and mental health; and those preferring marginalization (low sense of belonging to both cultures) had much lower scores. For life satisfaction, those preferring assimilation also scored high; and for mental health, those preferring separation also scored high.

The extension of the integration hypothesis to apply to members of the dominant national group is new. When they hold the multiculturalism expectation for how non-dominant group members should relate interculturally, there may well also be benefits for the dominant group. This may be due to their more open and tolerant orientation to cultural diversity, which in turn may provide a basis for their well-being when dealing with intercultural relations in a plural society. The MIRIPS project will evaluate the integration hypothesis among the dominant, as well as the non-dominant samples.

In sum, the integration hypothesis proposes that when individuals prefer the integration strategy, or have the multiculturalism expectation (that is, when they are doubly or multiply engaged), they will achieve higher scores on psychological, sociocultural and intercultural adaptation than when they prefer any of the other three strategies. Conversely, when individuals are marginalized (when they have no, or few engagements), they will achieve lower scores. Because one or the other form of social capital is present in the assimilation and separation strategies, mid-levels of adaptation are expected for the assimilation and separation strategies.

7   Design of the MIRIPS Study

The goal of the MIRIPS project is to evaluate the validity of these three hypotheses in different cultural groups living in varying intercultural contexts. If they are widely supported, then some general principles of intercultural relations may be established. Where they are not supported, the specific conditions that prevail in that context will need to be examined to discern why there is no support.

Each country research team employed the MIRIPS instrument in a way that met their research needs and their social conditions. Thus, the findings are not always comparable across countries. Nevertheless, the core concepts and the three hypotheses remain generally common, even if they were operationalized somewhat differently. These variations in conceptual and empirical aspects are identified in each chapter. Because of these variations, the goal of the MIRIPS project has *not been* to place all the data collected in all the societies into one data base, and thereby to carry out pan-cultural analyses (as was done, e.g., in the study of immigrant youth) (Berry et al., 2006). The balance of this book presents chapters outlining the studies out by colleagues in a number of countries. This is followed by an integrative chapter **that** provides an overview and evaluation of the findings from the project.

The structure of the book follows a geographic rationale. First are chapters from studies of Russian peoples in Eastern and Northern Europe (in Russia, Latvia, Azerbaijan, Estonia, Finland and Norway). Two Western European countries (Germany and Switzerland), five Southern European (Greece, Italy, Malta, Portugal and Spain) and two Asian countries (India and Hong Kong) follow. The sequence is completed by the presentation of findings from two traditional 'settler societies' (Australia and Canada).

7.1   *Questionnaire. Please see appendix for details*

Socio-demographic variables: Age, Gender, Education, Religion, Status (work), Status (ownership)

Ethnicity variables: Ethnic origin, Marriage preference, Neighbourhood ethnic composition, Place of birth

Intercultural variables: Social contacts, Cultural identity, Security, Acculturation strategies, Acculturation expectations, Perceived discrimination

Attitudes: Multicultural ideology, Tolerance/prejudice, Attitudes towards Immigration (kind, number, perceived consequences), and to Ethnocultural groups

Adaptation: Self-esteem, Life satisfaction, Psychological problems, Sociocultural competence.

Social Desirability

7.2   Context Variables (Not in Questionnaire)

In addition to variables that are assessed using the questionnaire with samples of individuals, we also gathered contextual information at the group level. For national societies as a whole, and for various component groups (regional, immigrant, ethnocultural), the national census and other forms of archival statistics were used.

These data can include:

1. Distribution of population by ethnic origin, language and religion in the national society and regional populations.
2. Percentage of immigrants in the national society and regional populations.
3. Public policies regarding diversity and intercultural relations. This variable reflects the degree to which a national society promotes pluralism.
4. Economic indicators of the national society, and the regional and immigrant/ethnic populations.
5. Historical factors that may influence intercultural relations.

References

Aleksynska, M. and Algan, Y. (2010). *Assimilation and Integration of Immigrants in Europe*. IZA DP No. 5185 http://ftp.iza.org/dp5185.pdf.

Alesina, A., Arnaud, D., Easterly, W., Kurlat, S. and Wacziarg, R. (2003). Ethnic Fractionalisation. *Journal of Economic Growth, 8*, 155–194.

Alesina, A., Harnoss, J. and Raporport, H. (2016). Birthplace diversity and economic prosperity. *Journal of Economic Growth, 21*, 101–138.

Ben-Shalom, U., and Horenczyk, G. (2003). Acculturation orientations: A facet theory perspective on the bidimensional model. *Journal of Cross-Cultural psychology, 34*, 176–188.

Berry, J. W. (1970). Marginality, stress and ethnic identification in an acculturated Aboriginal community. *Journal of Cross-Cultural Psychology, 1*, 239–252.

Berry, J.W. (1974).Psychological aspects of cultural pluralism. *Culture Learning, 2*, 17–22.

Berry, J.W. (1980). Acculturation as varieties of adaptation. In A. Padilla (Ed.), *Acculturation: Theory, Models and Some New Findings.* (pp. 9–25). Boulder: Westview Press.

Berry, J.W. (1984). Multicultural policy in Canada: A social psychological analysis. *Canadian Journal of Behavioural Science, 16,* 353–370.

Berry, J.W (1997). Immigration, acculturation and adaptation. *Applied Psychology: An International Review, 46,* 5–68.

Berry, J.W. (2003a). How shall we all live together? In M. Luik (Ed.) *Multicultural Estonia* (pp. 3–11). Tallinn: Estonian Integration Foundation.

Berry, J.W. (2003b). Conceptual approaches to acculturation. In K. Chun, P. Balls-Organista and G. Marin (Eds.). *Acculturation: Advances in Theory, Measurement and Application* (pp. 17–37). Washington: APA Books.

Berry, J. W. (2004). Fundamental psychological processes in intercultural relations. In D. Landis and J. Bennett (Eds.), *Handbook of Intercultural Research.* (3rd ed., pp. 166–184). Thousand Oaks: Sage Publications.

Berry, J.W. (2005). Acculturation: Living successfully in two cultures. *International Journal of Intercultural Relations, 29,* 697–712.

Berry, J.W. (2006) Attitudes towards immigrants and ethnocultural groups in Canada. *International Journal of Intercultural Relations, 30,* 719–734.

Berry, J. W. (2009). A critique of critical acculturation. *International Journal of Intercultural Relations, 33,* 561–371.

Berry, J.W. (2013). Achieving a global psychology. *Canadian Psychology, 54,* 55–61.

Berry, J.W. (2015). *Intercultural adaptation to acculturation.* Paper presented at Annual Conference, Canadian Psychological Association, Ottawa, June.

Berry, J.W. (2016). Diversity and equity. *Cross-Cultural and Strategic Management, 23,* 413–430.

Berry, J.W., and Hou, F. (2016). Acculturation and wellbeing among immigrants to Canada. *Canadian Psychology: Special Issue on Immigrants and Refugees in Canada, 57,* 254–264.

Berry, J.W., and Kalin, R, (1995) Multicultural and ethnic attitudes in Canada: An overview of the 1991 national survey. *Canadian Journal of Behavioural Science, 27,* 301–320.

Berry, J.W., and Kalin, R. (2000). Multicultural policy and social psychology: The Canadian experience. In S. Renshon and Duckitt, (Eds.), *Political Psychology: Cultural and Cross-Cultural Foundations* (pp. 263–284). London: MacMillan.

Berry, J.W., Kim, U., Power, S., Young, M., and Bujaki, M. (1989). Acculturation attitudes in plural societies. *Applied Psychology: An International Review, 38,* 185–206.

Berry, J.W., Phinney, J.S., Sam, D.L., and Vedder, P. (Eds.) (2006a). *Immigrant Youth in Cultural Transition: Acculturation, Identity and Adaptation across National Contexts.* Mahwah: Lawrence Erlbaum Associates.

Berry, J.W., Phinney, J.S, Sam, D.L., and Vedder, P. (Eds.) (2006b). Immigrant youth: Acculturation, identity and adaptation. *Applied Psychology: An International Review, 55,* 303–332.

Berry, J.W., Poortinga, Y.H., Breugelmans, S.M., Chasiotis, A., and Sam, D.L. (2011). *Cross-Cultural Psychology: Research and Applications.* 3rd edition. Cambridge: Cambridge University Press.

Berry, J. W., and Sabatier, C. (2010). Acculturation, discrimination, and adaptation among second generation immigrant youth in Montreal and Paris. *International Journal of Intercultural Relations, 34(3)*, 191–207.

Berry, J. W., and Sabatier, C. (2011). Variations in the assessment of acculturation attitudes: Their relationships with psychological wellbeing. *International Journal of Intercultural Relations, 35*, 658–669.

Bloemraad, I. (2011). The debate over multiculturalism: Philosophy, politics, and policy. Migration Information Source. www.migrationinformation.org/Fe ature/display.cfm?ID=854.

Bloemraad, I., and Wright, M. (2014). "Utter failure" or unity out of diversity? Debating and evaluating policies of multiculturalism. *International Migration Review, 48*, 292–334.

Bourhis, R., Moise, C., Perreault, S., and Senecal, S. (1997). Towards an interactive acculturation model: A social psychological approach. *International Journal of Psychology. 32*, 369–386.

Branscombe, N. R., Schmitt, M. T., and Harvey, R. D. (1999). Perceiving pervasive discrimination among African Americans: Implications for group identification and well-being. *Journal of Personality and Social Psychology, 77*, 135–149. *http://dx.doi.org/10.1037/0022- 3514.77.1.135.*

Chirkov, V. (2009) (Ed). Critical acculturation psychology. *International Journal of Intercultural Relations*, Special Issue, 33, 2.

Dona, G., and Berry, J.W. (1994). Acculturation attitudes and acculturative stress of Central American refugees in Canada. *International Journal of Psychology, 29*, 57–70.

Esses, V.M., Hodson, G., and Dovidio, J.F. (2003). Public attitudes toward immigrants and immigration: Determinants and policy implications. In C.M. Beach, A.G. Green and J.G. Reitz (Eds.), *Canadian Immigration Policy for the 21st Century* (pp. 507–535). Montreal, Canada: McGill Queen's Press.

Fearon, J. (2013). Ethnic and cultural diversity by country. *Journal of Economic Growth, 8*, 195–222.

Fleras, A. (2009). *The Politics of Multiculturalism: Multicultural Governance in Comparative Perspective.* New York: Palgrave.

Gezentsvey Lamy, M.,Ward, C., and Liu, J. (2013) Motivation for ethno-cultural continuity. *Journal of Cross-Cultural Psychology, 44*, 1047–1066.

Government of Canada (1971). *Multicultural Policy: Statement to House of Commons.* Ottawa.

Graves, T. D. (1967). Psychological acculturation in a tri-ethnic community. *Southwestern Journal of Anthropology, 23*, 337–350.

Gui, Y., Berry, J. W., and Zheng, Y. (2012). Migrant worker acculturation in China. *International Journal of Intercultural Relations. 36*, 598–610.

Hewstone, M., and Swart, H. (2011). Fifty-odd years of inter-group contact: From hypothesis to integrated theory. *British Journal of Social psychology, 50*, 374–386.

Horenczyk, G., Jasinskaya-Lahti, I., Sam, D.L., and Vedder, P. (2013). Mutuality in acculturation: Toward integration. *Zeitschrift für Psychologie*, *221*, 205–213.

Jetten, J., Branscombe, N., Haslam, A. et al. (2015). Having a lot of a good thing: Multiple important group memberships as a source of self-esteem. PLOS ONE; doi:10.1371/journal.pone. Accessed May 27, 2015.

Kalin, R., and Berry, J.W. (1996). Interethnic attitudes in Canada: Ethnocentrism, consensual hierarchy and reciprocity. *Canadian Journal of Behavioural Science*, *28*, 253–261.

Kesler, C., and Bloemraad, I. (2010). Does immigration erode social capital? The conditional effects of immigration-generated diversity of trust, membership, and participation across 19 countries, 1981–2000. *Canadian Journal of Political Science*, *43*, 319–347.

Koots-Ausmees, L., and Realo, A. (2015). The association between life satisfaction and self-reported health status in Europe. *Personality*, *29*, 647–657.

Lebedeva, N., and Tatarko, A. (2013). Immigration, acculturation and multiculturalism in post-Soviet Russia. *European Psychologist*, *18*, 169–178.

Liebkind, K. (2001). Acculturation. In R. Brown and S. Gaertner (Eds.), *Blackwell Handbook of Social Psychology* (Vol. 4, pp. 386–406). Oxford: Blackwell.

Navas, M., Garcia, M., Sanchez, J., Rojas, A., Pumares, P., and Fernandez, J. (2005). Relative acculturation extended model. *International Journal of Intercultural Relations*, *29*, 21–37.

Navas, M., Rojas, A. J., García, M., and Pumares, P. (2007). Acculturation strategies and attitudes according to the Relative Acculturation Extended Model (RAEM): The perspectives of natives versus immigrants. *International Journals of Intercultural Relations*, *31*, 67–86.

Nguyen, A.-M. D., and Benet-Martinez, V. (2013). Biculturalism and adjustment: A meta-analysis. *Journal of Cross-cultural Psychology*, *44*, 122–159.

Nieto, S., Matano, A., and Ramos, R. (2013). *Skill mismatches in the EU: Immigrants versus natives*. Discussion Paper 7701. Institute for the Study of Labour (IZA), Bonn, Germany. http://ftp.iza.org/dp7701.pdf.

Pettigrew, T., and Tropp, L. (2011). *When Groups Meet*. London: Psychology Press.

Plaut, V. C., Garnett, F. G., Buffardi, L. E., and Sanchez-Burks, J. (2011). What about me? Perceptions of exclusion and whites' reactions to multiculturalism. *Journal of Personality and Social Psychology*, *101*, 337–353.

Plaut, V. C., Thomas, K. M., and Goren, M. J. (2009). Is multiculturalism or colour-blindness better for minorities? *Psychological Science*, *20*, 444–446.

Putnam, R. D. (2007). Diversity and community in the twenty-first century. *Scandinavian Political Science*, *30*, 137–174.

Redfield, R., Linton, R., and Herskovits, M.J. (1936). Memorandum for the study of acculturation. *American Anthropologist*, *38*, 149–152.

Riek, B., Mania, E., and Gaertner, S. (2006) Intergroup threat and outgroup attitudes: A meta-analytic review. *Personality and Social Psychology Review*, *10*, 336–353.

Ryder, A., Alden, L., and Paulhus, D. (2000). Is acculturation unidimensional or bidimensional? *Journal of Personality and Social Psychology*, *79*, 49–65.

Sam, D.L and Berry, J.W (Eds.) (2016). *Cambridge Handbook of Acculturation Psychology* (2nd ed.). Cambridge: Cambridge University Press.

Safdar, S.,Lay, C., & Struthers, W. (2003).The process of acculturation and basic goals: Testing a multidimensional individual differences acculturation model with Iranian immigrants in Canada. Applied Psychology: An International Review, 52, 555–579

Schmitt, M, Branscombe, N. et al. (2014).The Consequences of Perceived Discrimination for Psychological Well-Being: A Meta-Analytic Review. *Psychological Bulletin*, 921–932.

Social Science Research Council. (1954). Acculturation: An exploratory formulation. *American Anthropologist*, *56*, 973–1002.

Stephan, W., Lausanne, R., Esses, V., Stephan, C., and Martin, T. (2005). The effects of feeling threatened on attitudes towards immigrants. *International Journal of Intercultural Relations*. *29*, 1–20.

Van de Vijver, F. J. R., Helms-Lorenz, M., and Felzer, M. J. A. (1999). Acculturation and cognitive performance of migrant children in the Netherlands. *International Journal of Psychology*, *34*, 149–162.

Van Oudenhoven, J. P., and Ward, C. (2012). Fading majority cultures: The effects of transnationalism and demographic developments on the acculturation of immigrants. *Journal of Community and Applied Social Psychology*. *23*, 81–97

Vertovec, S., and Wessendorf, S. (Eds.) (2010). *The Multiculturalism Backlash: European Discourses, Policies and Practices*. London: Routledge.

Vetic, R. (2016).Two complementary research strategies in acculturation studies. Paper in preparation.

Ward, C. (1996). Acculturation. In D. Landis and R. Bhagat (Eds.), *Handbook of Intercultural Training* (2nd ed., pp. 124–147). Newbury Park: Sage.

Ward, C., Bochner, S., and Furnham, A. (2001). *The Psychology of Culture Shock*. Sussex: Routledge.

Wright, M., and Bloemraad, I. (2012). Is there a trade-off between multiculturalism and socio-political integration? Policy regimes and immigrant incorporation in comparative perspective. *Perspectives on Politics*, *10*, 77–95.

2   Intercultural Relations in Russia

*Nadezhda Lebedeva, Victoria Galyapina, Zarina Lepshokova and Tatiana Ryabichenko**
National Research University Higher School of Economics, Russian Federation

1   Introduction

The Russian Federation is one of the most multicultural societies in the world, having more than 100 ethnic and cultural groups. It ranks in the middle of the ethnic diversity index; however, it is estimated that Russia is low on the migrant integration index, and estimated to be in the middle on the multiculturalism policy index. In this chapter, we present two studies of intercultural relations in two multicultural regions of the Russian Federation: Central Federal District (Moscow) and two republics in the North Caucasus (Kabardino-Balkar Republic and Republic of North Ossetia–Alania). For each study, we first present the local context of intercultural relations and related theoretical issues, the samples and the results of each regional study. Then we present a general discussion based on a comparative analysis of the three hypotheses in both regions. Finally, we consider the limitations of the studies and their possible implications.

2   Context of Intercultural Relations in the Russian Federation

The Russian Federation consists of 83 Federal Administrative Units, 21 of which are called 'National' Republics, named after the names of one or more of the most numerous ethnic groups living in this republic. According to UN estimates (United Nations, Department of Economic and Social Affairs, Population Division, 2015), the Russian Federation is the world's third-leading country in terms of the total immigrants living there (11.6 million). The immigrants mainly come

---

* The names after the first author appear in alphabetical order.

34

from the states of the former Soviet Union. In 2013, their overall share was 87.6%, with the relative contribution of Central Asian countries continuously on the rise (Vishnevsky, 2011; Zayonchkovskaya, Karachurina, Florinskaya & Mkrtchyan, 2015). The cultural diversity resulting from this migration and from the existing ethnic diversity of many Russian regions brings about complex problems of intercultural relations, and mutual acculturation and adaptation among different types of migrants, ethnocultural groups and the larger society (Lebedeva & Tatarko, 2013).

The two regions examined in this study differ substantially in their ethnic composition. In the first study (in the Moscow, Central Federal District), we investigated the mutual intercultural relations among members of the dominant group (ethnic Russians) and two groups of migrants: one from South Caucasus (Armenians, Georgians and Azerbaijanis) and another group from Central Asia (Uzbeks and Tajiks). In the second study, we studied the mutual intercultural relations between the dominant groups in two regions (Kabardians and Balkars in the Kabardino-Balkar Region [KBR] and Ossetians in the North Ossetia–Alania Region [RNO-A]) and ethnic Russians (who are minorities in these Republics of the Russian Federation in the North Caucasus).

2.1   Immigration to the Russian Federation

Russia's attractiveness for migrants from the former USSR is determined by a shared history over many centuries, the widespread use of the Russian language in interpersonal communication during the Soviet period, and a visa-free regime. Three main migration waves to Russia have been identified (Genov and Savvidis, 2011). The first consisted of ethnic Russians, or Russian native speakers with different ethnic backgrounds, who returned to Russia from the newly independent states after the collapse of Soviet Union in 1990s. Since the end of the 1990s, the ethnic composition and social structure of migration has changed. Migrants from Ukraine, Moldova, and states of the South Caucasus (Armenia, Georgia and Azerbaijan) formed the second wave of migration to Russia. In the third ongoing wave, the numbers of migrants from Central Asia have become predominant. The second and the third migration waves were mainly caused by the substantial economic gap between Russia and high levels of unemployment in some of the adjacent states (Zayonchkovskaya & Tyuryukanova, 2010; Genov & Savvidis, 2011; Di Bartolomeo, Makaryan & Weinar, 2014).

Despite the need of Russia's economy for labor migrants, the attitudes of Russians towards migration and migrants are rather negative. Among Russians the term 'migrants' is associated mostly with migrants from Central Asia and Caucasus regarded as a source of cultural threat and economic burden (Genov & Savvidis, 2011; Zayonchkovskaya, Poletaev, Doronina, Mkrtchyan & Florinskaya, 2014).

Studies conducted in Moscow showed that migrants from the different source countries differ from one another. Migrants from Armenia and Georgia are employed in factories, construction, transportation, education, healthcare, various services and trade. Most of them are professionally skilled and have jobs that mostly correspond to their educational level. The main reasons for young migrants from Armenia and Georgia to go abroad are better education and job opportunities (Poghosyan, 2011; Badurashvili, 2011). A similar picture appears in the case of migrants from Azerbaijan who are employed in the retail and wholesale trade, construction, factories and transportation (Yunusov, 2013). The vast majority of migrants from Central Asia are low-skilled workers. High unemployment rates and low wages, especially among the rural population in Central Asia, serve as powerful push factors for young and less skilled migrants who do not speak Russian and who are thus often perceived as culturally and socially distant by the host population in Russia (Di Bartolomeo et al., 2014; Zayonchkovskaya & Tyuryukanova, 2010). Migrants from Central Asia see migration to Russia as a strategy for success in life. Their decision to migrate is reinforced by the experience of those who have already emigrated and who have been able to improve the financial situation of their families (Di Bartolomeo et al., 2014). According to statistics, approximately 30% of officially employed foreign workers are concentrated in Moscow, and 43% are in the Central Federal District as a whole (Di Bartolomeo et al., 2014).

3   Evaluation of the MIRIPS Hypotheses

In these two studies, we examine the three MIRIPS hypotheses (Multiculturalism, Contact and Integration) in the three different cultural contexts in the two multicultural regions of Russia.

To test our hypotheses three path models were constructed. The theoretical model is presented in the Figure 2.1. The three hypotheses are shown as paths among the variables of security, contact and the integration strategy. In addition, we examined the role of the assimilation strategy in adaptation.

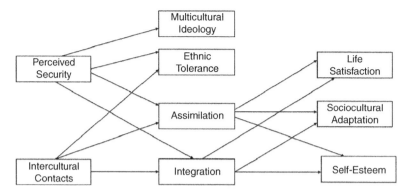

Figure 2.1. Theoretical model tested in the two studies.

4   Method

4.1   Measures

We used the following scales from the MIRIPS questionnaire: *Perceived security*, *Intercultural contacts*, *Ethnic tolerance*, *Multicultural ideology*, *Acculturation strategies* (of migrants and ethnic minorities) and *Acculturation expectations* (of ethnic majorities), *Life satisfaction* (Diener, Emmons, Larsen & Griffin, 1985), *Self-esteem* (Rosenberg, 1965), *Sociocultural adaptation scale* ((Wilson, 2013) (used with migrants and ethnic minorities only). *Age* and *duration of residence of migrants* in Russia were measured in years. Measures were translated into Russian and adapted for use in previous studies in Russia (Lebedeva & Tatarko, 2009). In the first study (of migrants from Central Asia to the Moscow region), questionnaires were translated into Uzbek and Tajik and adapted for use in Russia by our colleague J. Khojiev.

4.2   Data Processing

To test the three hypotheses, we followed a Structural Equation Modeling (SEM) approach (Kline, 1998). Seven path analyses were performed with three ethnic majority groups (Russians, Kabardians Balkars and Ossetians) and two groups of ethnic minorities: migrants (from South Caucasus and from Central Asia); and two groups of Russian minorities in KBR and RNO-A. These analyses were carried out separately using SPSS AMOS 20 software (Arbuckle, 2011).

Multivariate analysis of variance (MANOVA) and t-tests were used to examine the differences between means-of-the-scales scores across the different groups. As noted earlier, we also examine the role of the assimilation strategy. This is because a preference for assimilation plays and important role in intercultural relations and mutual adaptation of migrants and the larger society (Jasinskaja-Lahti, Horenczyk & Kinunen, 2011; Kus-Harbord, Ward, 2015; Lebedeva, Tatarko & Berry, 2016).

5   Results

5.1   *Study 1. Mutual Intercultural Relations between Migrants from South Caucasus and Central Asia and Ethnic Russians in Moscow*

The aim of the Study 1 was to test three hypotheses of intercultural relations: the multiculturalism hypothesis, the contact hypothesis, and the integration hypothesis in the Central Federal District of Russia (Moscow) with samples of the ethnic Russian majority and two groups of migrants (from South Caucasus and Central Asia).

Participants were 261 ethnic Russians, 227 migrants from Central Asia (123 Uzbeks and 104 Tajiks) and 274 migrants from South Caucasus (179 Armenians, 48 Azerbaijanis and 47 Georgians). A description of the sample is presented in Table 2.1.

The migrant data were collected in various locales in Moscow: the Federal Migration Service Centers; public markets or workplaces; local migrant organizations and universities. A snowball sampling procedure was used. Participation was voluntary; respondents were informed that their responses are anonymous.

Table 2.1. *Sample description: Study 1.*

Group	N	Male	%	Female	%	Range	Mean	SD
			Gender				Age	
Migrants from Central Asia	227	143	63.0	84	37.0	19 – 66	31.55	8.70
Migrants from South Caucasus	274	120	43.8	154	56.2	17 – 74	34.39	12.36
Ethnic Russians	261	130	49.8	131	50.2	18 – 69	36.28	14.87
Total	762	393	51.6	369	48.4	17 – 74	34.19	12.51

Results of Study 1

The average length of residence of migrants from Central Asia in Russia was 5.70 years (SD = 4.99). Most (62.9%) arrived in Russia during the previous five years. The average length of residence in Russia for the migrants from South Caucasus was higher: 11.92 years (SD = 6.78).

Descriptive statistics including means, standard deviations and reliability coefficients of measures for all three groups are presented in Table 2.2.

With respect to mean differences, integration is the most preferred acculturation strategy in both groups of migrants, as well as the preferred expectation of Russians. Assimilation preferences of migrants from Central Asia are higher in comparison with migrants from South Caucasus. South-Caucasian migrants reported more frequent intercultural contacts than other groups, and they are more socioculturally adapted than are Central Asian migrants. However, Central Asian migrants have higher scores on life satisfaction. The levels of perceived security and multicultural ideology of migrants from Central Asia are the highest in comparison with other groups.

Results for Migrant Samples in Moscow

Goodness-of-fit indicators of the path model are satisfactory in the sample of migrants from Central Asia (χ^2/df = 2.12, RMSEA =.07, CFI=.93, PCLOSE =.19) and are good in the sample of migrants from South Caucasus (χ^2/df = 1.66, RMSEA =.05, CFI =.96, PCLOSE =.46). Standardized regression weights and correlations between variables from the empirical models of the groups of migrants from Central Asia and South Caucasus are presented in the Table 2.3 using slash.

Multiculturalism hypothesis. In both groups of migrants, perceived security positively related to their multicultural ideology (β_{CA} =.26, p <.001; β_{SC} =.16, p <.01), but did not relate to their ethnic tolerance. We also found a positive relationship between perceived security and integration in both groups (β_{CA} =.14, p <.05; β_{SC} =.15, p <.01). Additionally, we found a positive relationship between perceived security and assimilation in the group of migrants from South Caucasus (β_{SC} =.12, p <.05).

Contact hypothesis. Intercultural contacts positively related to ethnic tolerance only in the group of migrants from Central Asia (β_{CA} =.13, p <.05). Intercultural contacts were not related to multicultural ideology or to acculturation strategies in either of the groups.

Integration hypothesis. The relationship between integration and self-esteem was positive in both groups (β_{CA} =.14, p <.05; β_{SC} =.30, p <.001),

Table 2.2. *Means, standard deviations and reliability coefficients for samples of migrants from Central Asia and South Caucasus and sample of majority group (Russians).*

Measures	Migrants from Central Asia (CA)			Migrants from South Caucasus (SC)			Russians			$F(2, 759)$	η^2	p
	Mean	SD	α	Mean	SD	α	Mean	SD	α			
SEC	4.07[a]	.74	.61	3.14[b]	.80	.50	3.50[c]	.70	.58	96.04	.20	<.001
IC	3.05[a]	1.05	.70	3.55[b]	1.15	.82	2.30[c]	1.25	.91	79.08	.17	<.001
TOL	3.29[a]	1.08	.52	3.02[b]	1.17	.63	3.03[b]	1.07	.69	4.60	.01	.01
MI	4.15[a]	.73	.63	4.03[b]	.76	.63	3.78[b]	.76	.64	15.33	.04	<.001
INT	4.39[a]	.74	.65	4.40[a]	.72	.71	3.91[b]	.73	.68	38.57	.09	<.001
AS	2.01[a]	.96	.70	1.79[b]	.74	.58	2.09[a]	.75	.70	9.62	.03	<.001
LS	3.35[a]	1.01	.74	3.09[b]	.92	.86	3.26[a]	.79	.81	8.14	.02	<.001
SE	4.36[a]	.70	.76	4.13[a]	.59	.60	4.14[b]	.52	.71	11.18	.03	<.001
SA	2.44[a]	1.07	.94	4.17[b]	.62	.81	–	–	–	508.37*	.50	<.001

Notes: Differences between groups were tested using MANOVA and Tukey's HSD. Values in the same row with different superscripts are significantly different (p <.05).
* $F(1, 499)$.

SEC – Security; IC – Intercultural contacts; TOL – Ethnic Tolerance, MI – Multicultural ideology, INT – Integration; AS – Assimilation; LS – Life satisfaction; SE – Self-esteem; SA – Sociocultural adaptation.

Table 2.3. *Standardized regression weights and correlations for the samples of migrants (Central Asia/South Caucasus).*

Predictors	IC	MI	TOL	INT	AS	SA	SE	LS
SEC	*.09/*	*.26***/*	−.05/	.14*/	−.05/	–	–	*.16**/*
	12	*16***	.12	.15**	.12*			*.04*
IC	–	–	.13*/	.07/	.07/	–	–	–
			−.08	.02	.10			
MI	–	–	.07/	*.13*/*	*−.29**/*	–	*.23***/*	–
			−.08	.34***	−.25***		.05	
TOL	–	–	–	−.05/	*−.15*/*	–	–	–
				.01	−.05			
INT	–	–	–	–	*−.18*/*	.03/	.14*/	.05/
					−.25***	.29***	.30***	.16**
AS	–	–	–	–	–	.19**/	−.12/	*.22***/*
						.06	.01	.22***
R^2		.07/.02	.02/.02	.03/.02	.01/.03	.03/.08	.04/.09	.05/.06

Notes: *p <.05; **p <.01; ***p <.001.
SEC – Security; IC – Intercultural contacts; MI – Multicultural ideology; TOL – Ethnic tolerance; INT – Integration; AS – Assimilation; SA – Sociocultural adaptation; SE – Self-esteem; LS – Life satisfaction. Correlations are in italics.
CA – Central Asia, SC – South Caucasus.

while the relationships of integration with life satisfaction and sociocultural adaptation were found only in the group of migrants from South Caucasus (β_{SC} =.16, p <.01 for life satisfaction; β_{SC} =.30, p <.001 for sociocultural adaptation). Furthermore, the assimilation strategy was positively related with life satisfaction in both groups (β_{CA} =.22, p <.001; β_{SC} =.22, p <.001), and with sociocultural adaptation (β_{CA} =.19, p <.01) in migrants from Central Asia.

Results for Ethnic Majority Russians in Moscow
Goodness-of-fit indicators of the model for the majority group are good (χ^2/df = 1.46, RMSEA =.04, CFI=.98, PCLOSE =.54). Standardized regression weights and correlations between variables are shown in the Table 2.4.

Multiculturalism hypothesis. The results for the Russians' sample showed that perceived security is a strong predictor of their multicultural ideology (β =.45, p <.001), but does not predict their ethnic tolerance. Perceived security positively related to their integration expectation (β =.17, p <.01) and negatively related to assimilation expectation (β = −.17, p <.01).

Table 2.4. *Standardized regression weights and correlations for the sample of the Russian majority group.*

Predictor	IC	MI	TOL	INT	AS	SE	LS
SEC	−.15*	.45***	−.02	.17**	−.17**	–	.11
IC		–	−.01	.18**	−.09	–	–
MI		–	.18**	.35***	−34***	−.02	–
TOL		–	–	−.01	−.12	–	–
INT		–	–	–	−.12	.17**	.15*
AS		–	–	−.12	–	−.03	.08
R²		.21	<.001	.05	.03	.03	.03

Notes: *p <.05; **p <.01; ***p <.001.
SEC – Security; IC – Intercultural contacts; MI – Multicultural ideology; TOL – Ethnic tolerance; INT – Integration; AS – Assimilation; SE – Self-esteem; LS – Life satisfaction. Correlations are in italics.

Contact hypothesis. Intercultural contacts were positively linked to the integration expectation (β =.18, p <.01) among ethnic Russians. No relationships between intercultural contacts and ethnic tolerance were found.

Integration hypothesis. Integration expectation of the majority group positively related to their life satisfaction (β =.15, p <.05) and self-esteem (β =.17, p <.01). For the assimilation expectation, no relationships were found.

5.2   Study 2. Mutual Intercultural relations in North Caucasus

In Study 2, we evaluated the three intercultural relations hypotheses in the North Caucasus region of the Russian Federation. This region is one of the most multicultural regions of Russia, with a rich history and complex inter-ethnic relations between numerous ethnic groups living there. We studied intercultural relations between titular ethnic groups (majority) and ethnic Russians (minority) in the Republic of North Ossetia–Alania (RNO-A) and the Kabardino-Balkar Republic (KBR).

The dynamics of the ethnic composition of the population of the North Caucasus has been characterized by an intensive outflow of ethnic Russians from the region at the end of the 1970s (Belozerov, 2001). In the 1990s, the process increased dramatically, but the overall trend has not changed: Russians are leaving the region (Vsesoyuznaya perepis' naseleniya, 2015; Itogi vserossiyskoy perepisi naseleniya 2002 goda, 2004; Itogi vserossiyskoy perepisi naseleniya 2010 g. v 11 T., 2012). In addition, the identity of Russians living in the North Caucasus was being transformed as they became aware of themselves as an ethnic minority (Soldatova, 1998; Vorobyev, 2001), although they are still the majority in the Russian Federation as a whole.

Several factors determined the choice of these republics in which to carry out the MIRIPS project. They are similar, in that both republics are multicultural, with the share of the titular ethnic groups being more than 50–70%, and the share of the Russian population about 20%. In addition, the share of Russians declined by 10–20% in both these republics between 2002 and 2010. There are also sharp differences, leading to the differences in interethnic relations in these republics. In RNO-A there is one titular ethnic group (the Ossetians, with 65.1% of the population); Muslims account for 8.7%, and Orthodox Christians for 91.2%. In KBR, there are two titular ethnic groups (the Kabardians, with 57% and the Balkars, with 12.6%); Muslims account for 72.0%, Orthodox Christians for 27.8%.

Interethnic attitudes in the republics also differ: in RNO-A the titular ethnic group (Ossetians) and ethnic Russians prefer equal-status interaction (Gutsunaeva, 2010). In contrast, in KBR the titular ethnic groups (Kabardians and Balkars) prefer intracultural contacts, while ethnic Russians prefer intercultural contacts (Sklyarova, 2008). In RNO-A, 63% of ethnic Russians are satisfied with their interethnic relations; in KBR less than half (40%) of ethnic Russians are satisfied with their interethnic relations (Denisova & Ulanov, 2003). Based on these data, we can characterise the intercultural context in North Ossetia as a 'close' cultural context, whereas in the KBR it is a 'distant' cultural context.

Method

Participants

In RNO-A the sample included members of the titular ethnic group, the Ossetians ($N = 340$), and the ethnic minority, the Russians ($N = 344$). In KBR, the sample included members of the titular ethnic groups, the Kabardians and Balkars ($N = 351$), and the ethnic minority, the Russians ($N = 335$). Table 2.5 provides the socio-demographic characteristics of these samples.

Table 2.5. *Gender and age characteristics of the sample.*

Respondents	N	Gender Characteristics		Age Characteristics			
		Male (N,%)	Female (N,%)	Min.	Max.	M	SD
RNO-A							
Russians	344	101 (30%)	243 (70%)	15	91	43.4	21.9
Ossetians	340	105 (31%)	235 (69%)	15	87	42.6	22.8
KBR							
Russians	335	125 (37%)	210 (63%)	14	90	40.7	19.6
Kabardians and Balkars	351	124 (35%)	227 (65%)	14	88	43.0	21.0

Results of Study 2

Table 2.6 presents the means and standard deviations for the measures and the results of the *t*-test for all four samples.

In KBR, the means of multicultural ideology, assimilation and life satisfaction were significantly higher in the sample of Kabardians and Balkars than in the sample of Russians. Intercultural contacts were assessed as being more intensive by Russians than by the members of the titular population. In RNO-A, means of intercultural contacts, multicultural ideology, ethnic tolerance, integration and self-esteem were significantly higher in the sample of Russians than in the sample of Ossetians, but means of assimilation and life satisfaction were significantly higher in the sample of Ossetians.

We examined the three hypotheses together by combining them into one model for each sample.

Results of the Study in RNO-A

Standardized regression weights and significance levels of the path models are good: for Ossetians – χ^2/df = 1.8; CFI =.994; RMSEA =.048; SRMR =.019; PCLOSE=.426; for Russians – χ^2/df = 1.4; CFI =.998; RMSEA =.038; SRMR =.015; PCLOSE =.521. The results of testing of three hypotheses of intercultural relations for Ossetians and Russians are presented in the Table 2.7.

Multiculturalism hypothesis. For Ossetians, their perceived security predicted the levels of support for multicultural ideology, ethnic tolerance and expectation of integration (β =.31, p <.001 and β =.14, p <.05, β =.32, p <.001, respectively). For the Russians, perceived security also predicted

Table 2.6. *Means, standard deviations and results of* **t**-*test for the samples of Russians/Kabardians and Balkars in KBR; Russians/Ossetians in RNO-A.*

Variables	KBR				RNO-A			
	M (R/KB)[a]	SD (R/KB)	T	Cohen's d	M (R/O)[b]	SD (R/O)	t	Cohen's d
Perceived security	3.37/3.48	.81/.87	1.74	.13	3.30/3.38	.82/.89	-1.07	.09
Intercultural contacts	3.31/2.77	1.09/1.19	-6.18**	.47	3.63/3.21	1.03/1.16	4.91***	.38
Multicultural ideology	3.81/3.95	.80/.71	-2.43*	.19	4.03/3.87	.72/.71	2.84**	.22
Ethnic tolerance	4.01/4.00	.92/.91	-0.12	.01	4.15/3.91	.93/.85	3.54***	.27
Assimilation	1.86/2.20	.88/1.09	-4.40***	.34	1.80/2.05	.86/.95	-3.71***	.28
Integration	3.71/3.67	.79/.89	-.73	.05	4.07/3.91	.93/.94	2.25*	.17
Self-esteem	4.11/4.18	.65/.67	1.37	.11	4.09/3.92	.72/.88	2.73**	.21
Life satisfaction	3.44/3.80	1.00/.77	5.27***	.40	3.23/3.39	.86/.88	-2.33*	.18
Sociocultural adaptation[c]	3.52	.92	–	–	3.62	.80	–	–

Notes: *p < .05, **p < .01, ***p < .001.
[a] Russians/Kabardians and Balkars; [b] Russians/Ossetians.
[c] measure of sociocultural adaptation is used in the groups of Russians only.

Table 2.7. *Standardized direct, indirect effects and intercorrelations for the sample of titular ethnic group and ethnic Russians in RNO-A (Ossetians/Russians).*

Predictor/ Outcome	IC	MI	TOL	AS	INT	SA		SE		LS	
						Dir.	Indir.	Dir.	Indir.	Dir.	Indir.
SEC	.10/ .18*	.31***	.14**/ .12*	.02/ -.18**	.32***/ .16**	/ .11*	/ .04**	.11*/ .24***	.04/ .05*	.24***/ .15***	.07**/ .01
IC	—	.37***	.04/ .19***	-.02/ .18***	.11*/ .34***	/ .11*	/ .06**	.03/ .13*	.00/ .05	.08/ .20***	.03*/ .04
MI		—	.41***/ .43***	.26***/ .36***	.40***/ .28***	—	—	—	—	—	—
TOL			—	-.14*/ .30***	.35***/ .25***	—	—	—	—	—	—

									AS
AS	–	–	–	–	/	–	.29*** /	–	.04/ .10
INT	–	–	–	-.13 *	/ .11 *	–	– .29*** .13*/ .00	–	.21*** /
									.19***
R^2	.10/ .14	.02/ .06	.01/ .06	.12/ .16	/ .09	.15/ .21	.15/ .14		

Notes: *p <.05; **p <.01; ***p <.001.
SEC – Security; IC – Intercultural contacts; MI – Multicultural ideology; TOL – Ethnic tolerance; AS – Assimilation; INT – Integration; SA – Sociocultural adaptation; SE – Self-esteem; LS – Life satisfaction.
Correlations are in italics.

multicultural ideology (β =.34, p <.001), ethnic tolerance (β =.12, p <.05) and their integration expectation (β =.16, p <.01).

Contact hypothesis. Among the Ossetians, their contacts with Russians positively and significantly affected their acculturation expectation of integration (β =.11, p <.05). The contacts of Russians with Ossetians positively and significantly affected their acculturation strategy of integration (β =.34, p <.001) and ethnic tolerance (β =.19, p <.001), but negatively and significantly affected their preference for assimilation (β = –.18, p <.001).

The integration hypothesis. A preference for the integration expectation among the Ossetians had a positive impact on their life satisfaction (β =.21, p <.001) and self-esteem (β =.13, p <.05). A preference for the integration strategy among the Russians had a significant positive impact on their life satisfaction (β =.18, p <.001) and sociocultural adaptation (β =.11, p <.05). We also found significant indirect effects of perceived security and intercultural contacts on their life satisfaction through the integration expectation among Ossetians.

Results of the Study in KBR

We tested all three hypotheses of intercultural relations simultaneously in two samples in KBR using path analysis. The results are presented in the Table 2.8. The data of titular ethnic groups of KBR and ethnic Russians of KBR are presented in the same table using slash.

Assessment of models' fit indicates that all the goodness-of-fit indices are exceptionally good in the sample of titular ethnic groups (χ^2/df=2.4; CFI=.97; RMSEA=.06; PCLOSE=.25) and in the sample of ethnic Russians (χ^2/df=2.1; CFI=.98; RMSEA=.06; PCLOSE=.32).

The multiculturalism hypothesis. Perceived security had significant positive effect on multicultural ideology in both groups of KBR (β_{KB} = 0.17, p <.01; β_{eR} =.22, p <.001), while the relationships between perceived security and ethnic tolerance were found only in the titular ethnic groups of KBR (β_{KB} = 0.12, p <.05).

The contact hypothesis. Intercultural contacts significantly and positively predicted both the assimilation (β_{KB} =.12, p <.05) and integration (β_{KB} =.13, p <.05) expectations among titular ethnic groups of KBR. In the group of ethnic Russians in KBR, their intercultural contacts with members of titular ethnic group positively related only with assimilation strategy (β_{eR} =.16, p <.01).

The integration hypothesis. The relationship between integration and self-esteem was positive only in the titular ethnic groups of KBR (β_{KB} =.18, p <.001), while in the group of ethnic Russians in KBR it is

Table 2.8. *Standardized regression weights and correlations for the samples of KBR (Kabardians and Balkars/ethnic Russians).*

Outcome Predictor	IC	MI	TOL	AS	INT	SA Dir.	SA Indir.	SE Dir.	SE Indir.	LS Dir.	LS Indir.
SEC	.01 / *.08*	.17** / *.22***	.12* / *.06*	.16** / *-.01*	-.05 / *.08*	/.00	/.00	.02 / *.14***	-.01 / *.14***	.12* / *.19***	.03*
IC	—	—	.04 / *-.02*	.12* / *.16***	.13* / *.03*	/.03	/.00	.06 / *.17***	.02 / *.17***	.11* / *.29***	.04*
MI	—	—	.36*** / *.35***	.34*** / *.29***	.22*** /	—	—	—	—	—	—
TOL	—	—	—	.23*** / *.35***	.26*** / *.38***	—	—	—	—	—	—
AS	—	—	—	—	—	.04	—	-.02 / *-.10*	—	.23*** / *-.03*	—
INT	—	—	—	—	—	.04	—	.18*** / *-.04*	—	-.07 / *.21***	—
R²	.03 / *.05*		.02 / *.00*	.04 / *.03*	.02 / *.01*	.07 / *.09*		.12 / *.05*			

Notes: *p <.05; **p <.01; ***p <.001.

SEC – Security; IC – Intercultural contacts; MI – Multicultural ideology; TOL – Ethnic tolerance; AS – Assimilation; INT – Integration; SA – Sociocultural adaptation; SE – Self-esteem; LS – Life satisfaction.

KB – Kabardians and Balkars, eR – ethnic Russians.

Correlations are in italics.

negative (β_{cR} = –.21, p <.001). Furthermore, assimilation expectation of members of titular ethnic groups of KBR was positively related to their life satisfaction (β_{KB} =.23, p <.001). Additionally, we found significant indirect effects of perceived security and intercultural contacts on life satisfaction through assimilation expectation among members of titular ethnic groups of KBR.

6   Discussion and Conclusions

We have presented the results of testing the three MIRIPS hypotheses of multiculturalism, contact and integration in the two multicultural regions of the Russian Federation: Central Federal District (Study 1) and North Caucasus (Study 2).

The results of the Study 1 showed that in all three groups the most preferred acculturation strategy/expectation is integration. These results coincide with the results of previous studies in Russia (e.g., Lebedeva, Tatarko & Berry, 2016), and other countries (e.g., Berry & Sabatier, 2011). Participants of the study were culturally different groups of migrants from two different regions of origin: Central Asia and South Caucasus. Moreover, these groups significantly differ in their duration of residence in Russia, and in their levels of adaptation. Despite these differences, we found some similarities in their patterns of acculturation. It is important that some of these patterns are similar to those of the host society members. For instance, in all three groups their perceived security predicted multicultural ideology (but not to their ethnic tolerance) and to the integration strategy/expectation. Integration was positively related to self-esteem of the members of all acculturating groups. These similarities support the mutual character of intercultural relations in these regions.

However, some differences in acculturation and adaptation were also found. The contact hypothesis was partially supported in the Russian majority and in migrants from Central Asia, but was not confirmed among migrants from South Caucasus. We believe that the latter group was already well adapted in Russia and that having close friends among Russians did not contribute to their acculturation preferences and tolerance, which were already relatively high.

The integration hypothesis was fully confirmed in the Russian majority group and in migrants from South Caucasus and partially confirmed with the migrants from Central Asia. In the group of migrants from Central Asia who are newcomers in comparison with migrants from South Caucasus, the assimilation strategy was positively related to their sociocultural adaptation. We believe that all the advantages of integration are achievable when migrants have more social capital (such as education, language knowledge and professional skills) to achieve good adaptation. However, these are less available among migrants from Central Asia.

In addition to integration, the assimilation strategy of migrants positively related to their life satisfaction in both groups. We suggest that migrants may regard assimilation as the best way to reduce perceived cultural and social differences in order to avoid negative attitudes from the host population. However, such a relationship was not found in the Russian majority; their integration expectations were the real predictors of their self-esteem and life satisfaction.

In addition, only in migrants from Central Asia did perceived security positively correlate with their life satisfaction, and multicultural ideology positively correlate with their self-esteem. The latter result is in line with findings for Turkish-Dutch and Moroccan-Dutch minorities that have the lowest social status in the Netherlands and face social rejection and discrimination (Verkuyten, 2009). The integration and assimilation acculturation strategies differ in their level of cultural maintenance. As we can see from the results obtained in all groups, maintenance of one's own culture increases a person's self-esteem.

In the Study 2, we tested three hypotheses of intercultural relations in two North Caucasus republics with different sociocultural contexts: in North Ossetia–Alania with the close cultural context and in the KBR with the distant cultural context. In RNO-A, the multiculturalism hypothesis received full support in both groups: the Ossetians and the Russians; perceived security predicted multicultural ideology and tolerance in both samples. These results are consistent with data obtained in other countries (e.g., Berry, 2006): measures of security correlated positively with positive intercultural attitudes and multicultural ideology. In KBR, the multiculturalism hypothesis was partially supported in both groups: perceived security predicted multicultural ideology, but did not predict preference for integration. Among members of titular ethnic groups of KBR, perceived security also predicted ethnic tolerance, which was not usually the case in the other samples.

Additionally, perceived security predicted the assimilation expectation among members of titular ethnic groups of KBR. This phenomenon can be explained by the group-threat theory (Bobo, 1999), which states that when a minority group challenges the societal position of the majority group by maintaining their own culture, the majority group will feel threatened and prefer the assimilation of a minority (Davies, Steele & Markus, 2008; Tip et al., 2012).

The contact hypothesis received partial confirmation in both groups in RNO-A. Intercultural contacts predicted a preference for integration in both samples and higher ethnic tolerance in the Russians. The Ossetians were willing to accept Russians on their own cultural terms and did not require them to give up their cultural heritage in order to be accepted in the larger society. Having Ossetian friends and frequent contacts with them promoted the orientation of the Russians to the integration strategy. These data partly confirm the results obtained earlier in the RNO-A by Gutsunaeva (2010), who noted that intercultural contacts significantly and positively correlated with positive attitudes towards integration.

The contact hypothesis in KBR was partially supported in both groups of KBR: contacts of members of titular ethnic groups with ethnic Russians were positively related to their integration and assimilation expectations, but were not related to ethnic tolerance. Among Russians in KBR, contacts with members of titular ethnic groups were related only to assimilation strategy. The results of our study demonstrated that intercultural contacts predicted a preference for assimilation among members of both samples in KBR. Allport's (1954) contact hypothesis identified four optimal conditions for contact to reduce prejudice: equal status of the groups in the situation, cooperation rather than competition, common goals and authority support. We suppose that the absence of all these conditions in KBR are the reasons why intercultural contacts predicted a preference for assimilation in both samples in KBR. A preference for assimilation emphasizes that minority group members should adapt to the majority culture and discard their own culture and group identity; and a preference for assimilation among members of the ethnic majority can serve as a justification for intolerant behaviour (Gieling, Thijs, Verkuyten, 2014). In general, we can postulate that intercultural contacts lead to the assimilation of Russians in KBR.

Regarding the integration hypothesis, the preference for the integration strategy among the Russians in RNO-A predicted their life satisfaction and sociocultural adaptation; and among the Ossetians the integration expectation predicted their life satisfaction and self-esteem. Thus, the integration hypothesis was fully supported in the Ossetians' sample and partially supported in the Russian sample. In part, our results are consistent with other research (Ward & Kennedy, 1994; Jasinskaja-Lahti, Horenczyk & Kinunen, 2011) who reported that integration promoted better psychological adaptation of immigrants. Previous studies have also shown that the integration expectations of the dominant group members predicted their psychological adaptation and well-being (Schmitz & Berry, 2009; Hui et al., 2015).

In KBR, the integration hypothesis was partially supported in the titular ethnic groups, but was not supported in the group of Russians. Among titular ethnic groups' members, their integration expectation positively related to their self-esteem. This result is consistent with data obtained in a study of ethnic majority in China (Li, Chongde, Tsingan, Donghui & Liqing, 2015). Among Russians in KBR, the integration strategy was significantly and negatively related to their life satisfaction, but was not significantly related to their self-esteem and sociocultural adaptation. These results are consistent with the results of the study of ethnic Russians in Estonia (Kus-Harbord & Ward, 2015), which revealed that interaction between the acculturation dimensions of maintenance and participation demonstrated that participation in Estonian culture was associated with lower life satisfaction under the conditions of high cultural maintenance.

Our findings highlight the importance of context (Ward, Fox, Wilson, Stuart & Kus, 2010) and are broadly in accordance with the Interactive Acculturation Model of Bourhis et al. (1997), which argued that the concordance or discordance of the acculturation preferences of minority and majority groups determines consensual, problematic and conflictual outcomes. The study of intercultural relations in Kabardino-Balkaria and Chechnya found that ethnic Russians in these republics preferred the integration strategy, while the titular population expected exclusion (Lepshokova, 2012). Related research has demonstrated that perceived discrepancies between one's own acculturation preferences and the out-group acculturation preferences predict lower levels of life satisfaction and negative intergroup attitudes (Pfafferott & Brown, 2006; Piontkowski et al., 2002; Ward, 2009; and Zagefka & Brown, 2002).

The role of context is manifested in the indirect effects of perceived security and intercultural contacts on well-being in the two republics. In RNO-A the integration expectation of the Ossetians mediated the effects of perceived security and intercultural contacts on their life satisfaction, while in KBR the assimilation expectation of members of titular ethnic groups of KBR plays such mediating role.

This means that in the 'close' cultural context (RNO-A), the integration expectation, and in the 'distant' cultural context (KBR), the assimilation expectation enhanced the positive effect of perceived security and intercultural contacts on well-being of the majority group members.

The summary of the results of testing the three hypotheses in both studies are presented in Table 2.9.

In general, we note that in each region the leading role in the confirmation of the hypotheses belongs to the majority. That is, if the hypothesis is

Table 2.9. *Results of the testing the three hypotheses in multicultural regions of Russia.*

	Study 1			Study 2			
Groups/Hypotheses	Migrants CA	Migrants SC	Russian Majority	Ossetians RNO-A	Russians RNO-A	Kabardians Balkars KBR	Russians KBR
Multiculturalism	Partial support	Partial support	Partial support	Full support	Full support	Partial support	Partial support
Contact	Partial support	No support	Partial support	Partial support	Partial support	Partial support	Partial support
Integration	Partial support	Full support	Full support	Full support	Partial support	Partial support	No support

fully supported in the dominant group, it is at least partially supported in the minority/migrant groups. And if it is partially supported in the dominant group, it has partial or no support in the non-dominant group. This indicates the responsibility of the majority group for mutual intercultural relations in each context.

There are some limitations of our studies. The samples were small, convenient, and we used the snowball sampling technique. Despite these limitations, our results enabled us to find various and interesting data about intercultural relations in different multicultural regions of the Russian Federation.

Acknowledgements

This work was supported by the Russian Science Foundation (Project No. 15–18-00029). The authors appreciate the help of Javokhir Khojiev in translating the questionnaires into the Uzbek and Tajik languages and gathering data among migrants from Central Asia.

References

Allport, G. W. (1954). *The Nature of Prejudice*. Reading, MA: Addison-Wesley.
Arbuckle, J. L. (2011). Amos (Version 20.0) [Computer Program]. Chicago: SPSS.
Badurashvili I. (2011) Out-migration from Georgia to Moscow and other destinations. In N. Genov & T. Savvidis (eds.), *Transboundary Migration in the Post-Soviet Space: Three Comparative Studies* (pp. 79–122). Frankfurt am Main: Peter Lang.
Belozerov, V. S. (2001) Russkiye na Kavkaze: evolyutsiya rasseleniya [Russians in the Caucasus: evolution of settlement]. In V. V. Chernous (Ed.), *Russkiye na Severnom Kavkaze: vyzovy XXI veka Sbornik nauchnykh statey [Russians in the North Caucasus: the challenges of the XXI century, the Collection of scientific articles.]* (pp. 27–45). Rostov-na-donu, Publ. SKNC VSH.
Berry, J. W. (2006). Mutual attitudes among immigrants and ethnocultural groups in Canada. *International Journal of Intercultural Relations, 30*(6), 719–734. doi: 10.1016/j. ijintrel.2006.06.004.
Berry J. W. & Sabatier, C. (2011). Variations in the assessment of acculturation attitudes: Their relationships with psychological wellbeing. *International Journal of Intercultural Relations, 35*, 658–669.
Bobo, L. D. (1999). Prejudice as group position: Microfoundations of a sociological approach to racism and race relations. *Journal of Social Issues, 55*(3),445–472. doi: 10.1111/0022–4537.00127.
Bourhis R.Y., Moïse L.C., Perreault S., & Senécal S. (1997). Towards an Interactive Acculturation Model: A social psychological approach. *International Journal of Psychology, 32*(6): 369–386. doi: 10.1080/ 002075997400629.

Davies, P. G., Steele, C. M., & Markus, H. R. (2008). A nation challenged: The impact of foreign threat on America's tolerance for diversity. *Journal of Personality and Social Psychology, 95*(2), 308–318. doi: 10.1037/0022-3514 .95.2.308.

Denisova, G. S., & Ulanov, V. P. (2003). *Russkiye na Severnom Kavkaze: analiz transformatsii sotsiokul'turnogo statusa.[Russian North Caucasus: An analysis of the transformation of the socio-cultural status.]* Rostov-on-Don: South Federal University.

Di Bartolomeo, A., Makaryan, Sh., & Weinar, A. (Eds.) (2014). *Regional migration report: Russia and Central Asia.* Florence, Italy: Migration Policy Centre, European University Institute.

Diener, E., Emmons, R. A., Larsen, R. J., & Griffin, S. (1985). The Satisfaction with Life Scale. *Journal of Personality Assessment, 49,* 71–75.

Genov, N., & Savvidis, T. (eds.) (2011) *Transboundary Migration in the Post-Soviet Space: Three Comparative Studies.* Frankfurt am Main: Peter Lang.

Gieling M., Thijs J., & Verkuyten M. (2014) Dutch adolescents' tolerance of Muslim immigrants: The role of assimilation ideology, intergroup contact, and national identification. *Journal of Applied Social Psychology, 44,* 155–165.

Gutsunaeva, S.V. (2010). *Strategii mezhetnicheskogo vzaimodeystviya osetin i russkikh, prozhivayushchikh v respublike Severnaya Osetiya – Alaniya* [*Strategy of interethnic interaction and Russian Ossetians living in the republic of North Ossetia – Alania*]. Candidate Dissertation. University of St. Petersburg, St. Petersburg, Russian Federation.

Hui, B.P.H., Chen, S. X., Leung, C. M., & Berry, J. W. (2015). Facilitating adaptation and intercultural contact: The role of integration and multicultural ideology in dominant and nondominant groups. *International Journal of Intercultural Relations, 45,* 70–84. doi: 10.1016/j. ijintrel.2015.01.002.

Itogi vserossiyskoy perepisi naseleniya 2002 goda (2004) [The results of the National Population Census of 2002]. V.4. Book 1. Moscow, Russian Federation: IPC 'Statistics of Russia'.

Itogi vserossiyskoy perepisi naseleniya 2010 g. v 11 T. (2012) T. 11. Svodnyye itogi Vserossiyskoy perepisi naseleniya 2010 goda [The results of the National Population Census of 2010. The 11 V. V. 11. Summary results of the national census in 2010] Retrieved from: www.gks.ru/free_doc/new_site/perepis2010/c roc/vol11pdf-m.html.

Jasinskaja-Lahti, I., Horenczyk, G., & Kinunen, T. (2011). Time and context in the relationship between acculturation attitudes and adaptation among Russian-speaking immigrants in Finland and Israel. *Journal of Ethnic and Migration Studies, 37*(9), 1423–1440.

Kline, R. B. (1998). *Principles and Practice of Structural Equation Modeling.* New York: Guilford Press.

Kus-Harbord, L., & Ward, C. (2015). Ethnic Russians in post-Soviet Estonia: Perceived devaluation, acculturation, well-being, and ethnic attitudes. *International Perspectives in Psychology: Research, Practice, Consultation, 4* (1), 66–81. doi: 10.1037/ipp0000025

Lebedeva, N. M., & Tatarko, A. N. (2013). Immigration and intercultural interaction strategies in post-Soviet Russia. In E. Tartakovsky (Ed.), *Immigration: Policies, Challenges and Impact* (pp. 179–194). New York: Nova Science.

Lebedeva, N. M., & Tatarko, A. N. (Eds.) (2009). *Strategii mezhkul'turnogo vzaimodejstvija migrantov i naselenija Rossii: Sbornik nauchnykh statey* [Strategies for the intercultural interaction of migrants and the sedentary population in Russia: A collection of scientific articles]. Moscow: RUDN.

Lebedeva, N., Tatarko A., & Berry J. W. (2016) Intercultural relations among migrants from Caucasus and Russians in Moscow. *International Journal of Intercultural Relations, 42*, 27–38.

Lepshokova, Z. (2012) Strategii adaptatsii migrantov i ikh psikhologicheskoye blagopoluchiye (na primere Moskvy i Severnogo Kavkaza) [Adaptation strategies of migrants and their psychological well-being (Case of Moscow and the North Caucasus)]. Moscow, Russia. Grifon.

Li, D., Chongde, L., Tsingan, L., Donghui, D., & Liqing, Z. (2015). The relationship between cultural identity and self-esteem among Chinese Uyghur college students: The mediating role of acculturation attitudes. *Psychological Reports, 117*(1), 302–318. doi:10.2466/17.07.pr0.117c12z8.

Pfafferott, I., & Brown R. (2006). Acculturation preferences of majority and minority adolescents in Germany in the context of society and family. *International Journal of Intercultural Relations, 30*, 703–717.

Piontkowski, U., Rohmann A., & Florack A. (2002). Concordance of acculturation attitudes and perceived threat. *Group Processes and Intergroup Relations, 5*, 221–232.

Poghosyan, G. (2011). Out-Migration from Armenia. In N. Genov and T. Savvidis (Eds.), *Transboundary Migration in the Post-Soviet Space: Three Comparative Studies* (pp. 39–78). Frankfurt am Main: Peter Lang.

Rosenberg, M. (1965). *Society and the Adolescent Self-Image.* Princeton, NJ: Princeton University Press.

Schmitz, P. G., & Berry, J. W. (2009). Structure of acculturation attitudes and their relationships with personality and psychological adaptation: A study with immigrant and national samples in Germany. In K. Boehnke (Ed.), *Proceedings of IACCP Congress.* Bremen. Retrieved from https://publications.hse.ru/chapters/139814898.

Sklyarova, D.V. Osobennosti etnicheskoy identichnosti studencheskoy molodezhi kabardinskoy, balkarskoy i russkoy etnogrupp [Features of ethnic identity of student's youth Kabardian, Balkar and Russian ethnic groups]. Avtoref. dis. ... kand. psikhol. nauk. Rostov na Donu, 2008, p. 25.

Soldatova, G.U. (1998). Psikhologiya mezhetnicheskoy napryazhennosti. [Psychology ethnic tensions]. Moscow, p. 265.

Tip, L. K., Zagefka, H., González, R., Brown, R., Cinnirella, M., & Na, X. (2012). Is support of multiculturalism threatened by... threat itself? *International Journal of Intercultural Relations, 36* (1), 22–30. doi: 10.1016/j.ijintrel.2010.09.011.

United Nations, Department of Economic and Social Affairs, Population Division (2015). *Trends in International Migrant Stock: The 2015 revision* (United Nations database, POP/DB/MIG/Stock/Rev.2015). Retrieved from www.un.org/en/development/desa/population/migration/data/estimates2/doc s/MigrationStockDocumentation_2015.pdf.

Verkuyten, M. (2009). Self-esteem and multiculturalism: An examination among ethnic minority and majority groups in the Netherlands. *Journal of Research in Personality, 43*(3), 419–427.

Vishnevsky, A. G. (2011). *Naselenie Rossii* 2009: *17-j ezhegodnyj demograficheskij doklad [Population ofRussia 2009: the 27th annual demographic report]*. Moscow: HSE.

Vorobyov, S.M. Etnopoliticheskiye protsessy na Severnom Kavkaze v postsovetskiy period. [Ethnopolitical processes in the North Caucasus in the post-Soviet period]. Cand. diss ... polit. sciences. Stavropol. 2001.

Vsesoyuznaya perepis' naseleniya (2015).[All Union Population Census]. *Demoscope Weekly*. 651–652 Retrieved from www.demoscope.ru/weekly/ssp/r us_nac_70.php?reg=50.

Ward, C. (2009). Acculturation and social cohesion: Emerging issues for Asian immigrants in New Zealand. In C.-H. Leong, & J.W. Berry (Eds.), *Intercultural Relations in Asia: Migration and Work Effectiveness* (pp. 3–24) Singapore: World Scientific.

Ward, C., & Kennedy, A. (1994). Acculturation strategies, psychological adjustment, and sociocultural competence during cross-cultural transitions. *International Journal of Intercultural Relations, 18*, 329–343. doi: 10.1016/0147–1767 (94)90036–1.

Ward, C., Fox, S., Wilson, J., Stuart, J., & Kus, L. (2010). Contextual influences on acculturation processes: The roles of family, community and society. *Psychological Studies, 55*(1), 26. doi:10.1007/s12646-010–0003-8.

Wilson, J. (2013). "Exploring the past, present and future of cultural competency research: The revision and expansion of the sociocultural adaptation construct" (Unpublished doctoral dissertation). Victoria University of Wellington, Wellington, New Zealand.

Yunusov A. (2013). The Demographic And Economic Framework Of Circular Migration in Azerbaijan. In A. Bara A. Di Bartolomeo, Z. Brunarska, Sh. Makaryan, M S. ananashvili, & A. Weinar (Eds). *Regional Migration Report: South Caucasus* (pp. 129–137). European University Institute, 2013.

Zagefka H., & Brown R. (2002). The relation between acculturation strategies, relative fit and intergroup relations: Immigrant-majority relations in Germany. *European Journal of Social Psychology, 32*, 171–188.

Zayonchkovskaya Zh., Karachurina L., Florinskaya Y., & Mkrtchan N. (2015) *Migratsiia naselenija* [Migration of population] In: Naselenie Rossii 2013: dvadcat' pervyj ezhegodnyj demograficheskij doklad [Population of Russia 2013: Annual 21st demographic report]. S. V. Zaharov, A. G. Vishnevskij; otv. red.: S. V. Zaharov. M.: Izdatel'skij dom NIU VShJe, 2015. P. 296–357.

Zayonchkovskaya, Zh. A., & Tyuryukanova, E. (Eds.) (2010). *Migratsiia i demograficheskii krizis v Rossii [Migration and the demographic crisis in Russia]*. Moscow: MAKS Press.

Zayonchkovskaya, Zh. A., Poletaev, D., Doronina, K. A., Mkrtchyan, N. V., & Florinskaya, Ju. F. (2014). Zashhita prav moskvichej v uslovijah massovoj migracii [Protection of the rights of Muscovites in conditions of mass migration]. In Upolnomochennyj po pravam cheloveka v gorode Moskve [Human Rights Commissioner in Moscow]. Moscow: ROO Centr migracionnyh issledovanij.

3   Intercultural Relations in Latvia and Azerbaijan

Nadezhda Lebedeva, Alexander Tatarko and Victoria Galyapina

National Research University Higher School of Economics, Moscow, Russia

1   Introduction

This chapter examines the intercultural relations between ethnic Russians who have continued to live in two newly independent states (Latvia and Azerbaijan) that emerged after the collapse of the USSR in 1991. Many former Russian citizens involuntarily changed their status from Soviet citizens with Russian nationality and became ethnic minorities – even people without citizenship – in these newly independent states. In this study, we are interested in whether patterns of intercultural relations between members of dominant group and the Russian minority in these countries are similar or different compared each with other. Latvia and Azerbaijan present two very different national contexts in which to examine this issue: because Latvia is very high in the diversity index, while Azerbaijan is in the middle. However, Latvia and Azerbaijan are similar on the other two indexes: they are at the bottom of the migrant integration index, and both are near the bottom on the multiculturalism policy index. We investigate the intercultural relations between members of the host population and ethnic Russians in these two countries with different trajectories of post-Soviet development, Latvia and Azerbaijan, guided by the three MIRIPS hypotheses (multiculturalism, contact, integration).

2   Context of Intercultural Relations in Latvia and Azerbaijan

2.1   Latvia

Demography. As noted earlier, Latvia is very high on the ethnic diversity index, indicating that it is a highly culturally diverse country, of just over two million people. Relations between the dominant ethnic group (the Latvians) and other ethnic groups play an important role in Latvia's domestic policy (Apine, 2010). Other ethnic groups therefore constitute a significant force in the shared experience of Latvian society. Ethnic Russians form the second-largest ethnic group by size (26.0%) after Latvians themselves (61.4%). Non-citizens represent around 15% of the population; of these, 64% were Russians. Russians are thus in a unique position owing to a change in their status. Before the Soviet Union broke up, Russians in Latvia were the ethnic majority in the whole USSR, but, after the fall, they immediately became the ethnic minority in the independent Latvia by numbers and by their status and power.

Modern European standards of democracy require Latvia to provide equal rights for both the dominant ethnic group and ethnic minorities when it comes to political participation. Latvia's official policy towards national minorities is defined as "integration while preserving cultural and ethnic identity" (Permanent Mission of the Republic of Latvia to the United Nations, 2016). In Latvia, national minorities are officially defined as Latvian citizens who differ from ethnic Latvians by their culture, religion or language and who have traditionally been living in Latvia for a long time and who consider themselves a part of the Latvian state and society. People who are not citizens of Latvia are not considered members of a national minority, but they still enjoy the same rights as national minorities unless the law places restrictions on them.

However, this definition presents a problem for national minorities, in particular for non-citizens residing in Latvia for an extended period of time (typically since the end of the Soviet Union). In 2014, there were 276,797 non-citizens residing in Latvia (12.77% of Latvia's total population; Ministry of Foreign Affairs of the Republic of Latvia, 2015). In comparison, citizens of the former Soviet Union who were residing in Russia or in other independent states (for instance, Lithuania, Azerbaijan, but not Estonia) after the fall of the Soviet Union received citizenship in these countries automatically.

Non-citizens of Latvia are not refugees; they are guaranteed almost the same rights as Latvian citizens; they have the right to reside permanently in Latvia and also have the same social guarantees as citizens. The main difference in rights is that non-citizens cannot vote or be elected and cannot hold public office or positions related to national security.

Policy. In 1994, Latvia adopted an official citizenship law that described the naturalization procedure that began in 1995. Naturalization is the process by which an applicant for citizenship is awarded Latvian citizenship after passing exams on the Latvian language and on the history of Latvia, and after swearing an oath to the Latvian Republic. But, in reality, this process better represents assimilation than integration because the purpose of naturalization is the gradual removal of the Russian language from daily communication. Language is, after all, one of the strongest ties people have with their culture. The second step in carrying out the assimilation policy towards the Russian minority in Latvia has its roots in education. In 1998, a new education law had a significant impact on the education of ethnic minorities in Latvia (Republic of Latvia, 1998). Before 1999, there were both "Latvian" schools and schools for ethnic minorities in Latvia. Teaching in schools for ethnic minorities was carried out in their native language (e.g., in Russian schools children were taught in Russian), and the state language (Latvian) was taught also as a special subject. The 1998 law introduced a new concept, referring to "schools using national minority educational programs". (Republic of Latvia, 1998) In this way, the Russian language started to gradually become less relevant in education. Therefore, we can conclude that although its declared integration policy is called "integration", Latvia is actually implementing a gradual assimilation policy for ethnic minorities. Education reform in Latvia has become a catalyst for dissent among the Russian-speaking population (Sytin, 2012; Skrinnik, 2009). Intercultural relations in Latvia are sometimes evaluated as a conflict-prone by experts (Rodin, 2013).

2.2   Azerbaijan

Demography. Russians have lived in Azerbaijan for more than 180 years since the middle of the nineteenth century. The first wave of Russian migration in Azerbaijan was during the period from 1830 to 1850. The second wave was in the late nineteenth – early twentieth centuries and was caused by the development of the oil industry. These Russians were employed mostly in the industrial and administrative sectors. They played the most important role in the development of Azerbaijan during the Soviet period (Kerimov, 2010).

The Russian language in Azerbaijan was not only the official language but also prevailed in everyday communication in the domestic sphere. During the Soviet period, Azerbaijan virtually became a Russian-speaking republic (Karavaev, 2008).

Russians emigrated en masse from Azerbaijan in the 1980–1990s after the collapse of the Soviet Union and the formation of the independent Republic of Azerbaijan. In the 30 years following the collapse of the Soviet

Union, the Russian population decreased from 475,000 to 180,000. Today, Russians in Azerbaijan amount to only 1.34% of the total population. They are the third-largest ethnic group in the republic (after Azerbaijanis and Lezgins; Perepisi naseleniya Azerbaydzhana, 2013). Russians who stayed in Azerbaijan after the collapse of the USSR received citizenship in this country automatically (Vykhovanets, 2005).

The reasons for the out-migration of Russians were numerous: unstable political situation; a long Armenian–Azerbaijani Nagorno-Karabakh conflict; the economic crisis; the destruction of the industrial sector where Russians traditionally worked; narrowing of the scope of the Russian language; increasing psychological discomfort of Russians, and so on (Popov, 2010).

3   Evaluation of the MIRIPS Hypotheses

We have evaluated the three hypotheses of intercultural relations (the multiculturalism hypothesis, the contact hypothesis and the integration hypothesis) in both the independent states of Latvia and Azerbaijan in order to reveal similarities and differences in mutual adaptation to changing socio-cultural contexts in the former soviet republics after the collapse of Soviet Union.

Latvia. There is a lack of previous research on intercultural relations in Latvia. However, while the declared policy in Latvia is called "integration", Latvia is actually implementing a gradual assimilation policy for ethnic minorities.

Studies show that in Latvia there is evidence for discrimination of ethnic minorities, especially against their languages, employment, participation in elections (Hughes, 2005; Ivlevs, 2008). The possible reasons of such a discriminatory policy are the desire of the Latvian government to protect the socio-economic status of the Latvians (Horowitz, 1998; Docquier, Rapoport, 2003); to eliminate the historical injustice based on preferential treatment of the Russian language and culture in the Soviet period (Horowitz, 1998); and the fear of ethnic Latvians that they will lose their language and culture (Hanovs, 2010). There is an opinion that in Latvia there are probably not a minority and majority, but two minority groups. This is because the Latvians still partly feel like a minority, and in some urban areas, they are a numerical minority, while the Russians have had minority status since 1992 (Rosenvalds, 2012). Both groups are afraid of losing their culture and language, and this hinders their mutual integration. This situation contributes to the fact that Latvia has developed two sustainable subcultures, formed on the basis of the Russian and Latvian languages (Muiznieks, 2010; Golubeva, 2010). These subcultures manifest themselves in the media as well as in everyday communication. Very few people are included in both subcultures; most people exist in the two separate parallel cultural worlds (Golubeva, 2010).

Researchers have described three possibilities for ethnic Russians in the Baltic states: a) they will either *assimilate* into ethnic Balts, b) they will *integrate* within the Baltic states and c) they will *separate* by becoming culturally and politically divergent from the Balts (Kronenfeld, 2005, p. 255). An empirical study conducted within Berry's acculturation framework demonstrated that integration is the most favored strategy for Latvian Russian and marginalisation is the least preferred one (Pisarenko, 2006).

The position of Russians is debated actively in Latvia and other Baltic states. Opinions about fate of Russians "range from the shrill cry of Latvian rightists that all Baltic Russians are an alien fifth column (and should be immediately deported), to the equally unsubtle view among some Russians that the Balts, with no independent culture of their own, should accept the Russians as their superiors" (Kronenfeld, 2005, p. 248). The rejection of Russians by Latvians is clearly associated with their large population in the country. One empirical study demonstrated a significant interactive relationship between the size of the Russian population and the strength of Latvian nationalism (Bloom, 2008). However, Russians are trying to adapt to this situation, and there is empirical evidence that Russophones in the Baltic states are in the process of forming a new, Baltic Russian, identity (Kronenfeld, 2005).

Azerbaijan. The findings of previous studies of intercultural relations in Azerbaijan in the post-Soviet period differ greatly. The data of conflict monitoring, based on the experts' interviews in 2003–2004, showed that the level of intercultural conflicts in Azerbaijan is higher than in other republics of the former USSR (Tishkov & Stepanov, 2004). However, in general, the results of many studies haven't shown significant problems in inter-ethnic relations in Azerbaijan. Members of all ethnic groups have a high level of ethnic tolerance, a willingness to work and study in multi-ethnic collectives, have interethnic friendships, aimed on inter-ethnic cooperation in different spheres (Guliev, 2012; Azerbaydzhan v 2006–2010 godakh. Sotsiologicheskiy monitoring, 2011; Faradov, 2011).

The Russian language is still widely used in everyday communication in Azerbaijan, and 47% of ethnic Azerbaijanis speak Russian (Musabekov, 2011). The Russian language is widespread among the Azerbaijani elite; it helps to make a good career (Karavaev, 2008). Not one Russian school has been closed, more than 109,000 school children (11%) and 20,000 university students are studying in Russian. In 2000, Baku Slavic University (BSU) was founded (Gavrilov, Kozievskaya & Yatsenko, 2008) where the language of instruction is Russian.

However, some studies have shown that the scope of the Russian language in Azerbaijan is being gradually reduced. Since the collapse of the USSR, anti-Russian propaganda has intensified. Russia was seen as an ally of Armenia in the Armenian-Azerbaijani conflict (Furman, Abbasov, 2001; Yunusov, 2001). Public opinion polls show that only a very small part of the population of Azerbaijan has positive attitudes towards Russia (Azerbaydzhan v 2006-2010 godakh. Sotsiologicheskiy monitoring, 2011).

Based on these data we can suppose that the context of intercultural relations between Azerbaijani and Russians provides good conditions for mutual integration due to the use of both languages in everyday communication and high ethnic tolerance.

In this study, we evaluate the three hypotheses of intercultural relations (the multiculturalism hypothesis, the contact hypothesis and the integration hypothesis) in both independent states of Latvia and Azerbaijan in order to reveal similarities and differences in mutual adaptation to changing socio-cultural contexts in the former soviet republics after the collapse of the Soviet Union.

4   Method

4.1   Samples

Table 3.1 presents the age and gender statistics for both samples.

The sample in Latvia included 699 adult respondents: Latvians (N = 363) and ethnic Russians (N = 336). The sample in Azerbaijan included 607 adult respondents: 300 Azerbaijanis and 307 ethnic Russians. See Table 3.1 for age and gender statistics. The study in Latvia was carried out in the city of Riga, which is the capital of this country.

Table 3.1. *Sample composition.*

Groups		Age		Gender
		M	SD	Male (%)
Latvians (Riga)	363	42.6	20.7	12.1
Ethnic Russians (Riga)	336	42.8	21.5	14
Azerbaijanis	300	46.6	20.1	43
Ethnic Russians (Baku)	307	45.8	21.6	29.3

The survey in Azerbaijan was mostly conducted in the city of Baku, the capital of the country. Eighty percent of ethnic Russians in Azerbaijan live in the city of Baku according to the census of the population in this country (Perepisi naseleniya Azerbaydzhana, 2013). Additionally, the survey was conducted in the two regions of Azerbaijan, where ethnic Russians live (Ismaillinsky and Khachmazsky).

4.2 Measures

The study used scales and items from the MIRIPS questionnaire. The items were translated into Russian and adapted for use in Russia (Lebedeva & Tatarko, 2009, 2013) and were translated into Latvian and adopted for use in Latvia by our colleague I. Plotka. All the Azerbaijanis were interviewed in Baku and filled out the questionnaire in Russian, because in Baku they speak Russian as well as the Azerbian language.

The following scales were used from the MIRIPS questionnaire: Perceived security; Intercultural contacts; Multicultural ideology; Intercultural strategies of non-dominant groups; Intercultural expectations of dominant groups; Ethnic tolerance; Life satisfaction; Self-esteem; and Demographic variables (gender, age and level of education).

4.3 Procedure

In Latvia, a snowball technique was used. Our Latvian colleagues interviewed Latvian and Russian university students first and then asked them to interview their ethnic Latvian and ethnic Russian friends, acquaintances, colleagues and relatives. For Russians, the survey was conducted in Russian; for Latvians it was conducted in Latvian.

The research in Azerbaijan was conducted by the Center for Research of Development and International Cooperation (SIGMA). They used convenience sampling in the survey process. For both Russians and Azerbaijanis, the survey was conducted in Russian.

4.4 Data Processing

For the testing of our three hypotheses, we used structural equation modeling (SEM) with AMOS version 20. We also used path analysis with AMOS version 19 (Arbuckle, 2010). This instrument allows the evaluation of a series of simultaneous hypotheses, taking measurement errors into account (see Bollen & Pearl, 2013). During the data processing, separate models were constructed for the each of the four samples.

5   Results

5.1   *Statistics*

Descriptive statistics, including means, standard deviations are presented in Table 3.2.

In the Table 3.2, there are several trends in the differences between respondents from Latvia and Azerbaijan.

Security. The level of perceived security is significantly higher in participants from Azerbaijan than in those from Latvia; and it is higher among the ethnic majority (the Azerbaijani) than among the Russians.

Contact. The Russians in Azerbaijan assessed intercultural contacts with the ethnic majority as more intensive than did the Russians in Latvia; this is expected, as the number of the Russians in Azerbaijan is relatively small. At the same time, the Latvians assessed the intensity of contacts with the Russians higher than the Russians themselves with the Latvians do. The ethnic majorities and minorities evaluated acceptability of multicultural ideology in these two countries in the same way, but there are differences between the countries: the level of acceptability of multicultural ideology in Azerbaijan is higher than in Latvia. The preference for integration is higher among the Russians in Azerbaijan compared to the Russians in Latvia.

Intercultural strategies and expectations. The preference for assimilation among ethnic majorities' members is higher than among Russians in both republics. The preference of assimilation among the Latvians is higher than among the Azerbaijani. The level of ethnic tolerance is higher in Azerbaijan, than in Latvia. Within the republics, it is higher among Russians in Latvia, and among the Azerbaijani in Azerbaijan.

Life satisfaction of the Russians in Azerbaijan is slightly higher than life satisfaction of the Azerbaijani themselves, but does not differ from that of the Russians in Latvia. Self-esteem of the Russians is statistically significantly higher among the Russians in Azerbaijan compared with the Russians in Latvia.

The overall pattern is that the comparison of the main variables between the groups and republics demonstrates that there is more successful mutual acculturation of the Azerbaijani majority and the Russian minority in Azerbaijan compared with Latvians and Russians in Latvia.

5.2   *The Results of Structural Equation Modeling*

We next tested all three hypotheses of intercultural relations in the combined models with all four samples using structural equation

Table 3.2. *Means, standard deviations, and t-tests for the four samples: Russians in Latvia, Latvians, Russians in Azerbaijan, and Azerbaijanis*

	M; σ				t-test, p			
	RL	La	RA	Az	RL–La	RA–Az	RL–RA	AZ–La
SEC	2.70; 0.66	2.69; 0.66	3.76; 1.41	4.29; 0.81	−.48	−7.3***	−13.9***	−26.8***
IC	2.66; 0.96	3.62; 0.95	3.65; 1.05	2.60; 1.11	−11.4***	11.8***	−11.0***	11.6***
MI	3.52; 0.81	3.36; 0.65	4.08; 0.67	4.19; 0.83	2.8**	−1.7	−9.5***	−13.8***
INT	3.98; 0.64	4.33; 0.63	4.38; 0.54	4.37; 0.82	.08	.05	−6.2***	−.78
ASS	1.76; 0.74	2.09; 0.73	1.44; 0.53	1.62; 0.89	.40	−2.9**	5.8***	7.4***
TOL	3.73; 0.92	3.45; 0.83	4.07; 0.84	4.24; 0.83	3.7***	−2.6**	−4.7***	−11.8***
LS	3.23; 0.89	3.15; 0.77	3.33; 0.95	3.16; 0.87	.07	2.3*	−.13	−.07
S-Est	4.05; 0.74	3.97; 0.58	4.25; 0.55	4.01; 0.67	.13	1.4	−3.6***	−.08

*p < .05; **p < .01; ***p < .001.

SEC, Security; IC, Intercultural contacts; MI, Multicultural ideology; INT, Integration; ASS, Assimilation; TOL, Ethnic tolerance; SCA, Sociocultural adaptation; LS, Life satisfaction; S-Est, Self-Esteem.

RL, Russians in Latvia; La, Latvians; RA, Russians in Azerbaijan; Az, Azerbaijanis.

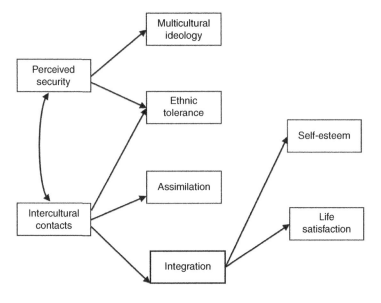

Figure 3.1. The tested model.

modelling. The tested model presented in the Figure 3.1 was built according to the three hypotheses. In fact, the empirical models have many more direct links than are shown; all of them are presented in the Tables 3.3 and 3.4.

The results for the Russian minority and Latvians in Riga are presented in Table 3.3. The data of Russian minority and Latvians in Latvia are presented in the same table using slash.

Assessment of the models' fits indicates that all the goodness-of-fit indices are exceptionally good for the Russian sample (χ^2/df= 2.2; CFI=.97; RMSEA=.06; PCLOSE=.27) as well as for the Latvian sample (χ^2/df=2.6; CFI=.98; RMSEA=.06; PCLOSE=.21).

The percentage of variance explained by socio-demographic variables (gender and age) is either equal to zero or very small (0.01–0.03). So, we can postulate, that age and gender do not play significant roles in these two models.

We now describe the results of the Russians in Latvia and Latvians. *Multiculturalism hypothesis.* Perceived security had a positive and significant effect on ethnic tolerance (β =0.28, p <.001) and multicultural

Table 3.3. *Standardized direct effects and correlations (Russians in Latvia/Latvians).*

Predictors	IC	MI	TOL	INT	ASS	S-Est	LS
SEC	-.02/ -.43***	.11*/ .52***	.89***/ .31***	.26***/ .57***	-.24***/ -.43***	.00/ 24***	.00/ .00
IC	—	.25***/ .23***	.03/.31***	.17**/ -.02	.15**/ .01	.00/.00	.00/ .30***
MI	.25***/ .23***	—	.08/.30***	-.08/ .61***	-.21***/ -.55***	.00/ -.27***	-.08/ -.08
TOL	.03/ .31***	.08/ .30***	—	.37***/ .23***	-.21***/ -.36***	.07/.09	-.08/ .28***
INT	.17**/ -.02	.08/ .61***	.37***/ .23***	—	-.35/ -.52**	.13*/.03	.18***/.09
ASS	.15**/ .01	-.21***/ -.55***	-.21***/ -.36***	-.35***/ -.52***	—	-.05/-.01	.04/-.12
R^2	—	.07/.22	.79/.19	.09/.32	.09/.18	.02/23	.05/10

*p < .05; **p < .01; ***p < .001. Correlations are in italics.
SEC, Security; IC, Intercultural contacts; MI, Multicultural ideology; INT, Integration; ASS, Assimilation; TOL, Ethnic tolerance; SCA, Sociocultural adaptation; LS, Life satisfaction; S-Est, Self-Esteem.

Table 3.4. *Standardized direct effects and correlations (Russians in Azerbaijan and Azerbaijanis).*

Predictors	IC	MI	TOL	INT	ASS	S-Est	LS
SEC	-.02/ -.43***	.11*/ .52***	.89***/ .31***	.26***/ .57***	-.24***/ -.43***	.00/ .24***	.00/ .00
IC	—	.25***/ .23***	.03/.31***	.17**/ -.02	.15**/ .01	.00/.00	.00/ .30***
MI	.25***/ .23***	—	.08/.30***	-.08/ .61***	-.21***/ -.55***	.00/ -.27***	-.08/ -.08
TOL	.03/ .31***	.08/ .30***	—	.37***/ .23***	-.21***/ -.36***	.07/.09	-.08/ .28***
INT	.17**/ -.02	.08/ .61***	.37***/ .23***	—	-.35/ -.52***	.13*/.03	.18***/.09
ASS	.15**/ .01	-.21***/ -.55***	-.21***/ -.36***	-.35***/ -.52***	—	-.05/-.01	.04/-.12
R²	—	.07/.22	.79/.19	.09/.32	.09/.18	.02/.23	.05/.10

*p <.05; **p <.01; ***p <.001. Correlations are in italics.
SEC, Security; IC, Intercultural contacts; MI, Multicultural ideology; INT, Integration; ASS, Assimilation; TOL, Ethnic tolerance; SCA, Sociocultural adaptation; LS, Life satisfaction; S-Est, Self-Esteem.

ideology (β =0.21, p <.001) in Latvians, but had no significant effect on either ethnic tolerance or multicultural ideology in Russians in Latvia. Therefore, this hypothesis has been supported in the Latvian sample, but not proved in the Latvian Russians.

Contact hypothesis. Intercultural contacts significantly and positively predicted the integration (β =0.25, p <.001) strategy of Latvian Russians, but had no significant effect on their ethnic tolerance. In Latvians, intercultural contacts affect neither tolerance nor the integration expectation. Therefore, the contact hypothesis has been partly confirmed in the Latvian Russians, but not in the Latvians.

Integration hypothesis. The integration expectation of Latvians had a significant and positive impact on self-esteem (β =0.14, p <.05), but had no significant impact on their life satisfaction. The preference for the integration strategy in Latvian Russians had no statistically significant impact on either measure of psychological adaptation. Therefore, the integration hypothesis has been partly supported with Latvians, but not with Latvian Russians.

Also, we have obtained additional results concerning the role of assimilation in the mutual acculturation of Latvians and Russians in Latvia. Perceived security had a significant positive impact on the preference for assimilation among Russians in Latvia (β =0.13, p <.05) and significant negative impact among Latvians (β = –0.13, p <.05). Moreover, intercultural contacts of Russians with Latvians also have significant positive effects on their assimilation preferences (β =0.22, p <.001), while intercultural contacts of Latvians with Russians had no effects on their assimilation expectations. Assimilation preferences had significant negative impact on the self-esteem of Latvian Russians (β = –0.42, p <.001) as well as of Latvians (β = –0.19, p <.05).

In addition, it is important to note that we found negative correlation between intercultural contacts and perceived security among Latvians (r=–0.18; p <.01). This means that the higher the intercultural contacts, the lower perceived security and vice versa. This unusual finding will be examined in the discussion.

We now examine the results of testing the three hypotheses in Azerbaijan with groups of Azerbaijanis and ethnic Russians (see Table 3.4). Assessment of the models' fits indicates that all the goodness-of-fit indices are exceptionally good for the Russian sample (χ^2/df= 1.5; CFI=.99; RMSEA=.04; PCLOSE=.59) as well as for the Azerbaijani sample (χ^2/df= 1.8; CFI=.99; RMSEA=.05; PCLOSE=.42).

The percentage of variance explained by socio-demographic variables (gender and age) is low in both samples except one case: age explains 10 percent of variance of multicultural ideology's impact in the Russian sample.

Multiculturalism hypothesis. The perceived security among Russians in Azerbaijan had a very strong positive effect on ethnic tolerance ($\beta = 0.89$, $p <.001$), significant positive effect on multicultural ideology ($\beta = 0.11$, $p <.05$) and the strategy of integration ($\beta = 0.26$, $p <.001$). At the same time, perceived security had a significant negative effect on assimilation strategy ($\beta = -0.24$, $p <.001$). Perceived security in the group of Azerbaijani also had significant positive effect on multicultural ideology ($\beta = 0.52$, $p <.001$), ethnic tolerance ($\beta = 0.31$, $p <.001$), and integration expectation ($\beta = 0.57$, $p <.001$). Therefore, we can conclude that the integration hypothesis has been fully supported in both Azerbaijanis and Russians in Azerbaijan.

Contact hypothesis. Intercultural contacts of Russians significantly and positively predicted both their preference for integration ($\beta = 0.17$, $p <.01$) and for assimilation ($\beta = 0.15$, $p <.01$), but did not predict their ethnic tolerance. Intercultural contacts of Azerbaijani significantly and positively predicted their ethnic tolerance ($\beta = 0.31$, $p <.001$), but did not predict intercultural expectations of integration and assimilation. Therefore, we can conclude that this hypothesis has been partly supported in both samples.

Integration hypothesis. The integration strategy in Russians in Azerbaijan significantly and positively predicted their life satisfaction ($\beta = 0.18$, $p <.001$) and self-esteem ($\beta = 0.13$, $p <.05$), while intercultural expectation of integration among Azerbaijanis had no significant impact on their life satisfaction and self-esteem. Therefore, the integration hypothesis has been partly supported with Russians in Azerbaijan and was not confirmed in the Azerbaijanis sample.

It is important to note that we found negative correlation between intercultural contacts and perceived security ($r=-0.43$; $p <.001$) in the sample of Azerbaijanis as we did in the Latvians in Riga.

6   Discussion

This study is the first to examine the mutual acculturation and intercultural relations of Russians who have become an ethnic minority in two very different post-Soviet societies. It has also compared them to each other and to the dominant populations in these two former Soviet republics. The independent states of Latvia and Azerbaijan are characterized by very different paths of post-Soviet development. This research gives the opportunity to compare the features of such intercultural relations and shed light on the role of the socio-cultural context and acceptability of multicultural ideology in this process.

We first discuss the results of evaluating the three hypotheses in both the countries. According to the first hypothesis (multiculturalism), the higher the perceived security, the higher are the intercultural adaptations, as assessed by support for multicultural ideology and ethnic tolerance (for both the minority group and the members of the larger society). For the sample of Latvians, perceived security does have significant impacts on both support for multicultural ideology and ethnic tolerance. However, in the sample of Russians in Latvia there are no significant impacts of perceived security on the acceptance of multicultural ideology and ethnic tolerance. In Azerbaijan, perceived security does have significant impacts on the support for multicultural ideology as well as on ethnic tolerance in both the dominant and the Russian minority groups. Thus the results of the study fully confirmed the multiculturalism hypothesis for three groups: the Latvians, the Azerbaijanis, the Russians in Azerbaijan, but do not support it for the Russian minority in Latvia. This support is important because the findings are from very different kinds of groups: they are with people who are not immigrants, but who have changed their dominant place in society for a minority one.

The contact hypothesis posits the positive impact of friendly intercultural contacts on the acceptance of "cultural others". With respect to tolerance, for Azerbaijanis, their intercultural contacts positively and significantly predicted their level of ethnic tolerance. However, intercultural contacts do not have any significant impact on such acceptance among Latvians. For the Russians in Latvia, having frequent friendly contacts among the host population positively and significantly affected their acculturation strategies of integration and assimilation, just as they did for the Russians in Azerbaijan. So the contact hypothesis is partially confirmed with three groups: Russians in Latvia, Russians in Azerbaijan and Azerbaijanis, but is not confirmed with Latvians. Again, this level of support is an important finding because of the atypical nature of the non-dominant groups in these studies.

According to the integration hypothesis, preference for the integration strategy promotes better psychological adaptation. Looking first at the minority Russians, in Latvia, contrary to the hypothesis, their preference for the integration strategy had no significant impact on their life satisfaction or self-esteem. However, among Russians in

Azerbaijan, the preference for the integration strategy has positive and significant impact on both measures of psychological adaptation (self-esteem and life satisfaction). Thus, we can conclude that the Russian minorities' preference for the strategy of integration contributed to their self-esteem and life satisfaction only in Azerbaijan.

For the majority groups, the preference for integration among the Latvians in Latvia promoted their self-esteem, but did not promote life satisfaction and self-esteem for the Azerbaijanis in Azerbaijan. Therefore, the integration hypothesis was partially supported in the host population in Latvia and in Russians in Azerbaijan, but it was not supported in the Russians in Latvia and the host population in Azerbaijan.

Thus, all three hypotheses received at least partial support only in one group – Russians in Azerbaijan. The multiculturalism hypothesis was not confirmed with the Russians in Latvia, the contact hypothesis was not supported with the Latvians in Latvia and the integration hypothesis was not supported with the Azerbaijanis in Azerbaijan and Russians in Latvia. The results of testing the hypotheses in these both countries are presented in the Table 3.5.

The most important questions are why these hypotheses did not receive support in these three groups: the Latvians in Latvia, the Russians in Latvia and the Azerbaijanis in Azerbaijan. To answer them we decided to analyze some relationships among the main pre-dictors in the models.

First, why perceived security did not predict acceptance of multi-cultural ideology and ethnic tolerance, and integration did not predict psychological well-being for Russians in Latvia? According to our

Table 3.5. *Comparison of the results of the hypotheses testing in Latvia and Azerbaijan.*

	Latvia		Azerbaijan	
Hypothesis	Latvians	Russians	Azerbaijanis	Russians
The multiculturalism hypothesis	fully supported	not supported	fully supported	fully supported
The contact hypothesis	not supported	partially supported	partially supported	partially supported
The integration hypothesis	partially supported	not supported	not supported	fully supported

results, low level of security positively and significantly correlated with preference for assimilation among Russians in Latvia. These findings require additional analysis of the socio-political and historical context in Latvia in order to understand the psychological outcomes of mutual acculturation of the minority and majority groups. Some parallels in the previous research on intercultural relations in Estonia (Kruusvall, Vetic & Berry, 2009) might shed light on our results. In Berry's (1997) terms, the Estonian formulation of integration policy incorporates only the participation dimension; the cultural-maintenance dimension is not part of the policy. Thus, the political terminology of integration is much closer to the acculturative expectation of assimilation. The ethnically connoted nation-state model equates integration with forced assimilation. Since the majority of Estonian Russians do not wish to assimilate, integration for them means "something to avoid". Therefore, the term *integration* itself has a negative meaning among ethnic Russians there (Kruusvall et al., 2009). Similarly, we described the Latvian context and policy as promoting assimilation more than integration, despite the opposite wording. This policy might explain why integration did not predict any positive outcomes for either of the groups in Latvia. According to our data, we have different correlations of assimilation with ethnic tolerance and with preference for integration in both groups in Latvia: in Russians these correlations are significant and negative, while in Latvians they are significant and positive. This means that preference for assimilation has different meanings for the Russian minority and the Latvian majority: for Russians it is connected with intolerance and lack of integration; in Latvians it is connected with tolerance and integration. Perhaps for Latvians, assimilation and integration have very close meanings, which is not true for Latvian Russians. The latter avoid such a type of integration, and it didn't contribute to their psychological well-being.

The second question is: why was the contact hypothesis not supported among Latvians? We obtained a significant negative relationship between security and contact in the Latvian sample. This means that intercultural contacts may make Latvians feel less secure or vice versa: low security impedes intercultural contact. Latvians have low levels of security and high levels of intercultural contact. Moreover they assessed the intensity of their intercultural contacts much higher than Russians did, despite the fact that Latvians are a numerical majority in Latvia. Probably this subjective evaluation of excessive intercultural contacts does not promote acceptance of Russians among Latvians. We also obtained a negative relationship between security and contact in Azerbaijanis, but the nature of this relationship is different: a discordance of high perceived security and low intercultural contacts. Such a combination does not impede the contact hypothesis, and contacts promote ethnic tolerance among Azerbaijanis.

But why was the integration hypothesis not supported with Azerbaijanis? Our results have shown that the integration expectation among Azerbaijanis does not promote their life satisfaction and self-esteem. We suppose that the integration of Russians is due to their low proportion in Azerbaijan (1.34%), and the relatively positive mutual attitudes did not significantly contribute to the psychological well-being of Azerbaijanis. At the same time, acceptance of multicultural ideology demonstrated unexpected and disturbing negative relationship with the self-esteem of Azerbaijanis ($\beta = -.27$; $p < .001$). This means that psychological well-being of the host population of Azerbaijan is sensitive to multicultural ideology, and the latter could reduce the self-esteem of Azerbaijanis. Probably the very small proportion of Russians and their reduced influence on the situation in the republic could explain why relatively positive intercultural relations still existed in Azerbaijan.

What are possible implications of our study? We see the main directions for national integration in Latvia as follows: to facilitate friendly intercultural contacts between Latvians and Russians, while at the same time providing a sense of cultural security (and reducing a sense of threat) in both groups. Differences between integration and assimilation should be more articulated in the multicultural ideology and multicultural policy in Latvia to provide better conditions for the integration of ethnic minorities, which is beneficial for both sides. As to Azerbaijan, the current intercultural relations between Russians and Azerbaijanis are characterized by mutual positive attitudes and the context in the republic provides good grounds for the integration of Russians. But the role of multicultural ideology should be more articulated in public discourse of this country.

There are some limitations of our study. The first limitation concerns the samples which reduces the generalizability of the findings: they are not representative for Azerbaijan as well as for Latvia because data were collected mostly in the capitals of these countries (Baku and Riga). The second limitation concerns the snowball sampling technique, in which respondents were recruited from a narrow circle of friends and acquaintances. To overcome these limitations, we plan to test these three hypotheses in neighbouring countries to compare the findings obtained in different socio-cultural contexts. This approach should allow us to assess the general character of these hypotheses, as well to identify some cultural and national specifics.

Acknowledgements

This work was supported by the Russian Science Foundation (Project No. 15-18-00029). The authors appreciate the help of Professor Irina Plotka and Dr. Tatiana Kanonire in gathering data and providing details of the sociocultural context in Latvia.

References

Apine, I. (2010). Latvian scientists about the traditions of recognition and acceptance of Russians (other ethnic minorities) in Latvia. *Ethnicity, 1*, 29–57.
Arbuckle, J. L. (2010). *IBM SPSS Amos 19 user's guide*. Crawfordville, FL: Amos Development Corporation.
Azerbaydzhan v 2006–2010 godakh. Sotsiologicheskiy monitoring (2011) [Azerbaijan in 2006–2010. Sociological monitoring]. Retrieved from http://pandia.ru/text/77/285/72964.php.
Berry, J. W. (1997). Immigration, acculturation and adaptation. *Applied Psychology: An International Review, 46*, 5–68.
Bloom, S. (2008). Competitive assimilation or strategic non-assimilation? The political economy of school choice in Latvia. *Comparative Political Studies, 41* (7), 947–970.
Bollen, K. A., & Pearl, J. (2013). Eight myths about causality and structural equation models. UCLA Cognitive Systems Laboratory Technical Report (R-393), July 2012. In S. L. Morgan (Ed.), *Handbook of Causal Analysis for Social Research* (pp. 301–328). New York: Springer.
Docquier, F., & Rapoport, H., (2003). Ethnic discrimination and the migration of skilled labor. *Journal of Development Economics, 70*, 159–172.
Faradov, T. (2011) Problema optimizatsii mezhetnicheskikh otnosheniy v Azerbaydzhane [The problem of optimization of inter-ethnic relations in Azerbaijan]. http://forum.atc.az/showthread.php?t=11999.
Furman, D.E., & Abbasov A. (2001). Azerbaydzhanskaya revolyutsiya [Azerbaijan Revolution] *Azerbaydzhan i Rossiya: obshchestvo i gosudarstvo [Azerbaijan and Russia: society and the state]*. Moscow: Summer Garden.
Gavrilov, K., Kozievskaya E., & Yatsenko E. (2008). Russkiy yazyk na postsovetskikh prostorakh [Russian language in the post-Soviet expanse] *Demoskop Weekly [Demoscope Weekly], 329–330*, 14–27, April 2008. Retrieved from www.demoscope.ru/weekly/2008/0329/tema03.php.
Golubeva M. (2010). Multiculturalism as Imperialism: Condemnation of Social Diversity within a Discourse of Threat and Blame. In M. Golubeva and R. Gould (Eds.), *Shrinking Citizenship. Discursive Practices that Limit Democratic Participation in Latvian Politics* (pp. 157–170). New York: Rodopi.

Guliev, V.M.O. (2012). Problemy analiza kachestva zhizni naseleniya respubliki Azerbaydzhan [The problems of the analysis of the quality of life of the population in the Republic of Azerbaijan]. *Teoriya i praktika obshchestvennogo razvitiya. [Theory and practice of social development], 3,* 317–321.

Hanovs, D. (2010). *Neiespȩamā integrācija* [Impossible integration]. Retrieved November 29, 2011, from http://politika.lv/article/neiespejama-integracija.

Horowitz D.L. (1998). Structure and strategy in ethnic conflict: A few steps towards synthesis. In B. Pleskovicand J.E. Stiglitz, (Eds.), *Annual World Bank Conference on Development Economics* (pp. 345–370). The World Bank.

Hughes J. (2005). 'Exit' in deeply divided societies: Regimes of discrimination in Estonia and Latvia and the potential for Russophone migration. *Journal of Common Market Studies, 43*(4), 739–762.

Ivlevs A. (2008). Are Ethnic Minorities More Likely to Emigrate? Evidence from Latvia. Retrieved June 29, 2011, from www.nottingham.ac.uk/gep/documents/papers/2008/08-11.pdf.

Karavaev, A. (2008). Russkaya rech' i kul'tura v stranakh SNG (na primere Azerbaydzhana): issledovaniye fonda «Naslediye Yevrazii» [Russian language and culture in the CIS countries (for example, Azerbaijan): Research Fund 'Eurasia Heritage'] *Informatsionno-Analiticheskiy Tsentr, [Information-Analytical Center]*. Retrieved from www.fundeh.org/about/articles/40/.

Kerimov, E. (2010). Russkiye Azerbaydzhana [Russians of the Azerbaijan]. *Zhurnal IRS-Naslediye [Journal IRS-Heritage], 3* (45), 54–65.

Kronenfeld, D. A. (2005). The effects of interethnic contact on ethnic identity: Evidence from Latvia. *Post-Soviet Affairs, 21*(3), 247–277.

Kruusvall, J., Vetik, R., & Berry, J. W. (2009). The strategies of inter-ethnic adaptation of Estonian Russians. *Studies of Transition States and Societies, 1,* 3–24.

Lebedeva, N. M., & Tatarko, A. N. (2013). Immigration and intercultural interaction strategies in post-Soviet Russia. In E. Tartakovsky (Ed.), *Immigration: Policies, challenges and impact* (pp. 179–194). New York: Nova Science.

Lebedeva, N. M., & Tatarko, A. N. (Eds.). (2009). *Strategii mezhkul'turnogo vzaimodejstvija migrantov i naselenija Rossii (Strategies for the intercultural interaction of migrants and the sedentary population in Russia).* Moscow: RUDN.

Ministry of Foreign Affairs of the Republic of Latvia (2015). Naturalisation (Naturalizācija). Retrieved from www.mfa.gov.lv/en/policy/society-integration/citizenship/naturalisation.

Muiznieks N. (2010). Social integration: A brief history of an idea. In N. Muiznieks (ed.), *How Integrated Is Latvian Society? An Audit of Achievements, Failures and Challenges* (pp. 15–32). Riga: University of Latvia Press.

Musabekov, R. (2011). Nezavisimyy Azerbaydzhan i etnicheskiye men'shinstva [Independent Azerbaijan and ethnic minorities]. Retrieved

from www.kavkazoved.info/news/2011/12/06/nezavisimyj-azerbajdzhan-i-et
nicheskie-menshinstva-i.html.

Perepisi naseleniya Azerbaydzhana (2013). [Population Censuses of Azerbaijan].
Retrieved from http://web.archive.org/web/20121130101713/http://www.azstat
.org/statinfo/demoqraphic/en/AP_/1_5.xls.

Pisarenko, O. (2006). The acculturation modes of Russian speaking adolescents
in Latvia: Perceived discrimination and knowledge of the Latvian language.
Europe-Asia Studies, 58(5), 751–773.

Permanent Mission of the Republic of Latvia to the United Nations (2016).
Integration politics in Latvia: A multi-faceted approach (Integrācijas politika
Latvijā: daudzpusīga pieeja. Retrieved from www.mfa.gov.lv/en/newyork/soci
ety-integration/integration-policy-in-latvia-a-multi-faceted-approach.

Popov, E. (2010). Russkiye v Azerbaydzhane [Russians in Azerbaijan] Stoletiye.
Informatsionno analiticheskoye izdaniye fonda istoricheskoy perspektivy [Century.
Information analytical publication fund of historical perspective], September.
Retrieved from /www.stoletie.ru/rossiya_i_mir/russkije_v_azerbajdz
hane_2010-08-25.htm?CODE=russkije_v_azerbajdzhane_2010-08-
25&PAGEN_2=2

Republic of Latvia. (1998). Education law (Izglītības likums). Retrieved from w
ww.minelres.lv/NationalLegislation/Latvia/Latvia_Education_excerpts_Englis
h.htm.

Rodin, M.Y. (2013). Etnopoliticheskiye konflikty i natsional'naya identichnost'
v Latvii [Ethno-political conflicts and national identity in Latvia].
In Etnicheskiye konflikty v stranakh Baltii v postsovetskiy period: Sbornik statey
pod redaktsiyey A. V. Gaponenko [Ethnic conflicts in the Baltic countries in the post-
Soviet period: Collection of articles edited by A.V. Gaponenko] (pp. 27–60). Riga:
Institute of European Studies.

Rozenvalds, J. (2012). The Political Culture of Latvian Russian-Speakers in
a Comparative Perspective. Conference paper. Association for the
Advancement of Baltic Studies. Chicago 26–28 April.

Skrinnik, V.M. (2009). Rossiyskaya diaspora v stranakh Baltii: sotsial'no-
politicheskiy diskurs i problemy konsolidatsii [The Russian diaspora in the
Baltic States: the socio-political discourse and the consolidation of the pro-
blem]. Uchenyye zapiski [Scientific notes], 2, 126–131.

Sytin, A. (2012). Referendum o statuse russkogo yazyka kak proyavleniye krizisa
latviyskoy gosudarstvennosti: Referendumo russkom yazyke i latviyskaya gosu-
darstvennost' [A referendum on the status of the Russian language as
a manifestation of Latvian statehood crisis: Russian Language Referendum as
a Crisis of Latvian Statehood], slovo.ru: baltiyskiy aktsent [slovo.ru: baltic accent],
1, 7–13.

Tishkov, V.A., & Stepanov, V.V. (2004). Izmereniye konflikta. Metodika
i rezul'taty etnokonfessional'nogo monitoringa Seti EAWARN v 2003
godu [Measurement of the conflict. The methodology and the results of ethno-
religious monitoring of Network EAWARN in 2003]. (pp. 305–322).
Moscow. Institute of Ethnology and anthropology Russian Academy of
Sciences.

Vykhovanets, O. (2005) Priobreteniye grazhdanstva v stranakh SNG i Baltii (obzor zakonodatel'stva) [Acquisition of citizenship in the CIS and Baltic countries (legislative review)]. Retrieved from www.archipelag.ru/agenda/pov estka/naturalization/doklad/enclosure3/.

Yunusov, A.S. (2001). *Etnicheskiye i migratsionnyye protsessy v postsovetskom Azerbaydzhane [Ethnic and Migration processes in post-Soviet Azerbaijan].* Retrieved from http://chairs.stavsu.ru/geo/Conference/c1-67.htm.

4 Intercultural Relations in Estonia

Raivo Vetik, Maaris Raudsepp, Jüri Kruusvall, Larissa Kus-Harbord, Marianna Makarova and Aune Valk
Tallinn University, Estonia

1 Introduction

The Republic of Estonia regained independence in 1991, after being incorporated in the Soviet Union for half a century. A major feature of the Estonian context lies in the fact that as many as one-third of the current Estonian population is of foreign origin. Ethnic Russians form the biggest minority group, comprising about 26 per cent of the total population; altogether there are representatives of more than 100 different ethnic groups among the population. Among MIRIPS countries, Estonia ranks very high (second) on the Diversity Index, but low on the Integration Index. It is not represented on the policy index, but is estimated to be low.

2 Context of Intercultural Relations in Estonia

2.1 Immigration

Although a small number of Russians have lived in Estonia for centuries, the majority arrived during the Soviet period (1945 to 1991). While immediately after the Second World War the Estonian population was ethnically very homogeneous (97% were ethnic Estonians), in the 1989 census more than a third of the population were Russian-speaking people, due to migration from other parts of the Soviet Union. The increase of the Russian-speaking migrant population from 26,000 in 1945 to 602,000 in 1989 is a contextual factor having a major impact on intercultural relations in Estonia (Vetik, 1993). Other immigrant origins (i.e., not countries of the former Soviet Union) of the Estonian population are Finland and Poland, but their numbers are very small according to the last population census of 2011.

2.2   Policies

During the Soviet period, the official policies and institutions strongly supported the structural integration of Russian-speaking immigrants in Estonia. These migrants worked mostly at all-Union enterprises and had privileges in getting housing; a separate Russian-language education system was established, and key spheres in the economy as well as in political institutions operated in the Russian language. As a result of the Soviet period, there are currently two rather segregated societies in Estonia with minimal interaction both in structural and cultural domains. Integration policies carried out in Estonia since the end of the 1990s have been aiming at overcoming such segregation, but the results can be regarded as successful only partly at best, since Russians often perceive these policies as assimilation pressure.

3   Evaluation of the MIRIPS Hypotheses in Estonia

Due to this socio-historical context, Estonia represents a very interesting case for academic research, highlighting several features that have not received enough attention in acculturation literature so far. For example, one can argue that the Russian-speaking population in Estonia represents an untypical category of "semi-immigrants" or "accidental diasporas" (Vetik & Helemäe, 2011; Brubaker, 1996). They have acquired their in-between status involuntarily as a result of new state boundaries being drawn between Estonia and Russia when Estonia regained independence. The post-independence nationalising policies and the new social boundaries they have triggered tend to construct Russians as "immigrants" in Estonia, which is perceived as discriminatory by most of them (Vetik & Helemäe, 2011). Ethnic Estonians, on the other hand, represent an atypical category of "threatened majority". Threat perceptions related to the arrival of a large number of immigrants over a comparatively short time can be found in many other countries as well, but the Estonian case is specific due to Russia's expansive foreign policies that aim to maintain control over the so-called near abroad. One of the measures Russia has adopted is the policy of "compatriots", claiming to represent the interests of Russians in the republics of the former Soviet Union, where they form a considerable minority group. Thus, perceptions of mutual threat by both the minority and the majority groups are an important feature of the intercultural context in Estonia, forming fertile ground for reactive ethnicity (Nimmerfeldt, 2011).

This study examines intercultural and acculturation issues in Estonia, guided by the three hypotheses on which the MIRIPS project is based. The relevance of the multiculturalism hypothesis is directly related to the historical context of the intercultural relations. As noted earlier, there are widespread threat perceptions among both minority and majority groups. However, the peculiarity of the Estonian case lies in the fact that there is no history of deeply rooted inter-ethnic conflict at the grass-roots level. The relevance of the contact and integration hypotheses can be related to the history of segregation between the two cultural groups in Estonia that was described earlier.

4 Method

4.1 Samples

The data for the study were collected in May 2015 by the polling company Saar Poll among both the Russian-speaking and ethnic Estonian adult populations. Proportional random sampling was based on the 2011 census in Estonia. The survey questionnaires were filled out during face-to-face interviews, and the response rate was 48 per cent. The final sample consisted of 501 Russian-speaking and 510 ethnic Estonian respondents (54% female, mean age 48 [range 18 to 74 years]). Participation in the survey was voluntary and confidential.

4.2 Measures

The measures used in the survey were drawn from those in the MIRIPS questionnaire, supplemented by other relevant measures. These other measures are now described.

Ethnic identity. Four items were adapted from existing research (Mlicki & Ellemers, 1996). They correspond to MIRIPS *Cultural identity* scale items) to measure ethnic identification (e.g., "I feel that I am Estonian/Russian", "I am proud that I am Estonian/Russian", "I am glad that I am Estonian/ Russian", with majority or minority groups, respectively). Participants rated all items on a 5-point scale (1 – disagree, 5 – agree), with higher scores indicating higher levels of ethnic identification.

National identity. The items which were used to measure ethnic identity (adapted from Mlicki & Ellemers, 1996) were applied to measure national identity (e.g., "I feel that I am a part of Estonian society", "I am proud that I am part of Estonian society").

Russian-speaking community identity. The same items that were used to measure national identity (adapted from Mlicki & Ellemers, 1996) were used to measure Russian community identity (e.g., "I am proud of belonging to the Russian-speaking community in Estonia").

The *Intergroup anxiety* measure was adapted from Stephan and Stephan (1985). Participants were asked to indicate their feelings if they were the only Russian/Estonian person in an interpersonal interaction situation with outgroup members (Estonians/Russians). On a scale from 1 (completely disagree) to 5 (completely agree), participants rated 8 items: nervous, depressed, good (reversed), infringed, safe (reversed), relaxed (reversed), afraid to do something wrong, confident (reversed). Higher scores indicate higher levels of intergroup anxiety.

Outgroup feelings were measured using the MIRIPS "feeling thermometer".

Ingroup bias. Participants also rated their feelings towards their ingroup on this "feeling thermometer". Ingroup bias scores were obtained by subtracting the outgroup rating from the ingroup rating.

Outgroup trust. Three items adapted from Paolini, Hewstone and Cairns (2007) were used to measure outgroup trust (e.g., "Most Estonians/Russian-speaking minorities are trustworthy"). All items were measured on a 5-point agreement/disagreement scale (1 – strongly disagree; 5 – strongly agree).

Measures of contact. The subjective level of outgroup contacts was measured by a set of questions on the relative prevalence of various outgroup contacts ("How many of the people with whom you interact more closely belong to other ethnicity than yourself?"). The categories were relatives, friends, neighbours, colleagues, hobby companions and contacts in the social media (1 – majority, 2 – half, 3 – some, 4 – none). In the analysis we used two composite indexes – an *index of voluntary contact* (summation of outgroup contacts with friends, hobby companions and in social media). And an *index of involuntary outgroup contacts* (summation of outgroup contacts with relatives, neighbours and colleagues).

Social status of a minority group. The perceived relative status of a minority group and minority culture measure was adapted from Louis, Duck, Terry, Schuller & Lalonde (2007). The participants were asked, "How much is Russian culture / Russian ethnic group appreciated compared to other minorities, compared to Estonian culture/Estonian ethnic group?" (1 – less, 2 – rather less, 3 – equally, 4 – rather more, 5 – more).

Legitimacy of minority status. The perceived legitimacy of the relative status of a minority group measure was adapted from Louis et al. (2007). A summation index of items such as "The status of Russian-speaking people in Estonia compared to Estonians is the way it should be", "Russian-speaking people in Estonia have deserved their present status" and "Differences in status between ethnic groups are fair" was used. All items were measured on a 5-point agreement/disagreement scale (1 – strongly disagree, 5 – strongly agree).

Perceived respect towards the ingroup was measured using a summation index of items from the collective self-esteem scale, which was adapted from Luhtanen and Crocker (1992) and applied to national, ethnic and Russian community identity measures.

A *support for minority rights* scale was used to measure the contact outcomes for the majority group members. The measure was adapted from Ariely (2011). The respondents were asked, "How ready would you be to take actions in order to improve the position of Russian-speaking persons in Estonia?" There were 4 items (e.g., to defend the rights of Russian minority in an open debate) to rate on a four-point scale, ranging from 1 – certainly not ready to 4 – certainly ready.

Intercultural strategies. These strategies were assessed by using items based on the two dimensions (of culture maintenance and culture adoption), rather than by the four scales that assess the four strategies. Two cultural maintenance items were adapted from Berry (1997) (e.g., "Russians in Estonia should maintain their religion, culture and language"); two *culture adoption* items were adapted from Bourhis et al. (1997) (e.g., "It is important that Russians in Estonia embrace Estonian culture and traditions").

Expected intercultural strategies. In the minority questionnaire, an additional measure (based on Piontkowski, Rohmann & Florack, [2002] and Horenczyk [1996]) was used to identify the perception of majority group intercultural strategies expectations by the minority group. The same items as in the *Intercultural strategies* measure were used, with the difference that they were to be evaluated by minority group members "as a typical Estonian would evaluate them".

Economic situation. Participants had to choose one out of five answers to describe their family's economic situation (1 – "We have enough money to satisfy our needs and we are able to save"; 5 – "We have to limit our consumption a lot and we do not cope with our level of income"). Higher scores indicate a lower economic situation for a family.

Two scales from the MIRIPS instrument were used as in the main questionnaire.

The *multicultural ideology* scale from MIRIPS was used as an indicator of the perceived norms of intergroup relations.

Psychological adaptation and well-being were measured using the two MIRIPS scales: *life satisfaction* and *self-esteem*.

The participants also provided information on demographic variables (e.g., gender, age, level of education, ethnicity, citizenship, place of living, work status).

5   Results

We present the results for each hypothesis, preceded by a short discussion of the theoretical basis in Estonia and followed by a specific discussion of each hypothesis. A general discussion of all the results together follows this results section.

5.1   Multiculturalism Hypothesis

Previous studies in Estonia have shown that realistic political and economic threats were negatively related to outgroup attitudes and low support for affirmative action among the majority ethnic group (Kus, 2011). It has been found that minority Russians with high ethnic pride rated outgroups more positively than Russians with low ethnic pride (Valk, 2000). However, more recent research demonstrated that Russian-speaking participants with stronger ethnic identity showed more outgroup derogation and negative stereotypes of Estonians (Raudsepp, 2009), and more negative outgroup attitudes (Kus, 2011) than those with weaker ethnic identity. Among majority Estonians, previous research (e.g., Kus, 2011; Raudsepp, 2009) has indicated that stronger ethnic identity among Estonians is related to negative, distrusting and distancing outgroup attitudes, lower support of cultural heterogeneity and more restrictive views towards the entitlement of political, social and economic rights for a minority group.

We evaluate the multiculturalism hypothesis among the ethnic minority Russian and majority populations in Estonia by investigating how ethnic identity relates to intergroup relations under conditions of low and high intergroup anxiety. In line with the multiculturalism hypothesis, we propose: (1) intergroup anxiety is expected to be a significant predictor of intergroup relations, specifically of negative outgroup feelings, outgroup distrust and ingroup bias; (2) we expect to find a significant interaction between intergroup anxiety and ethnic identity (and community identity for the Russian ethnic minority group). In detail, under conditions of low intergroup anxiety (low threat), ethnic (and community) identity will be related to positive outgroup feelings, outgroup trust and lower ingroup bias, while under conditions of high intergroup anxiety (high threat) the opposite direction of relationships is expected.

A series of multiple linear regressions were performed to predict (a) outgroup feelings, (b) outgroup trust and (c) ingroup bias.

Minority Russian Participants

In the *prediction of outgroup feelings*, demographic variables explained 11 percent of variance in the initial step. With identity and intergroup anxiety variables entered into the model, the following step explained the additional 14 percent of variance in outgroup feelings. While ethnic and community identities did not contribute significantly to the prediction, intergroup anxiety was a significant negative predictor or outgroup

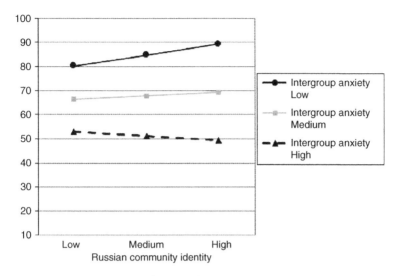

Figure 4.1. Outgroup feelings of Russian-speaking minorities.

feelings ($\beta = -.39$, p <.001). Additionally, the effects of region of living and family's economic situation remained significant: in comparison to individuals from the capital Tallinn, those from Northeastern Estonia ($\beta = .26$, p <.001) or the rest of the country ($\beta = .26$, p <.001) showed more positive outgroup attitudes; and a lower economic situation of the family predicted outgroup attitudes negatively ($\beta = -.08$, p =.05). The last step explained another 3 per cent of variance in outgroup feelings. This was due to the significant contribution of the interaction between community identity and intergroup anxiety.

To interpret the interaction term, the simple slope analysis (Jose, 2013) was conducted. The results (see Figure 4.1) revealed that under the condition of low intergroup anxiety (low threat), Russian community identity predicts positive feelings towards Estonians (slope = 6.40, t = 3.82, p <.001). The relationship between Russians' community identity and outgroup feelings was non-significant with medium (slope = 2.01, t = 1.63, p =.10) or high (slope = −2.37, t = −1.50, p =.13) perceptions of intergroup anxiety. This supports the multiculturalism hypothesis.

In the *prediction of outgroup trust*, demographic variables explained 10 per cent of variance in the initial step. The next step explained another 12 per cent of variance in outgroup trust, including identity and intergroup anxiety variables in the model. Similarly, ethnic and community identities showed no significant relationship with outgroup trust, while

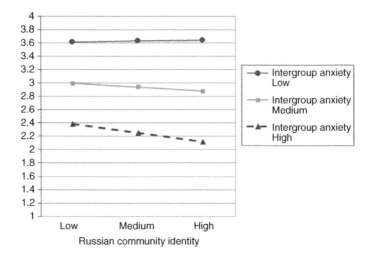

Figure 4.2. Outgroup trust of Russian-speaking minorities.

intergroup anxiety contributed significantly to the prediction of outgroup trust ($\beta = -.36$, p <.001). Some demographic variables also remained significant predictors: Russian-speaking individuals from Northeastern Estonia ($\beta =.23$, p <.001) and the rest of the country ($\beta =.18$, p <.001) showed higher outgroup trust than those from the capital Tallinn; individuals with lower family's economic situation ($\beta = -.16$, p <.001) showed lower outgroup trust. The interaction between community identity and intergroup anxiety was significant in the next step, explaining another 1 per cent of variance in outgroup trust.

The simple slope analysis indicated (see Figure 4.2) that when intergroup anxiety is perceived high (high threat), greater Russian community identity is related to lower outgroup trust (slope = –0.19, t = –2.04, p <.05). The relationship between Russians' community identity and outgroup trust is non-significant with low (slope = 0.02, t = 0.29, p =.77) or medium perceptions of intergroup anxiety (slope = –0.08, t = –1.07, p =.28). These results support the multiculturalism hypothesis.

In *prediction of ingroup bias*, demographic variables explained 20 per cent of variance in the ingroup bias in the initial step. Russian community identity and intergroup anxiety contributed significantly to the prediction of ingroup bias in the next step, accounting for another 10 per cent of variance. Additionally, region of living and family's economic position remained significant predictors from among the

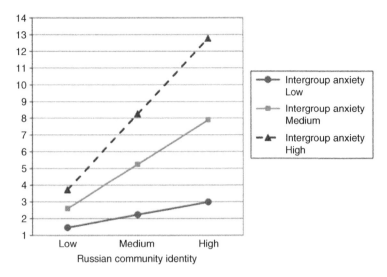

Figure 4.3. Ingroup bias of Russian-speaking minorities.

demographic variables, showing that Russian-speaking individuals with a better economic situation (β =.12, p <.01) and those living in Northeastern Estonia (β = −.35, p <.001) or the rest of the country (β = −.33, p <.001) showed lower ingroup bias than those living in the capital Tallinn. In the next step, the interaction between community identity and intergroup anxiety was significant, accounting for another 2 per cent of variance in ingroup bias.

The simple slope analysis showed (see Figure 4.3) that when inter-group anxiety is perceived to be high (slope = 6.53, t = 4.53, p <.001) or medium (slope = 3.82, t = 3.47, p <.001), greater Russian community identity is related to greater ingroup bias. The relationship between Russians' community identity and ingroup bias is non-significant with low perceptions of intergroup anxiety (slope= 1.10, t = 0.76, p =.45). These results support the multiculturalism hypothesis.

Majority Estonian Participants
In the *prediction of outgroup feelings, outgroup trust* and *ingroup bias* among majority participants, region of residence alone explained 7 per cent, 2 per cent and 3 per cent of variance, respectively. Including Estonians' ethnic identity and intergroup anxiety in the models of regression accounted for another 14 per cent, 8 per cent and 12 per cent of variance, respectively. Ethnic identity contributed significantly only to the prediction

of ingroup bias (β <.26, p <.001), showing that greater ethnic identity predicted greater ingroup bias. Intergroup anxiety was a significant negative predictor of outgroup feelings (β < -.37, p <.001) and outgroup trust (β < -.28, p <.001), and a significant positive predictor of ingroup bias (β <.25, p <.001). Additionally, Estonian-speaking residents of Tallinn showed more negative outgroup feelings (β =.16, p <.001), less outgroup trust (β =.16, p <.001) and more ingroup bias (β < -.14, p <.01) than participants residing in other regions of Estonia (except Eastern Estonia). At the same time, Estonian-speaking participants from Tallinn showed more positive outgroup feelings (β = -.17, p <.001) and less ingroup bias (β =.09, p <.05) than those residing in the region of Eastern Estonia. None of the three interaction terms between Estonians' ethnic identity and intergroup anxiety were significant.

In summary, consistent with our first prediction, intergroup anxiety significantly predicted negative outgroup feelings, outgroup distrust and ingroup bias. For our second hypothesis, we found support among the Russian minority but not among the Estonian majority participants.

Discussion of the Multiculturalism Hypothesis

The results for both majority (Estonian-speaking) and minority (Russian-speaking) participants showed that intergroup anxiety as a form of threat is negatively associated with intergroup outcomes. High perception of intergroup anxiety predicted more negative outgroup feelings, less outgroup trust and more ingroup bias. We further investigated interactive effects between ethnic identity and intergroup anxiety in the prediction of intergroup relations. The ethnic identity of Estonian and Russian-speaking individuals showed no significant relationships with outgroup feelings or outgroup trust, and these relationships remained unchanged with different levels of intergroup anxiety. Greater ethnic identity among Estonians and community identity among Russians predicted greater ingroup bias. However, for Russian-speaking individuals a positive relationship between their community identity and ingroup bias existed only with high or medium levels of intergroup anxiety, while with low levels of intergroup anxiety this relationship become non-significant. Similarly to ingroup bias, under conditions of high perceived intergroup anxiety, Russians' community identity significantly predicted outgroup distrust. Additionally, Russians' community identity was significantly related to positive outgroup feelings when intergroup anxiety was perceived to be low. These results among minority participants are in line with the multiculturalism hypothesis, while no support for the multiculturalism hypothesis was found among majority participants.

Previously, evidence for the multiculturalism hypothesis was found among majority Estonians with political but no economic threat as moderators, showing that with low perceived political threat ethnic identity predicted positive outgroup attitudes (Kus, 2011). Political threat could possibly undermine the sense of security for Estonians more strongly than intergroup anxiety. The average score of intergroup anxiety indicated that Estonian participants tended to disagree with experiencing feelings that underlie intergroup anxiety. As a limitation, the current study did not include MIRIPS variables of cultural and economic security. It is also possible that high scores of ethnic identity (i.e., agreement with statements including pride, joy, importance of belonging to one's ethnic group) could have prevented obtaining significant results with other variables.

Support for the multiculturalism hypothesis among minority Russians was found with their community identity, but not ethnic identity. Russians' community identity predicted positive outgroup attitudes with low perceived threat, and greater ingroup bias and outgroup distrust with high perceived threat. Russians' ethnic identity may transpire beyond Estonian borders, while identification with the Russian community in Estonia is likely to include more visible and active involvement with one's ethnic community, which, therefore, presents a rather politicised identity. The Russian-speaking community is perceived as a homogenous group by the majority group and is an object of ethnic politics and policies. Ethnic community identity may lay the foundation to be more sensitive towards one's intergroup situation, including intergroup threat.

5.2   Contact Hypothesis

In keeping with this hypothesis, we presume a negative relation between outgroup contact and group anxiety for both majority and minority groups. Second, for the majority group we expect that outgroup contacts are positively related to behavioural measures of outgroup positivity (support to minority rights and practical activities to promote these rights). Third, for the minority group we expect that outgroup contact is positively related to individual self-esteem.

To evaluate the contact hypothesis, correlation analyses were performed with indexes of contact and intergroup outcome measures separately for the Estonian majority and the Russian-speaking minority. The impact of the variation of three different contact conditions – common (national) identity, intergroup norms (level of multicultural ideology), perceived equality of groups and perceived respect for the ingroup were also analysed. Low and high levels of contact conditions were determined by using a median split of the respective summed indexes separately for Estonian and Russian-speaking respondents. In the case of the index of relative group appreciation, comparison groups were defined according to the measurement scale distribution (perceived lower status of Russians <3, perceived equal status =3, perceived higher status >3).

Majority Estonian Participants

In line with the contact hypothesis, all the forms of outgroup contacts studied are negatively related to group anxiety and positively related to support for minority rights and practical actions promoting minority rights (see Table 4.1). Variations of common identity have relatively greater impact on the positive intergroup effects of involuntary contacts. Variation of intergroup norms has less impact on the contact relations with anxiety but greater impact on the relations between contact and behaviour outcomes: when support for multiculturalism ideology is low, outgroup contacts are more strongly related to a readiness to support the minority; when support for the multiculturalism ideology is high, outgroup contacts are more strongly related to proactive behaviour.

Perceived group equality is the only contextual factor that eliminates the correlation between outgroup contact and anxiety, which is observed in all other conditions. Perceived respect towards the ingroup has a strong impact: in conditions of low perceived respect, outgroup contacts (especially voluntary) have stronger relations with outgroup helping behaviour (practical support for the minority). In low perceived respect conditions, voluntary contacts have a stronger impact on anxiety and outgroup helping.

Minority Russian Participants

In line with the hypothesis, all the forms of outgroup contacts reduce group anxiety and are positively related to self-esteem. Those with a high sense of national belonging demonstrate stronger positive relations between outgroup contacts and self-esteem and stronger negative relations between outgroup contacts and group anxiety, compared to those with a low sense of national belonging. Voluntary contacts are more strongly related to anxiety reduction, and involuntary contacts more strongly enhance self-esteem among those who support the multiculturalism ideology less. For those who perceive a relatively low status of their ingroup, outgroup contacts are positively related to individual self-esteem.

The anxiety-reducing effect of outgroup contacts is stronger in conditions of perceived equal or higher status of Russians, whereas self-esteem is more strongly related to outgroup contacts if the ingroup status is perceived as being lower. In case of low perceived respect towards the ingroup, any contacts with the majority enhance psychological adaptation (by supporting individual self-esteem). Contacts operate as a group anxiety-reducing device more strongly in this group. Thus, voluntary and

Table 4.1. *Correlations of voluntary and involuntary outgroup contacts with outcome measures in various contact conditions.*

Contact outcomes	Contact conditions	ESTONIANS		RUSSIANS	
		Voluntary contact	Involuntary contact	Voluntary contact	Involuntary contact
Anxiety		-0.15***	-0.1**	-0.24***	-0.16**
	Low national identity	-0.15*	ns	ns	-0.15*
	High national identity	-0.16*	-0.19**	-0.26***	-0.16**
	Low norms	Ns	-0.13*	-0.31***	-0.18*
	High norms	-0.13*	ns	-0.21***	-0.16**
	Lower status of Russians	Ns	ns	-0.15**	0.15**
	Equal status of Russians	Ns	ns	-0.5***	-0.4***
	Higher status of Russians	Ns	ns	-0.65***	-0.4**
	Low respect	-0.2**	-0.18*	-0.32***	-0.25***
	High respect	Ns	ns	-0.18*	-0.15*
Estonian's support towards minority rights / Russian's self-esteem		0.24***	0.16***	0.26***	0.19***
	Low national identity	0.23***	ns	0.23***	0.13*
	High national identity	0.26**	0.29***	0.25**	0.24***
	Low norms	0.27***	0.21***	0.25***	0.24***
	High norms	Ns	ns	0.27***	0.16**
	Lower status of Russians	0.29***	ns	0.28***	0.22***
	Equal status of Russians	0.2**	0.25**	0.24**	ns
	Higher status of Russians	0.2*	0.17**	ns	ns
	Low respect	0.33***	0.22**	0.41***	0.34***
	High respect	0.17*	0.19**	ns	Ns

Table 4.1. (*cont.*)

Contact outcomes	Contact conditions	ESTONIANS		RUSSIANS	
		Voluntary contact	Involuntary contact	Voluntary contact	Involuntary contact
Practical support (Estonians only)	Low national identity	0.25***	0.21***		
	High national identity	0.24***	0.15*		
	Low norms	0.22***	Ns		
	High norms	0.31***	0.23***		
	Lower status of Russians	0.34***	Ns		
	Equal status of Russians	0.27**	Ns		
	Higher status of Russians	0.21*	0.31**		
	Low respect	0.34***	0.19**		
	High respect	Ns	ns		

* p< 0.05, **, p<0.01, ***p<0.001.

involuntary contacts with the majority compensate for a general sense of low respect towards the minority group.

Discussion of the Contact hypothesis

Both *voluntary and involuntary contacts* have effects that confirm the contact hypothesis; we found no relations that would indicate an increase of outgroup negativity. Contact and positive intergroup outcomes (support towards the minority group), as well as positive individual outcomes (self-esteem) are moderated by contextual variables (the perceived equality of groups, multiculturalism norms, perceived respect towards the ingroup) that enhance or limit the contact effects.

The asymmetric positions of majority and minority groups are reflected in different patterns of relationships between outgroup contacts and outcome variables. Among Russians, the anxiety-reducing effect of outgroup contacts is stronger than among Estonians. Voluntary contacts are especially effective in conditions of perceived equal or higher status, and low respect. The anti-anxiety effect of involuntary contacts among Russians was greater in conditions of equal or higher perceived status. For minority group members, irrespective of context variation, both voluntary and involuntary contacts with the majority group are positively related to individual self-esteem, more strongly in the condition of perceived lower status of Russians and perceived low respect. Therefore, self-esteem may be considered as an indicator of successful psychological adaptation by the minority in a plural ethnic context.

Among Estonians, a coherent relationship with all kinds of outgroup contacts was revealed in positive attitudes and practical actions to support minority rights. Relations were strongest in the condition of high national identity, low multiculturalism norms and low perceived respect. Voluntary contacts are more effective in the condition of perceived lower status of Russians, and involuntary contacts are more effective when the status of Russians is perceived to be higher, as well as in conditions of high respect.

In general, the contact hypothesis was supported, and some variations in respect to different contact contexts were revealed (see also Kruusvall & Raudsepp, 2012).

5.3   Integration Hypothesis

The integration hypothesis proposes that when individuals and groups seek integration they will be more successful in achieving a higher levels of adaptation, in the psychological, sociocultural and intercultural domains, than if they engage only one or the other of the cultural groups. Previous research generally supports the hypothesis. However, Estonia represents a theoretically interesting case, highlighting the fact that in a polarised multi-ethnic context, the integration strategy might not be available for minorities. As noted by Berry (1997), "integration can only be chosen and successfully pursued by non-dominant groups when the dominant society is open and inclusive in its orientation towards cultural diversity. Thus a mutual accommodation is required for integration to be attained, involving the acceptance by both groups of the right of all groups to live together as culturally different peoples". Thus, it may be that the integration hypothesis may not hold in Estonia. For example, in the assimilationist Estonian context, some previous empirical evidence found that higher levels of well-being are achieved, depending on the acculturation realm, either by the assimilation or separation groups (Kus-Harbord & Ward 2015; Kruusvall, Vetik, & Berry 2009).

In this study, we chose to assess the four strategies endorsed by the participants through the use of two underlying dimensions, and by splitting the two dimensions of cultural maintenance (Berry, 1997) and culture adoption (Bourhis et al., 1997; Dona & Berry, 1994). The culture adoption questions have been chosen due to the peculiarities of the Estonian context described earlier. These questions bring in the idea of *asymmetry* of the acculturation field, in which only one side of the relationship has to make efforts to adapt to the culture of the other side. This, in turn, automatically assumes the existence of a social hierarchy between the majority and minority groups. Such a hierarchy has been assumed and discussed initially by Berry (1997) regarding the conditions in which the integration strategy is possible at all.

Results in the Russian Sample

The four acculturation strategy groups of Russians were obtained by dividing the summary indices of acculturation dimensions at the mean points of cultural maintenance, first with contact and second with culture adoption. Only the model with cultural maintenance and adoption was retained for further analyses, as the model with cultural maintenance and contact proved to be biased towards a high proportion of those in the integration strategy. Table 4.2 provides information about the distribution of these strategies and their relationships with adaptation variables.

The integration group of respondents has a high preference for maintaining Russian culture (mean 5.0), and a moderately positive preference for adopting Estonian culture (3.9). They live more often in Northeastern Estonia, which is 80% Russian-speaking and an economically less developed region of Estonia. This might partly explain certain contradictions found in the outcomes of their psychological and economic adaptation. On the one hand, their economic situation is worse off compared to all the

Table 4.2. *Results of the Russian-speaking respondents (percentages and means on a 5-point scale) for four strategies.*

	integration	assimilation	separation	marginalisation
types	22%	23%	34%	19%
Acculturation				
Cultural maintenance	5.0**	3.9***	4.9**	3.7***
Culture adoption	3.9**	4.0**	2.4***	2.7***
Intercultural relations				
The % who have many outgroup friends	29	32	17	9
Intergroup anxiety	2.6*	2.3***	2.6*	2.7*
Outgroup trust	3.3*	3.5***	3.1*	3.2*
Outgroup feelings	74***	82***	66**	67**
Legitimacy of minority status	1.7*	1.9**	1.6**	1.8*
Economic and psychological well-being				
Economic situation	2.9***	3.3*	3.4*	3.4*
Non-working (%)	47	25	5	46
Life satisfaction	2.7*	2.9*	2.8	2.8
Support for minority rights	4.0***	3.5**	3.8***	3.5**

Note: Asterisks indicate a number of significant differences between the acculturation groups, i.e., one asterisk shows that this group differs significantly ($p < 0.05$) from one other group.

other groups (2.9 vs. 3.3 and 3.4). This can be seen in the lower level of assessments given to their economic situation, the highest proportion of elderly and non-working respondents among them and slightly lower satisfaction with life (2.7, compared to 2.8 and 2.9). In such a context, it is understandable that they exhibit higher readiness for action in support of minority rights compared to the other groups (4.0, compared to 3.5–3.8). On the other hand, however, they report having relatively high number of Estonian friends (29%) and warm feelings towards Estonians (74/100).

The assimilation group of respondents has a balanced preference on the two dimensions (means of 3.9 on cultural maintenance and 4.0 on cultural adoption). They live more often in predominantly Estonian-language regions of Estonia, where there are more opportunities to be in contact with Estonians and Estonian culture. In this context, they exhibit the warmest feelings for Estonians (82/100), as they have relatively more Estonian friends, more trust for the Estonians and less anxiety while being among Estonians. They are relatively more satisfied with their lives (2.9), and they feel relatively less status inequality compared to the Estonians. This might explain their lower readiness for action to protect the minority rights of Russian-speaking people (3.5).

The separation group of respondents has a high preference for cultural maintenance (4.9) and a low preference for adoption of the Estonian culture (2.4). This group represents more working-age Russian-speaking people who live more often in Tallinn and in other regions of Estonia where the Estonian language predominates. Despite better opportunities for contact with Estonians, they have relatively fewer Estonian friends (17%) and feel cooler towards Estonians (66/100). This might be due to the fact that they also exhibit a higher perception of status inequality between majority and minority groups and a comparatively high readiness for action to protect Russian minority interests (3.8).

The marginalisation group of respondents has low preference on both dimensions (3.7 and 2.7). They tend to live in Tallinn and the Northeastern region of Estonia. There are more young and retired age-cohorts in this group, which is reflected in the high proportion of non-working people among them (46%). Their economic well-being outcomes are at an average level, while their readiness for action to protect the interests of Russian-speaking people is lower compared to the other groups. In addition, they have fewer Estonian friends (9%), and their feelings towards Estonians are cool (67/100).

With respect to the relationship between acculturation strategies and psychological adaptation, Table 4.2 reveals that those in the assimilation group have higher life satisfaction than those in the other groups. With respect to economic indicators of sociocultural adaptation (economic situation and proportion), those in the integration group have lower scores. With respect to intercultural adaptation (anxiety and trust), those in the assimilation group have the most positive scores compared to the other groups; and for outgroup feelings, the integration and assimilation groups are more positive than those in the separation and marginalization group.

Comparing the social situation of the four acculturation groups it is important to note the following: nearly two-thirds of the integration group (59%) are over the age of 55 (this age bracket makes up only about a third in the other groups); nearly half (43%) of them live in the economically worse-off region of Northeastern Estonia (in other groups the share was 21–31%); and nearly half (47%) of them are currently not participants in the labour market (with the respective figure being 46% for the marginalisation group, 25% for the assimilation group and 5% for the separation group).

Discussion of the Integration Hypothesis

In this discussion, we focus on the results of Russian-speaking respondents[1]. When interpreting the attitudes of the Russian acculturation groups, we first compare these with the acculturation expectations of

---

[1] We did the analysis of the Estonian-speaking respondents as well; however, due to space limits we do not include a discussion of detailed results in this chapter.

the Estonians, and with how the Russians perceive the acculturation expectations of the Estonians. First, we see that Estonians prefer multiculturalism (24%) at about the same level as Russians perceive that Estonians expect multiculturalism (25%), and the Russian-speakers prefer the integration strategy (22%). This represents a fair degree of similarity in the way to engage intercultural relations.

Second, for the melting pot, Estonians have an expectation that Russians should assimilate (32%), compared to the perception of the Russian-speaking population that Estonians expect them to assimilate (37%). The Russians themselves prefer a much lower level of assimilation (23%). This represents a large discordance between the views of the Russian minority and the Estonian majority.

Third, for segregation, Estonians have an expectation that Russians should separate (28%), compared to the perception of the Russian-speaking population that Estonians expect them to separate (22%). The Russians themselves prefer a much higher level of separation (34%). Again, this represents a large discordance between the views of the Russian minority and the Estonian majority.

Fourth, for marginalisation Estonians hold a low expectation (14%) that Russians should be excluded, which is similar to the perception of the Russian-speaking population that Estonians expect them to separate (12%). The Russians themselves have a much higher level of marginalisation (19%). Again, this represents a large discordance between the views of the Russian minority and the Estonian majority.

In sum, when examining the Russians' own preferences in selecting their own acculturation strategies, what stands out is the more frequent occurrence of separation and marginalisation (34% and 19%), compared to the share of expectations attributed to the Estonians (22% and 12%, respectively). This can be interpreted as a reaction to the presumed assimilation pressure from the Estonians, which was evident in the high assimilation expectation rate described earlier.

To better contextualize the discussion, we look in detail at how the different Russian-speaking acculturation groups perceive the acculturation expectations of the Estonians. As the representatives of the Russian integration group see it, Estonians have left them with two main acculturation options: integration or separation. It can be presumed that separation is mostly perceived in terms of a threat that would damage their already worse-off economic situation. Separation is perceived negatively, also due to the fact that they already live in a relatively isolated region of Estonia with a mostly Russian-speaking population. Therefore, it is logical that this group prefers integration, which is also supported by their strong sense of ethnic community as well as warmer feelings and a higher level of trust towards Estonians.

Respondents in the Russian assimilation group perceive the expected acculturation choices to be integration and assimilation. On the one hand, this group is characterised by a higher level of satisfaction with life, a presumed better level of Estonian language skills (residing more often in the mostly Estonian language regions and in Tallinn), as well as positive attitudes towards Estonians (low anxiety, higher trust and positive feelings, etc.). At the same time, they exhibit a lower sense of belonging to the Russian-speaking community in Estonia. Representatives of the separation group first and foremost sense the pressure to assimilate (46%, followed by separation at 23%). Their negative assessment of the state policies is demonstrated by the lowest perceived fairness of socio-economic status of the minority group. However, the indicators for individual coping and satisfaction are relatively good for this group (including a high level of employment). Their attitudes towards Estonians are more negative (in terms of feelings and trust) and they have fewer friends, although only a few of them live in Northeastern Estonia, where there are fewer opportunities for contacts. The marginalisation group also perceives a strong pressure to assimilate from the Estonians (49%, followed by marginalisation at 22%); however, unlike the separation group, this group has a significantly lower sense of belonging to the Estonian Russian community. This is what creates their culturally marginal situation; they do not want to assimilate and become Estonian (their feelings towards the Estonians are the coolest, and they also have the fewest friends among Estonians); however, they also have the least warm feelings towards belonging to the Russian community. The representatives of this type mostly live in Tallinn (53%) and Northeastern Estonia, with many of them unemployed (46%) and young (15–39 years).

6   General Discussion

Analysing the results of the evaluation of the three hypotheses together reveals the importance of social positioning in explaining the acculturation processes in Estonia. We note that the characteristics of respondents in the four strategy and expectation groups correspond well with their theoretical meaning: those in the integration and assimilation groups have a large number of Estonian friends, warm feelings towards Estonians and higher out-group trust compared to those in the separation and marginalisation groups. These findings provide validation for the meaning of these four groups.

First, the data on intercultural adaptation clearly show that, regardless of their acculturation group, most Russian-speaking respondents perceive a lower cultural status for their minority group, as well as socio-economic discrimination; in contrast, most Estonians do not. For example, when comparing the value of Russian culture compared to Estonian culture in the society, all four Russian-speaking acculturation groups exhibit average results ranging from 1.6 to 2.0 (on a 5-point scale). When it comes to the legitimacy level of the minorities' socio-economic status, all four Russian-speaking acculturation groups perceive it on average as ranging from 1.6 to 1.8, and their readiness for action to improve the minority's situation is expressed in figures ranging from 3.5 to 4.0. For Estonians, however, all these indicators fall clearly at the other end of the scale, compared to Estonian Russians, which shows that in their opinion, Estonian Russians have no reason to feel either cultural endangerment or social discrimination. These opposing attitudes can be interpreted in terms of inter-cultural positioning on an asymmetrical acculturation field, where the majority aims to justify the status quo and thereby to reproduce their higher position, while the minority is critical of the status quo with the objective of achieving a more equal status. Social positioning as a key factor of the acculturation processes is confirmed by a correlation between two types of attitudes in intercultural adaptation: the lower an acculturation group are in their valuation of Russian culture and the legitimacy of their group's socio-economic status in Estonian society, the more negative are the attitudes among the group in their relations with Estonians. Our data reveal the existence of this type of correlation. The data also reveal that the two opposites are the separation and assimilation groups as the first of these tends to perceive the acculturation field in terms of domination by the majority, while the second in terms of socialization of the minority.

Compared to other groups, the Russian separation group is the most likely to perceive that Russian culture is not valued (1.6) and that their group's socio-economic status is not legitimate (1.6), and as a reaction the attitudes of this group towards Estonians are the most reserved. For example, trust towards Estonians (3.1) and feelings towards them (66) are weakest among the separation group. In the assimilation group, all these attitudes show polar opposite results, so it can be said that since the group is least likely to perceive that the Russian culture is not valued and that their group's status is not legitimate (2.0 and 1.9, respectively), their attitudes towards Estonians are the most open ones. For example, their trust (3.5) and feelings towards Estonians (82) are the highest. Figures on intercultural adaptation that characterise the separation group are very close to those exhibited by the marginalisation group. Analysing how the minority group perceives the majority attitudes shows that these two groups are also characterised by a strong perception of the pressure to assimilate from the Estonians. Across two questions about acculturation strategies that are related to the opinion of the Russian-speaking respondents about their perception of how Estonians feel about maintaining Russian culture, the mean responses of these groups are 3.7 and 3.4, respectively, showing a strong opposition to the averages of the integration (4.8) and assimilation (4.1) groups.

Russian-speaking integration and assimilation groups by definition are similar, in that compared to the other groups, they show a stronger wish to adopt the Estonian language and culture. In order to interpret this attitude in the context of the Estonian acculturation field, there are two possibilities. First, these groups sense neither threat towards their culture nor discrimination in the labour market as acutely as the other groups do; therefore, they are more open towards adopting the Estonian language and culture. Second, this attitude does not express a lack of threat perceptions, but rather dissatisfaction with their socio-economic position and the consideration that Estonian language skills might be an important factor in improving their position. Our data show that for the first option, where threat and discrimination are not acutely perceived, the assimilation and integration groups strongly distinguish themselves on one side and the separation and marginalisation groups on the other. The first groups have significantly more positive feelings (82 and 74 points vs. 66 and 67 points) and higher trust (averages of 3.3 and 3.5 vs. 3.1 and 3.2) towards Estonians, and lower intergroup anxiety (with averages of 2.3 and 2.6 vs. 2.6. and 2.7). With the other interpretation option, however, what stands out is the uniqueness of the integration group in the Estonian acculturation field. More specifically, compared to other groups, this group expresses a significantly higher readiness towards activities that are geared towards improving the socio-economic position of the minority group (their average is 4.0, whereas the assimilation and marginalisation groups have an average of 3.5, and the integration group 3.8). This demonstrates that compared to other groups they are more critical of their group's lower socio-economic status, and they are ready to act in order to improve their position.

This kind of analysis yields a significant conclusion about how to understand acculturation strategies in the context of a polarized and asymmetrical acculturation field. It can be claimed that, in such a context, the choice of the integration strategy is not an expression of better adaptation outcomes and greater resources compared to the other groups, which is presumed by the integration hypothesis. Rather it is an expression of their wish for a more successful adaptation. Thus, this group is more dissatisfied with their lower social position (their life satisfaction indicator is lower compared to all the other groups) and more ready to act in protection of in-group interests[2]. Considering the socio-economic indicators described earlier, it cannot be concluded in any way that the choice of the integration strategy for this group is based on greater resources compared to other groups. Instead, it can be claimed

---

[2] This interpretation is supported by the fact that the corresponding questionnaire question is worded to probe the wish of the respondent, not the actual situation.

that in the context of weaker socio-economic adaptation, this group simply cannot afford to separate. The representatives of this group sense that they need additional resources for a more successful adaptation, and they see the integration strategy in terms of an opportunity for gaining these resources. Following the same logic of positioning in the social field, the separation group's better economic adaptation outcomes can be explained by the fact that those who are economically better off can afford separation as a form of cultural resistance to perceived assimilation pressures. However, among the assimilation group, their comparatively higher economic adaptation outcomes, as compared to the integration and marginalisation groups, are translated into more active participation in the larger society, as its members perceive the Estonian acculturation field mostly in terms of socialization, instead of domination.

In conclusion, despite the polarised acculturation field, intercultural contacts play a potentially positive role in Estonian society, which is corroborated by the positive correlations found in the study between the existence/subjective volume of communication and positive attitudes towards the other group. Favourable contacts present the means for decreasing threat perceptions and for increasing self-confidence of the minority; moreover, these contacts also encourage the minority to protect their rights and the majority to accept multiculturalism.

Acknowledgement

The study reported in this chapter was funded by the Research Council of Norway, through the European Economic Area (EEA) program funding, grant number EMP 138.

References

Ariely, G. (2011). Spheres of citizenship: The role of distinct perceived threats in legitimizing allocation of political, welfare and cultural rights in Israel. *International Journal of Intercultural Relations, 35* (2), 213–225.

Berry, J. W. (1997). Constructing and expanding a framework: Opportunities for developing acculturation research. *Applied Psychology: An International Review, 46* (1), 62–68.

Bourhis, R. Y., Moise, L. C., Perreault, S., & Senécal, S. (1997). Towards an Interactive Acculturation Model: A social psychological approach. *International Journal of Psychology, 32* (6), 369–386.

Brubaker, R. (1996) *Nationalism Reframed: Nationhood and the National Question in the New Europe,* Cambridge: Cambridge University Press.

Dona, G., & Berry, J. W. (1994). Acculturation attitudes and acculturative stress of Central American refugees. *International Journal of Psychology, 29* (1), 57–70.

Horenczyk, G. (1996). Migrant identities in conflict: Acculturation attitudes and perceived acculturation ideologies. In G. M. Breakwell & E. Lyons (Eds.), *Changing European identities: Social psychological analyses of social change.* International Series in Social Psychology (pp. 241–250). Woburn, MA: Butterworth-Heinemann.

Jose, P. E. (2013). ModGraph-I: A programme to compute cell means for the graphical display of moderational analyses: The internet version, Version 3.0. Victoria University of Wellington, Wellington, New Zealand. Retrieved from http://pavlov.psyc.vuw.ac.nz/paul-jose/modgraph/.

Kruusvall, J., Vetik, R., & Berry, J. W. (2009). The strategies of inter-ethnic adaptation of Estonian Russians. *Studies of Transition States and Societies, 1* (1), 3–24.

Kruusvall, J., & Raudsepp, M. (2012). Perspectives of Interethnic Relations in Different Contact Conditions. In R. Vetik (Ed.), *Nation-Building in the Context of Post-Communist Transformation and Globalization: The Case of Estonia* (pp. 157–181). Bern: Peter Lang Verlag.

Kus, L. (2011). "Is there a shared history? The role of contextual factors in the psychology of inter-ethnic relations in Estonia". (Doctoral thesis). Victoria University of Wellington, Wellington.

Kus-Harbord, L., & Ward, C. (2015). Ethnic Russians in post-Soviet Estonia: Perceived devaluation, acculturation, well-being, and ethnic attitudes. *International Perspectives in Psychology: Research, Practice, Consultation, 4*(1), 66–81.

Louis, W. R., Duck, J. M., Terry, D. J., Schuller, R. A., & Lalonde, R. N. (2007). Why do citizens want to keep refugees out? Threats, fairness and hostile norms in the treatment of asylum seekers. *European Journal of Social Psychology, 37*(1), 53–73.

Luhtanen, R., & Crocker, J. (1992). A collective self-esteem: Self-evaluation of one's social identity. *Personality and Social Psychology Bulletin, 18* (3), 302–318.

Mlicki, P. P., & Ellemers, N. (1996). Being different or being better? National stereotypes and identifications of Polish and Dutch students. *European Journal of Social Psychology, 26* (1), 97–114.

Nimmerfeldt, G. (2011). Sense of belonging to Estonia. In R. Vetik & J. Helemäe (Eds.), *The Russian Second Generation in Tallinn and Kohtla-Järve: The TIES Study in Estonia* (pp. 203–226). Amsterdam: Amsterdam University Press.

Paolini, S., Hewstone, M., & Cairns, E. (2007). Direct and indirect intergroup friendship effects: Testing the moderating role of the affective-cognitive bases of prejudice. *Personality and Social Psychology Bulletin, 33* (10), 1406–1420.

Piontkowski, U., Rohmann, A., & Florack, A. (2002). Concordance of acculturation attitudes and perceived threat. *Group Processes and Intergroup Relations, 5* (3), 221–232.

Raudsepp, M. (2009). Ethnic self-esteem and intergroup attitudes among the Estonian majority and the non-Estonian minority. *Studies of Transition States and Societies, 1*(1), 36–51.

Stephan, W. G., & Stephan, *C. W. (1985). Intergroup anxiety. *Journal of Social Issues, 41*(3), 157–175.

Valk, A. (2000). Ethnic identity, ethnic attitudes, self-esteem and esteem towards others among Estonian and Russian adolescents. *Journal of Adolescent Research, 15*(6), 637–652.

Vetik, R. (1993), 'Ethnic Conflict and Accomodation in Post-Communist Estonia', *Journal of Peace Research, 30* (3): 271–280.

5   Intercultural Relations in Finland

Asteria Brylka,[1, 2, †] *, Inga Jasinskaja-Lahti*[1] *and Tuuli Anna Renvik*[3]

1 Department of Social Research University of Helsinki
2 Institute for Social Innovation and Impact University of Northampton
3 Open University University of Helsinki
† At the time of the MIRIPS-FI project, the author was associated with the University of Helsinki.

Funding

This research was funded by the KONE Foundation [grant number 31–219].

1   Introduction

With growing globalization and migration, research on intergroup relations in ethnoculturally diverse societies has become a world-wide scientific endeavor. This is mainly because challenges of everyday life in culturally plural societies continue to call for more research-based knowledge to help understand and support immigrant integration in a manner that meets the needs of individuals, groups and societies. Although Finland is only moderate on the ethnic diversity index, it is high on both the migrant integration and multiculturalism policy indexes. This makes Finland one of the more accepting and inclusive societies in the MIRIPS project.

2   Context of Intercultural Relations in Finland

2.1   Demography

Finland has been facing challenges related to the integration of immigrants for only the last twenty years. At present, there are 289,000 foreign-born nationals in Finland (Statistics Finland, 2014) which constitutes around 5 per cent of the country's total population. This demographic change in Finland is a result of different processes: (1) the large-scale immigration of Russians and Russian Finns after the collapse of the Soviet Union; (2) the eastward enlargement of the European Union (EU) resulting in noticeable, labor-driven immigration from neighboring Estonia and (3) the ongoing reception of asylum-seekers from the Horn of Africa region and the Middle East. In addition, the most common reasons for immigrating to Finland include family reunification and marriages (54%), working (18%), studying (10%) and asylum seeking (10%) (Nieminen, Sutela & Hannula, 2015).

Demographic, cultural and social changes related to immigration call for more research that will address ways to ensure successful integration of immigrants and positive intergroup relations in society. In the MIRIPS framework, such research also needs to better acknowledge that both integration and intergroup relations require mutual efforts of both majority group members and immigrants. To properly address the notions of mutuality and reciprocity within the context of immigrant integration, a closer merger between acculturation theory and social psychology of intergroup relations is required. Such research will fulfil the urgent need of finding measures helping to strengthen and adjust the country's multicultural integration policy to the changing context, and to prevent intergroup tensions now and in the future.

2.2   Policy

As noted earlier, the official multiculturalism policy of Finland fares well in international comparisons. For example, Finland is consistently among the top countries in the migrant integration index that focuses on labor market mobility, rights to family reunion, equality issues in health care and education, political participation of immigrants, access to permanent residence and nationality, and measures taken against discrimination (MIPEX, 2015). However, in the aftermath of the so-called refugee crisis in Europe in 2015–2016, there has been considerable social and political pressure to tighten Finland's immigration policy, especially when it comes to family reunion and the rights of migrants who do not have papers. Moreover, as pointed out by Saukkonen (2013), we should keep in mind that it is not enough to consider the degree of multiculturalism in a country solely on the basis of rules and recommendations: The grassroots level of practices and the attitudes of lay people may not be in line with official policies. He has also pointed out (Saukkonen, 2014) that in Finland, as in many other Northern European countries, integration policy has responded relatively slowly to societal changes caused by immigration, and the implementation of policy actions is suboptimal in relation to formal objectives.

3 Evaluation of the Multiculturalism Hypothesis in Finland

In the Finnish MIRIPS study, we examined only the multiculturalism hypothesis and did not evaluate the contact or integration hypotheses directly. We focused on the intergroup relations between majority Finns and Russian-speaking immigrants in Finland. The reason for studying this particular group of immigrants is twofold. First, Russian-speakers are the biggest immigrant group in Finland: Immigrants from Russia and the former Soviet republics are the largest foreign-born group in the country (slightly over 1 percent of the total population; Statistics Finland, 2014). While Russian immigration noticeably increased right after the collapse of the Soviet Union, it has remained relatively steady over the following years. Moreover, Russian-language speakers constitute one of the oldest ethnic minority groups in Finland, the settlement of which dates back to the beginning of the nineteenth century when Finland became a part of the Russian Empire.

Second, the relationships between Finns and Russian-speakers are characterized by historical and political antagonisms that pose specific requirements for scientific research focusing on means to overcome barriers for mutual integration. Although in 1917 Finland became a sovereign state, due to the country's close proximity to the Soviet Union, Russians remained a vivid part of Finnish history. The most important problems for the bilateral relations between the two countries involved armed conflicts during World War II, as the result of which Finland lost some of its territories to the Soviet Union in 1945. In the post-war era, the Soviet influence over Finland became more subtle, but it significantly affected Finnish politics and trade (Allison, 1985). Therefore, the Finnish-Russian (Soviet) relations in the twentieth century were rather conflictual and are most likely one of the reasons for quite strong and pervasive prejudice against immigrants from Russia and from the post-Soviet republics among Finns, and the low standing of this group in the Finnish ethnic hierarchy over the years (Jaakkola, 2005, 2009).

To investigate the intergroup relations between Finns and Russian-speaking immigrants, we conducted four studies utilizing as well as broadening the methodology of the MIRIPS project. In this chapter, we summarize the results of four studies published by the first author and her colleagues (Brylka, Mähönen & Jasinskaja-Lahti, 2015a; Brylka, Mähönen & Jasinskaja-Lahti, 2015b; Brylka, Mähönen, Schellhaas & Jasinskaja-Lahti, 2015; Mähönen, Brylka & Jasinskaja-Lahti, 2014).

The four studies are 1. 'Threats and gains, and attitudes towards minority groups'; 2. 'Ownership of the country and mutual attitudes of majority and minority members'; 3. 'The role of ethnic superiority in outgroup attitudes and support for multiculturalism' and 4. 'Cultural discordance and support for minority groups' collective action'.

These studies contribute to our understanding of the premises of and dynamics involved in the multiculturalism hypothesis. The second to fourth studies were also included in the doctoral dissertation in social psychology of the first author. We have looked closely at (1) social psychological outcomes of acculturation (intergroup attitudes, endorsement of multiculturalism and support for minority group's collective action); and (2) the role of identity processes and threat perceptions in shaping the aforementioned outcomes of acculturation. Thus, our four studies not only test the social psychological processes outlined in the interactive acculturation model by Bourhis, Moïse, Perreault & Senécal (1997), but also extend our understanding of this model.

3.1   *Theoretical Issues*

In our studies of the multiculturalism hypothesis, we highlight the notions of mutuality and reciprocity as crucial for understanding intergroup relations in general and the functioning of multicultural hypothesis in particular. We see mutual efforts of majority members and immigrants to be the necessary prerequisites of promoting confidence in and feeling of security about their own cultural identities and their place in the larger society. In our studies, we aimed at bridging social psychological and acculturation theorizations which focus on the role of identities in predicting and shaping intergroup relations (see Horenczyk, Jasinskaja-Lahti, Sam & Vedder, 2013). Specifically, we have studied three indicators of the quality of intergroup relations that allowed us to explore the multiculturalism hypothesis among majority Finns and Russian-speaking immigrants in Finland: (i) positive intergroup attitudes (Study 1, 2 and 3); (ii) the endorsement of the multicultural ideology (Study 3); and (iii) support for collective action towards egalitarian change in society (Study 4).

These three indicators vary with the degree of engagement dedicated by an individual to promoting good-quality relations with other groups in society. While favorable intergroup attitudes reflect relatively passive positive orientation towards outgroups, support for multiculturalism requires more active engagement in acknowledging and promoting ethno-cultural diversity. Even greater social engagement and dedication to equality of intergroup relations is needed to support collective action of the minority outgroup or one's own minority ingroup. Therefore, examining these three indicators allows for deeper insight into identity-related processes behind the different levels of engagement in promoting positive intergroup relations in culturally diverse societies by majority and minority group members. Next, we describe the specific theoretical models tested in each of our four studies.

3.2   Previous Research

Study 1: Threats and Gains, and Attitudes towards Minority Groups

The multiculturalism hypothesis proposes that feeling secure in one's ethno-cultural place in society will provide a basis for accepting those who are culturally different. In contrast, as proposed in Chapter 1, when such security is undermined or threatened, the opposite reaction will be present. Previous research has corroborated the role of perceived threats in explaining the association between strong national identification and opposition to immigration among majority group members (e.g., Bizman & Yinon, 2001a, 2001b). In this study, we suggest that the association between high national identification and more negative attitudes towards immigrants may be inhibited by gains perceived to result from immigration. To test this assumption, two competitive models were examined. In the first model, based on social identity theory (Tajfel & Turner, 1979), we tested whether the perception of more gains than threats could prevent national identification from negatively impacting attitudes towards immigrants; in the second model, based on integrated threat theory (Stephan & Stephan, 2000), we tested if the negative association between national identification and outgroup attitudes is merely due to perceiving more threats than gains resulting from immigration. In addition, we investigated whether the nature of the studied associations changed when a distinction between (1) personal versus group and (2) realistic versus symbolic threats and gains was introduced.

Study 2: Ownership of the Country and Mutual Attitudes of Majority and Minority Members

Intergroup relations between majority members and immigrants are often characterized by negotiations over the groups' rights, responsibilities and power to dictate rules. Recently, two interesting and useful concepts have been proposed that help us to better understand the differences in standings towards these issues: *autochthony* (Ceuppens & Geschiere, 2005; Gausset, Kenrick & Gibb, 2011; see also Martinovic & Verkuyten, 2013) and *psychological ownership* (Verkuyten, Sierksma & Martinovic,

2015). While autochthony refers to feelings of ownership derived from the belief of primary occupancy of a territory, psychological ownership of the country refers to possessive feelings held by individuals towards their country of birth (majority members) or residence (minority members) (cf. Pierce, Kostova & Dirks, 2001, 2003). As shown by Martinovic and Verkuyten (2013), high national identifiers claim stronger autochthony and thus also more right to regulate immigration and intergroup relations. This finding was corroborated for psychological ownership among children whose entitlement to the territory gave them more rights to regulate the rules of playing (Verkuyten et al., 2015).

In contrast to this previous research, which focused on the majority point of view only, in this study we examine whether immigrants also experience feelings of psychological ownership of the country, and whether these feelings explain the relationship between national identification and intergroup attitudes among both majority Finns and Russian immigrants.

Study 3: The Role of Ethnic Superiority in Outgroup Attitudes and Support for Multiculturalism

Previous research among *majority* members has focused mainly on factors explaining negative attitudes towards immigration and immigrants, and support for multiculturalism (e.g., Hodson, Dovidio & Esses, 2003; Verkuyten & Martinovic, 2006). In these studies, high national identification, especially if too narrowly and ethnically defined, was seen as one of the key elements preventing national majority groups from being more inclusive. In contrast, studies focusing on the association between ethnic identification and outgroup attitudes among *minority* group members and *immigrants* often show that high ethnic identifiers have more positive attitudes towards the majority group (e.g., Staerklé, Sidanius, Green & Molina, 2005) and that they more strongly endorse multiculturalism (e.g., Verkuyten & Martinovic, 2006). However, the question remains whether all forms of ethnic identification are similarly beneficent.

In this study, we aim to identify those ethnic identity dimensions that may prevent immigrants from engaging in positive intergroup relations with the majority. Specifically, we examine the roles of the affective-cognitive and the ethnic superiority aspects of ethnic identification in outgroup attitudes towards majority Finns, and in the endorsement of multiculturalism among Russian immigrants. Ethnic superiority (an identity dimension resembling blind patriotism; Schatz, Staub & Lavine, 1999) and collective narcissism (Bizumic & Duckitt, 2008; Golec de Zavala, Cichocka, Eidelson & Jayawickreme, 2009) are conceptualized in this study as a perception of the exaggerated worthiness of one's ethnic ingroup. We tested whether positive emotional identification with one's own ethnic group translates into more negative attitudes towards the majority group and less support for multiculturalism if combined with too pronounced feelings of ethnic superiority.

Study 4: Cultural Discordance and Support for Minority Groups' Collective Action

Previous research strongly recommends moving towards more complex and truly reciprocal models of integration (Horenczyk et al., 2013), as envisaged by Berry (1980) and elaborated by Bourhis and his colleagues (1997). Thus, while in Studies 1 to 3 we focused on the reciprocity of integration by addressing the dynamics of intergroup relations among majority Finns and Russian-speaking immigrants separately, in this study, we aim to better incorporate the idea of reciprocity at the level of measurement. Moreover, instead of focusing on intergroup attitudes, we examine support for collective action, which is a more active and behavioural way of challenging intergroup inequalities than only having positive outgroup attitudes.

Thus, in Study 4 we investigate the degree and the role of cultural discordance (a disagreement between majority and minority group members on the preferred degree of minority groups' cultural maintenance; Piontkowski, Rohmann & Florack, 2002) in support for an egalitarian change in ethno-culturally diverse society from the perspective of both majority Finns and Russian immigrants. Specifically, we examine whether perceived cultural discordance is associated with support for a minority group's collective action among both minority and majority group members, and whether intergroup emotions of anxiety and trust mediate this association. The association between cultural discordance and support for collective action has not been previously examined, which was the first novelty of this study. The second novelty concerned examining this association also among members of the national majority group, as research on support for minority groups' collective action among majorities is rather scarce (but see Mallett, Huntsinger, Sinclair & Swim, 2008).

4   Method

4.1   Samples

The data for this study were collected by Professor Inga Jasinskaja-Lahti and her research team in the Department of Social Research at the Faculty of Social Sciences, the University of Helsinki. The representative sampling was conducted by the Finnish National Population Register Center.

The inclusion criteria for the majority group members were Finnish as the mother tongue, being born in Finland, and residing in the country at the time of the survey. The criteria for the Russian immigrants were Russian as the mother tongue, being born in the former Soviet Union or the Russian Federation, and having moved to Finland no later than January 1, 2008.

The data were collected between June and November 2012 with the use of a postal survey. The questionnaire included not only the core questions of the international MIRIPS study, but also other scales needed to address the research questions posed by the Finnish research team. Participation in the study was voluntary and confidential. The response rate to the survey was 33.5% (n = 334; 57% female, M_{age} = 46) for the majority and 39.0% (n = 313; 77% female, M_{age} = 45) for the minority sample. The final majority and minority sub-samples used in the present study remained regionally representative. However, when compared to the initial sub-samples, in the final sub-samples there were more women (original majority sample: 48% female; original minority sample: 67% female), and the respondents were older than the non-respondents (original majority sample: M_{age} = 41; original minority sample: M_{age} = 40).

4.2   Measures

The four studies were developed not only to examine the multicultural-ism hypothesis of the MIRIPS project but also to further develop the theoretical models used to explain the dynamics involved in this multi-culturalism hypothesis. To give a more social-psychological insight into these issues, the original MIRIPS questionnaire was slightly modified to better fit the Finnish national context and complemented with some additional measures. The original MIRIPS scales used in the sub-studies were: cultural identity [14], acculturation attitudes and expecta-tions (cultural maintenance) [16; A and B] and multicultural ideology [18]. The added scales were: psychological ownership of Finland, per-ceived ethnic superiority, perceived acculturation attitudes of outgroup members (cultural maintenance), perceived threats and gains resulting from immigration[1], intergroup anxiety, outgroup trust, support for col-lective action and outgroup attitudes (eight-item scale).

---

[1] To assess the multiculturalism hypothesis, we used the scale of perceived threats and gains. Although this scale is a conceptual opposition of the original MIRIPS security scale [15], it builds on the integrated threat theory of Stephan and Stephan (2000; see also Stephan, Renfro & Davis, 2008) and more closely resembles the MIRIPS 'perceived consequences of immigration' sub-scale of the 'attitudes towards immigration [20]' scale.

Psychological ownership of Finland at the individual and group level was measured with two items adapted from the Psychological Ownership Scale of Van Dyne and Pierce (2004) originally used in the organizational context. Perceived ethnic superiority was measured with a four-item scale adapted from Roccas, Sagiv, Schwartz, Halevy and Eidelson (2008). A three-item scale was used to assess attitudes towards the cultural maintenance of Russian immigrants from the perspective of an average outgroup member (i.e., a Russian immigrant for native Finnish participants and vice versa). Perceived threats and gains resulting from Russian immigration to Finland were measured with a 12-item five-point bipolar scale. The definitions of threats and gains were based on the distinction made by Stephan and colleagues (2008), and the bipolar form of the scale was adapted from Schwartz (2007). The items were developed for this study to tap the degree of different types of (1) personal versus group and (2) realistic versus symbolic threats and gains perceived to result from immigration from Russia to Finland. An overall threats/gains index score, reflecting a relative difference between perceived threats and gains was computed by summing individual scores on 12 items. Corresponding index scores were also calculated for personal versus group and realistic versus symbolic threats and gains. A positive index score indicates that more gains than threats were perceived, whereas a negative index score indicates that a participant perceived more threats than gains. Intergroup anxiety was measured with a six-item measure adapted from Stephan and Stephan (1985), reflecting how participants would feel during an interpersonal interaction with outgroup members. Outgroup trust was measured with three items adapted from Paolini, Hewstone and Cairns (2007). Outgroup attitudes were measured with an eight-item scale previously used in the present intergroup context by Jasinskaja-Lahti, Liebkind and Solheim (2009). More information about the scales used in each sub-study can be found in the original publications.

4.3   Statistical Analysis

Statistical analyses for all four studies were conducted with SPSS software. All hypotheses were tested with conditional process analysis (Hayes, 2013) using the PROCESS tool for SPSS. In Study 1, the hypotheses were tested with the moderation and the mediation analysis; in Study 2 and Study 4, the hypotheses were tested with the moderated mediation model with the group's status (majority versus minority) as the moderator; in Study 3, the moderation analysis was applied. In all Studies 1 to 4, the strength and significance of conditional and indirect effects were assessed with a non-parametric bootstrapping method using 10,000 resamples. In Study 2 and 4, the moderation of the indirect effects by group status was assessed with the test of equality of the conditional indirect effects between the groups called the index of moderated mediation (see Hayes, 2015). All regression coefficients and the indirect effects are reported in an unstandardized form (*B*).

5   Results

5.1   Study 1

The aim of Study 1 was to clarify the nature of the relationship between national identification of majority Finns, their joint perception of threats and gains resulting from Russian immigration to Finland and attitudes towards Russian-speaking immigrants. Specifically, it was examined whether the joint perception of threats and gains resulting from immigration *moderated* or *mediated* the relationship between national identification and outgroup attitudes. It was also examined whether introducing the distinction between personal versus group, and realistic versus symbolic threats and gains added to our understanding of the role of perceived threats and gains in the investigated relationship.

The testing of the proposed moderation effect has shown that there was no interaction between national identification and the perception of threats and gains resulting from Russian immigration. Thus, when participants identified more strongly as Finns, it was always linked to more negative attitudes towards Russian-speaking immigrants, regardless of whether the participants perceived more or fewer threats in relation to gains. As regards the testing of mediation (see Figure 5.1), the results showed that with increasing national identification of majority Finns, the perception of threats over gains resulting from Russian immigration to Finland was also stronger. This perception, in turn, was further associated with more negative attitudes towards Russian-speaking immigrants. Therefore, with stronger national identification, majority Finns tend to perceive more threats than gains to result from Russian immigration, and this translates into more negative attitudes towards Russian-speakers residing in the country. This pattern of results was present regardless of whether different types of threats and gains were examined jointly or whether they were divided into personal versus group, or realistic versus symbolic threats and gains.

5.2   Study 2

In Study 2, we examined whether psychological ownership of a country mediates the association between national identification and mutual attitudes among majority Finns and Russian-speaking immigrants in Finland.

The results show (see Table 5.1) that when majority members identified more strongly as Finns and Russian-speaking immigrants identified more strongly with Finnish society, they both felt stronger psychological ownership of Finland. However, while this stronger ownership of Finland was linked to more negative attitudes towards Russian-speaking immigrants among majority Finns, it was linked to more positive attitudes towards majority Finns among immigrants.

Table 5.1. *Bootstrapped indirect effects of national identification on outgroup attitudes via psychological ownership of Finland for Finns (n = 334) and Russian-speaking immigrants (n = 313).*

	Psychological ownership			
Group membership	B	SE	LL CI	UL CI
Finns	−0.20*	0.04	−0.323	−0.094
Immigrants	0.05*	0.02	0.016	0.087

Note: *At least $p < .05$. LL CI and UP CI = lower and upper level of the bias corrected confidence intervals for $\alpha = .05$.

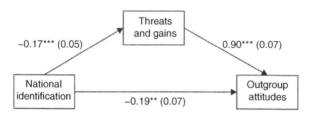

Figure 5.1. Predictors of the majority members' attitudes towards Russian-speaking immigrants in Finland ($N = 335$): Mediation model.

5.3   Study 3

The aim of Study 3 was to investigate the role of perceived ethnic superiority of the ingroup in Russian-speaking immigrants' attitudes towards majority Finns and in their support for multiculturalism. Specifically, we

Table 5.2 *Regression analysis on the predictors of outgroup attitudes and support for multiculturalism among Russian-speaking immigrants (n = 312).*

	Outgroup attitudes (Y1)		Multicultural ideology (Y2)	
	B	*SE*	B	*SE*
Constant	4.29**	0.07	1.41**	0.38
Sex (0 = male)	0.06	0.07	0.21*	0.07
Age	0.00	0.00	0.00	0.00
Years of education	0.01	0.01	0.01	0.01
Ethnicity (0 = Russian)	0.09	0.06	0.08	0.07
Cultural identity (CI)	−0.02	0.03	0.44**	0.08
Perceived superiority (PS)	−0.12**	0.04	0.43**	0.13
CI x PS	0.01	0.03	−0.11**	0.03

Note: *$p < .01$. **$p \leq .001$.

examined whether perceived ethnic superiority of the ingroup moderated the association between the affective-cognitive aspect of ethnic identification and attitudes towards majority Finns and support for multiculturalism, respectively.

The obtained results (Table 5.2) show that while the strength of ethnic identification was not associated with more negative attitudes towards majority Finns, feelings of ethnic superiority of Russians were associated with more negative outgroup attitudes. As regards the relationship between ethnic identification and support for multiculturalism, stronger ethnic identification was linked to stronger support for multiculturalism only among those immigrants who did not have strong feelings of ethnic superiority over other ethno-cultural groups in society.

5.4   Study 4

Study 4 investigated the previously unexplored association between perceived cultural discordance and support for the minority group's collective action, and the role of two affective mediators – intergroup anxiety and outgroup trust – in this relationship among both majority Finns and Russian-speaking immigrants.

The findings in Table 5.3 show that when the association between perceived cultural discordance and support for collective action is analyzed, group status is an important moderator to be considered. Among majority Finns, those participants who perceived stronger cultural discordance were more negatively oriented towards the collective action of

Table 5.3. *Bootstrapped indirect effects of cultural discordance on support for collective action via intergroup anxiety and outgroup trust for Finns (n = 274) and Russian-speaking immigrants (n = 228).*

	Intergroup anxiety				Outgroup trust			
Group membership	B	SE	LL CI	UL CI	B	SE	LL CI	UP CI
Finns	−0.14*	0.04	−0.219	−0.075	−0.13*	0.03	−0.202	−0.073
Immigrants	0.02	0.02	−0.011	0.069	0.04*	0.03	0.001	0.112

Note: *At least $p < .05$. LL CI and UP CI = lower and upper level of the bias corrected confidence intervals for $\alpha = .05$.

Russian-speaking immigrants. Besides this direct relationship, perceived cultural discordance was associated with support for the minority group's collective action also indirectly, through intergroup emotions of intergroup anxiety and outgroup trusts. Specifically, those Finns who perceived cultural discordance experienced stronger intergroup anxiety and trusted the outgroup less, which in turn was reflected in less support for the collective action of Russian-speaking immigrants.

Among Russian-speaking immigrants, as expected based on the previous results (Barlow, Sibley & Hornsey, 2012; Rohmann, Florack & Piontkowski, 2006), intergroup anxiety did not play any role in the association between perceived cultural discordance and support for the ingroup's collective action. However, those Russian-speaking immigrants who perceived stronger cultural discordance felt less trust towards majority Finns, and they, in turn, supported collective action of the ingroup more firmly.

6   Discussion and Conclusions

The last decades have witnessed a growing trend in theory and research on acculturation and immigrant integration which lays emphasis on the context and mutuality of the acculturation process (e.g., Horenczyk et al., 2013). What is still lacking, however, are attempts to overcome the barriers of concepts and models traditionally used or isolated from each other, and to suggest new and fresh ways to show and study the nuances of intergroup relations as experienced in everyday intergroup interactions. In this chapter, we have presented four studies, which show how identity is strategically used to monitor intergroup relations by both majority- and minority-group members. The results show that both parties involved in intergroup interactions are sensitive to each other's claims, and when

these claims are defined too exclusively or provocatively, ingroup identification rather undermines than supports positive intergroup relations in
society. Altogether, our results support the multiculturalism hypothesis
stating that when individuals feel secure about their own cultural identities, different groups are more positive towards each other, but when
identities are threatened, mutual hostility occurs.

In our four studies, we examined the three pillars of positive intergroup
relations that differ in the degree of engagement in promoting positive
intergroup relations in diverse societies: intergroup attitudes, the endorsement of multiculturalism and support for collective action towards
egalitarian change in society.

Positive intergroup attitudes. At the primary level of engagement reflected
in intergroup attitudes, our studies make three important contributions.
The first contribution demonstrates that threats and gains perceived to
result from immigration mediate but do not moderate the association
between ingroup identification and attitudes towards Russian-speaking
immigrants among majority Finns (Study 1). In line with previous theorizations (Stephan & Stephan, 2000) and results (e.g., Aberson &
Gaffney, 2009; Stephan et al., 2002), stronger Finnish national identification was associated with less favourable attitudes towards Russian-
speaking immigrants due to stronger perceptions of threats over gains.
Interestingly, however, realistic threats and gains played a much more
significant role than symbolic threats and gains. This finding suggests that
in relatively young immigration contexts like Finland, threats (and gains)
related to society's economy and security may be more important for
intergroup relations than threats to the culture and way of life. Overall,
the finding showing that different threats to the identity of the majority
group result in more negative attitudes towards minority groups, which
are seen as the source of these threats, supports the multiculturalism
hypothesis.

We also identified a new social psychological mechanism explaining the
relationship between national identification and intergroup attitudes
among both majority and minority members, namely psychological ownership of a country (Study 2). While among majority Finns, psychological
ownership of Finland had an exclusionary character, it was inclusionary
among Russian-speaking immigrants. Specifically, among majority Finns
psychological ownership of Finland reinforced by national identification,
elicited more negative attitudes towards immigrants. This negative indirect effect may derive from rather essentialist representations of
Finnishness (Varjonen, Arnold & Jasinskaja-Lahti, 2013), which anchor
Finnish national belonging in Finnish bloodlines and linguistic heritage,
and exclude immigrants from the national ingroup. In contrast, among

immigrants psychological ownership of Finland was reinforced by identification with Finnish society and further linked to more positive attitudes towards majority Finns, who most likely were perceived by the immigrants as members of the common national ingroup. These findings show that among immigrants, both national identification and psychological ownership of Finland operate at the superordinate level of identification, in line with the common ingroup identity model (Gaertner & Dovidio, 2000).

The third contribution concerns the role of perceived ethnic superiority of the ingroup in the association between the affective-cognitive aspect of immigrants' ethnic identification and attitudes towards the national majority group (Study 3). The findings showed that perceived ethnic superiority of one's own minority group was associated with less positive attitudes towards majority Finns among Russian-speaking immigrants. Perceived ethnic superiority, however, did not moderate the relationship between affective-cognitive aspects of ethnic identification and outgroup attitudes. These results show that the mere perception of ethnic superiority, which is likely to be a reactive result of perceived discrimination towards one's own minority group, is detrimental for attitudes towards the national majority. Thus, the last two contributions again support the multiculturalism hypothesis linking the security of identities with more favourable outgroup attitudes.

Support for multiculturalism. With respect to the engagement of individuals in a more active promotion of cultural diversity in the country – that is, endorsing multiculturalism – our studies shed more light on the conditions under which immigrants support this ideology (Study 3). Previous research among minority members has shown that even high ethnic identification in terms of emotional and cognitive attachment to the ethnic ingroup is not detrimental to intergroup relations and it supports the endorsement of multiculturalism. However, as the fourth contribution of our present research we found that when immigrants perceive their ethnic ingroup as superior to other groups in society, the positive association between ethnic identification and support for multiculturalism disappears. Thus, this finding highlights the need of acknowledging the multidimensionality of ethnic identification when intergroup attitudes in diverse societies are investigated. As indicated by previous theorizations (e.g., Roccas et al., 2008) and the multiculturalism hypothesis, the obtained results corroborate that while some (secure) aspects of ethnic identification are constructive and contribute to more positive intergroup relations, other (non-secure) dimensions of ethnic identification do not necessarily support ethnocultural diversity.

Support for collective action. Concerning the most active and engaged form of support for ethno-cultural diversity (that is, support for the minority group's collective action), our research broadens the understanding of this form of intergroup solidarity and its underlying processes among majority group members and immigrants (Study 4). For the first time, we have shown that the stronger majority Finns perceive Russian-speaking immigrants as wishing to maintain more of their heritage culture than the majority group approves, the stronger is intergroup anxiety and the lower trust towards these immigrants. These two intergroup emotions are, in turn, linked to lower support for Russian-speaking immigrants' collective struggle towards more social equality and equal participation in society. For Russian-speaking immigrants, stronger perception that majority Finns allow them to preserve Russian culture to a lesser extent than the immigrants wish is linked to lower trust towards the majority group, which in turn is associated with stronger support for the ingroup's collective action. Also the sole perception of cultural discordance directly triggers support for the ingroup's collective action. Therefore, these findings constitute the fifth novelty of the present research and highlight the previously signalized (e.g., van Zomeren, Leach & Spears, 2012) importance of emotional processes in intergroup relations. At the same time, these findings are very strongly supporting the multiculturalism hypothesis by showing the importance of secure identities in intergroup solidarity.

The presented results corroborate the important roles of identity-related determinants and the security of majority and minority identities in intergroup relations in plural societies. They also offer practical implications for improving intergroup relations in terms of guidelines for practices that would promote social equality and facilitate accommodation of immigrants into society already upon their arrival. The results point to the need to prevent or change negative attitudes of majority group members and immigrants towards each other. This could be done, for instance, by promoting among the national majority a more inclusive, citizenship-based understanding of national identification (Study 2) that would result in more positive intergroup attitudes among majority and minority members.

Moreover, secure ethnic identification should be promoted, and the possible perception of one's minority ingroup being superior to other groups in society (ethnic superiority) should be discouraged among those immigrants who wish to maintain their cultural heritage in the host country (Study 3). The promotion of constructive and secure dimensions of ethnic identification and positive, non-exclusive pride over one's ethno-cultural background should contribute to more favourable intergroup attitudes and stronger support for multiculturalism among majority and minority groups alike. In general, intergroup respect should be promoted, so that no group in society would feel that its cultural background and identity are threatened; different groups should also feel that they have a confident sense of place in the plural society (as originally proposed in the multiculturalism hypothesis by Berry, Kalin & Taylor, 1977). In such a case, in line with the multiculturalism hypothesis, there would be no need for exclusive intergroup attitudes and excessive bolstering of one's ingroup's value.

With growing ethno-cultural diversity, more equal social relationships between all groups in society should be endorsed by, for example, supporting the collective struggle of immigrants towards equal rights and social participation. As shown in Study 4, it is especially important to promote secure identities among members of majority and minority groups, as they are likely to result in lower intergroup anxiety and alleviated outgroup trust, both of which play a crucial role in support for intergroup solidarity (see, e.g., Pettigrew & Tropp, 2006).

Finally, our study accentuates the reciprocity of intergroup relations, thus dividing the responsibility for immigrants' socio-cultural adaptation and integration to the host society between majority members and immigrants. Despite the fact that the national majority group has always more power in shaping the social context of intergroup relations than minority groups (see Berry, 2001; Bourhis et al., 1997; Navas et al., 2005), it is important that both the majority group and immigrants become more conscious of their joint contribution to the degree of inclusiveness and peacefulness of the intergroup context.

Acknowledgements

We would like to thank Emma Nortio and Elena Waschinski (Department of Social Psychology, University of Helsinki, Finland) for their help in data collection and coding.

References

Aberson, C. L., & Gaffney, A. M. (2009). An integrated threat model of explicit and implicit attitudes. *European Journal of Social Psychology*, *39*, 808–830.

Allison, R. (1985). *Finland's Relations with the Soviet Union, 1944–84*. London: Macmillan.

Barlow, F. K., Sibley, C. G., & Hornsey, M. J. (2012). Rejection as a call to arms: Inter-racial hostility and support for political action as outcomes of race-based rejection in majority and minority groups. *British Journal of Social Psychology*, *51*, 167–177.

Berry, J.W. (1980). Acculturation as varieties of adaptation. In A. Padilla (ed.), *Acculturation: Theories and some new findings*. Westview Press

Berry, J. W. (2001). A psychology of immigration. *Journal of Social Issues*, *57*, 615–631.

Berry, J. W., Taylor, D. M., & Kalin, R. (1977). *Multiculturalism and Ethnic Attitudes in Canada*. Ottawa, Canada: Minister of State for Multiculturalism.

Bizman, A., & Yinon, Y. (2001a). Intergroup and interpersonal threats as determinants of prejudice: The moderating role of in-group identification. *Basic and Applied Social Psychology*, *23*, 191–196.

Bizman, A., & Yinon, Y. (2001b). Perceived threat and Israeli Jews' evaluations of Russian immigrants: The moderating role of Jewish and Israeli identity. *International Journal of Intercultural Relations*, *25*, 691–704.

Bizumic, B., & Duckitt, J. (2008). "My group is not worthy of me": Narcissism and ethnocentrism. *Political Psychology*, *29*, 437–453.

Bourhis, R. Y., Moïse, L. C., Perreault, S. & Senécal, S. (1997). Towards an interactive acculturation model: A social psychological approach. *International Journal of Psychology*, *32*, 369–386.

Brylka, A., Mähönen, T. A., & Jasinskaja-Lahti, I. (2015a). National identification and attitudes towards Russian immigrants in Finland: Investigating the role of perceived threats and gains. *Scandinavian Journal of Psychology*, *56*, 670–677.

Brylka, A., Mähönen, T. A., & Jasinskaja-Lahti, I. (2015b). National identification and intergroup attitudes among members of the national majority and immigrants: Preliminary evidence for the mediational role of psychological ownership of a country. *Journal of Social and Political Psychology*, *3*, 24–45.

Brylka, A., Mähönen, T. A., Schellhaas, F. M. H., & Jasinskaja-Lahti, I. (2015). From cultural discordance to support for collective action: The roles of intergroup anxiety, trust and group status. *Journal of Cross-Cultural Psychology*, *46*, 897–915.

Ceuppens, B., & Geschiere, P. (2005). Autochthony: Local or global? New modes in the struggle over citizenship and belonging in Africa and Europe. *Annual Review of Anthropology*, *34*, 385–407.

Gaertner, S. L., & Dovidio, J. F. (2000). *Reducing Intergroup Bias: The Common Ingroup Identity Model*. Philadelphia: Psychology Press.

Gausset, Q., Kenrick, J., & Gibb, R. (2011). Indigeneity and autochthony: A couple of false twins? *Social Anthropology*, *19*, 135–142.

Golec de Zavala, A., Cichocka, A., Eidelson, R., & Jayawickreme, N. (2009). Collective narcissism and its social consequences. *Journal of Personality and Social Psychology*, *97*, 1074–1096.

Hayes, A. F. (2013). *Introduction to Mediation, Moderation, and Conditional Process Analysis: A Regression-Based Approach*. New York: The Guilford Press.

Hayes, A. F. (2015). An index and test of linear moderated mediation. *Multivariate Behavioral Research*, *50*, 1–22.

Hodson, G., Dovidio, J. F., & Esses, V. M. (2003). Ingroup identification as a moderator of positive-negative asymmetry in social discrimination. *European Journal of Social Psychology*, *33*, 215–233.

Horenczyk, G., Jasinskaja-Lahti, I., Sam, D. L., & Vedder, P. (2013). Mutuality in acculturation. *Zeitschrift für Psychologie, 221*(4), 205–213.

Jaakkola, M. (2005). *Suomalaisten suhtautuminen maahanmuuttajiin vuosina 1987–2003 [Finns' attitudes towards immigrants in years 1987–2007]*. Helsinki, Finland: Ministry of Labour.

Jaakkola, M. (2009). *Maahanmuuttajat suomalaisten näkökulmasta: Asennemuutokset 1987–2007 [Immigrants from the perspective of Finns: Change in attitudes 1987–2007]*. Helsinki, Finland: City of Helsinki Information Center.

Jasinskaja-Lahti, I., Liebkind, K., & Solheim, E. (2009). To identify or not to identify? National disidentification as an alternative reaction to perceived ethnic discrimination. *Applied Psychology, 58*(1), 105–128.

Mähönen, T. A., Brylka, A., & Jasinskaja-Lahti, I. (2014). Perceived ethnic superiority and immigrants' attitudes towards multiculturalism and the national majority. *International Journal of Psychology, 49*, 318–322.

Mallett, R. K., Huntsinger, J. R., Sinclair, S., & Swim, J. K. (2008). Seeing through their eyes: When majority group members take collective action on behalf of an outgroup. *Group Processes and Intergroup Relations, 11*, 451–470.

Martinovic, B., & Verkuyten, M. (2013). 'We were here first, so we determine the rules of the game': Autochthony and prejudice towards out-groups. *European Journal of Social Psychology, 43*, 637–647.

Migrants Integration Policy Index MIPEX (2015). Retrieved from www.mipex.eu/.

Navas, M., García, M., Sánchez, J., Rojas, A. J., Pumares, P., & Fernandez, J. S. (2005). Relative acculturation extended model (RAEM): New contributions with regard to the study of acculturation. *International Journal of Intercultural Relations, 29*, 21–37.

Nieminen, T., Sutela, H., & Hannula, U. (2015). Ulkomaista syntyperää olevien työ ja hyvinvointi Suomessa 2014 [Work and well-being of foreigners in Finland 2014]. Helsinki, Finland: Statistics Finland.

Paolini, S., Hewstone, M., & Cairns, E. (2007). Direct and indirect intergroup friendship effects: Testing the moderating role of the affective and cognitive bases of prejudice. *Personality and Social Psychology Bulletin, 33*, 1406–1420.

Pettigrew, T. F. & Tropp, L. R. (2006). A meta-analytic test of intergroup contact theory. *Journal of Personality and Social Psychology, 90*, 751–783.

Pierce, J. L., Kostova, T., & Dirks, K. T. (2001). Toward a theory of psychological ownership in organizations. *Academy of Management Review, 26*, 298–310.

Pierce, J. L., Kostova, T., & Dirks, K. T. (2003). The state of psychological ownership: Integrating and extending a century of research. *Review of General Psychology, 7*, 84–107.

Piontkowski, U., Rohmann, A., & Florack, A. (2002). Concordance of acculturation attitudes and perceived threat. *Group Processes and Intergroup Relations, 5*, 221–232.

Roccas, S., Sagiv, L., Schwartz, S., Halevy, N., & Eidelson, R. (2008). Toward a unifying model of identification with groups: Integrating theoretical perspectives. *Personality and Social Psychology Review, 12*, 280–306.

Rohmann, A., Florack, A., & Piontkowski, U. (2006). The role of discordant acculturation attitudes in perceived threat: An analysis of host and immigrant attitudes in Germany. *International Journal of Intercultural Relations, 30*, 683–702.

Saukkonen, P. (2013). *Erilaisuuksien Suomi [Finland of diversities]*. Helsinki, Finland: Gaudeamus.

Saukkonen, P. (2014). Multiculturalism and cultural policy in Northern Europe. *The Nordic Journal of Cultural Policy/Nordisk Kulturpolitisk Tidsskrift*, *16*(02), 178–200.

Schatz, R. T., Staub, E., & Lavine, H. (1999). On the varieties of national attachment: Blind versus constructive patriotism. *Political Psychology*, *20*, 151–174.

Schwartz, S. (2007). Universalism, values, and the inclusiveness of our moral universe. *Journal of Cross-Cultural Psychology*, *38*, 711–728.

Staerklé, C., Sidanius, J., Green, E. G. T., & Molina, L. (2005). Ethnic minority-majority asymmetry and attitudes towards immigrants across 11 nations. *Psicologia Politica*, *30*, 7–26.

Statistics Finland (2014). *Foreign-language speakers account for 90 per cent of the population growth in 2013*. Retrieved from www.stat.fi/til/vaerak/2013/vaera k_2013_2014-03-21_tie_001_en.html.

Stephan, W. G., Boniecki, K. A., Ybarra, O., Bettencourt, A., Ervin, K. S., Jackson, L. A., McNatt, P. S., & Renfro, C. L. (2002). The role of threats in the racial attitudes of Blacks and Whites. *Personality and Social Psychology Bulletin*, *28*, 1242–1254.

Stephan, W. G., Renfro, C. L., & Davis, M. D. (2008). The role of threat in intergroup relations. In U. Wagner, L. R. Tropp, G. Finchilescu & C. Tredoux (Eds.), *Improving intergroup relations: Building on the legacy of Thomas F. Pettigrew* (pp. 55–72). Malden, MA: Blackwell.

Stephan, W. G., & Stephan, C. W. (1985). Intergroup anxiety. *Journal of Social Issues*, *41*, 157–175.

Stephan, W. G., & Stephan, C. W. (2000). An integrated threat theory of prejudice. In S. Oskamp (Ed.), *Reducing prejudice and discrimination. The Claremont Symposium on applied social psychology* (pp. 23–45). Mahwah, NJ: Lawrence Erlbaum Associates, Inc.

Tajfel, H., & Turner, J. (1979). An integrative theory of intergroup conflict. In M. A. Hogg & D. Abrams (Eds.), *Intergroup relations* (pp. 94–109). Philadelphia: Psychology Press.

Van Dyne, L., & Pierce, J. L. (2004). Psychological ownership and feelings of possession: Three field studies predicting employee attitudes and organizational citizenship behavior. *Journal of Organizational Behavior*, *25*, 439–459.

van Zomeren, M., Leach, C. W., & Spears, R. (2012). Protesters as "passionate economists": A dynamic dual pathway model of approach coping with collective action. *Personality and Social Psychology Review*, *16*, 180–199.

Varjonen, S., Arnold, L., & Jasinskaja-Lahti, I. (2013). 'We're Finns here, and Russians there': A longitudinal study on ethnic identity construction in the context of ethnic migration. *Discourse and Society*, *24*, 110–134.

Verkuyten, M., & Martinovic, B. (2006). Understanding multicultural attitudes: The role of group status, identification, friendships, and justifying ideologies. *International Journal of Intercultural Relations*, *30*, 1–18.

Verkuyten, M., Sierksma, J., & Martinovic, B. (2015). First arrival and collective land ownership: How children reason about who owns the land. *Social Development*, *24*, 868–882.

6 Intercultural Relations in Norway

David L. Sam,[1] *Raivo Vetik,*[2] *Marianna Makarova*[2]
and Maaris Raudsepp[2]

1 *University of Bergen, Norway*
2 *Tallinn University, Tallinn, Estonia*

1 Introduction

Norway is a country that has experienced substantial emigration over the centuries, but has recently has become a country of immigration. On the ethnic diversity index, Norway is very low, but it is high on the integration index, and around the middle of the policy index. This present chapter focuses on Russians[1] in Norway and should be considered in tandem with the chapter on intercultural relations in Estonia. The Estonian chapter was primarily interested in the acculturation of Russian-speakers in a society that for about half a century was ruled by the Soviet Union during its incorporation into the Soviet Union. Norway is a country that has a different historical relationship with the Soviet Union and with Russia. Whereas Russians in Estonia constitute a major minority group, they are much less numerous in Norway. These two chapters are both based on a joint project examining all three MIRIPS hypotheses. This chapter first presents a brief description of the Norwegian intercultural context, and is followed by a presentation of the three hypotheses, the findings and a discussion.

1.1 The Context of Intercultural Relations in Norway

The Norwegian anthropologist, Fredrik Barth (1962; 1981), described a community as an arena where people continually create and recreate their society and culture. Russians in Norway are creating their local culture out of the history, experiences and expectations of their ethnic Norwegian hosts on the one hand, and out of their own history,

---

[1] The use of the term "Russians" within the context of the Norwegian study refers to Russian speakers from Russia, the former Soviet Union and Eastern Europe. When Russians are referred to in the context of Estonia, it refers to "Russians speakers" in the country.

experiences and expectations on the other. Because acculturation outcomes are the result of contact between two groups, any study of Russians' acculturation without a look at Norway as a society to which immigrants are adapting to would be incomplete. And while the focus is on Russians, what happens to members of the larger Norwegian society is also examined. This represents the mutual perspective taken in this project.

2   Immigration

Up until the middle of 1990s, Norway was not an attractive destination for immigrants. Indeed, until the early 1960s, there was net emigration from Norway instead of immigration (Brochmann & Hammar, 1999). After the Second World War, Norway started receiving guest-workers, notably Pakistanis, Moroccans and Turks, in small numbers, but this shot up following the discovery and extraction of oil. In 1975, Norway, like many Western European countries put a stop to labor immigration (Kgl. Res, 1975). However, this did not stop immigration to Norway altogether. Family reunification and individuals fleeing from political and ethnic conflicts, notably Vietnamese and Chileans, were admitted in large numbers to Norway (Brochmann, 1999). In 1992, there were fewer than 200,000 immigrants in Norway, constituting less than 4.5% of the total Norwegian population. Up until the start of this century, the five largest immigrant groups in Norway were from Pakistan, Sweden, Denmark, Vietnam and the United Kingdom (Bjertnæs, 2000). The relative sizes of the ethnic groups have changed drastically in recent years.

Recent political and ethnic conflicts such as those in the Balkans, the Horn of Africa and Syria have all contributed to the numbers of immigrants coming to Norway. Although Norway is not part of the European Union (EU), it is associated with the EU through its membership in the European Economic Area (EEA) and the European Free Trade Association (EFTA). Membership in these associations comes with free movement between Norway and EU countries, resulting in the high influx of Eastern Europeans, particularly Polish and Lithuanians, into the country.

In 2016, there were approximately 850,000 immigrants living in Norway, representing 16.3% of the total Norwegian population (SSB, 2016). These immigrants come from 223 different countries: Poland, Lithuania, Sweden, Somalia and Germany are the five largest national groups.

In 2000, there were fewer than 2000 Russians (i.e., those defining themselves as Russians) in Norway. This number increased to approximately 3,700 a year later, and presently there are over 20,000 Russians living in Norway, making them the twelfth-largest national group in the country. The majority of the Russians (17,000) are first generation; and over half of them (57%) are females having arrived in Norway as part of the family reunification program.

2.1   Policy

As noted earlier, Norway is near the middle of the multiculturalism policy dimension. A few studies of Norwegian attitudes to immigrants were carried out prior to the 1990s. A 1987 study on Norwegian attitudes to immigrants concluded that Norwegians were generally positive towards immigrants, and saw immigrants as making positive contribution to the Norwegian economy and culture (Hernes & Knudsen, 1987). The researchers also pointed out that negative Norwegian attitudes were not directed at the immigrants themselves, but towards government institutions for the way immigrants were treated. More specifically, immigrants were perceived as getting more benefits from the government than Norwegians. Against this background, close to 80 per cent of the respondents did not approve of the government increasing public spending on immigrants in order to maintain their cultural heritage. And 70 per cent were of the opinion that immigrants needed to conduct their lives in line with Norwegian culture, in short to assimilate. A 1993 survey (of 3000 respondents) found that 80 per cent Norwegians would prefer that immigrants kept to Norwegian traditions and customs, and were skeptical about immigrants sticking to their own culture and traditions (Nytt fra Universitet i Bergen, 1993).

Recent studies all suggest that Norwegians have positive attitudes to immigrants, and in some areas, it is even more positive. For instance, a 2015 study found that fewer Norwegians than before found it uncomfortable if their child wanted to marry an immigrant (SSB, 2015). The proportion was 40 per cent in 2002, dropping to around 25 per cent in 2013 and to 17 per cent in 2015. Other findings of this study were that 73 per cent believed that immigrants make important contribution to Norwegian working life; and about the same percentage concurred that immigrants enrich the Norwegian cultural life. However, about 1 in 4 Norwegians thought immigrants abused the social welfare system, and about the same proportion saw immigrants as representing a source of insecurity in society. Finally, 87 per cent agreed that immigrants irrespective of nationality should have the same job opportunities as Norwegians. On the whole, females and younger people were more positive towards immigrants.

3   Method

3.0   Procedure

Data collection was undertaken by the Estonian Social and Market Research Company (Saar Poll). The data collection was a web-based survey with native Norwegians using a pre-recruited Computer Assisted Web Interview (CAWI) panel of approximately 58,000 members in Norway. The web-link questionnaire was randomly sent to the Norwegian panel without a new prior consent. The Russian survey was also CAWI and was carried out in two steps: (1) a phone call was made to potential participants to solicit their participation. When consent was given, (2) a link with the questionnaire was sent to the person. If the respondent did not answer, an email reminder was sent, and when necessary, a phone call was made. Contacts of 4000 randomly selected adult Russians were obtained through the Norwegian tax registry, with the goal of surveying between 300 and 500 Russians, calling each person up to four times in the course of two weeks. Only 33.11 per cent of Russians who consented to taking part in the study completed the online survey. It is important to note that Norwegians and Russians were drawn from different pools of samples for the study.

Ethical clearance for carrying out the study was obtained from the Norwegian Centre for Research Data, and permission to recruit participants for the study was obtained from the tax registry.

3.1   Samples

In all there were 752 participants (252 Russians and 500 Norwegians). The mean age of the participants was 48.22 (SD = 17.15) years. Norwegian participants were significantly older than the Russians (t $_{(750)}$ = 10.59; p <.001); Norwegians being approximately 11 years older (Mean $_{(Nor)}$ = 51.84; SD = 18.37) vs. Mean $_{(Rus)}$ = 40.98; SD = 11.41). There was an uneven gender distribution in the two national groups: Females made up 75 per cent (n = 189) in the Russians sample, compared with 46.6 per cent (n = 267) in the Norwegian sample. The majority of the Russians (55.6%) migrated to Norway for the purposes of marriage or because of family; 18.7 per cent of the Russian sample migrated to Norway primarily to work, and 11.5 per cent migrated to Norway because they were unhappy with the situation in Russia. The Russians on average had lived 10 years in Norway (Mean = 10.51, SD = 5.20 years). On the whole, more Russians had acquired higher education than their Norwegian counterparts: 56.7 per cent Russians compared with 39.0 per cent Norwegians had a university degree.

Furthermore, 31 per cent and 16.3 per cent of Russians, respectively, had a Masters or PhD degree, compared with 15 per cent and 2.2 per cent Norwegians, respectively. In terms of employment, 70 per cent of the Russians were employed, compared with only 54.0 per cent of Norwegians. However, there were more Russians who described themselves as unemployed compared with Norwegians: 9.9 per cent vs. 5.8 per cent. Close to 1 in 3 (29.6%) of the Norwegians were retired, compared with 3.8 per cent of Russians. About the same percentage of Norwegians and Russians were self-employed, 4.4 per cent Norwegians vs. 4.0 per cent Russians were self-employed, and 60 vs. 69 per cent of Russians and Norwegians respectively reported that they were employed in an area that corresponded with their education. About half of the participants (51.5%) indicated that they were economically sound. Only 4 per cent of the participants indicated that they could not make ends meet. These percentages are slightly higher among Norwegians 53.2 per cent vs. 48.0 per cent have enough to the extent of being able to save; and 5.0 per cent Norwegians vs. 2.0 per cent Russians, could not make ends meet. Nearly 1 in 3 (30.2%) of the Russian participants were living in Oslo and Akerhus county of Norway.

3.2   Measures

The measures used in Norway were mostly identical to the ones used in Estonia. However, some scales were used in only one of the two countries. The scales that differ in Norway (Security and Multicultural Ideology) are reported on in this chapter. Not using some scales in both countries implies that some analyses could not be replicated in this chapter. Moreover, the scales in Norway and Estonia are combinations of the MIRIPS scales, and ones developed specifically for some specific theoretical models we wanted to test in the two countries. Thus, a direct comparison of some findings may not be consistent with those arising from other MIRIPS studies internationally. Furthermore, the statistical analyses in the two countries were independently carried out, so that different statistical tools were used to address the same hypothesis.

To a large extent, most of the scales had very good reliabilities ranging from $\alpha = 0.75$ to 0.93, in both samples. A few scales, particularly Security and Multicultural ideology showed very low internal consistency for both samples, when the items were grouped into sub-scales based on theory. Using exploratory factor analysis, it was possible to identify some items that could be used to create acceptable sub-scales. Using Eigen values greater than 1 as a criterion, two factors could be extracted in both the Multiculturalism and Security scales.

However, only one of the two factors yielded an acceptable reliability in both Security and Multicultural Ideology; thus, we have kept with only a single factor. The Security scale, made up of four items, is a combination of cultural (e.g., language) and economic (e.g., financial prosperity) items. Similarly, the Multicultural Ideology scale is made up of five items and covers issues like accepting that the Norwegian society is made up of ethnic groups and that ethnic minorities be helped to preserve their cultural heritage.

4   Results

4.1   Descriptive statistics

Table 6.1 shows some descriptive statistics for the main scales (and items) used in the study.

Acculturation and intercultural strategies and expectations are central to any discussion of mutual intercultural relations. We therefore begin with how participants responded to them. "Cultural maintenance" and

Table 6.1. *Means, standard deviation and internal consistencies (alphas) of main scales.*

	Russians			Norwegians		
	Alpha	Mean	SD	Alpha	Mean	SD
National identity	.82	4.01	.94	.93	4.53	.86
Ethnic identity	.89	4.33	.92	.89	4,57	.73
Multicultural ideology	.83	3.58	.86	.69	3.26	.98
Security	.74	3.49	.88	.58	3.44	.96
In-group feeling		68.89	20.57		70.63	19.04
Out-group feeling		72.80	21.14		55.29	18.08
In-group bias		15.28	22.60		−.533	20.96
Out-group trust	.87	3.91	1.03	.89	3.47	1.02
Perceived discrimination	.81	1.93	.93	.89	1.96	.96
Self-esteem	.80	4.20	.82	.87	4.17	.52
Life satisfaction	.86	3.81	1.03	.91	3.88	.93
Voluntary contact	.80	3.13	.64	.72	2.27	.81
Involuntary contacts	.62	3.30	.58	.45	2.05	.78
Perceived social status	.77	2.66	.75	.83	2.40	.90
Intergroup anxiety	.82	2.23	.87	.86	2.36	.82
Legitimacy of status	.79	3.10	1.00	.79	2.74	.78
Defend social right		3.43	1.15		3.70	1.25
Intervene verbally		*3.82*	1.07		3.86	1.18

"contact and participation" are the underlying bases for the operationalization of these two strategies. In previous research, the second dimension has been operationalised in various ways with a focus on "contact", "identification" and or "adoption" (see Berry & Sabatier, 2011; Snauwaert, Soenens, Vanbeselaere & Boen, 2003). In this study, the second dimension used both contact and adoption domains. The contact dimension was assessed by looking at social relationships (e.g., "having friends among Norwegians", and "spending free time with them"). The cultural adoption domain was assessed by accepting Norwegian culture (e.g., "embracing Norwegian culture"). Since there was very little variance in the contact measures, the "adoption" questions were used in the creation of the strategies and expectations. Median split was used to extract four strategies: Integration, Assimilation, Separation and Marginalization. Similarly, median split was used to extract the intercultural expectations of Multiculturalism, Melting-pot, Segregation and Exclusion.

Based on the percentage of participants falling into the four strategies, Integration is the most preferred strategy (endorsed by 41% of the Russians) and Marginalization is the least preferred strategy (endorsed by 12%). However, the majority of Norwegians (62.0%) expected a melting-pot intercultural strategy for Russians and 4.7 per cent expected them to segregate. Figure 6.1 shows how Russians endorsed

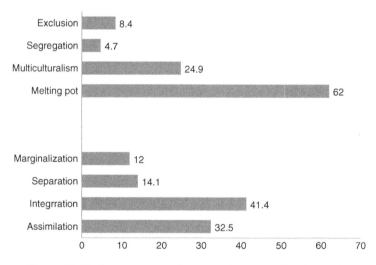

Figure 6.1. Preferred acculturation strategies among Russians and intercultural expectations of Norwegians.

acculturation strategies, and how Norwegians endorsed intercultural expectations for Russians.

A series of analyses were carried out to verify whether these strategies and expectations were related to the demographic factors of gender, length of residence and area of residence (i.e., city/urban area vs. village/rural area). Whereas there was a significant difference in preferred acculturation strategy among Russians between males and females ($\chi^2_{(3)} = 14.76$; p <.01), there was no such difference with respect to area of residence. Relatively more females than males preferred integration and assimilation (45.0% vs. 30.0% for Integration; 34.9% vs. 25.0% for Assimilation). Length of residence was unrelated to preferred acculturation strategy ($F_{(3, 240)} = .39$, p >.05). Area of residence was also unrelated to preferred acculturation strategies ($\chi^2_{(3)} = 1.50$, p >.01).

With respect to perceived social acceptance in Norwegian society[2], neither group perceived Russians as being highly appreciated in the society (i.e., their mean scores were below the theoretical mid-point of the scale; see Table 6.1 for means and standard deviations), Russians saw themselves as less appreciated within the society than Norwegians did of Russians ($t_{(632)} = 3.90$, p <.001; $d = .31$). Russians, nevertheless saw their minority status in the society as more legitimate than Norwegians did ($t_{(683)} = 3.83$, p <.001; $d = .27$). Among Russians, preferred acculturation strategies was unrelated to perceived social status ($F_{(3, 205)} = 1.05$, p >.05). Norwegians who expected that Russians will adopt multiculturalism perceived Russians as belonging to higher social status than those endorsing the other intercultural expectations, except for those endorsing segregation ($F_{(3, 415)} = 4.15$, p <.01, $\eta^2 = .03$).

In line with the perceived social status of Russians in Norway, and the legitimacy of this status, Norwegians are significantly more ready to defend the social rights of Russians than the Russians themselves ($t_{(660)} = 2.07$, p <.01), but not particularly more ready to intervene verbally.

4.2   Multiculturalism Hypothesis

This hypothesis proposes that individuals who feel secure in their identity are psychologically more likely to accept those who are culturally different from them. This acceptance entails lower levels of ethnocentrism and more positive views of multiculturalism. Berry and Ward (2016) have also reported that dominant group members who are more accepting of

---

[2] Participants were asked to rate four items such as "Russians are . . . than other immigrants and group culture", where the response categories on a 5-point scale were "less appreciated" (1) and "more appreciated" (5).

a multicultural ideology have higher levels of self-esteem and life satisfaction. In this study, we used hierarchical multiple regression analyses to examine this hypothesis. We separately sought to predict various forms of ethnocentrism (i.e., In-group feeling; Out-group feeling; In-group bias; Out-group trust), Multicultural ideology and psychological adaptation (self-esteem and satisfaction with life). As predictors, we used Ethnic and National identity; Inter-group anxiety and Security, and we controlled for the demographic factors of age, gender and economic situation. Because regional area of residence and duration of sojourn in Norway were unrelated to acculturation strategies, and also to a number of the outcomes (e.g., self-esteem, satisfaction with life, multicultural ideology and out-group trust), these demographic factors were not included in the analyses.

Table 6.2 shows the regression analyses for testing the multiculturalism hypothesis. This hypothesis was to a large extent supported in both the Russian and Norwegian samples of this study. After controlling for demographic effects (which generally accounted for less than 5% of the explained variance), the main predictors contributed an additional 8 to 20 per cent to the explained variance in the different outcomes examined. In Step I, where the demographic variables were entered into the model, in about half of the instances, the explained variance was insignificant. In some few cases (e.g., life satisfaction), the demographic variables accounted for over 20 per cent of the explained variance. Nevertheless, the predictors entered on Step II still made a substantial contribution to the explained variance. In the final Step, all the models became significant. The four predictors (i.e., Ethnic identity, National Identity, Inter-group anxiety and Security) varied in their contribution, although there seem to be some consistent patterns. For instance, among Russians, Security was positively related to In-group feelings, Out-group feelings, Out-group trust, Multicultural Ideology and Life satisfaction. That is, the more individuals felt secure, the more positive were their feelings about their own group, and about the out-group, and they had more trust in the out-group, more acceptance of multiculturalism and more life satisfaction. Both ethnic and national identities were related to higher out-group feelings, a higher multicultural ideology score and better satisfaction with life. However, while ethnic identity was related to high in-group bias, national identity was related to low in-group bias.

Results similar to those of the Russians were found among Norwegians: High feelings of security were related to high Out-group feeling, high Out-group trust, high Multicultural ideology scores and better life satisfaction. Security was also related to low In-group feelings. A high Ethnic identity score was related to high In-group feelings and high In-group bias. Inter-group anxiety was negatively related to out-group feeling, self-esteem and life satisfaction among both Russians and Norwegians. Intergroup

Table 6.2. *Predicting ethnocentric tendencies: Multicultural ideology, Satisfaction with life and Self-esteem.* ★

	RUSSIANS							NORWEGIANS						
	In-group feeling	Out-group feeling	In-group bias	Out-group trust	MCI	Self-esteem	Life Satis	In-group feeling	Out-group feeling	In-group bias	Out-group trust	MCI	Self-esteem	Life satis
Predictors														
Age	.02	.10	-.07	.11	.11	-.09	-.12[a]	.01	-.05	.04	.01	-.07[a]	.12[b]	.19[c]
Gender	.11[a]	.11	.04	.05	.04	.18[b]	.13[a]	-.05	.00	-.04	.03	.06	.05	.02
Eco Sit	.00	-.12	.03	-.16[b]	.07	.02	-.36[c]	-.04	.04	-.07	-.03	-.04[b]	-.15[c]	-.38[c]
Eth Identity	.31[c]	.14[a]	.19[b]	.04	.29[c]	.10	.11[a]	.48[c]	-.02	.42[c]	.05	-.09[a]	.23[c]	.29[c]
Nat Identity	.04	.31[c]	-.27[c]	.25[c]	-.03	.15[a]	.22[c]	.03	.06	.00	.01	.02	.09	.00
In-grp anxiety	-.10	-.15[a]	-.05	.12	.06	-.22[b]	-.26[c]	.12	-.20[c]	.17[c]	-.22[c]	-.09	-.21[c]	-.10[b]
Security	.16[a]	.19[b]	-.06	.32[c]	.27[c]	.02	.12[a]	-.11[b]	.33[c]	-.38[c]	.50[c]	.68[c]	.05	.13[c]
F-stats – I	2.39	2.30	.71	3.25[a]	1.84	3.25[a]	18.76[c]	2.33	.60	2.14	4.41[b]	4.68[c]	12.17[c]	63.28[c]
F-stats – II	5.80[c]	7.11[c]	4.38[c]	10.26[c]	4.73[c]	4.69[c]	19.03[c]	20.82[c]	13.90[c]	28.05[c]	37.09[c]	62.67[c]	13.66[c]	45.50[c]
R²–I	.04	.03	.01	.05	.03	.05	.21	.02	0.00	.01	.03	.03	.10	.28
R²-II	.17	.25	.14	.27	.14	.14	.40	.25	.15	.31	.37	.49	.19	.41

★ Beta co-efficient at the Step II of the regression model are reported.

a = p <.05; b = p <.01; c = p <.001 F-Stats – I = F statistics at Step I; F-Stats – I = F statistics at Step II; R² – I = R-square at Step I; R² – II = R2 at Step II; R2 – II – R2 at
Eco-sit = Economic situation; Eth ident = Ethnic identity; Nat iden = National identity; In-grp anxiety = Inter-group anxiety.

anxiety was also related to low Out-group trust and high In-group bias among Norwegians.

4.3 Contact Hypothesis

This hypothesis postulates that under appropriate conditions, bringing members from different groups together will reduce prejudice. To test this hypothesis, we examined the correlation between two forms of contact: Voluntary and Involuntary (as operationalized in the Estonia chapter); and different indicators of ethnocentrism (as used in examining the multiculturalism hypothesis). In addition, we included perceived discrimination (whether discrimination will be lowered); Inter-group anxiety (whether this will be less); support for ethnic minority rights (whether being in contact with other groups increases support for them); ethnic and national identity (whether being in contact other ethnocultural groups increases one's own ethnic/national identity) and whether preferred acculturation and intercultural strategy is related to contact. Because acculturation and intercultural strategies and expectations are categorical and contact is continuous, one-way ANOVA was performed here. Separate analyses were run for Russians and for Norwegians.

Table 6.3 shows Pearson correlation coefficient of relationships among contact on one hand and ethnocentric measures. Among Russians, In-group feelings are associated with more contact. Involuntary contact is associated with high In-group feelings, but not for Out-group feelings.

Table 6.3. *Pearson's correlations between two forms of contact and ethnocentric tendencies, identity and discrimination.*

	RUSSIANS		NORWEGIANS	
	Voluntary	Involuntary	Voluntary	Involuntary
In-group feeling	$.14^a$	$.16^a$	$-.10^a$	$-.08$
Out-group feeling	$.14^a$	$.09$	$.05$	$.17^c$
In-group bias	$.02$	$.07$	$-.21^c$	$-.13^b$
Out-group trust	$.10$	$.10$	$.02$	$-.01$
Inter-group anxiety	$-.21^b$	$-.23^c$	$-.09^+$	$-.06$
Multicultural ideology	$.09$	$.12$	$-.21^c$	13^b
Support minority group activities	$.14^a$	$.06$	$.09$	$.06$
Discrimination	$-.14^a$	$-.25^c$	$.13^b$	$.14^b$
Ethnic identity	$.03$	$.01$	$-.24^c$	$-.22^c$
National identity	$.25^c$	$.21^a$	$.18^c$	$.17^c$

Notes: a = p <.05; b = p <.01 and c = p <.001; p =.056; + = p =.56.

Among Norwegians, voluntary, but not involuntary contact, is associated with reduced in-group feelings, and involuntary contact is associated with increased out-group feelings. These findings generally seem to suggest that the more contact Russians and Norwegians have, the more positive are their feelings towards the other group. Among Norwegians, while contact is associated with low In-group bias, this is not the case for Russians; contact is not associated with their In-group bias. Among Norwegians, contact is associated with stronger multicultural ideology, but this is not the case for Russians. There was no significant relationship between level of contact and multicultural ideology. Not surprising, perceived discrimination is associated with lower contact among Russians. For Norwegians, perceived discrimination was positively related to contact: high contact level is related to more perceived discrimination. For both Russians and Norwegians, national identity is *increased* when there is more contact, be it voluntary or involuntary. The association between ethnic identity and contact is different for the two groups: contact is not associated with level of ethnic identity among Russians. Among Norwegians, contact is associated with low ethnic identity (Voluntary, $r = -.24$, $p < .001$; Involuntary $r = -.22$, $p < .001$). Among Russians, Inter-group anxiety was negatively related to contact ($r = -.21$ and $r = -.23$, respectively, for voluntary and involuntary contact), namely, the more contact Russians had, the lower their inter-group anxiety. No such relationship was found among the Norwegians.

Regarding the relationship between acculturation strategies and contact, we found significant differences between both voluntary and involuntary contact and the intercultural expectations of Norwegians: ($F_{(3, 480)} = 16.10$, $p < .001$; $\eta^2 = .11$ – Involuntary contact), where the significant difference was between Marginalization and all the other strategies, and also between Assimilation and Integration. Individuals who expected Russians to assimilate were those who had lowest involuntary contact, followed by those expecting Russians to go into separation; ($F_{(3, 480)} = 17.37$; $p < .001$; $\eta^2 = .10$ – voluntary contact), where the difference was between Marginalization and all the other strategies, as well as between Assimilation and integration.

No significant difference was found between acculturation strategies and contact, neither for involuntary contact ($F_{(3, 243)} = .92$; $p > .05$) nor for voluntary contact ($F_{(3, 243)} = .26$; $p > 0.05$) when it comes to the Russians. In the area of intercultural strategies, a borderline difference was found among Norwegians: ($F_{(3, 401)} = 2.55$; $p = 0.56$ – Involuntary contact); and a significant difference ($F_{(3, 401)} = 3.13$; $p < 05$; $\eta^2 = .10$) when there is voluntary contact. The significant difference was between multiculturalism and melting-pot. For Russians, no significant difference was found in the type of contact and acculturation and intercultural strategies.

Looking at the various ways the contact hypothesis has been examined here, the general conclusion is that the hypothesis is only partially supported, more so among Russians and less so among the Norwegians.

4.4   Integration Hypothesis

This hypothesis proposes that when members of non-dominant groups seek integration by being "doubly engaged" in both their heritage culture and in the larger society, they will be more successful in achieving a higher level of adaptation.

Before examining this hypothesis, we compared Russians and Norwegians on two forms of adaptation: psychological and intercultural. For psychological adaptation, we compared them on self-esteem and life satisfaction; and for intercultural adaptation, we compared them on perceived discrimination, multicultural ideology and inter-group anxiety. In the area of psychological adaptation, no significant difference was found between Russians and Norwegians in life satisfaction ($t_{(745)}$ =.90; p >.05). A difference however was found in the area of self-esteem ($t_{(737)}$ = 8.99; p <.001), with Russians reporting higher self-esteem. When it comes to intercultural adaptation, significant difference was found between the two groups in the areas of multicultural ideology ($t_{(739)}$ = 4.46; p <.001) and Inter-group anxiety ($t_{(725)}$ = 2.07; p <.05) but not in perceived discrimination ($t_{(723)}$ =.333; p >.05). Russians reported higher scores on multicultural ideology and lower scores on inter-group anxiety than their Norwegian counterparts.

The integration hypothesis was examined by comparing the mean scores of the acculturation and intercultural strategies of Russians on the two psychological adaptation outcomes (self-esteem and satisfaction) and three intercultural adaptation outcomes (Multicultural ideology, inter-group anxiety and perceived discrimination). A univariate general lineal model was performed where age and gender were included as covariates.

Comparing Russians' satisfaction with life by different acculturation strategies, gender and age, a significant effect was found for the overall model ($F_{(8, 247)}$ = 2.91, p <.001, η^2 =.09); significant differences were also observed on self-esteem and acculturation strategies ($F_{(3, 247)}$ = 4.12, p <.01, η^2 =.05), and age ($F_{(1, 247)}$ = 7.92, p <.01, η^2=.03). There was no main effect between gender and self-esteem. Russians preferring assimilation reported the highest level of life satisfaction, and those preferring separation had the lowest life satisfaction score. Russians preferring assimilation, rather than integration reported the highest life satisfaction. The significant difference was not between Russians who prefer assimilation compared with integration, but the difference was between Russians who prefer assimilation compared with those who prefer separation.

Similarly the overall model comparing Russians' acculturation strategy on self-esteem taking into consideration age and gender found a significant difference ($F_{(8, 242)}$ = 2.15, p <.05, η^2 =.07). There was no effect between acculturation strategies and self-esteem ($F_{(3, 242)}$ = 1.09, p =.35). However, a significant main effect was found for gender ($F_{(1, 242)}$ = 8.86, p <.01, η^2 =.04) with females reporting higher self-esteem than males. In effect self-esteem levels could not be differentiated on the basis of their acculturation strategy.

The overall model for Multicultural ideology was significant ($F_{(8, 235)}$ = 4.96, p <.001, η^2 =.14), and there was a significant main effect for acculturation strategies ($F_{(3, 235)}$ = 6.90, p <.001, η^2 =.08); but not gender and not for age. Individuals who preferred integration had the highest Multicultural ideology score, and this was significantly higher than for the other acculturation strategies, except for separation. Individuals endorsing assimilation had the lowest Multicultural ideology scores.

The overall model for inter-group anxiety and for perceived discrimination were not significant. Neither were the main effects significant. For lack of space, the details of the statistics have not been reported here.

An examination of the integration hypothesis among Norwegians was done by looking at the relationship between multicultural ideologies on the one hand, and psychological adaptation (self-esteem and satisfaction with life) and intercultural adaptation (i.e., perceived discrimination and inter-group anxiety) on the other hand. Results indicated that multicultural identity was significantly related with all the outcomes: Self-esteem (r =.11, p <.05); Life-satisfaction (r =.12, p < 0.01); Inter-group anxiety (r = –.20, p <.00) and perceived discrimination (r = –.24, p <.001). These results suggest that Norwegians who embrace multicultural ideology report better psychological and intercultural adaptation.

The consistency of the correlation between multicultural ideology and psychological and intercultural adaptation among Norwegians led us to explore this relationship among Russians as well. Multicultural ideology was not related to any of the adaptation outcomes examined among the Russians here.

The earlier results suggest mixed support for the integration hypothesis. Of the five outcomes examined among Russians, support was gained for only one outcome (multicultural ideology). Among Norwegians, however, higher acceptance of multiculturalism predicts better psychological and intercultural adaptation.

5 Discussion

The results of this study suggest that the three MIRIPS hypotheses gain variable support in the two samples. The multiculturalism hypothesis gains the strongest support, while the integration and contact hypotheses gain partial support. And whereas the integration hypothesis gains strong support among Norwegians, the contact hypothesis gains more support among Russians. Before drawing any firm conclusions, the results need to be understood within the Norwegian context, particularly the asymmetric nature of the relationships within the society and the historical presence of Russians in Norway.

This project was developed with the assumption that intercultural relations in multicultural societies are influenced by the asymmetric positioning of the groups within the society between the acculturating group and the larger society. In the past, research has often been one-sided, where only the non-dominant group was the focus. The MIRIPS project was designed to allow all sides to be examined together (see Horenzcyk, Jasinskaja-Lahti, Sam & Vedder, 2013 for a discussion). An approach of this present study was to examine how Russians and Norwegians perceive the social status of Russians in Norway. The answer to this issue gives some indication of the asymmetric nature between the two groups. We found that neither group perceived Russians to be highly appreciated in the society, although Russians have a more positive view of their own position than their Norwegian counterparts do. Moreover, Russians view their status within society to be appropriate (acceptable, with their score above the theoretical mid-point of the scale). However, Norwegians viewed Russians in a less appreciated position. As a democratic country, and being ranked highly when it comes to human rights (Freedom in the World, 2016), defending the rights of Russians is perhaps nothing peculiar. This finding should also be understood within the context of Norway's relatively high migrant integration score among all participating countries. Russians as a minority group may find themselves at a disadvantage in fighting for their own rights in a country where they constitute less than 0.4 per cent of the total population. It should also be noted that current Russian conflicts with Ukraine and with the West are probably making Russians take a low profile in supporting social actions in their own defense.

5.1 Multiculturalism Hypothesis

The multiculturalism hypothesis receives the strongest support in this study among Russians and Norwegians. Being secure in one's identity was associated with higher out-group trust, and lower perceived discrimination and better adaptation. Feelings of security together with a strong identity are related to a number of outcomes that can likely result in harmonious relations in multicultural societies. Is it possible to claim that multiculturalism has the potential for positive outcomes among individuals and for the larger society? The data for this study are based on only two groups; but if similar finding are found for other groups in Norway, it will be plausible to assume that multiculturalism may be good for intercultural relations in Norway.

A challenge that many contemporary societies face is how to promote a thriving multicultural society where the different ethnocultural groups can co-exist. Politicians such as former British prime minister David Cameron and German chancellor Angel Merkel (not withstanding her current welcoming policy towards refugees and asylum-seekers) have made claims that multiculturalism has failed, it is obvious that these countries have not made much efforts to ensure that conditions are in place for equitable intercultural. While some countries seem to have allowed some degree of cultural maintenance, they cannot show efforts to promote equitable and full participation in the activities by all cultural communities in the larger society.

5.2   Contact Hypothesis

The contact hypothesis receives only partial support in this study; this support is stronger among Russians than among Norwegians. Of particular significance is that among Russians, both perceived discrimination and inter-group anxiety are associated with inter-group contact, be it voluntary or involuntary. The situation is different for Norwegians: inter-group contact for Norwegians is associated with high perceived discrimination, and voluntary inter-group contact also associated with lower multicultural ideology. In-group bias is, however, associated with low inter-group contact among Norwegians. What these findings suggest is that while inter-group contact may lower ethnocentrism among Norwegians, the reduction is perhaps not strong enough to have a positive effect on perceived discrimination. What is not clear in this study is the ethnicities of people engaging in the inter-group contact, which perhaps could shed some light on these findings. More specifically, the various ethnocultural groups may belong to a specific position in an ethnic hierarchy. It is possible that the inter-cultural contact with groups low on the hierarchy may yield a significant change in ethnocentrism when contact takes place. Similarly, if a third cultural group were included in this study, and we were able to ascertain their position relative to Russians on the hierarchy, we might have been able to see the extent of prejudice. In this study we only have information on how Russians' perceive their own social status, and how Norwegians perceive Russians on social status. It would have been good to see how Norwegians see themselves on social status, and how Russians perceive them.

One possible reason for the partial support of the contact hypothesis may be that the analysis did not control for many of the conditions (e.g., common goals; inter-group cooperation; and support for authorities, laws and customs) that were proposed by Allport (1954) to be necessary for the best contact hypothesis results. The two groups in this study were certainly not of equal status.

It is equally important to remember that the central premise of the contact hypothesis is that contact will reduce prejudice. However, the indicators used as proxies of prejudice might not have been the best. According to Allport (1954), prejudice is a favourable or an unfavourable feeling towards a person or an object that is not based on experience; more specifically, feelings that are reached prior to having an experience with the group or the object. A characteristic feature of prejudice, according to Brewer (1999), is favouritism towards one's group. The recognition of this favouritism has led to a number of other theories that suggest that favouritism can lead to In-group bias, (perceived) discrimination, out-group distrust and intergroup anxiety, and these are what were examined here. Again, some of these measures were based on only a single item, and this could probably account for the partial support gained for this hypothesis.

5.3   Integration Hypothesis

The integration hypothesis received only partial support in Norway. Consistent with findings from several studies (see, e.g., Abu-Rayya & Sam, 2017), Integration is the strategy Russians in Norway most prefer. This preference is related to gender, but not to how long the person has lived in the country. Russians in Norway are not very different from other immigrant groups in Norway in their preferred acculturation strategies (see Sam, 1994). Even though the majority of the Russians preferred integration to the other strategies, individuals preferring this strategy did not report any better psychological or intercultural adaptation compared with those who preferred the other strategies. Individuals who preferred assimilation reported the highest self-esteem, but this was not different from individuals who preferred Integration. Moreover, the effect of acculturation strategies on self-esteem is rather small. It should be noted that Russians actually reported higher self-esteem than Norwegians, and for Russians preferring assimilation to score highest on self-esteem may be self-pride on their part for their personal achievement, such as being highly educated compared with Norwegians). It could be that Russians who preferred assimilation were more economically sound; however, this was not the case. Again, it is important to remember that the majority of the Russians came to Norway because of family, rather than for economic reasons.

The area where the integration hypothesis gained support was with respect to Multicultural Ideology. This was the case for both Norwegians and Russians. It should be added that support for this hypothesis in the area of multicultural ideology was arrived at using different statistical analysis for Norwegians and Russians. Among Russians, this is based on comparing adaptation across the four acculturation strategies. In contrast, for Norwegians, this finding is based on correlations. A question that needs further clarification is whether the two groups view and understand multicultural ideology similarly or differently. Based on the asymmetrical acculturation field, this is possible: Estonians and Russians occupy different positions in the acculturation field, and multicultural ideology means different things to them. In the absence of information on Norwegians' own acculturation strategy preferences, no easy answer can be provided to this question.

Multicultural ideology centers around promoting multiculturalism within the society (Sam, in press), and integration is an individual's attitude towards cultural maintenance and participation within the larger society. It goes without saying that wanting to maintain one's cultural heritage at the same time as adopting Norwegian cultural values may be a prerequisite to being welcomed into the larger society. As Berry (1997) points out, integration is possible in a welcoming society, where welcoming means ethnocultural groups other than the dominant group are encouraged to maintain their cultural heritage, as well as giving them the opportunity to interact with members of the larger society. In addition, having programs for maintaining the non-dominant group's culture, is essential. For Norwegians, a positive multicultural ideology is a prerequisite to creating an environment that makes multiculturalism possible. For Russians, multicultural ideology means being willing to integrate.

This limited support for the integration hypothesis in Norway may be that the measures of acculturation and intercultural strategies as used in this study were not the best. Only two items each went into the two main dimensions of the strategies, and no internal consistency could be established. Perhaps more valid measures of the contact and adoption domains might have supported the hypothesis.

5.4 Conclusions

The results from this study support many features of the hypotheses that were based on the multiculturalism policy and practice in Canada. This support is particularly the case for the multiculturalism hypothesis. Studies examining the multiculturalism hypothesis to date are not as extensive as those that have examined the other two hypotheses. Gaining support for the multiculturalism hypothesis in this study is a positive contribution to our understanding the hypothesis and adds to available studies that can be used for meta-analysis.

With respect to the contact and integration hypotheses, there is widespread and convincing support in the existing literature (see Nguyen & Benet-Martinez, 2013; Pettigrew, Tropp, Wagner & Christ, 2011, for meta-analytic reviews of these two hypotheses). Taking together support for the multiculturalism hypothesis and the partial support for the contact and integration hypotheses arising from this study (along with this previous support for these two hypotheses), we believe that social scientists are well armed to propose policies that may change the pessimistic views on multiculturalism that have been raised by some heads of states.

Acknowledgement

The study reported here was funded by the Research Council of Norway, through the European Economic Area (EEA) program funding, grant number EMP 138.

References

Abu-Rayya, H. M., & Sam, D. L. (2016). Is integration the best way to acculturate? A reexamination of the bicultural-adaptation relationship in the "ICSEY dataset" using the bilineal method. *Journal of Cross-Cultural Psychology*, *48* (3): 287–293. DOI: 0022022116685846.

Allport, G. W. (1954). *The Nature of Prejudice*. Reading, MA: Addison-Wesley.

Barth, F. (1962). *The Role of the Entrepreneur in Social Change in Northern Norway*. Oslo: Universitietsforlaget. Oslo, Norway.

Barth, F. (1981). *Process and Form in Social Life*. London: Routledge and Kegan Paul.

Berry, J.W. (1997). Immigration, acculturation, and adaptation. *Applied Psychology: An International Review*, *46* (1),46–68.

Berry, J. W., & Sabatier, C. (2011). Variations in the assessment of acculturation attitudes: Their relationships with psychological well-being. *International Journal of Intercultural Relations*, *35*, 658–669.

Berry, J. W., & Sam, D. L. (2016). *Theoretical perspectives*. In D. L. Sam & J. W. Berry (eds). *The Cambridge Handbook of Acculturation Psychology*. 2nd edition. (pp 11–29). Cambridge: Cambridge University Press.

Berry, J. W., & Ward, C. (2016). Multiculturalism. In D. L. Sam & J. W. Berry (eds). *The Cambridge Handbook of Acculturation Psychology*. 2nd edition. (pp. 441–63). Cambridge: Cambridge University Press.

Bjertnæs, M. K. (2000). Innvandring og innvandrere. Oslo: Statistics Norway. http://ssb.no/befolkning/artikler-og-publikasjoner/innvandring-og-innvan drere-2000.

Brewer, M. B. (1999). The psychology of prejudice: Ingroup love and outgroup hate. *Journal of Social Issues*. *55*, 429–44.

Brochman, G. (1999). Re-drawing lines of control: The Norwegian welfare state dilemma. In G. Brochmann & T. Hammar, T. (Eds.). *Mechanism of Immigration Control: A Comparative Analysis of European Regulation Practices* (pp. 203–232) Berg: Oxford, UK.

Brochmann, G., & Hammar, T (Eds.) (1999). *Mechanism of Immigration Control: A Comparative Analysis of European Regulation Practices*. Berg: Oxford, UK.

Freedom in the world (2016). Anxious dictators, wavering democracies: Global freedom under Pressure. https://freedomhouse.org/report/freedom-world/free dom-world-2016 (accessed October 6, 2016).

Hernes, G., & Knudsen, K. (1987). Over grensen: Om holdning til innvandrere og asylsøkere. *Tidsskrift for samfunnsforskning*, *30*, 27–60.

Horenczyk, G., Jasinskaja-Lahti, I., Sam, D. L. & Vedder, P. (2013). Mutuality in acculturation: Towards an integration. *Zeitschrift für Psychologie*, *221*, 205–213.

Kgl. Res, (1975). *Kongelig resolusjon av 19.1.1975 Om Innvandringsstopp*. Oslo: Ministry of Interior.

Nguyen, A.-M. T., & Benet-Martinez, V. (2013). Biculturalism and adjustment: A meta-analysis. *Journal of Cross-Cultural Psychology*, *44*(1),122–159.

Nytt fra Universitet i Bergen (1993), Litt toleranse overfor innvandrere. *Nytt fra Universitet i Bergen, Nr. 6*. Bergen: Universitet i Bergen.

Pettigrew, T. F., Tropp, L. R., Wagner, U., & Christ, O. (2011). Recent advances in intergroup contact theory. *International Journal of Intercultural Relation*, *35*, 271–280.

Sam, D. L. (1994). Psychological adjustment of young immigrants in Norway. *Scandinavian Journal of Psychology*, *35*, 240–253.

Sam, D. L. (in press). Multiculturalism. In F. M. Moghaddam, (Ed.). *The SAGE Encyclopedia of Political Behavior*. Thousand Oaks, CA: SAGE.

Sam, D. L., & Berry, J. W. (Eds.). (2016). *The Cambridge Handbook of Acculturation Psychology*, 2nd edition. Cambridge: Cambridge University Press.

Snauwaert, B., Soenens, B., Vanbeselaere, N. & Boen, F. (2003). When integration does not necessarily imply integration. Different conceptualizations of acculturation orientations lead to different classifications. *Journal of Cross-cultural Psychology*, *34*, 231–239.

SSB (2015). Attitudes towards immigrants and immigration, 2015. www.ssb.no /en/befolkning/statistikker/innvhold/aar/2015-12-11.

SSB. (2016). Innvandrere og norskfødte med innvandrerforeldre, 1. januar 2016. https://ssb.no/befolkning/statistikker/innvbef. Accessed October 1, 2016.

7 Intercultural Relations in Germany

Katja Hanke

GESIS-*Leibniz Institute for the Social Sciences*
Jacobs University Bremen

Marieke van Egmond and Anette Rohmann
University of Hagen

Klaus Boehnke

Jacobs University Bremen, Germany
National Research University Higher School of Economics,
Russian Federation

1   Introduction

Germany has a history of more than forty years of large-scale, primarily economic migration. At present, Germany is close to the middle on the diversity and integration indexes, and below the middle on the policy index. Because of the recent arrival of around one million refugees from West Asia, Germany is an important country to examine and understand views about intercultural relations during this period of transition.

2   Context of Intercultural Relations in Germany

2.1   Immigration

Almost 16 million (20%) people in Germany have a "migration background" (which is 20% of the population). This term does not only mean all immigrants and all foreigners who were not born in Germany, but also refers to individuals who were born in Germany and who have German citizenship, but who have at least one parent who was born outside of Germany (Bundesregierung, 2014).

Migration to Germany is often thought of in terms of the large number of invited guest workers (*Gastarbeiter*) who predominately originated in Southern Europe (Italy, Spain, Greece, later Turkey, but also in South Korea). The high death toll that resulted from World War II led to a shortage in the workforce during the 1950s and to work migration in the 1960s and

1970s. During that time, German policy makers assumed that guest workers would stay for two or three years to make money and would then leave Germany again. Max Frisch, the Swiss playwright and novelist, is quoted with the statement that "we called for workers, and it was human beings who came". In hindsight, Frisch was correct, since many of the incoming guest workers, especially the Turks, settled in Germany and later brought their families (Zick et al., 2001). The children of these migrants, who were born in Germany but to non-German parents were not granted German citizenship automatically until a reform of this law took place in 1998. The premise for automatic citizenship since then is that one parent should have lived in Germany for at least eight years prior to the birth of the child and have permanent residency (Auswärtiges Amt, 2015).

More recently, Germany has seen an increase in intra-European migration (Statistisches Bundesamt, 2014). The largest groups of migrants originate from countries that joined the EU in 2004 (e.g., Poland, Hungary) and 2007 (e.g., Romania). The second-largest group is formed by people from the Southern European countries that have been hit hardest by the financial crisis that commenced in 2008, such as Spain and Greece. Both of these latter countries have a much longer migration history with Germany (with a Greek background currently being the fourth-largest group of migrants in Germany, after people from Turkey, Poland and Italy, Statistisches Bundesamt, 2012). The fact that dual citizenship was restricted until 2014 forced migrants to choose between their German and non-German citizenships. This complicated the development of identities that are not mono-cultural. Permitting dual citizenship has thus been viewed as a positive step to support the formation of hybrid identities among children of the second and third generations (Owers, 2015). On the other hand, it is crucial that such identities be seen as compatible. A recent longitudinal study conducted among Turkish and Russian migrants in Germany, for example, revealed that in the case of strong self-perceived incompatibilities between identity components, a combination of a strong identification with both the host and one's ethnic group may foster destructive forms of political mobilization such as radicalization (Simon, Reichert & Grabow, 2013).

And, of course, the most recent arrivals from West Asia have changed the composition of the migrant population in Germany and have become a matter of political and policy discussion and debate.

2.2   Policies

Until now, there have been no concrete policies in place that regulate or even foster the social integration of migrants into German society.[1]

---

[1] It has only been with the extremely recent arrival of over one million refugees, many of them escaping the Syrian civil war, that integration efforts have been explicitly discussed

For the generations of migrants that arrived over the last decades, German politics have failed to implement multicultural policies that would have ensured "true integration" (Schmitt-Rodermund & Silbereisen, 2008, p. 89). This has led to numerous proclamations from mostly conservative politicians that multiculturalism is a doomed concept in Germany (Modood, 2006). Most prominently, federal chancellor Angela Merkel insisted in 2006 that multiculturalism has failed.[2] Notably, Rita Süssmuth, former president of the Lower House of German Parliament (the *Bundestag*), said in response to Merkel's remark about the failure of multiculturalism that "Multiculturalism is not a concept, it is a fact. Thus, one cannot claim that all has failed" (Das Gupta, 2010). Indeed it cannot be denied that immigration is inherently part of contemporary Germany and that the country is a truly multicultural society (at least in demographic terms). However, due to the lack of policies that support multiculturalism in Germany, neither for migrants nor for the majority population, we expect varying findings when it comes to assessing the three MIRIPS hypotheses.

Hence, we will assess the intercultural relations of participants who identify with being German as well as with their home culture (coined as bicultural) and compare them to those who only identify with an ethnic identity.

3   Evaluation of the MIRIPS Hypotheses in Germany

3.1   *Previous Research*

It should be clear that the migration context in Germany differs from those in classical settler societies that deal with immigration constructively (Berry, Phinney, Sam & Vedder, 2006; Boehnke et al., 2016; Pfafferott & Brown, 2006; Zick et al., 2001). During the early part of the twentieth century, the majority of incoming migrants were Polish workers who quickly assimilated into German society. This is largely due to the rather small cultural distance and similarity in religious beliefs and low visibility of Polish workers (Böttinger, 2005). Another group of migrants that is not necessarily seen as "foreign" arrived in Germany after World War II. This group consisted of people who were ethnically German, but resided beyond the country's borders, in Eastern Europe

and defined in the political sphere as well as in public discourse (Boehnke, Deutsch & Boehnke, 2016).
[2] Angela Merkel recently acknowledged that Islam is a part of Germany and that Germany is an immigration country (www.faz.net/aktuell/politik/ausland/europa/angela-merkel-sieht-deutschland-als-einwanderungsland-13623846.html).

and the former Soviet Union. They *returned* to Germany after the war (called *Aussiedler* and after 1992 *Spätaussiedler*). They were granted German citizenship immediately, based on their descent *(jus sanguinis)*, in spite of the fact that their families had not lived in Germany for a considerable time, sometimes several hundreds of years (Zick, Wagner, Van Dick & Petzel, 2001).

Research shows that most Germans think of people with a Turkish migration background when they hear the word *Gastarbeiter* and *Ausländer (foreigner*; Asbrock, Lemmer, Becker, Koller & Wagner, 2014), ignoring ethnic differences among migrants from Turkey, such as Turkish/Kurdish and other significant groups (Yükleyen, 2012). Asbrock and colleagues (2014) found that respondents tended to be more prejudiced when they associated Turks with the term "foreigner" than with another group. This finding is in line with other research, which has found a hierarchy between ethnic groups in the German context, with Turks being perceived as both a symbolic threat (cultural values) as well as a realistic threat (economic status) (Hagendoorn, 1995).

Members of the German majority more often perceive foreigners as a threat rather than as an enrichment to society. In particular, migrants with a Muslim background (approximately 4 million, or 5% of the population) are exposed to negative attitudes (see, e.g., Hafez & Schmidt, 2015; Mühe, 2016; Kunst, Tajamal, Sam & Ulleberg, 2012; Van der Noll, 2014). Although Germany is not the only Western European country to struggle with islamophobic attitudes, the problem is pervasive and growing (Fekete, 2009; Saeed, 2007; Taras, 2012). Moreover, studies on the acculturation of Muslim youth have been misinterpreted and misused in the general media and even in reports by the Federal Ministry of Internal Affairs (e.g., Frindte, Boehnke, Kreikenbom & Wagner, 2012; also see Owers, 2015). Findings were negatively toned in public statements, while encouraging aspects were neglected. The then minister of the interior later admitted to parliament that he had leaked slanted information about Frindte et al.'s (2012) study to the largest German tabloid, which published an article that painted rather a dark picture of the willingness of young Muslims to integrate, which fed into the resentments towards Muslims and mistrust in foreigners.

In an international comparative study, Berry et al. (2006) found that in Germany, 40 per cent of migrant youth of Turkish descent had a so-called *diffuse* (or marginalization) acculturation profile suggesting that they do not know where they belong. These results were interpreted as a consequence of the fact that Germany lacked public policies for the successful structural and psychological integration of immigrants (Berry et al., 2006). Furthermore, this study revealed that Germans preferred a culturally homogenous society and therefore reject cultural diversity as a way of living together (Berry et al., 2006). These findings are mirrored in more recent comparisons by the Multiculturalism Policy Index, in which Germany scored 2.5 points, where a score of under 3 is considered weak. This score of 2.5 was based on the evidence that there is no explicit recognition or affirmation of multiculturalism, no multicultural school curriculum, the lack of representation of migrants in public media, controversy surrounding dress codes, the absence of dual citizenship regulations (before 2014), little funding of ethnic groups, limited mother tongue instruction and no policy on affirmative action.

In contrast, there are also public voices that argue that the increasing arrival of migrants is an opportunity for Germany. Germany is facing a dramatic demographic shift due to its aging population. This demographic shift results in a "rapidly aging workforce" (Jackson & Debroux, 2016, p. 8). The decrease in birthrates of previous years, as well as increased longevity, has led to an uneven distribution of age groups; there is the saying that the population pyramid is developing into a population mushroom (Borgmann, 2005). At the societal level, this demographic shift created a situation in which the social welfare system is in serious jeopardy because there are fewer younger working people to financially support and contribute to the system. Thus, there is hope that the current inflow of refugees could help overcome these gaps and make up for the shortage of skilled employees contributing to the social welfare system.

Recent research highlights the dynamic nature of acculturation and intercultural relations, especially the interplay between minority and majority attitudes and their mutual perceptions. There is correlational and experimental evidence from studies conducted in Germany that show that discordant acculturation attitudes are associated with higher levels of symbolic and realistic threat (Rohmann, Florack & Piontkowski, 2006; Rohmann, Piontkowski & van Randenborgh, 2008). Perceived acculturation attitudes of outgroup members do influence the acculturation attitudes of both minority and majority group members (Celeste, Brown, Tip & Matera, 2014; Zagefka, Tip, Gonzalez, Brown & Cinnirella, 2012). Moreover, in a German multilevel survey, a negative intergroup climate (higher amounts of prejudice) was related to a stronger desire for cultural maintenance expressed by immigrants (Christ, Asbrock, Dhont, Pettigrew & Wagner, 2013).

In short, it can be concluded that an expectation of formal integration (i.e., speaking the language, going to school or having a job) dominates the German multicultural landscape. An explicit focus on the acculturation processes (in the sense of subjectively experienced belongingness and acceptance) is typically lacking from public debates. For this reason, the extent to which migrants feel that they belong and are being accepted takes a central role in the present chapter. The other strategy that has been discussed is the role that marginalization plays in the development of radicalization tendencies (Lyons-Padilla, Gelfand, Mirahmadi, Farooq & van Egmond, 2015).

The study in this chapter investigates intercultural relations in Germany with two samples from German participants and three other samples with diverse migration backgrounds. Furthermore, we examine how the feelings of well-being of migrants and the majority are related to their feelings of security and intergroup contact.

3.2   Theoretical Issues

The multiculturalism hypothesis proposes that confidence in one's own identity and place in society leads to the acceptance of culturally different others. In this study, we operationalize confidence in one's own identity and place in society as feeling secure in Germany. We evaluate this hypothesis in several independent studies, using a variety of instruments. To measure security, we use the security measure of the MIRIPS questionnaire, which also taps into realistic and symbolic experiences of threat. We also include life satisfaction as a proxy of "feeling secure of one's place in society", since specifically for Germans it can be a signifier of feeling secure if they are satisfied with their lives. Furthermore, identification with the nation is used as a proximal measure of feeling secure in one's society of residence.[3] Acceptance of culturally different others is operationalized by asking how much sympathy respondents have for specific out-groups.

For the contact hypothesis, we assess the conditions under which contact is associated with higher levels of acceptance and positive out-group attitudes among minority members. We operationalize "contact" through the degree of fulfillment of the need to feel connected to Germans. We assume that feeling connected predicts perceptions of warmth (measured by warmth and friendliness), competence (measured by competence and capability) and lower coldness (measured by cold and arrogant) of Germans. These stereotypes are taken from Cuddy and Fiske's (2007) stereotype content model and are used as an operationalization of out-group attitudes. Furthermore, we assess the extent to which a minority's perceptions of majority acculturation attitudes function as a barrier to the

---

[3] High levels of identification with the nation of residence may be a highly ambivalent indicator of feelings of security in the case of Germany due to the highly negative connotation that nationalism has in Germany, given the nation's role in World War II.

development of positive perceptions. Specifically, we assess if the relationship between contact, reported by minority group members, and tolerance is moderated by the extent to which minority group members have the impression that majority group members desire such contact as well.

The integration hypothesis proposes that a double engagement with both the culture of origin and the majority society should positively affect the well-being of migrants. We empirically evaluate this hypothesis by assessing two outcomes in relation to the integration strategy. First, we examine the notion of flourishing, which refers to respondents' self-perceived success in important areas of life, such as relationships, self-esteem, purpose and optimism (Diener et al., 2009). The eight-item scale to assess flourishing provides a single psychological well-being score. Second, we examine sociocultural competence, to see if this form of adaptation is higher among respondents who can be identified as pursuing the integration acculturation strategy. In one of the studies reported, we also include self-reported fluency in German, which we see as an overarching facilitator of contact, integration, and a multicultural lifestyle.

4   Method

4.1   Samples

German Majority.[4] We drew two samples from the German majority population.

Sample 1: Data were collected via diverse online forums and Facebook groups targeting a sample of majority members (respondents with German citizenship, who were born in Germany and identified as being German) with the aim of getting a more or less equal representation of all federal states within Germany. This endeavor was quite successful. Hence, there is a relatively balanced representation of each federal state in this data set. However, this is not a random probability sample. The mean age was 28.24 (SD = 10.11, range: 17–80), 33.5% were male participants with a total sample size of $N = 603$.

---

[4] Data collection for Majority Sample 1 and two of individuals with a migration background was conducted within the framework of a larger overarching research project on the topic of belongingness. This research project was funded within the framework of the European Commission's Marie Curie-Skłodowska scheme. For Majority Sample 2 and a sample of Greek migrants, data collection was designed on the basis of the MIRIPS study. It should be noted that scales that are not reported in this chapter referred to the specific out-group of people with a Turkish migration background.

Sample 2: A second data set of majority/"native" Germans originated from a study conducted at the University of Hagen. A total sample of 276 student participants was recruited. Since 20 of these participants indicated a migration background, they were excluded, reducing the final sample size to N = 256. The University of Hagen is Germany's only public distance-learning university and has a majority of non-traditional students. This implies that this sample includes a wider range of age groups than a traditional student sample. The mean age was 32.11 (SD = 10.41, range: 18–75), and participants were 26 per cent male.

We also drew two samples from the German minority population.

Sample 1a and 1b. Diverse migration background. Data were collected online using diverse online forums and Facebook groups. The target population was migrants and individuals with a migration background. Data were collected from two different populations: one sub-sample included persons solely associating with their own ethnic group (*ethnic sample:* $N = 135$, $M_{age} = 27.41$, $SD_{age} = 7.91$, age range: 16–59; male = 41.5%). The other sub-sample was individuals associating both with being German and with their own ethnic group (*bicultural sample:* $N = 241$, $M_{age} = 28.01$, $SD_{age} = 9.31$, age range: 16–60; male = 31.1%). Both the ethnic sample and the bicultural sample were mixed regarding the make-up of ethnicities with people predominately originating from Turkey, Eastern European countries and the Middle East (in the ethnic sample), and from Turkey, Eastern Europe, Latin America, as well as Western Europe (in the bicultural sample). It should be noted that the terms *ethnic* and *bicultural* do not imply that the sampled individuals are engaged *only* with their home culture as distinct from being doubly engaged with both home and host culture.

Sample 2. Greek background: A sample of 396 participants (33% male) was recruited from German-Greek communities, which meant that all participants had a least one Greek parent. Despite their Greek background, a little over half of all participants (54%) had been born in Germany. Data were collected via an online survey distributed through social media. Participants were 40 years old on average (SD = 12.37) with a range between the ages of 16 and 84. Seventy-two percent of the participants indicated that they were religious and the majority of participants were employed (75%) or in school (15%), with the others being homemakers (3%), pensioners (4%) or unemployed (2%).

4.2   Measures

An overview of all measures with their sources and psychometric properties of each sample is included in Table 7.1.

Table 7.1. *Overview of measures and samples, means and standard deviations.*

Sample	Concept (#items, Cronbach's alpha)	Source	IV /DV*	M (SD)	
German Majority 1	Feeling secure (6,.79)	Haenni Hoti, Heinzmann, Müller & Buholzer (2017)	IV	4.46 (1.24)	
	Sympathy towards different ethnic groups (4,.80)	Rippl, Baier & Boehnke (2007)	DV	4.14 (1.03)	
	Integration orientation (9,.82)	Adapted version based on Haenni Hoti, Heinzmann, Müller, & Buholzer (2017)	IV	5.77 (.84)	
	Separation orientation (7,.76)			5.05 (.82)	
	Assimilation orientation (6,.68)			4.90 (.83)	
	Stereotypes – warmth (2,.77), cold (2,.77),	Cuddy et al. (2007)		4.41 (1.14) 4.19 (1.19)	
	competence (2,.86)			5.35 (.94)	
German Majority 2	Tolerance (11,.89)	MIRIPS Questionnaire	DV	4.31 (0.67)	
	Identification with the nation (3,.77)	MIRIPS Questionnaire	IV	3.66 (.92)	
	Life Satisfaction (5,.83)	MIRIPS Questionnaire	IV	3.98 (0.73)	
	Security (12,.72)	MIRIPS Questionnaire	IV	2.41 (0.53)	
				Ethnic	Bicultural
Ethnic/bicultural sample (sample 1a and 1b)	Multicultural/Integration Orientation (9;.83/.87)	Adapted version based on Haenni Hoti, Heinzmann, Müller & Buholzer (2017))	IV	5.93 (1.31)	6.17 (0.77)
	Flourishing (8,.88/.87)	Diener et al., (2009)	DV	45.16 (7.17)	45.58 (7.36)

Table 7.1. (*cont.*)

Sample	Concept (#items, Cronbach's alpha)	Source	IV /DV	M (SD)	
	Socio-Cultural Competence (23,.93/.93)	Based on MIRIPS Questionnaire and Ward and Kennedy (1999)	DV	5.31 (1.18)	5.76 (1.02)
	General Belongingness – Acceptance subscale (6,.89/.91)	Malone, Pillow & Osman (2011)	IV	5.41 (1.07)	5.57 (1.04)
	Basic Needs Fulfillment – Feeling connected to Germans (3,.78/.84)	La Guardia, Ryan, Couchman & Deci (2000)	IV	3.88 (1.31)	3.89 (1.32)
	Stereotypes warmth (2,.84/.82): cold (2,.77/.66), competence (2,.78/.68)	Cuddy et al. (2007)	DV	4.42 (1.51) 4.18 (1.46) 5.12 (1.06)	4.43 (1.40) 4.33 (1.32) 5.52 (0.86)
Greek minority (sample 2)	Acculturation orientation (6, Cultural maintenance dimension: .86; Contact dimension:.69)	Zagefka & Brown (2002)	IV	5.48 (1.43) / 5.97 (.77)	
	Perceived host country acculturation preference (5, Cultural maintenance dimension: .89; Contact dimension: .74)	Zagefka & Brown (2002)	IV	5.57 (1.49) / 3.98 (1.56)	
	Life satisfaction (5,.89)	MIRIPS Questionnaire	DV	4.70 (1.31)	
	Well-being (7,.80)	Wydra, 2014	DV	4.96 (.95)	
	German fluency (4,.79)	MIRIPS Questionnaire	IV	4.84 (.37)	

Note: * IV = Independent Variable, DV = Dependent Variable.

5   Results

5.1   The Multiculturalism Hypothesis

In Majority Sample 1, multiple hierarchical regressions tested the predictive power of feeling secure to explain variance in feeling sympathy for (acceptance of) different ethnic out-groups represented in a single composite score (Africans, Bulgarians, Romanians and Croatians) with Majority Sample 1. In the first block, age and gender (sympathy score: M_{women} = 4.28, SD = 1.03, M_{men} = 3.84, SD = .96) were entered. In the second and last block, feeling secure was entered. The variance inflation factor (VIF) was below 2, indicating no problems with multicollinearity[5]. Age (β = −.10, p < .05) and gender (β = −.18, p < .001) were significant indicating that the younger the participants, the more sympathy towards these groups and that female participants had more sympathy for these groups. After entering feelings of security, age became insignificant and feeling secure (β = .25, p < .001) explained 6% of additional variance indicating that feeling secure contributes uniquely to explain variations in feeling sympathy. There were still gender differences (β = −18, p < .001). The overall model did not explain much of the variance (11%) in feelings of sympathy, but it points to the fact that a variety of other variables may play a role in explaining variations in feeling sympathy for certain out-groups.

In Majority Sample 2, we tested if there is an effect of security on tolerance, over and above the effects of national identity and life satisfaction. Life satisfaction was used as a proxy for one's confidence in one's place in society, given the problematic nature of measuring German national identity. This was tested using identification with the nation-state and generalized tolerance. A similar multiple hierarchical regression model as before was conducted with generalized tolerance as the dependent variable. Age and gender were entered in the first block again. In the second block, identification with the nation and life satisfaction were entered as measures of one's own identity and confidence in place in society. Security was entered in the third and last block. In this sample, neither age nor gender significantly affected tolerance (p's > .1). Both national identity (β = −.35, p < .001) and life satisfaction (β = .32, p < .001), however, significantly contributed to the explanation of tolerance (ΔR^2 = .15). It should be noted that whereas life satisfaction is a positive predictor of tolerance towards others, identification with the nation is a relatively strong negative predictor of tolerance in the German

---

[5] Multicollinearity did not emerge as a problem in any of the subsequently reported regression analyses. We, thus, refrain from stating this for all other analyses reported in this chapter.

context. The addition of feelings of security ($\beta = -.65$, $p < .001$) further enhanced the explained variance ($\Delta R^2 = .35$). The direction of this effect was positive, in line with the stated multiculturalism hypothesis. Notably, the inclusion of security in Block 3 renders insignificant the effects of identification with the nation and of life satisfaction. The overall model explains an impressive amount of 50.9 per cent of the variance.

5.2   The Contact Hypothesis

In order to test the influence of positive contact (conceptualized for the Minority Ethnic and Bicultural samples as feeling connected to Germans) to predict out-group attitudes (conceptualized for the ethnic/bicultural sample as warmth, coldness and competence stereotypes about Germans), we employed multiple hierarchical regressions.

Ethnic sample. We tested three multiple hierarchical regression models with warmth, competence, and cold stereotypes towards the out-group as outcome variables, respectively. We entered age and gender again in the first block and feeling connected to Germans in Block 2. The first dependent variable was warmth stereotypes. Neither age nor gender was significant. Feeling connected to Germans as a proxy of positive contact significantly predicted warmth stereotypes ($\beta = .23$, $p < .05$; $\Delta R^2 = .05$) and explained 5 per cent of unique variance in warmth stereotypes. Model 1 explained 8 per cent of the variance in warmth stereotypes. We yielded a similar result for the prediction of competence stereotypes ($\beta = .28$, $p < .01$; $\Delta R^2 = .08$). This second model also explained 8 per cent of the variance in competence stereotypes. The last model tested used coldness stereotypes as the outcome variables. Feeling connected to Germans was a significant negative predictor for coldness stereotypes ($\beta = -.25$, $p < .05$; $\Delta R^2 = .06$), and the overall model explained 6 per cent of the variance in cold stereotypes. In other words, people whose need for connectedness with Germans is fulfilled, perceived Germans as warmer, more competent and less cold.

Bicultural sample. We tested the same models (with feeling connected to Germans as a predictor) as earlier. Model 1 (predicting warmth stereotypes): feeling connected to Germans was a significant positive predictor for warmth stereotypes ($\beta = .28$, $p < .001$; $\Delta R^2 = .08$), and the overall model explained 9 per cent of the variance in warmth stereotypes. Model 2 (predicting competence stereotypes): feeling connected to Germans was not a significant predictor ($\beta = .096$, $p = .192$). Model 3 (predicting coldness stereotypes): feeling connected to Germans was a significant negative predictor ($\beta = -.28$, $p < .001$; $\Delta R^2 = .08$), and the overall model explained 8 per cent of the variance in cold stereotypes.

In other words, if the need to feel connected to Germans is fulfilled, positive stereotypes about Germans increase while negative ones decrease. This finding rests on the assumption that the feeling of connectedness is a form of positive contact with Germans.

Greek Sample

A possible condition under which contact could be associated with a positive perception of German majority members for the sample of Greek migrants was identified as the expectation that the Greeks have the acculturation expectation that majority members hold. The main premise would be that if one is willing to engage in contact, but one has the impression that host country members do not desire this contact, that one will have a more negative perception of the out-group, despite one's own willingness to engage in contact.

For the sample of Germans–Greeks, we, therefore, conducted a moderation analysis (PROCESS, Model 1) with own contact with Germans as the predictor variable and perceived discrimination (i.e., lack of perceived acceptance) as the dependent variable. The effect of one's own willingness to seek contact on levels of discrimination that was experienced is reduced by the extent to which one perceives majority members as desiring contact as well ($F[1,397] = 7.42, p < .05, \Delta R^2 = .02$) and supporting the cultural maintenance of migrants ($F[1,397] = 4.79, p < .05, \Delta R^2 = .01$). We also tested for the moderating effects of perceived cultural distance and language proficiency on this relationship, but neither of these two variables were found to significantly affect the relationship between own willingness to engage in contact and the (absence of) discrimination.

German majority sample 1. Further pursuing the idea that a positive self-image promotes positive attitudes towards migrants among the German majority sample 1, we investigated the correlations between the integration, separation and assimilation expectations (that is, the acculturation expectations from Germans towards migrants) and the stereotypes used earlier with the difference that the stereotypes refer to the own in-group (auto-stereotypes). Interestingly, an integration orientation was positively associated with coldness auto-stereotypes ($r[458] = .16, p < .001$) and negatively with warmth ($r[459] = -.15, p < .001$) and competence stereotypes ($r[459] = -.09, p < .05$). This means that the more Germans expect migrants to be doubly engaged in German society and their heritage culture, the more pronounced was their coldness auto-stereotype, and the less pronounced were the warmth and competence auto-stereotypes about Germans. A separation/segregation expectation was positively associated with coldness ($r[458] = .16, p < .001$) and competence auto-stereotypes ($r[459] = .13, p < .01$). In other words, the more Germans expect migrants to keep to their own culture, the more pronounced the coldness and competence stereotypes about Germans. An assimilation / melting pot expectation was positively associated with warmth ($r[459] = .15$, p $< .001$) and competence stereotypes ($r[459] = .29$, p $< .001$). The more Germans expect migrants to assimilate into German society, the more pronounced the warmth and competence auto-stereotypes. This is an interesting finding, since it suggests that feeling good about your own group by holding warmth and competence stereotypes is actually associated with the expectation that the minority should assimilate while having an integration orientation. Instead, migrants are expected to engage in both host and home culture, when Germans perceive their own group as colder, less warm and less competent. Thus, if Germans feel good about themselves by perceiving the typical German as warm and competent, the less there is an expectation that migrants should integrate and the higher the expectation that migrants should assimilate. This reflects Baumeister's and colleagues' (1996) review about the danger of high self-esteem.

5.3   The Integration Hypothesis

We used multiple hierarchical regressions analysis again and tested the integration hypothesis in the different samples. Specifically, we tested whether an integration orientation and the feeling of belonging and to be accepted, predict flourishing and sociocultural competence in the ethnic sample as well as in the bicultural sample.

Ethnic Sample

We conducted a multiple hierarchical regression model with *flourishing* as the dependent variable, age, and gender (Block 1) as our control variables, integration operationalized as integration orientation (Block 2) and general belongingness (Block 3) as the predictors. Age and gender were not significant. Integration orientation was significant and explained 26 per cent of unique variance in flourishing ($\beta = .52, p < .001; \Delta R^2 = .26$). Belongingness was also significant and explained 10 per cent of the additional variance ($\beta = .33, p < .001$). The integration orientation was still significant but dropped ($\beta = .45, p < .001$) after belongingness was added. The whole model explained 39 per cent of the variance.

The second multiple hierarchical regression model with *sociocultural competence* as the dependent variable made use of the same predictors. Age and gender in Block 1 were not significant. Block 2 with integration orientation was significant and explained 13 per cent of unique variance in sociocultural competence ($\beta = .36, p < .001; \Delta R^2 = .13$). Belongingness explained an additional 19 per cent of the variance (β = .45, p < .001, ΔR^2 = .19). The integration orientation was still significant but dropped (β = .26, p < .05) after belongingness was added. The overall model explained 35 per cent of the variance.

Bicultural Sample

To examine *flourishing*, we entered age and gender again in the first block, integration orientation in Block 2 and general belongingness in Block 3. The dependent variable was flourishing. An integration orientation significantly predicted flourishing (β = .28, p < .001; ΔR^2 = .08) and explained 8 per cent of additional variance in flourishing. However, when the feeling to belong (β = .62, p < .001; ΔR^2 = .36) was added to the regression it explained an additional 36 per cent of the variance in flourishing. The integration orientation was still significant but dropped (β = .15, p < .05) after belongingness was added. The whole model explained 43 per cent of the variance.

In another multiple hierarchical regression model, we used *sociocultural competence* as a dependent variable. In Block 1, we controlled for age and gender, which were not significant. In Block 2, we added integration orientation and in Block 3 again general belongingness. Integration orientation was a significant predictor (β = .24, p < .01; ΔR^2 = .06) and explained 6 per cent of the variance in our dependent variable. General belongingness was also significant (β = .37, p < .001; ΔR^2 = .13) and explained 13 per cent of unique additional variance in sociocultural competence. The integration orientation was still significant but dropped (β = .16, p < .05) after belongingness was added. The whole model explained 21 per cent of the variance.

German-Greek Sample. A multiple hierarchical regression analysis was conducted with subjective well-being as the dependent variable. Age and gender were included in Block 1. The two acculturation dimensions of cultural maintenance and contact with Germans were entered as predictors in Block 2, and German language fluency was included in Block 3 for exploratory purposes. Neither age nor gender was significantly related to well-being. The inclusion of the two acculturation dimensions significantly improved the amount of explained variance of the model, with (ΔR^2 = .02). A closer inspection of the regression weights revealed that only *contact with Germans* formed a significant predictor of well-being (β = .11, p < .05), but not *cultural maintenance* (β = .08, p > .05). The inclusion of German fluency, however, further significantly improved the prediction of well-being with ΔR^2 = .02. The inclusion of this variable in Block 3 (β = .13, p < .05) even eliminates the effect of contact with Germans. In total, however, the model still explains a mere 4.4 per cent of the variance. The same model was run with the dependent variable of life satisfaction, but no significant effects were found.

6   Discussion

Overall, a substantial amount of the obtained German results support the three MIRIPS hypotheses. Despite a relatively low level of explained variance in some of the models, there is evidence that the core principles of security, contact and integration are indeed associated with positive outcomes for both migrants and majority members in the German context, but that other variables may also play an important role.

For the multiculturalism hypothesis, the feeling of being secure in one's own country predicted more sympathy towards out-groups in majority sample 1. However, for the majority sample 2, it is interesting to note the relatively strong negative effect of identification with the nation state. In the original formulation of the multiculturalism hypothesis (Berry et al., 1977), it was emphasized that feeling confident or secure in one's place in society was not the same as having a strong national identity or a high positive own-group evaluation. Indeed, we find that a sense of security and identification with the nation show highly diverse relationships with tolerance. The negative relationship between national identity and the acceptance of others is consistent with ethnocentrism theory and empirical findings (LeVine & Campbell, 1972). In other more recent research, national identity was related to negative attitudes towards asylum seekers among individuals with an essentialist conception of their group as well (Pehrson, Brown & Zagefka, 2009).

The relationship between national identity and tolerance towards or rejection of other groups is complex. When studying the relationship between national identification and prejudice, it seems crucial to take into account the nature of national identity.

It could be argued that in Germany, the view of national identity as an overarching mutual identity for all citizens is not appropriate. In some settler societies (e.g., USA: "E pluribus unum") or in some highly diverse societies (e.g., Indonesia: Bhinneka Tunggal Ika, translated as "Unity in Diversity"; Suparlan, 2003) is likely to backfire in the German context. One may, however, also want to discuss to what extent the "nation" as an object of identification is a historically outdated exclusionist concept, even beyond the specific German context. The current populist waves that rock many European countries (but also in the UK and the United States) might suggest that the nation (and the identification with it) is less a safe haven, but rather a concept mainly meant to keep "the other" out. Our results undoubtedly suggest that policies that aim to enhance levels of individual life satisfaction are more likely to achieve the desired results for tolerance than forging increased identification with geopolitical entities.

Our analyses were only able to provide a limited assessment of the contact hypothesis that asks *when* contact is associated with positive out-group perceptions. We found that when the need to relate to Germans is fulfilled for the migrants, the migrants endorsed less negative stereotypes and more positive stereotypes about Germans. It is also possible to argue in the other direction: if migrants hold more positive stereotypes of Germans, the motivation to fulfil the need of feeling connected to Germans is satisfied. Since we have cross-sectional data, we cannot draw causal conclusions. However, we find the first-mentioned direction to be more in line with related research that has found that a negative intergroup climate is related to a stronger desire for cultural maintenance among migrant samples in Germany (Christ, Asbrock, Dhont, Pettigrew & Wagner, 2013).

Furthermore, there was an interesting pattern for the German data regarding the relationship between acculturation expectations and stereotypes about Germans (also see Hanke, van Egmond & Rohmann, 2016). The patterns could be interpreted as follows: Germans who feel good about themselves, expressed by the positive stereotypes they hold about their own in-group, are more inclined to expect migrants to assimilate towards the typical German person (i.e., to be like us); and those who do not feel positively about Germans and hold more negative auto-stereotypes are more prone to expect migrants to integrate (i.e., to expect them to develop a German identity that is enriched by their own cultural background). This pattern could be interpreted as a superiority complex (Hoorens, 1995): due to the dark past of Germans, there is a hidden inferiority complex which may play out overtly as a superiority complex. This means that Germans who endorse positive stereotypes about themselves feel that they are on the moral high ground, which justifies the belief that it is desirable to be like Germans. People who overtly acknowledge the problematic sides of holding a German national identity may, on the other hand, believe that it is not appropriate to force people from different origins to be like Germans. Further research will need to investigate the underlying psychological processes that shape these dynamics. The significant moderation that was found for the acculturation expectations of the majority from the migrant perspective, points to the need for the receiving society to create a positive context of reception. It highlights the truly *mutual* nature of intercultural relations.

Regarding the integration hypothesis (the positive effect of a double engagement with both the culture of origin and host country), our results confirm that desiring contact with the host country culture is indeed associated with higher levels of well-being. In the interpretation of these results, however, it should be considered that the Greek sample for which these analyses were conducted are reported to be relatively highly integrated and assimilated into German society in general. This community is also not at the heart of the heated multiculturalism discussion that is taking place in public discourse at the moment, nor is it exposed to high levels of assimilation expectations, xenophobia or discrimination.

It is, therefore, reasonable to assume that this result might not replicate to migrants with a Muslim background. The potential policy implications of the relatively strong effect of language fluency that is found for well-being, which eliminates the effect of mere contact are important to note as well. For the recently arrived group of refugees, the requirement to learn German is stated in the first sentence of the Integration Information website of the Federal Office for Migration and Refugees, and is explicitly set as the first condition for formal integration (Bundesamt für Migration und Flüchtlinge, 2016). In light of the finding for the Greek sample, one might also speculate that time since the initial migration move could be a moderator. Clearly, for new arrivals double engagement is best for well-being; however, later for the second and third generation, both double engagement (integration) and assimilation may offer greater well-being After four and more generations, it might predominantly be assimilation that promises well-being, and upholding double engagement might even become a source of ill-being. How long one should preserve one's roots is an open question. Furthermore, it is particularly striking that a general sense of belonging and feeling accepted is associated with a higher level of socio-cultural competence and more success in life. If belonging is interpreted as an indication of a secure sense of one's place in society, there is clear evidence to suggest that, as hypothesized, such a feeling is important for the positive psychological development of migrants.

Although Germany faces large challenges, the current results are promising in the sense that the mechanisms that are hypothesized to facilitate the development of positive intercultural relations are likely to function as expected in the German context. Our results do speak in favor of an inclusion of the psychological domain in the design of integration policies so that dimensions such as belongingness and security are taken into consideration, over and above mere formal integration (e.g., employment or school success).

Since our studies do not have representative samples or longitudinal data, the generalizability of our findings is limited, as well as the extent to which causal claims can be made. The way certain constructs were assessed could be improved as well in future research, such as a more sensitive measure of German national identity. Nonetheless, our findings are in line with contemporary acculturation research in both the German and international context, which is impressive given the diverse samples that were included and different instruments that were employed, both in the German studies and in the international literature on acculturation and intercultural relations.

In conclusion, we would like to highlight the need to study acculturation as a dynamic process in its broader ecological context in the future (Demes & Geeraert, 2014; Ward & Geeraert, 2016). A deeper knowledge about the role of familial, institutional and societal contexts for acculturation processes will be particularly valuable to inform adequate integration policies.

Acknowledgment

This research was partly supported by the Marie Curie Career Integration Grant (CIG) by the European Commission (FP7-PEOPLE-2012-CIG-321963) awarded to the first author. Klaus Boehnke's contribution to this chapter was in part prepared within the framework of the Basic Research Program at the National Research University Higher School of Economics (HSE) and supported within the framework of a subsidy granted to the HSE by the Government of the Russian Federation for the implementation of the Global Competitiveness Program. We would also like to acknowledge the contribution of Mesut Celenk, Slieman Halabi, Andrea Seekatz and Jannis Salapatas, who were responsible for data collection.

References

Asbrock, F., Lemmer, G., Becker, J. C., Koller, J., & Wagner, U. (2014). "Who are these foreigners anyway?" The content of the term foreigner and its impact on prejudice. *Sage Open, 4* (2). doi: 2158244014532819.

Auswärtiges Amt. (2015). *Staatsangehörigkeitsrecht* [Citizenship law]. Retrieved from: www.auswaertiges-amt.de/DE/EinreiseUndAufenthalt/Staatsangehoeri gkeitsrecht_node.html.

Baumeister, R., Smart, L., & Boden, J. (1996). Relation of threatened egotism to violence and aggression: The dark side of high self-esteem. *Psychological Review, 103,* 5–33. http://dx.doi.org/10.1037/0033-295X.103.1.5.

Berry, J.W., Kalin, R., & Taylor, D.M. (1977). *Multiculturalism and Ethnic Attitudes in Canada.* Ottawa: Ministry of Supply and Services.

Berry, J. W., Phinney, J. S., Sam, D., & Vedder, P. (2006). *Immigrant Youth in Cultural Transition: Acculturation, Identity and Adaptation Across National Contexts.* Mahwah, NJ: Erlbaum.

Böttinger, H. (2005). *Migration in Deutschland. Analysen und Perspektiven* [Migration in Germany. Analyses and perspectives]. Göttingen: Sierke.

Boehnke, M., Deutsch, F., & Boehnke, K. (2016). ‚Open House' oder ‚Closed Shop': Einwanderung nach Deutschland als Zielkonflikt mit Gewaltpotenzial? ['Open house' or 'closed shop': Immigration to Germany as a conflict of objectives with the potential for violence?]. In M. Johannsen, B. Schoch, M. M. Mutschler, C. Hauswedell & J. Hippler (Eds.), *Friedensgutachten 2016* (pp. 166–180). Berlin: LIT Verlag.

Borgmann, C. H. (2005). *Social Security, Demographics, and Risk*. Berlin: Springer.

Brückner, G. (2014, March 7). *Ausländerzahl in Deutschland 2013 auf Rekordniveau* [Number of foreigners in Germany in 2013 at a record level]. Retrieved from www.destatis.de/DE/PresseService/Presse/Pressemitteilungen/2014/03/P D14_081_12521.html.

Bundesamt für Migration und Flüchtlinge (2016). *Welcome to Germany*. Retrieved from www.bamf.de/EN/Willkommen/willkommen-node.html.

Bundesregierung (2014) *Datenblatt zum 7. Integrationsgipfel* [Specifications of the 7th Integration Summit]. https://www.bundesregierung.de/Content/DE/Artik el/IB/Artikel/Integrationsgipfel/2014-11-28-Datenblatt.html.

Christ, O., Asbrock, F., Dhont, K., Pettigrew, T. F., & Wagner, U. (2013). The effects of intergroup climate on immigrants' acculturation preferences. *Zeitschrift für Psychologie, 221* (4), 252–257. doi: 10.1027/2151-2604/a000155.

Christ, O., Schmid, K., Lolliot, S., Swart, H., Stolle, D., Tausch, N., Al Ramiah, A., Wagner, U., Vertovec, S., & Hewstone, M. (2014). Contextual effect of positive intergroup contact on outgroup prejudice. *Proceedings of the National Academy of Sciences, 111*, 3996–4000. doi: 10.1073/pnas.1320901111.

Cuddy, A. J. C., Fiske, S. T., & Glick, P. (2007). The BIAS map: Behaviors from intergroup affect and stereotypes. *Journal of Personality and Social Psychology, 92* (4), 631–648. doi: http://dx.doi.org/10.1037/0022-3514.92.4.631.

Das Gupta, O. (2010, May 17). Süssmuth-Interview "Wir brauchen eine Leitkultur des Zusammenlebens" [Süssmuth interview: "We need a primary culture for co-existence"]. Retrieved from: www.sueddeutsche.de/politik/suess muth-interview-wir-brauchen-eine-leitkultur-des-zusammenlebens-1.316671.

Demes, K. A., & Geeraert, N. (2014). Measures matter scales for adaptation, cultural distance, and acculturation orientation revisited. *Journal of Cross-Cultural Psychology, 45*(1), 91–109. doi:10.1177/0022022113487590.

Diener, E., Wirtz, D., Tov, W., Kim-Prieto, C., Choi, D., Oishi, S., & Biswas-Diener, R. (2009). New measures of well-being: Flourishing and positive and negative feelings. *Social Indicators Research, 39*, 247–266. doi:10.1007/s11205-009-9493-y.

Fekete, L. (2009). *A Suitable Enemy: Racism, Migration and Islamophobia in Europe*. London: Pluto Press.

Frindte, W., Boehnke, K., Kreikenbohm, H., & Wagner, W. (2012). *Lebenswelten junger Muslime in Deutschland*. Berlin: Bundesministerium des Innern. [Life worlds of young Muslims].

Haenni Hoti, A., Heinzmann, S., Müller, M., & Buholzer, A. (2017). Psychosocial adaptation and school success of Italian, Portuguese and Albanian students in Switzerland: Disentangling migration background, acculturation and the school context. *Journal of International Migration and Integration, 18* (1), 85–106. doi: 10.1007/s12134-015-0461-x.

Hafez, K., & Schmidt, S. (2015). *Die Wahrnehmung des Islams in Deutschland* [The perception of Islam in Germany]. Gütersloh: Bertelsmann Stiftung.

Hagendoorn, L. (1995). Intergroup biases in multiple group system: The perception of ethnic hierarchies. In W. Stroebe & M. Hewstone (Eds.), *European Review of Social Psychology* (pp. 199–228). Chichester, UK: Wiley.

Hanke, K., van Egmond, M.C., & Rohmann, A. (2016). *Acculturation and Wellbeing among German Migrants*. Manuscript in preparation.

Hoorens, V. (1995). Self-favoring biases, self-presentation, and the self-other asymmetry in social comparisons. *Journal of Personality, 63*, 793–817. doi: 10.1111/j.1467-6494.1995.tb00317.x.

Jackson, K., & Debroux, P. (2016). HRM responses to ageing societies in Germany and Japan: Contexts for comparison. *Management Revue.* 27(1–2), 5–13. doi: 10.1688/mrev-2016-Introduction.

Kunst, J. R., Tajamal, H., Sam, D. L., & Ulleberg, P. (2012). Coping with Islamophobia: The effects of religious stigma on Muslim minorities' identity formation. *International Journal of Intercultural Relations, 36*, 518–532. http://dx.doi.org/10.1016/j.ijintrel.2011.12.014.

La Guardia, J. G., Ryan, R. M., Couchman, C. E., & Deci, E. L. (2000). Within-person variation in security of attachment: A self-determination theory perspective on attachment, need fulfillment, and well-being. *Journal of Personality and Social Psychology, 79* (3), 367–384. doi: http://dx.doi.org/10.1037/0022-3514.79.3.367.

LeVine, R. A., & Campbell, D. T. (1972). *Ethnocentrism: Theories of Conflict, Ethnic Attitudes, and Group Behavior*. New York: Wiley.

Lyons-Padilla, S., Gelfand, Mirahmadi, H., Farooq, M., & van Egmond, M. (2015). Belonging nowhere: Marginalization & radicalization risk among Muslim immigrants. *Behavioral Science & Policy, 1* (2), 1–12. https://behavioralpolicy.org/article/belonging-nowhere-marginalization-radicalization-risk-among-muslim-immigrants/.

Marques, J., Vincze, O., Garate, J. F. V., & Rovira, D. P. (2006). Dealing with collective shame and guilt. *Psicologia Politica, 32*, 59–78.

Modood, T., Triandafyllidou, A., & Zapata-Barrreo, R. (2006). European challenges to multicultural citizenship: Muslims, secularism and beyond. In T. Modood, A. Triandafyllidou, R. Zapata-Barrreo (Eds.), *Multiculturalism, Muslims and Citizenship. A European Approach* (pp. 37–56), London & New York: Routledge.

Mühe, N. (2016). Managing the stigma: Islamophobia in German schools. *Insight Turkey, 18* (1), 77–95.

Pehrson, S., Brown, R., & Zagefka, H. (2009). When does national identification lead to the rejection of immigrants? Cross-sectional and longitudinal evidence for the role of essentialist in-group definitions. *British Journal of Social Psychology, 48*, 61–76. doi: 10.1348/014466608X288827.

Rohmann, A., Florack, A., & Piontkowski, U. (2006). The role of discordant acculturation attitudes in perceived threat: An analysis of host and immigrant attitudes in Germany. *International Journal of Intercultural Relations, 30*, 683–702. http://dx.doi.org/10.1016/j.ijintrel.2006.06.006.

Rohmann, A., Piontkowski, U., & van Randenborgh, A. (2008). When attitudes do not fit: Discordance of acculturation attitudes as an antecedent of intergroup threat. *Personality and Social Psychology Bulletin, 34,* 337–352. doi: 10.1177/ 0146167207311197.

Saeed, A. (2007). Media, racism and Islamophobia: The representation of Islam and Muslims in the media. *Sociology Compass, 1* (2), 443–462. doi:10.1111/j. 1751-9020.2007.00039.x.

Simon, B., Reichert, F., & Grabow, O. (2013). When dual identity becomes a liability: Identity and political radicalism among migrants. *Psychological Science, 24* (3), 251–257. doi: https://doi.org/10.1177/0956797612450889.

Schmitt-Rodermund, E., & Silbereisen, R. K. (2008). Well-adapted adolescent ethnic German immigrants in spite of adversity – The protective effects of human, social, and financial capital. *European Journal of Developmental Psychology, 5,* 186–20. http://dx.doi.org/10.1080/17405620701557290.

Statistisches Bundesamt (2012). Ausländische Bevölkerung – Fachserie 1 Reihe 2 – 2011, Wiesbaden. Suparlan, P. (2003). Bhinneka Tunggal Ika: Keanekaragaman Sukubangsa atau Kebudayaan? [Unity in diversity: Ethnic or cultural diversity]. *Antropologi Indonesia, 72,* 24.

Taras, R. (2012). *Xenophobia and Islamophobia in Europe.* Edinburgh: Edinburgh University Press.

Owers, D. (2015). From immigrants to fundamentalists: Changing portrayals of Muslim identities in Europe (No. 52/2015). Working Paper, Institute for International Political Economy Berlin.

Pfafferott, I., & Brown, R. (2006). Acculturation preferences of majority and minority adolescents in Germany in the context of society and family. *International Journal of Intercultural Relations, 30,* 703–717. http://dx.doi.org/10 .1016/j.ijintrel.2006.03.005.

Van der Noll, J. (2014). Religious toleration of Muslims in the German public sphere. *International Journal of Intercultural Relations, 38,* 60–74. http://dx.doi .org/10.1016/j.ijintrel.2013.01.001.

Ward, C., & Geeraert, N. (2016). Advancing acculturation theory and research: The acculturation process in its ecological context. *Current Opinion in Psychology, 8,* 98–104. http://dx.doi.org/10.1016/j.copsyc.2015.09.021.

Wydra, G. (2014). Der Fragebogen zum allgemeinen habituellen Wohlbefinden (FAHW und FAHW-12). Entwicklung und Evaluation eines mehrdimensionalen Fragebogens. Retrieved from: www.sportpaedagogik-sb.de/pdf/FAHW-Manual.pdf.

Yükleyen, A. (2011). *Localizing Islam in Europe: Turkish Islamic Communities in Germany and the Netherlands.* New York: Syracuse University Press.

Zagefka, H., & Brown, R. (2002). The relationship between acculturation strategies, relative fit and intergroup relations: Immigrant-majority relations in Germany. *European Journal of Social Psychology, 32*(2), 171–188. doi: 10.1002/ejsp.73.

Zagefka, H., Tip, L. K., González, R., Brown, R., & Cinnirella, M. (2012). Predictors of majority members' acculturation preferences: Experimental evidence. *Journal of Experimental Social Psychology, 48* (3), 654–659. doi: https:// doi.org/10.1016/j.jesp.2011.12.006.

Zick, A., Wagner, U., van Dick, R., & Petzel, T. (2001). Acculturation and prejudice in Germany: Majority and minority perspectives. *Journal of Social Issues, 57,* 541–55. doi: 10.1111/0022-4537.00228.

8   Intercultural Relations in Switzerland

Andrea Haenni Hoti[1]*, Sybille Heinzmann*[2]*, Marianne Müller*[1, 3, 4]*, Alois Buholzer*[1] *and Roland Künzle*[1]

1 *University of Teacher Education, Lucerne, Switzerland*
2 *University of Teacher Education, St. Gallen, Switzerland*
3 *Zurich University of Applied Sciences, Switzerland*
4 *Swiss Federal Institute of Technology Switzerland*

1   Introduction

Switzerland is one of the most diverse societies in the world, ranking near the top of the diversity index.[1] With approximately 24 per cent of foreign residents it is one of the countries with the highest share of foreign residents in the European context (OECD, 2014). However, it only ranks in the middle of the integration index and near the bottom on the multicultural policy index. Given this imbalance, Switzerland is a particularly interesting setting to examine the integration hypothesis. The Swiss study focuses on immigrant youth with Italian, Portuguese and Albanian backgrounds.

2   Context of the Study

2.1   Demography and History

Of the foreign resident population, 294,359 are Italian and 238,432 Portuguese. Since the Albanian population in Switzerland stems from different countries of origin[2], their numbers are more difficult to estimate on the basis of these statistics: 79,437 have a Kosovan, 61,631 a Macedonian and 1,132 an Albanian nationality (Bundesamt für Statistik, 2013a).

Of the three groups surveyed in this study, the Italians have the longest tradition of immigration into Switzerland: After the Second World War, Italians were recruited as temporary guest workers in order to satisfy the

---

[1] This contribution is a revised and shortened version of a journal article: see Haenni Hoti, Heinzmann, Müller & Buholzer, 2015.
[2] Kosovo, Macedonia, Albania, Serbia, Montenegro.

demand for labour in Switzerland (FIMM, 2011, p. 2). During the depression in the 1970s, the work permits of many of these guest workers were no longer renewed so that they could no longer stay in Switzerland. After the recovery of the economy, labour was once again intensively recruited up until the 1990s, this time predominantly from former Yugoslavia and Portugal (Fibbi et al., 2010, p. 19). The immigrants from former Yugoslavia were to a large extent Albanians from Kosovo and Macedonia (Burri Sharani et al., 2010). During the Balkan Wars in the 1990s, the immigration from this area changed. More and more people came to Switzerland (in particular from Bosnia-Herzegovina and Kosovo) because they were fleeing from displacement and genocide (von Aarburg & Gretler, 2008, p. 5). At the same time Switzerland tightened its immigration policy. This largely prevented (Kosovo-) Albanians from immigrating as working migrants. In addition, they were confronted with an increasingly restrictive asylum policy. In contrast, immigrants from the EU (such as Italians or Portuguese) could basically work and reside in Switzerland and bring their family members to Switzerland thanks to agreements with the EU enabling the free movement of persons. Such a categorization of people into 'wanted' and 'unwanted' with its legal inequality of treatment and discrimination were criticized by the Swiss Commission against Racism among others (Eidgenössische Kommission gegen Rassismus, 1996). Consequently, Italian, Portuguese and Albanian immigrants are confronted with different historical, economic, political and legal conditions in Switzerland. In particular, Portuguese immigrants, the group with the youngest history of immigration into Switzerland, find comparatively favourable conditions in Switzerland thanks to the agreement with the EU enabling the free movement of persons and the good economic situation in Switzerland (Fibbi et al., 2010, p. 20).

2.2   *Educational Opportunities of Italian, Portuguese and Albanian Migrants in Switzerland*

There are several differences between adolescents with an Italian, Portuguese and Albanian migration background with regard to their educational situation in Switzerland: Adolescents with an Italian migration background are usually second- or even third-generation immigrants who have established themselves in Switzerland and are socially accepted (Bolzmann, Fibbi & Vial, 2003, p. 210). Compared to the other two groups, there are also more Italian students attending the more demanding school type in secondary school, which prepares for grammar school (Bundesamt für Statistik, 2013b). In contrast, it is particularly Albanian students (included in the category 'former Yugoslavia') who can be more commonly found in school types with basic exigencies (54%) compared to Portuguese (42%) and Italian students (37%). Of the special needs students, 12 per cent are from former Yugoslavia, 7 per cent are Portuguese and 4 per cent are Italians. Albanian adolescents, who are also mostly born in Switzerland, are more commonly affected by negative prejudices against their ethnic group and by discrimination on the apprenticeship market, particularly if they are male (Imdorf, 2008). There are, consequently, significant differences between the three groups studied in terms of their educational opportunities and career perspectives.

Based on these official statistics and migration studies, we expected that the migration background of the students would have an impact on their psychosocial adaptation such as life satisfaction and on their educational success in terms of educational aspirations and reading skills in the local language of instruction (German). In other words, we expected to find group differences, with Italians showing the highest and Albanians showing the lowest values on these target variables with Portuguese lying in between. In addition, the Swiss study in the MIRIPS project focused on testing the integration hypothesis, according to which the acculturation strategy of integration among migrants is associated with a better psychosocial adaptation[3] and higher school success[4] in the receiving country than assimilation, separation or marginalization (see introduction of this book).

3   Research on the Integration Hypothesis in Education

Some studies have examined the relationship between acculturation strategies and school outcomes. In a Swedish study with young grown-up migrants, it was found that the integration strategy is most effective for educational success in Sweden (Nekby, Rödin & Özcan, 2007). However, Makarova and Birman (2015, p.16) conclude from their content analysis of 29 studies that the positive impact of integration on the academic achievement of migrant students is not entirely clear and that its effectiveness depends on a diversity-friendly school context.

With respect to a minority orientation ('separation') research results are inconsistent, with negative and no effects being found in some studies (Makarova & Birman, 2015). There are also studies, however, that point to the advantages of a minority orientation in relation to educational success in the receiving country (see Gibson, 1988; Suinn,

---

[3] In the Swiss MIRIPS study, psychosocial adaptation encompasses life satisfaction, self-efficacy beliefs and sociocultural competence.
[4] School success was measured by means of the following indicators: school satisfaction, educational aspirations and German reading skills.

2010 for studies among Asian-Americans). It seems to be beneficial for school success if the keeping of one's own traditional lifestyle within the family is combined with a belief in the chances of school success and economic possibilities in the receiving country. In a study by Stuart, Ward and Adam (2010) with Muslim youth in New Zealand, a minority orientation also constituted an important resource for psychological and educational adaptation.

There are also studies where a strong majority orientation ('assimilation') turned out to be more favourable than integration (or at least equally favourable) for psychosocial adaptation or school success (Baysu, Phalet & Brown, 2011; Oh, Koeske & Sales, 2002; Trickett & Birman, 2005). In the study by Baysu et al. (2011) with Turkish Belgian young adults, the assimilation strategy was associated with higher school success, whereas the effectiveness of the separation strategy and the integration strategy depended on school contextual factors such as experienced discrimination and perceived identity threat. The authors concluded that in an assimilationist school environment the assimilation strategy may facilitate school adaptation and educational success of migrants by fulfilling the norms of the dominant culture.

There are also studies which point to the need to examine the acculturation strategies of groups with different migration backgrounds within the same national context (Andriessen & Phalet, 2002; Motti-Stefanidi, Pavlopoulos, Obradovic & Masten, 2008). In the Greek study of Motti-Stefanidi et al., migrant students from the former Soviet Union had a stronger minority and a lower majority orientation than did Albanian students. Nonetheless both migrant groups experienced similar difficulties in school adjustment. In the Dutch study by Andriessen and Phalet (2002), there was a positive relationship between an open attitude towards intercultural contact (e.g., assimilation at school) and school adaptation among adolescents of Moroccan origin whereas for the Turkish adolescents integration and a minority orientation ('separation') turned out to be more beneficial.

The Swiss MIRIPS study aims to answer the following research questions:

1. What influence do different acculturation strategies of migrant adolescents exert on their psychosocial adaptation and school success? Based on the integration hypothesis, we assume that integration is beneficial for the psychosocial adaptation and for school success.
2. What influence does the migration background of the adolescents exert on their psychosocial adaptation and school success? The assumption is that students with an Italian migration background will exhibit a better psychosocial adaptation and a higher educational success than students

with a Portuguese background. Both of these groups will exhibit a better psychosocial adaptation and a higher educational success than students with an Albanian migration background.

4   Method

4.1   Samples

The Swiss MIRIPS-study was carried out in urban areas of German-speaking Switzerland. The convenience sample consisted of 90 culturally heterogeneous school classes with at least 30 per cent of students classified as foreigners. In total there were 1526 8th grade students aged between 12 and 18 years (14.4 years on average). Forty-nine percent were girls and 51 per cent boys. Twenty-four percent of the respondents attended a school type with higher exigencies (type A), 41 per cent attended a school type with medium exigencies (type B) and 28 per cent attended a school type with basic exigencies (type C). Another 6 per cent attended a secondary school with general exigencies in the city of Basel. In order to be able to compare Italians, Portuguese and Albanians with respect to the relationship between acculturation strategies, psychosocial adaptation and school success, school classes comprising several students with an Italian (n=161), Portuguese (n=106) and/or Albanian (n=295) migration background were preferably recruited. As far as their nationality is concerned, 37 per cent of the participants were Swiss, 26 per cent were dual citizens and 37 per cent had a foreign citizenship. The vast majority of the participating adolescents (81%) were born in Switzerland.

4.2   Instruments

The instruments for the data collection consisted of an online questionnaire and a German reading test for the students and an online questionnaire for their class teacher. Besides demographic information, the questionnaire for the students contained scales from the MIRIPS project. These instruments were adapted for the Swiss context and the language competencies of the participants.

4.2.1   Scales in the Student Questionnaire
Acculturation Strategies: The two-scale approach (measuring minority and majority orientation) was used as a starting point for the generation of the *acculturation scales* (Donà & Berry, 1994). This approach was complemented with a third orientation, called the 'multicultural orientation' (see Table 8.1). The adolescents were asked about their attitudes and

behaviours with regard to different domains (traditions, language acquisition, choice of friends and partner, food and music), about their well-being among people of the same/ of a different/ of many different nationalities, and about their interest in events of their country of residence/ country of heritage/ worldwide (sports, politics, economy, etc.). They could respond to the questions on a 5-point scale ranging from 'not at all true' to 'totally true'. Because of two different perspectives (majority versus minority), separate factor analyses were carried out for Swiss adolescents and adolescents belonging to 'another national group'. Consequently, two Cronbach Alpha values are provided for the acculturation scales. Out of the 3-factor solution for the Swiss (total variance explained: 42.3%) and the 4-factor solution for the non-Swiss (total variance explained: 46.5%), the two scales 'majority orientation' and 'multicultural orientation' could be generated with corresponding items. The scale 'minority orientation' was generated for the non-Swiss only.

Out of the 27 items in the questionnaire focusing on acculturation strategies, 16 items were used to generate the three acculturation scales. The 'majority-orientation' (assimilation) scale is characterized by a wish on the part of the adolescents for cultural adaptation of immigrants to the local mainstream culture of German-speaking Switzerland (five items, $\alpha=.51$[5] for non-Swiss/.66 for Swiss, sample item: *"Portuguese should adapt to the traditions of the Swiss"* [version for Portuguese students]). The 'multicultural-orientation' scale points to an openness towards and an interest in different cultures on the part of the respondents (five items, $\alpha=.60$ for non-Swiss/.68 for Swiss, sample item: *"As an Italian I feel at ease among people from many different countries"* [version for Italian students]). The 'minority-orientation' (separation) scale is characterized by an orientation of the adolescents towards their heritage culture (or the heritage culture of their parents) (six items, $\alpha=.72$ for non-Swiss only, sample item: *"As an Albanian I feel at ease among Albanians"* [version for Albanian students]) (see Table 8.1).

Psycho-social adaptation: For the assessment of the psychological adaptation of the adolescents, the MIRIPS instruments were used. The two subscales 'life satisfaction' (six items, $\alpha=.87$) and 'self-doubts and fear of failure' (six items, $\alpha=.85$) were complemented with a scale on self-efficacy beliefs from the LiMA[6] project (eight items, $\alpha=.91$). This latter is based on the 'general self-efficacy' instrument of Schwarzer and Jerusalem

[5] The low Cronbach alpha can be explained by the large array of topics covered by the acculturation scale and the relatively few items.
[6] Linguistic Diversity Management in Urban Areas: http://wissenschaft.hamburg.de/exzellenz-wissenschaft/1791744/lexc-14-09-linguistic-diversity-management-in-urban-areas/ .

(1999). Sociocultural competence was assessed by means of an adapted scale by Ward and Kennedy (1999) (fourteen items, α=.89).

Table 8.1 provides an overview of the scales derived from the student questionnaire and their psychometric properties.

Table 8.1. *Scales in the student questionnaire and their psychometric properties.*

Scales (Number of Items)	Original Source	Cron-bach Alpha	Total Variance Explained
Acculturation strategy "majority orientation" (assimilation) (5)	Donà & Berry (1994)	.51 /.66	–
Acculturation strategy "minority orientation" (separation) (6)		.72	
Acculturation strategy "multicultural orientation" (5)	Haenni Hoti et al. (2013)	.60 /.68	
Life satisfaction (6)	Diener, Emmos, Larsen &	.87	
Self-doubts and fear of failure (6)	Griffin (1985); Rosenberg (1965)	.85	60.1%
Self-efficacy beliefs (8)	Schwarzer & Jerusalem (1999)	.91	61.5%
Sociocultural competence (14)	Ward & Kennedy (1999)	.89	43.1%
Subjective feelings of security[7] (6)	Berry, Kalin & Taylor (1977)	–	–
School satisfaction (7)	QUASSU[8] (2001) Zentrum Schulent wicklung (2004)	.73	38.6%
Quality of teacher-student relationship: respect (6)	Zentrum Schulent wicklung (2004)	.76	54.7%
Quality of teacher-student relationship: equity (7)	Abs, Diedrich, Sickmann & Klieme (2007)[9]	.94	
Quality of student-student relationship: solidarity (5)	QUASSU (2001)	.78	58.6%
Quality of student-student relationship: equity (7)	Abs et al. (2007)	.94	
Adapted teaching methods to students' needs (7)	QUASSU (2001)	.85	44.2%
Achievement expectations of the teachers (4)	Abs et al. (2007)	.72	
Extent of multicultural education at school (8)	Haenni Hoti et al. (2013)	.87	53.6%
Perceived violence at school (9)	Abs et al. (2007)	.89	55.6%

[7] The Rasch Analysis yielded a person separation index of .62.
[8] DFG-project, Quality of school and teaching (Ditton & Merz, 2000).
[9] DIPF-project, Evaluation of the BLK-model program learning and living democracy.

Educational success: The first indicator for educational success was school satisfaction. The scale 'school satisfaction' was developed on the basis of instruments of the DFG-Projects "Quality of school and teaching" (Ditton & Merz, 2000) and the project "political orientations of students within the framework of recognition at school" (Zentrum für Schulentwicklung, 2004; seven items, $\alpha=.73$). Second, the students' educational aspirations were assessed by asking them what educational degree they are striving for.[10] The third indicator for educational success was the students' reading skills in German, the local language of instruction.

4.2.2   German Reading Test

The adolescents' German reading skills were assessed by means of reading tasks from the PISA studies 2000–2006 (OECD n.d.). The test consisted of a prose text ('Police'), on the one hand, and a non-continuous text based on pictures/graphs (working population) on the other hand. The following three reading processes were assessed: accessing information, interpreting a text and evaluating a text / thinking about a text. First, a Rasch scale was constructed from the tasks of the German reading test using the program RUMM 2030. Since the German reading tasks were not able to cover the whole spectrum of reading abilities among the students and since the preconditions for a regression would not have been met when using the Rasch scale, a sum score was used for the German reading skills.

4.3   Data Analysis

In a first step the data from the student questionnaire were analysed by means of factor analyses using SPSS version 19, and scales were created on this basis. Principal axis factoring was used as the extraction method, and Varimax and Oblim rotation was used. The scale for the construct 'security' was generated by means of Rasch analysis using the program RUMM 2030 (Andrich, Sheridan & Luo, 2010).

To examine the relationships between acculturation strategies of the adolescents on the one hand and their psychosocial adaptation and school success on the other hand, multilevel regression analyses were carried out.

In a first step the influence of socio-demographic variables, including the migration background and school-contextual variables, on the adolescents'

---

[10] The following answer categories were available: secondary school degree, 2-year apprenticeship, 3- or 4-year apprenticeship, 3- or 4-year apprenticeship with maturity, grammar school degree, university degree, none of these degrees.

subjective feeling of security was analysed, since the notion of security played a crucial role in the international MIRIPS project. In the next step, the influence of these variables on acculturation strategies was analysed. In the third step, the scales on psychosocial adaptation were used as response variables. As a fourth and last step, models were developed in which the different school success variables (school satisfaction, educational aspirations, German reading skills) served as response variables. All the other variables (socio-demographic variables, acculturation strategies, psychosocial adaptation, subjective feeling of security, school context) were taken into account as potential explanatory variables in these models. In these regression models, the predictors were examined including non-linear terms and interactions as well as potential random class effects. The variable selection was based on the Akaike information criterion (AIC). All regression analyses were carried out with the program R, version 2.14.0 (R Development Core Team, 2011).

5   Results

5.1   Influence of Acculturation Strategies on Life Satisfaction

The influence of acculturation strategies on the life satisfaction of adolescents with a migration background was analysed by means of a multiple regression analysis since there was no significant class effect. Rather than using the three single acculturation scales as potential explanatory variables, a categorization was used for this analysis. This categorization was carried out on the basis of the endorsement of the different acculturation strategies by the participants, including the endorsement of more than one acculturation strategy. Endorsement of a particular acculturation strategy was defined as a mean of ≥ 3 across all the items of the corresponding scale. This corresponds to an endorsement of the answer category 'true' or 'totally true' on average. The subsample used for this analysis consists of participants of all national groups except Swiss nationals. The assignment of the participants to a certain national group was based on their subjective feeling of group belonging. Table 8.2 displays the result of this analysis. The (bi-) national identification as Italian, Portuguese or Albanian did not have a significant impact on their life satisfaction. Of the demographic variables only gender played a significant role: boys have a higher life satisfaction than girls. Of the school-related factors, the quality of social relationships at school and the extent of multicultural education are positively related to the life satisfaction of adolescents with a migration background. The more respected and appreciated the adolescents feel by their teachers the higher their life

Table 8.2. *Results of the regression analysis on the life satisfaction of adolescents with a migration background.*

	Regression Coefficient	Standard Error	P-Value
(Intercept)[11]	1.52	0.28	<.000
Gender (male)[12]	0.54	0.10	<.000
Teacher-student-relationship: respect	0.33	0.10	0.001
Student-student-relationship: equity	0.28	0.09	0.002
Student-student-relationship: solidarity	0.29	0.10	0.003
Multicultural education at school	0.24	0.08	0.004
Feelings of security	0.71	0.09	<.000
Feelings of security ^2	−0.07	0.04	0.087
Multicultural orientation[13]	0.16	0.18	0.368
Minority orientation	0.59	0.17	0.000
Minority orientation–multicultural orientation	0.45	0.16	0.005
Majority orientation	0.09	0.45	0.832
Majority orientation–multicultural orientation	0.47	0.31	0.127
Majority orientation–minority orientation	0.34	0.32	0.297
Majority orientation–minority orientation–multicultural orientation	1.00	0.21	<.000

(n=1094; R^2=.23)

satisfaction is (see Table 8.2). Besides the teacher-student relationship, the student-student relationship is also important for the life satisfaction of the adolescents: The more the participants agree that all students in the class are treated equally irrespective of their cultural background or skin colour and the more they agree that the students in the class stick together, the higher their life satisfaction is. Furthermore, the life satisfaction of students with a migration background increases with the extent of multicultural education and the discussion of racial discrimination in the class. On top of this, the social context plays a role: There is a relationship between the subjective feeling of security in terms of crime, poverty and unemployment and the life satisfaction of the adolescents. This

---

[11] The Intercept in Table 8.2, Table 8.3 and Table 8.4 corresponds to the estimated value for the target variable if all the continuous explanatory variables are set to zero. With categorical variables, the regression coefficient indicates to what extent students from the category in question differ from students in the reference group. With continuous variables, the regression coefficient indicates how much the target variable changes if this continuous variable changes by the value 1.

[12] The reference category 'female' is not listed in Table 8.2.

[13] The reference category 'endorsement of no acculturation strategy' is not listed in Table 8.2 or any of the following tables. Significant effects between different categories of acculturation strategies were determined by means of the Tukey's post-hoc test.

relationship is not linear, however (see Table 8.2). The effect of a higher sense of security on life satisfaction manifests itself mainly among those participants who evaluate the situation in Switzerland as very insecure and less so among those whose feeling of security is medium or high.

In terms of the influence of acculturation strategies on the life satisfaction of adolescents with a migration background, the analysis yields the following result (see Table 8.2): The endorsement of a minority orientation or a combined majority-minority-multicultural orientation turns out to be beneficial for the participants' life satisfaction, whereas the endorsement of no orientation, which can be considered cultural marginalisation, is unfavourable for life satisfaction. Adolescents with a migration background who orient themselves towards the cultural frame of their heritage culture (or the heritage culture of their parents) have a higher life satisfaction than culturally marginalised adolescents. This suggests that not only a minority orientation and social networking with members of their own cultural group constitute an important source of life satisfaction for adolescents with a migration background, but also the integration of all three types of acculturation strategies turns out to be a better strategy in terms of life satisfaction than either the lack of any strategy or a multicultural strategy alone. The majority orientation does not appear as a significant positive predictor of life satisfaction in this analysis. This may be due to the fact that an endorsement of a majority orientation in isolation (without the concomitant endorsement of other orientations), which can be considered cultural assimilation, is relatively rare among the migrant adolescents who participated in the study (1%, n=14).

5.2   Influence of Acculturation Strategies on Educational Aspirations

We now analyse which factors influence the educational aspirations of adolescents with a migration background. Higher educational aspirations are conceptualized as an indicator of educational success. We speak of higher educational aspirations if the adolescents aim for a university degree or a vocational school diploma with maturity. Table 8.3 shows the results of the multi-level analysis. Somewhat surprisingly, the (bi-) national identification of the students did not appear as a predictor in this model. This means that there are no differences between immigrants from an Italian, Portuguese or Albanian background in terms of their educational aspirations. Of the demographic variables, the length of residence in Switzerland plays a significant role: Adolescents who have been in Switzerland for less than five years have higher educational aspirations than adolescents who were born in Switzerland. With increasing length of residence in Switzerland, the

Table 8.3. *Results of the multi-level analysis of the educational aspirations of adolescents with a migration background.*

	Regression Coefficient	Standard Error	P-Value
(Intercept)	−1.95	0.56	0.001
Length of residence < 5 years[14]	0.59	0.27	0.030
Length of residence 5 to 9 years	0.23	0.29	0.425
Length of residence more than 9 years	−0.11	0.27	0.689
11–50 books at home[15]	0.53	0.18	0.002
51–100 books at home	0.78	0.23	0.001
More than 100 books at home	1.35	0.25	<.000
Type of school with medium exigencies[16]	−1.15	0.23	<.000
Type of school with basic exigencies	−1.87	0.25	<.000
Type of school with general exigencies	−1.44	0.38	0.000
Percentage of Swiss nationals and binationals in the school class	1.28	0.54	0.018
Achievement expectancy of teachers	0.41	0.15	0.007
Multicultural orientation[17]	0.82	0.28	0.003
Minority orientation	0.24	0.26	0.356
Minority orientation-multicultural orientation	0.10	0.25	0.683
Majority orientation	−0.91	0.78	0.245
Majority orientation–multicultural orientation	0.96	0.47	0.043
Majority orientation–minority orientation	0.89	0.47	0.056
Majority orientation–minority orientation-multicultural orientation	0.24	0.33	0.465

(n−1074)

educational aspirations of adolescents with a migration background decrease. Once they have been living in Switzerland for five years, migrants no longer differ from adolescents with a migration background that were born in Switzerland (see Table 8.3). The extent to which the adolescents strive for higher levels of education also depends on the educational resources of the family (measured in terms of the number of

[14] The reference category is youth 'born in Switzerland'.

[15] The reference category is youth with '0–10 books at home'.

[16] The reference category which is not listed in Table 8.3 is students who are enrolled in a school type with higher exigencies (type A). A school type with medium exigencies corresponds to school type B and a school type with basic exigencies corresponds to school type C. The school type 'general exigencies' corresponds to the "Weiterbildungsschule" in the canton Basel city.

[17] The reference category is 'endorsement of no acculturation strategy'. Significant effects between different categories of acculturation strategies were determined by means of the Tukey's post-hoc test.

books at home) (see Table 8.3). With an increasing number of books at home, the adolescents tend to strive for a higher educational degree.

The following school-related factors contribute to the explanation of higher educational aspirations of students with a migration background: type of school, the percentage of Swiss nationals and binationals (students that feel that they belong to Switzerland as well as at least another nation) in the class, as well as the achievement expectation of the teacher (see Table 8.3). The lower the exigencies of the attended school type, the lower the expectation to achieve a higher educational level among the students with a migration background (see Table 8.3). The higher the percentage of Swiss and binational students in the class is, the more students with a migration background report striving for a higher educational degree (see Table 3). It seems that attending a more demanding school type and going to school with more Swiss and binational classmates contributes to higher expectations of adolescents with a migration background in relation to their professional goals. In addition, higher achievement expectations of the teacher go hand in hand with higher educational aspirations of the students (see Table 8.3). The more the respondents agree that their teachers encourage them to learn more and give their best, the more likely they are to have higher educational aspirations. As far as acculturation strategies are concerned, the endorsement of a multicultural orientation is more beneficial in terms of educational aspirations than the endorsement of no acculturation strategy (see Table 8.3). The other acculturation strategies, including combinations of acculturation strategies that can be considered an instance of integration did not have a significant effect on the students' educational aspirations. Besides these individual explanatory variables, there were significant class effects with regard to students' educational aspirations.

5.3   Influence of Acculturation Strategies on German Reading Skills

The mastery of German, the local language of instruction, is another indicator of school success. In order to analyse the influence of acculturation on German reading skills, a multi-level analysis was carried out (see Table 8.4). Again the migration background of the students did not have a significant impact: Italians, Portuguese and Albanians did not differ in their German reading skills. But other demographic variables played a role. Boys exhibited higher reading skills than the girls, a fact that may be attributable to the selected tasks which may have been easier for boys than girls. Migrant adolescents whose families have high educational resources (more than 51 books at home) exhibited higher German reading skills than those whose families have fewer (11–50 books) or very few

Table 8.4. *Results of the multi-level analysis of the German reading skills of adolescents with a migration background.*

	Regression-Coefficient	Standard Error	P-Value
(Intercept)	4.37	0.58	<.001
Gender (male)[18]	0.27	0.12	0.032
11–50 books at home[19]	0.14	0.15	0.337
51–100 books at home	0.53	0.20	0.008
More than 100 books at home	0.46	0.22	0.036
German and another language spoken at home[20]	−0.31	0.27	0.238
Another language than German spoken at home	−0.74	0.28	0.008
Type of school with medium exigencies[21]	−1.17	0.28	<.001
Type of school with basic exigencies	−1.83	0.29	<.001
Type of school with general exigencies	−2.26	0.45	<.001
Percentage of Swiss nationals and binationals in the school class	2.76	0.63	<.001
Multicultural orientation[22]	0.78	0.24	0.001
Minority orientation	0.63	0.22	0.004
Minority orientation–multicultural orientation	0.88	0.21	<.001
Majority orientation	−0.31	0.57	0.589
Majority orientation–multicultural orientation	0.63	0.40	0.112
Majority orientation–minority orientation	0.69	0.42	0.099
Majority orientation–minority orientation–multicultural orientation	0.83	0.28	0.028

(n=1116; ICC=.13)

(0–10 books) educational resources. Besides gender and the educational resources of the family, language use in the family also played a role: Students who speak another language than German at home had lower test scores than students who speak both German and another language at home. The best results were achieved by those respondents who grow up monolingual with German (see Table 8.4).

Of the school-related factors only school type and the percentage of Swiss and binational students in a class played a significant role (see Table 8.4). The best reading skills in the local language of instruction

[18] The reference category is 'female'.
[19] The reference category is youth with '0–10 books at home'.
[20] The reference category is youth with 'German spoken at home'.
[21] The reference category is students who are enrolled in a 'type of school with higher exigencies'.
[22] The reference category is 'endorsement of no acculturation strategy'. Significant effects between different categories of acculturation strategies were determined by means of the Tukey's post-hoc test.

were exhibited by students with a migration background who attend a school type with higher exigencies. Students who attend a school type with lower exigencies or the "Weiterbildungsschule" had lower scores in the German reading test. The higher the percentage of Swiss and binational students in the class is, the better the German reading skills of the respondents (see Table 8.4). As far as acculturation strategies are concerned, the analysis revealed that a multicultural orientation and the combination of multicultural and minority orientation are more advantageous than the endorsement of no acculturation strategy (see Table 8.4). Adolescents with a migration background who appreciate cultural diversity and can handle it and adolescents who orient themselves to both the heritage culture (of their parents) and cultural diversity (this can be seen as a specific instance of cultural integration) exhibit higher German reading skills than marginalised adolescents who do not seem to orient towards any cultural frame of reference. The multicultural orientation and the cultural integration seem to be the acculturation strategies adopted by the more successful students with a migration background (as measured by their reading skills in German). The other acculturation strategies, such as the majority orientation (cultural assimilation), did not have a significant effect on the reading skills of students with a migration background (see Table 8.4). Furthermore, there are significant differences between the school classes in relation to their German reading skills (see Table 8.4).

6   Discussion and conclusion

The three main groups in this study (students with an Italian, Portuguese and Albanian migration background) did not differ with respect to their psychosocial adaptation, educational aspirations or their reading skills in German. This is a surprising result, given the different educational opportunities and career perspectives these students face in Switzerland. Rather than the migration background per se, it is the family's educational resources, the acculturation strategies and the school context which are important for the explanation of their psychosocial adaptation and their educational success.

As far as the relationship between acculturation strategies and psychosocial adaptation among immigrant adolescents is concerned, a combination of all three acculturation strategies (including the openness and appreciation of cultural diversity) and a minority orientation (separation) were shown to be beneficial for the psychosocial adaptation (as measured by life satisfaction). The results of the Swiss MIRIPS-study primarily support the insights from those studies that point to the advantages of integration for the psychosocial adaptation of immigrants (Abubakar, van de Vijver, Mazrui, Arasa & Murugami, 2012; Berry et al., 2006; Ferguson et al., 2012; Nguyen & Benet-Martínez, 2013; Portes & Rumbaut, 2001). However, the form of the integration strategy that turned out to be beneficial in this study is more comprehensive and includes a multicultural orientation. In addition, these results are more in keeping with studies that found positive effects of a minority orientation (separation) on the psychosocial adaptation of migrants (Abubakar et al., 2012; Andriessen & Phalet, 2002; Ferguson et al., 2012; Motti-Stefanidi et al., 2008; Stuart et al., 2010) than with studies that found positive effects of a majority orientation (that is assimilation) (Baysu et al., 2011; Oh et al., 2002; Trickett & Birman 2005).

With respect to the relationship between acculturation strategies and educational success in the receiving country, the present results also partially support the insights from studies that point to the advantages of integration (Berry et al., 2006; Ferguson et al., 2012; Nekby et al., 2007; Nguyen & Benet-Martínez, 2013; Portes & Rumbaut, 2001). In our study, however, integration refers to a combination of a multicultural- and a minority-orientation and not to a combination of a majority- and a minority-orientation. The multicultural orientation (in isolation or in combination with the minority orientation) seems to be the preferred strategy of the better performing (measured with German reading skills) and educationally more ambitious students with a migration background. However, the results do not support the findings of studies which point to the positive effects of separation for educational success and adaptation (Ferguson et al., 2012; Gibson 1988; Stuart et al., 2010; Suinn, 2010). The same goes for studies whose results argue for advantages of assimilation for educational success in the receiving country (Baysu et al., 2011; Motti-Stefanidi et al., 2008; Trickett & Birman, 2005). On the basis of these empirical findings, Swiss schools and teachers who aim for cultural assimilation of students with a migration background seem to be less able to justify their actions than schools and teachers who aim for cultural integration and who appreciate the cultural diversity of their students.

The study also points to some school-contextual factors which seem to foster psychosocial adaptation and educational success of adolescents with a migration background. The quality of social relationships at school seems to be one such factor: A teacher-student relationship which is characterized by mutual respect and appreciation, which fosters solidarity among the students, and the sense of equal treatment irrespective of social, cultural, and religious background seems to contribute to a good psychosocial adaptation. This confirms previous findings that teachers are not only instrumental for the educational achievement but also for the social and emotional well-being of their students (Gagné, Shapka & Law, 2012; Vedder, Boekarts & Seegers, 2005).

Besides the experience of sound social relationships and non-discrimination, the extent of intercultural teaching also plays a role: A school which enables the students to learn about cultural diversity and to deal with issues such as immigration and racism seems to contribute to a successful psychosocial adaptation of their students with a migration background by strengthening and appreciating their cultural identity. Furthermore, a positive relationship has been shown to exist between the achievement expectations of the teachers and the educational aspirations of students with a migration background. Teachers can play a key role in the maintenance of initially relatively high educational aspirations of immigrant adolescents. It seems crucial that teachers have appropriately high expectations for immigrant students and that they believe in their achievement potential (Tenenbaum & Ruck, 2007). In this respect, schools should continue to optimize the chances of adolescents from socially disadvantaged families with (and without) a migration background to achieve higher educational qualifications.

References

Abs, H. J., Diedrich, M., Sickmann, H., & Klieme, E. (2007). *Evaluation im BLK-Modellprogramm Demokratie lernen und leben: Skalen zur Befragung von Schüler/-innen, Lehrer/-innen und Schulleitungen. Dokumentation der Erhebungsinstrumente 2006*. Frankfurt am Main: Deutsches Institut für Internationale Pädagogische Forschung.

Abubakar, A., van de Vijver, F. J. R., Mazrui, L., Arasa, J., & Murugami, M. (2012). Ethnic identity, acculturation orientations, and psychological well-being among adolescents of immigrant background in Kenya. In C. Garcia Coll (Ed.), *The Impact of Immigration on Children's Development* (pp. 49–63). Basel: Karger.

Andrich, D., Sheridan, B., & Luo, G. (2010). *RUMM 2030. Rasch Unidimensional Measurement Models Software*. Perth, WA: RUMM Laboratory.

Andriessen, I., & Phalet, K. (2002). Acculturation and school success: A study among minority youth in the Netherlands. *Intercultural Education, 13*(1), 21–36.

Baysu, G., Phalet, K., & Brown, R. (2011). Dual identity as a two-edged sword: Identity threat and minority school performance. *Social Psychology Quarterly, 74*(2), 121–143. Doi: 10.1177/0190272511407619.

Berry, J. W., Kalin, R., & Taylor, D. (1977). *Multiculturalism and Ethnic Attitudes in Canada*. Ottawa: Ministry of Supply and Services.

Berry, J. W., Phinney, J. S., Sam, D. L., & Vedder, P. (2006). *Immigrant Youth in Cultural Transition: Acculturation, Identity, and Adaptation across National Contexts*. New Jersey: Lawrence Erlbaum Associates.

184   *Haenni Hoti, Heinzmann, Müller, Buholzer and Künzle*

Bolzmann, C., Fibbi, R., & Vial, M. (2003). *Secondas – Secondos. Le processus d'intégration des jeunes adultes issus de la migration espagnole et italienne en Suisse.* Zürich: Seismo Verlag.

Bundesamt für Migration (2012). *Ausländerinnen, Ausländer und Asylsuchende in der Schweiz. Das Bundesamt für Migration BFM – seine Aufgaben kurz erklärt.* Bern: BFM. www.alexandria.admin.ch/broschuere-bfm-d.pdf. Accessed 19 September 2013.

Bundesamt für Statistik (2013a). *Bestand der ständigen ausländischen Wohnbevölkerung nach Staatsangehörigkeit Ende Dezember 2011 und 2012.* https://www.sem.admin.ch/sem/de/home/publiservice/statistik/auslaenderstatistik/archiv/2016/12.html. Accessed 17 September 2013.

Bundesamt für Statistik (2013b). *Schülerinnen, Schüler und Studierende 2011/12. Lernende nach Bildungsstufe, Bildungstyp und Staatsangehörigkeit 2011/12* (T2). www.bfs.admin.ch/bfs/portal/de/index/themen/15/03.html. Accessed 20 September 2013.

Burri Sharani, B., Efionayi-Mäder, D., Hammer, S., Pecoraro, M., Soland, B., Tsaka, A., & Wyssmüller, C. (2010). *Die kosovarische Bevölkerung in der Schweiz.* Bern: Bundesamt für Migration.

Diener, E., Emmos, R. A., Larsen, R. J., & Griffin, A. (1985). The Satisfaction with Life Scale. *Journal of Personality Assessment, 49,* 71–75.

Ditton, H., & Merz, D. (2000). *Qualität von Schule und Unterricht: Kurzbericht über erste Ergebnisse einer Untersuchung an bayrischen Schulen.* Katholische Universität Eichstätt & Universität Osnabrück.

Donà, G., & Berry, J. W. (1994). Acculturation attitudes and acculturative stress of Central American refugees. *International Journal of Psychology, 29,* 57–70.

Eidgenössische Kommission gegen Rassismus (1996). *Stellungnahme zum Drei-Kreise-Modell des Bundesrats über die schweizerische Ausländerpolitik.* www.ekr.admin.ch/dokumentation/00143/index.html. Accessed 19 September 2013.

Ferguson, G., Bornstein, M. H., & Pottinger, A. M. (2012). Tridimensional acculturation and adaptation among Jamaican adolescent-mother dyads in the United States. *Child Development, 83*(5), 1486–1493.

Fibbi, R., Bolzmann, C., Fernandez, A., Gomensoro, A., Kaya, B., Maire, C., Merçay, C., Pecoraro, M., & Wanner, P. (2010). *Die portugiesische Bevölkerung in der Schweiz.* Bern: Bundesamt für Migration.

FIMM (Forum für die Integration der Migrantinnen und Migranten) (2011). *Kurze Migrationsgeschichte der Schweiz.* Bern: FIMM.

Gagné, M. H., Shapka, J. D., & Law, D. M. (2012). The impact of social contexts in schools: Adolescents who are new in Canada and their sense of belonging. In C. Garcia Coll (Ed.), *The Impact of Immigration on Children's Development* (pp. 17–34). Basel: Karger.

Gibson, M. A. (1988). *Accommodation without Assimilation: Sikh Immigrants in an American High School.* Ithaca, NY: Cornell University Press.

Haenni Hoti, A., Heinzmann, S., Müller, M., & Buholzer, A. (2015). Psychosocial adaptation and school success of Italian, Portuguese and Albanian students in Switzerland: Disentangling migration background, acculturation and the school context. *Journal of International Migration and Integration.* Doi: 10.1007/s12134-015-0461-x Link: https://link.springer.com/article/10.1007/s12134-015-0461-x.

Haenni Hoti, A., Heinzmann Agten, S., Müller, M., Buholzer, A., & Künzle, R. (2013). *Akkulturation, psychosoziale Adaptation und Bildungserfolg von Jugendlichen mit Migrationshintergrund. Zusammenfassung zentraler Forschungsergebnisse des MIRIPS-Projekts*. Luzern: Pädagogische Hochschule Luzern.

Imdorf, C. (2008). Der Ausschluss "ausländischer" Jugendlicher bei der Lehrlingsauswahl – ein Fall von institutioneller Diskriminierung? In K. S. Rehberg (Ed.), *Die Natur der Gesellschaft. Verhandlungen des 33. Kongresses der Deutschen Gesellschaft für Soziologie, Kassel, 2006*. (pp. 2048–2058). Frankfurt a. M.: Campus Verlag.

Makarova, E., & Birman, D. (2015). Cultural transition and academic achievement of students from ethnic minority backgrounds: A content analysis of empirical research on acculturation. *Educational Research*, doi: 10.1080/00131881.2015.1058099.

Motti-Stefanidi, F., Pavlopoulos, V., Obradovic, J., & Masten, A. S. (2008). Acculturation and adaptation of immigrant adolescent in Greek urban schools. *International Journal of Psychology*, *43*, 45–58.

Nekby, L., Rödin, M., & Özcan, G. (2007). Acculturation identity and educational attainment. IZA Discussion Paper No. 3172. Bonn: Institute for the Study of Labour.

Nguyen, A.-M. D., & Benet-Martínez, V. (2013). Biculturalism and adjustment: A meta-analysis. *Journal of Cross-Cultural Psychology*, *44*(1), 122–159.

OECD (2014). *International migration policies and data. Stocks of foreign population*. www.oecd.org/els/mig/keystat.htm. Accessed 17 October 2014.

OECD Programme for International Student Assessment n.d. *PISA – freigegebene Beispielaufgaben mit Bewertungen von PISA 2000 bis PISA 2006: PISA – Lesen*. http://pisa.educa.ch/de/aufgabenbeispiele. Accessed 19 December 2012.

Oh, Y., Koeske, G. F., & Sales, E. (2002). Acculturation, stress, and depressive symptoms among Korean immigrants in the United States. *Journal of Social Psychology*, *142*(4), 511–526.

Portes, A., & Rumbaut, R. G. (2001). *Legacies: The story of the immigrant second generation*. Berkeley: University of California Press.

QUASSU (2001). *DFG-Projekt "Qualität von Schule und Unterricht". Skalenbildung Hauptuntersuchung, Schülerfragebogen*. www.quassu.net/SKALE N_1.pdf. Accessed 5 February 2013.

R Development Core Team (2011). *R: A language and environment for statistical computing*. R Foundation for Statistical Computing, Vienna, Austria.

Rosenberg, M. (1965). *Society and the Adolescent Self-Image*. Princeton, NJ: Princeton University Press.

Schwarzer, R., & Jerusalem, R. (1999). *Skalen zur Erfassung von Lehrer- und Schülermerkmalen. Dokumentation der psychometrischen Verfahren im Rahmen der Wissenschaftlichen Begleitung des Modellversuchs Selbstwirksame Schulen*. Berlin: Freie Universität Berlin.

Stuart, J., Ward, C., & Adam, Z. (2010). Current issues in the development and acculturation of Muslim youth in New Zealand. *Bulletin (of the International Society for the Study of Behavioural Development)*, *58*(2), 9–13.

Suinn, R. M. (2010). Reviewing acculturation and Asian Americans: How acculturation affects health, adjustment, school achievement, and counseling. *Asian American Journal of Psychology*, *1*, 5–17.

Tenenbaum, H. R., & Ruck, M. D. (2007). Are teachers 'expectations different for racial minority than for European American students? A meta-analysis. *Journal of Educational Psychology, 99*(2), 253–273.

Trickett, E. J., & Birman, D. (2005). Acculturation, school context, and school outcomes: Adaptation of refugee adolescents from the former Soviet Union. *Psychology in Schools, 42*(1), 27–38.

Vedder, P., Boekarts, M., & Seegers, G. (2005). Perceived social support and well-being in school, the role of student's ethnicity. *Journal of Youth and Adolescence, 34*(3), 269–278.

Von Aarburg, H.-P., & Gretler, S. B. (2008). *Kosova-Schweiz. Die albanische Arbeits- und Asylmigration zwischen Kosovo und der Schweiz (1964–2000).* Vienna: LIT Verlag.

Ward, C., & Kennedy, A. (1999). The measurement of sociocultural adaptation. *International Journal of Intercultural Relations, 56*, 1–19.

Zentrum für Schulforschung und Fragen der Lehrerbildung (ZSL) (2004). *Skalenhandbuch zum Schülerfragebogen aus dem Projekt "Politische Orientierungen bei Schülern im Rahmen schulischer Anerkennungsbeziehungen".* Diskurse zu Schule und Bildung. Werkstatthefte des ZSL (Heft 24). Halle/Saale: Martin-Luther-Universität Halle-Wittenberg.

9 Intercultural Relations in Greece[1]

Vassilis Pavlopoulos and Frosso Motti-Stefanidi
National and Kapodistrian University of Athens, Greece

Whoever is not Greek, is a barbarian.
[cited by] Maurus Servius Honoratus

Hellenes are called those who share our upbringing,
rather than our common nature.
Isocrates

1 Introduction

Situated at the crossroads of three continents (Europe, Asia and Africa), Greece has repeatedly witnessed extended population movements through the centuries and, at present, is the destination of many fleeing the conflicts in West Asia. Migration has played an important role in shaping the ethnic identity of modern Greeks. As a result of these long-term and current migration flows, the contemporary intercultural situation in Greece is a complex one. At present, the diversity of the Greek population is moderate on the diversity index and is low on both the integration and policy indexes. As a result of these long-term and current migration flows, the contemporary intercultural situation in Greece is currently in flux.

2 Context of Intercultural Relations in Greece

The most prominent testimony to this complexity is to be found in the Greco-Turkish Population exchange that was decided at Lausanne in 1923, thus putting an end to what is now known as the 'Asia Minor Catastrophe' in Greece or the 'War of Independence' in Turkey. Almost 1,300,000 Anatolian Greeks and 500,000 Muslims from Greece were forced to become refugees and denaturalized from their homelands. Beyond the unspeakable human pain and suffering, a side effect from the

[1] The Greek contribution to the MIRIPS project was funded in part by a grant from the Special Account for Research Grants of the National and Kapodistrian University of Athens.

Lausanne convention was the formation of one of the most homogeneous countries in Europe in terms of language, religion and ethnic sense of belonging. On the other hand, various developments led to several waves of Greek emigration in the past two centuries, motivated mostly by employment search. Nowadays the Greek diaspora is estimated to comprise more than 5,000,000 people of Greek descent scattered across 140 countries all over the world (Tziovas, 2009).

2.1   Immigration

The cultural homogeneity of the modern Greek state has been challenged in the last decades of the twentieth century. The collapse of the communist regimes in Eastern Europe triggered large flows of immigrants, most of them undocumented, that rapidly and unexpectedly transformed Greece into a receiving society. Among them were a number of ethnic Greeks from the former Soviet Union (called Pontian Greeks) and from south Albania (Northern Epirus Greeks). Cavounidis (2013) examined the impact of these immigration flows on the economic and social landscape of the country, before and during the economic crisis of 2008. She highlights the abrupt change from a relatively homogeneous to a diverse population, the expansion of informal employment and the substitution of family-based enterprises by migrant wage-labour. During this period, she underlines the continuation of unauthorized inflows of migrants with limited absorption into the labour market, the expansion of return migration and a new wave of emigration by the young generation nationals.

The 2011 national census shows that the proportion of immigrants in the total population in Greece is 8.4 per cent. The largest group by far is from Albania (53%), followed by Bulgaria (8%), Romania (5%), Pakistan (3.7%), Georgia (3%), Ukraine (1.9%), UK (1.7%), Cyprus (1.5%), Poland (1.5%) and India (1.2%) (Hellenic Statistical Authority, 2014)[2]. Caution is necessary before any conclusions are drawn with regard to the sociodemographic profile of these groups as it varies considerably by country of origin, which reflects the dynamics of pull and push factors for migration. For example, Ukrainians are mostly women, while Pakistanis are predominantly men. In terms of education, EU

---

[2] The census data do not differentiate between documented and irregular immigrants; furthermore, they fail to capture the recent flows of refugees and asylum seekers washed up on the Greek islands in an attempt to enter EU through the Eastern Mediterranean route. Their number skyrocketed to 885,386 in 2015, from 50,834 in 2014 and 24,799 in 2013 (Frontex, 2016). Although in their vast majority they are migrants in transit, a number of them were trapped in Greece after the closing of the borders by the Former Yugoslav Republic of Macedonia in March 2016.

citizens share a similar profile with Greeks, while citizens from non-EU countries have fewer years of schooling. On the other hand, they are mostly economic immigrants, which means that they contribute to the same employment sectors (i.e., construction, agriculture, tourism and, in general, low-skilled jobs), independently of their educational status. Their official unemployment rate has been comparable to the one of the national population. The consequences of the economic crisis are more evident for non-EU citizens who witnessed a shocking increase in their unemployment rate, from 11 per cent in 2009 to 34 per cent in 2014 (about 26% for Greeks).

2.2   State Policies and Public Attitudes

Greek governments were slow to respond to the challenges of immigration and multiculturalism. Immigration policies in the 1990s and 2000s were largely characterized by a reactive approach to irregular migration and informal employment (Triandafyllidou, 2014). Until the early 1990s, the relevant issues were regulated by a law that dated back to the 1920s and the Asia Minor Catastrophe. For quite a long time, Greece has been notorious for its failing asylum system, and soon concerns started to rise with regard to the degrading conditions of detention of pending asylum seekers.

Greek nationality has been based predominantly on the *jus sanguinis* principle (i.e., based on ancestry). A series of regularization programmes were implemented in 1998, 2001, 2005 and 2007. In 2010, a new naturalization law was adopted incorporating several *jus soli* components (based on place of birth), but it was declared anti-constitutional by the Council of State in early 2013. The latest (2014) migration code introduced several improvements in the codification of the legal provisions and in aligning Greek legislation with EU directives, but still, as Triandafyllidou (2014) points out, it remained a management law and was a step back with respect to political participation and citizenship of second-generation immigrants. A new anti-racism law (2014) is relevant to the climate for immigration and intercultural relations. It toughened criminal sanctions for incitement to hatred, discrimination and violence, and declared Holocaust denial a criminal act.

Attitudes of Greek citizens towards immigration, as depicted in national polls and social surveys, have been on the negative side. In Eurobarometer studies, Greek attitudes rejecting non-EU citizens were considerably higher than the European average (European Commission, 2015). In another study, Greece was the only case among 17 European countries where the number of friends from minority groups did not significantly reduce levels of hostility towards immigrants (McLaren, 2003). It is important to understand how these dynamics of intergroup relations are affected by socioeconomic factors. As Adamczyk (2016) notes, the initially negative views of Greeks towards Albanian immigrants were gradually transformed to become more tolerant through the prism of the labour demands of the country's developing economy in the 2000s, but then xenophobic tendencies reappeared under the pressures of the recent economic and refugee crisis.

3   Evaluation of the MIRIPS Hypotheses in Greece

3.1   *Previous findings*

Some of the issues addressed in the three MIRIPS hypotheses have been subject to empirical studies in Greece in the past two decades. Unfortunately, this growing body of evidence is largely ignored by policy makers. There have been two lines of research. The first examines acculturation processes and adaptation outcomes for immigrants, thus falling within the framework of the integration hypothesis. The second line is in the construction of identity, views of immigrants and inter-cultural attitudes from the point of view of the Greek population. These studies provide evidence of the role of security and of contact in intergroup relations.

With respect to the integration hypothesis, there are studies examining the links between acculturation strategies and the adaptation of immigrants. In a study of 601 adult immigrants coming from 35 countries, Besevegis and Pavlopoulos (2008) found that the integration and assimilation strategies yielded the most positive adaptation outcomes and separation the most negative. Comparable findings emerged from a stratified sample of 1,843 immigrants throughout the country (Pavlopoulos, Dalla, Georganti & Besevegis, 2011). Individuals with a preference for integration had the most balanced profile in a set of non-psychological adaptation indicators, such as income, housing, physical health, political participation and language competence. Assimilation followed, though with increased health problems. Marginalized and, to a lesser extent, separated immigrants were clearly on the negative side of adaptation.

Various aspects of acculturation and adaptation of immigrant youth in the school context have been examined both cross-sectionally and long-itudinally by the Athena Studies of Resilient Adaptation, an international collaborative project focusing on risk and protective factors in the course of positive youth development in Greek urban schools. This research group has shown that immigrant status posed a risk on academic competence and peer popularity of Albanian and Pontian adolescents (Motti-Stefanidi et al., 2008) over and above resources and other social risks (Anagnostaki, Pavlopoulos, Obradović, Masten & Motti-Stefanidi, 2016). Parental school involvement moderated the effect of immigrant status on achievement, while peer popularity of minority immigrants increased significantly over three years in high school (Motti-Stefanidi, Asendorpf & Masten, 2012). In what concerns acculturation orientations, involvement in Greek culture was a salient predictor of school adjustment, and involvement in one's ethnic culture was positively related to subjective well-being (Motti-Stefanidi, Pavlopoulos, Obradović & Masten, 2008).

High levels of perceived discrimination in Greece have been confirmed in international studies. According to joint OECD and EU data (2015), 35 per cent of immigrants felt discriminated against ranking Greece first in perceived discrimination. This was especially true for those born abroad, as compared to naturalised immigrants, which reflects the *jus sanguinis* principle characterising laypeople's beliefs as well as state policies. On the other hand, in a study of Albanian immigrants in Greece (Iosifides, Lavrentiadou, Petracou & Kontis, 2007) participants acknowledged from their personal experience that close social contact with Greeks for a relatively long period of time reduces prejudice, xenophobic behaviour and discrimination quite substantially (also see Motti-Stefanidi, Asendorpf & Masten, 2012). Individual characteristics, such as personality traits, self-esteem, school grades and peer popularity, were also shown to buffer against translating perceived group discrimination of immigrant youth into experiences of personal discrimination (Motti-Stefanidi & Asendorpf, 2012).

From the perspective of the general population, a number of studies have examined the acculturation of immigrants and entitlement to citizenship using the tools of discursive and rhetorical social psychology. In contrast to the dynamic element of mutual accommodation, embedded in the definition of acculturation in the MIRIPS project, Greek participants seemed to legitimize their right to decide upon the acculturation process of others. The preferred adaptation outcome was assimilation of immigrants into Greek society. Still, this was limited to such aspects as Greek education, language learning and contribution to the economy, leaving out cultural elements such as shared ideas and norms (Sapountzis, 2013). In the same realm, Figgou (2015) revealed the chameleon-like properties of the politics of social exclusion, such as drawing a clear distinction between legal and illegal immigrants. Flexible ingroup recategorization (Sapountzis, Figgou, Bozatzis, Gardikiotis & Pantazis, 2013) and perceived incompatibility between national, ethnic and religious identities (Chryssochoou & Lyons, 2010) were found to serve similar purposes, such as questioning biculturalism, excluding immigrants of specific ethnic descent, or even inoculating oneself against accusations of prejudice.

3.2   *Theoretical issues*

The Greek MIRIPS project examines all three hypotheses. In addition, some theoretical extensions in the present Greek study are rooted in social psychological theories of intergroup relations. These refer to the dynamic processes that shape cultural orientations; social categorization and identity; the ingroup/outgroup distinction; the majority/minority asymmetric distribution of power; and political discourse in Greek society.

A recent shift in the literature of intercultural relations has been towards more encompassing approaches. One of these is the Integrated Threat Theory (ITT) of prejudice (Stephan & Stephan, 2000), which deals with the components, antecedents and consequences of perceived threat. As noted in Chapter 1, this theory phrases the multiculturalism hypothesis in reverse terms: lack of security is considered as threat. ITT identifies four types of threats: realistic threats (relative to economic welfare and political power); symbolic threats (against a person's beliefs, morals, and values); intergroup anxiety (feelings of discomfort when engaging with outgroup members); and negative stereotypes. In line with the multiculturalism hypothesis, ITT predicts that a sense of threat (e.g., in the form of undermining cultural identity of nationals, or experiencing discrimination by immigrants) will lead to rejection of the outgroup. ITT also addresses the contact hypothesis, because perceived threat is expected to lead to less willingness for intercultural contact and engagement with the outgroup.

With respect to the integration hypothesis, we take into consideration the warning of Van Acker and Vanbeselaere (2011) that results from studies using different conceptualizations of acculturation expectations may not be comparable. An example is to be found in the bidimensional frameworks developed by Berry (1980) and by Bourhis, Moïse, Perreault & Senécal (1997). In the former, the second dimension refers to a preference for having contact and engagement with other groups in the larger society, while in the latter, the second dimension refers to adopting the culture of the larger society. Therefore, the interpretation of the four acculturation strategies may not be the same, as was the case in a recent study with dominant group members in the Greek context (Sapountzis, 2013).

In addition to evaluating each of the three MIRIPS hypotheses separately, we also sought to build a structural equation model that integrates and explores the three hypotheses simultaneously. On the basis of the literature reviewed earlier, we expected that (a) for the Greek sample, pathways from national identification and contact to acculturation expectations will be mediated by security and intergroup attitudes; and (b) for the immigrant sample, the pathway from contact to adaptation will be mediated by security and acculturation strategies.

4   Method

4.1   Samples

The samples in the study were Greeks and first-generation immigrant adults living in Greece and residing in the region of Attiki and the wider Athens metropolitan area. They were recruited using the snowball method by 18 undergraduate Psychology students who were trained to act as research assistants in the context of their degree thesis.

The Greek sample (N = 449) consisted of 252 women and 197 men. Their mean age was 37.9 years (SD = 11.9; range: 19–69 years) and 171 were married, among them 6 with a spouse of different ethnicity. In terms of schooling, 163 had a university degree and 90 obtained a Master's or PhD diploma, while 7 dropped out of school after nine years of compulsory education. Their occupational status was quite diverse, as 212 were full-time employed, 50 had a part-time job, 85 were self-employed, 26 had retired, 32 were students and 42 did not work. On the contrary, it was a more coherent group in terms of religion: 360 were Christian Orthodox and 72 declared themselves to be atheists or with no religion. Their economic status indicates they were mostly middle-class, since 278 reported that they were (just) able to pay for everyday expenses, 83 had difficulty covering basic needs and 87 earned extra money for monthly savings.

Immigrant participants (N = 147) comprised 98 females and 49 males. They came from 24 countries, as follows: 65 from Albania, 14 from Balkan neighbouring countries (Bulgaria, Romania), 46 from Eastern Europe (Georgia, Moldavia, Poland, Russia, Ukraine), 16 from Western countries (Belgium, Canada, Finland, France, Italy, the Netherlands, Spain, UK), 2 from Asia (Pakistan, Philippines), 2 from Africa (Burundi, Seychelles), 1 from Egypt, and 1 from Brazil. Their mean age was 36.3 years (SD = 12.8; range: 18–67 years) and their mean length of stay in Greece was 16.2 years (SD = 8.3; range: 1–39 years). With regard to marital status, 79 were married, of whom 19 had a spouse of different ethnic origin. In terms of education, 16 had completed nine years of schooling, 42 had studied Upper High School, 33 had graduated from university and 6 had a master's or PhD degree. Their occupational status varied from full-time ($N = 55$) and part-time job ($N = 29$) to self-employment ($N = 16$), while 4 were pensioners, 15 were students and 28 did not work. About half of them ($N = 73$) reported a moderate economic status, 45 were not able to cover their everyday needs, and 28 could afford some extra savings. In terms of religion, 71 were Christian Orthodox, 13 Roman Catholic, 26 declared Christians with no further specification, 12 Muslims and 25 reported no religion or did not answer.

It should be noted that, with the exception of age, the earlier socio-demographic profiles differ significantly between the two groups, the Greeks having more years of formal education, higher occupational and economic status, and being more homogeneous in terms of religion than immigrants. These differences are in line with the official data provided by the Hellenic Statistical Authority (2011 census), which attests to the ecological validity of the study.

4.2   Measures and Procedure

Data were collected using the MIRIPS questionnaire. Questions were translated and back-translated from English into Greek and Albanian. However, more than 90 per cent of participants preferred to take the questionnaire in Greek. Detailed information on the measures and their descriptive statistics are presented in Table 9.1.

Scoring instructions followed the MIRIPS guidelines, with only a few minor adjustments. No total scores for Security were calculated, on the basis of low reliability; instead, we measured two more concrete domains (i.e., Cultural and Socioeconomic Security) that derived from exploratory principal components analyses of the 13 items of the Security scale, after testing for factorial invariance between the two groups. Similarly, we identified three components for Psychological Problems (i.e., Somatic Symptoms, Anxiety, Depression) and for Sociocultural Adaptation (i.e., Interpersonal Relations, Culture Learning, Intercultural Competence), but in these cases we preferred to use the total scores, as their subscales were highly inter-correlated. One exception to this was Intercultural Competence, which we used as a proxy for intergroup anxiety of Greeks guided by the Integrated Threat Theory. Reliability of all scales was calculated separately for the two groups, the resulting coefficients ranging from acceptable to very high (see Table 9.1).

Questionnaires were administered on an individual basis after informed consent was obtained, which focused on the principles of anonymity, confidentiality, privacy and minimal disturbance. Participation was voluntary, and there were no rewards other than a verbal expression of gratitude. In a few cases, data collection took the form of a structured interview due to the limited reading skills of immigrant participants. No participant decided to withdraw from the study during or after data collection.

5   Results

5.1   Descriptive Statistics

Descriptive statistics and reliability coefficients of all variables for both samples are presented in Table 9.1, and inter-correlations among variables in both samples are in Table 9.2.

A series of 2 (immigrant status) by 2 (gender) analyses of variance revealed that, compared to Greeks, immigrants reported higher Intercultural Contact ($\eta^2 = .34$), lower Greek identification ($\eta^2 = .10$), lower preference for Separation ($\eta^2 = .05$) and Marginalization ($\eta^2 = .14$), lower level of Discrimination ($\eta^2 = .27$) and a less favourable profile of psychological adaptation with lower Self-Esteem ($\eta^2 = .01$), less Life Satisfaction ($\eta^2 = .02$) and more Psychological Problems ($\eta^2 = .01$).

Overall, gender effects were small. Significant differences were found in adaptation, with women reporting more Life Satisfaction ($\eta^2 = .01$) and higher Sociocultural Adaptation ($\eta^2 = .02$), independently of immigrant status. Also, immigrant women scored higher than immigrant men in ethnic identification ($\eta^2 = .03$). No significant immigrant status by gender interactions were found.

Most correlations were in the expected direction. With regard to the multiculturalism hypothesis, in the Greek sample, Cultural Security correlated positively with Multicultural Ideology and negatively with Prejudice and the Perceived (negative) consequences of Immigration. Cultural Security also correlated negatively with National Identity and with three of the Acculturation Expectations (positively with Integration, and negatively with Assimilation and Separation). The socio-economic component of security did not relate to any variables of interest, except for the adaptation indices of Greeks. For the immigrant sample, Cultural Security correlated positively with their National Identity, positively with their preference for Integration, and negatively with Marginalisation.

With respect to the contact hypothesis, the Intercultural Contact of Greeks was associated positively with their Multicultural Ideology and Self-Esteem, and negatively with their National Identity, Prejudice and Attitudes rejecting Immigrants. In the immigrant sample, the only significant correlation with Intercultural Contact was with their National Identity.

Table 9.1. *Descriptive statistics and alpha reliabilities of the MIRIPS variables for the Greek and immigrant participants.*

	Group	# items	Alpha	M	SD	Min	Max
Contact and Identity							
Intercultural Contact	Gr	2	.73	1.88	1.03	1.00	5.00
	Im	2	.70	3.78	1.10	1.00	5.00
National (Greek) Identity	Gr	4	.85	4.02	0.80	1.50	5.00
	Im	4	.79	3.33	0.91	1.00	5.00
Ethnic Identity	Gr	–	–	–	–	–	–
	Im	4	.83	4.04	0.83	1.00	5.00
Security							
Cultural	Gr	4	.60	3.70	0.72	1.75	5.00
	Im	2	.61	3.51	0.96	1.50	5.00
Socio-economic	Gr	9	.60	2.27	0.49	1.00	3.56
	Im	8	.70	2.28	0.54	1.00	4.25
Acculturation							
Integration	Gr	4	.64	3.94	0.60	1.25	5.00
	Im	4	.68	4.12	0.58	2.75	5.00
Assimilation	Gr	4	.69	1.97	0.63	1.00	5.00
	Im	4	.71	1.95	0.61	1.00	4.00
Separation	Gr	4	.63	2.41	0.59	1.00	4.50
	Im	4	.67	2.09	0.56	1.00	4.00
Marginalization	Gr	4	.70	2.30	0.60	1.00	4.75
	Im	4	.74	1.70	0.55	1.00	3.50
Intergroup Relations							
Discrimination	Gr	5	.82	3.67	0.71	1.00	5.00
	Im	5	.80	2.54	0.82	1.00	5.00
Multicultural Ideology	Gr	10	.85	3.43	0.67	1.00	5.00
	Im	–	–	–	–	–	–
Prejudice	Gr	11	.87	2.07	0.67	1.00	4.64
	Im	–	–	–	–	–	–
Attitudes to Immigration	Gr	11	.91	2.81	0.81	1.09	4.91
	Im	–	–	–	–	–	–
Adaptation							
Self-Esteem	Gr	10	.85	3.95	0.57	2.10	5.00
	Im	10	.84	3.84	0.64	2.20	5.00
Life Satisfaction	Gr	5	.82	3.35	0.72	1.20	5.00
	Im	5	.75	3.11	0.65	1.60	5.00
Psychological Problems	Gr	15	.90	2.50	0.64	1.00	4.47
	Im	15	.91	2.28	0.64	1.00	4.00
Sociocultural Adaptation	Gr	20	.86	4.12	0.51	2.15	5.00
	Im	20	.85	4.19	0.54	2.25	4.19

Note: Gr: Greek ($N = 449$); Im: Immigrant ($N = 147$). Security scores are not directly comparable between Greek and immigrant participants due to the different number and/or content of the scales used. Acculturation measures refer to *expectations* from the side of native Greeks and to *strategies* from the side of immigrants. Similarly, discrimination refers to *attributed* (by native Greeks) or *perceived* (by immigrants) instances of devalued identity of immigrants in the Greek society. High scores on Attitudes to Immigration indicate negative evaluations.

Table 9.2. *Pearson correlation coefficients among the MIRIPS variables for the Greek (bottom left; N = 449) and immigrant (top right; N = 147) participants.*

	IC	EI	NI	CS	SS	In	As	Se	Ma	Di	MI	Pr	AI	SE	LS	PP	SA
Intercultural Contact	—	-.03	.23**	-.03	.04	.01	.09	-.10	-.01	-.03				-.03	-.05	-.03	.11
Ethnic Identity		—	.06	.16*	.10	.17*	-.23**	.18*	-.35***	-.11				.13	.00	-.24**	.19*
National Identity	-.10*		—	.15	.09	.11	.28***	-.13	-.12	-.16*				.01	.09	.08	.00
Cultural Security	.08		-.40***	—	.27***	.14	-.02	-.10	-.16*	-.16*				.11	.12	-.03	-.00
Socioeconomic Security	-.02		.06	.19***	—	-.12	.08	.03	.06	-.01				.02	.07	-.09	-.06
Integration	.03		-.10*	.19***	-.01	—	-.13	-.29***	-.42***	-.03				.23**	.10	.04	.21**
Assimilation	-.06		.20***	-.32***	.10*	-.05	—	.12	.46***	.11				-.26**	-.05	.06	-.10
Separation	-.07		.21***	-.27***	-.01	-.46***	.12*	—	.30***	.24**				-.16*	-.10	-.13	-.09
Marginalization	.18***		-.05	-.09	.04	-.24***	.20***	.26***	—	.31***				-.39***	-.11	.13	-.30***
Discrimination	.13**		-.31***	.37***	-.07	.05	-.24***	.05	.05	—				-.34***	-.28***	.27***	-.21*
Multicultural Ideology	.21***		-.40***	.52***	.09	.26***	-.40***	-.17**	-.03	.44***	—						
Prejudice	-.18***		.41***	-.60***	-.06	-.42***	.38***	.36***	.08	-.40***	-.65***	—					
Attitudes to Immigration	-.16***		.47***	-.57***	-.24***	-.27***	.28***	.28***	.01	-.40***	-.67***	.67***	—				
Self-Esteem	.13**		.25***	.01	.05	.04	.08	-.04	-.04	-.05	-.11**	.13**	.16***	—	.52***	-.30***	.51***
Life Satisfaction	.03		.21***	.03	.19***	-.01	.04	.02	-.03	-.01	.02	.03	.00	.48***	—	-.36***	.32***
Psychological Problems	-.09		-.16***	-.16***	-.22***	.02	.03	.08	.07	.02	-.07	.05	.10*	-.42***	-.43***	—	-.48***
Sociocultural Adaptation	.04		.16***	.12*	.16***	.10*	-.08	-.09	-.06	-.08	.06	-.06	-.04	.48***	.35***	-.48***	—

Note: * $p < .05$; ** $p < .01$; *** $p < .001$.

For the integration hypothesis, in the immigrant sample, there were significant positive correlations between a preference for Integration and both Self-Esteem and Sociocultural Adaptation, and negative correlations of Assimilation, Separation and Marginalization with Self-Esteem. In the Greek sample, there were no significant correlations between their acculturation expectations and their adaptation.

A number of demographic factors were examined for their relationships with the psychological variables. These findings are not described in detail due to space limitations. They suggest, however, that demographics should be taken into account as covariates in further analyses. In short, more education of Greeks was related to higher Cultural Security and to more favourable intercultural attitudes, while in the immigrant sample education correlated positively with Self-Esteem and Sociocultural Adaptation, and negatively with Separation, Marginalization and Perceived Discrimination. Economic status correlated positively with Psychological and Sociocultural Adaptation. Finally, length of residence in Greece of immigrants was associated with higher preference for Integration and lower for Separation, more Satisfaction with Life, but also more Psychological Problems.

5.2   Hypotheses Testing

To evaluate the multiculturalism hypothesis, a series of hierarchical multiple regressions were conducted for the prediction of intercultural attitudes and acculturation strategies from Security. Demographic factors (i.e., gender, age, education level, economic status and – in the case of immigrants – length of stay in Greece) served as covariates in Block 1, while the two indicators of Cultural and Socioeconomic Security were introduced in Block 2. The dependent variables were Perceived Discrimination and acculturation strategies of immigrants, on the one hand, and intercultural attitudes and acculturation expectations of Greeks, on the other.

In the Greek sample, after accounting for demographics, security explained 30.5 per cent of the variance of Multicultural Ideology, 30.3 per cent of Prejudice, 40.2 per cent of Attitudes to Immigration, 3 per cent of Integration, 12.1 per cent of Assimilation and 4.4 per cent of Separation. No significant amount of variance was accounted for Marginalization. The earlier findings were mainly due to Cultural Security, which predicted higher agreement with Multicultural Ideology ($\beta = .57$, $p < .001$), lower Prejudice ($\beta = -.58$, $p < .001$), less rejecting Attitudes to Immigration ($\beta = -.61$, $p < .001$), higher expectations for Integration ($\beta = .18$, $p < .001$) and lower for Assimilation ($\beta = -.36$, $p < .001$) and Separation ($\beta = -.22$, $p < .001$). Socioeconomic Security contributed only in the prediction of negative Attitudes to

Immigration ($\beta = -.14$, $p < .001$), and of expectations for Assimilation ($\beta = .16$, $p < .001$).

In the immigrant sample, there was not much variance for Security to explain after demographic factors were taken into account. However, Cultural Security was related to lower levels of Perceived Discrimination ($\beta = -.16$, $p = .049$, $\Delta R^2 = .026$), higher preference for Integration ($\beta = .18$, $p = .032$, $\Delta R^2 = .038$), and lower for Marginalization ($\beta = -.18$, $p = .029$, $\Delta R^2 = .031$). The effect of Socioeconomic Security was non-significant.

For the contact hypothesis, a series of hierarchical multiple regressions were run in order to predict intercultural attitudes and acculturation from intercultural contact. The effect of the same set of demographic factors was partialled out in Block 1, along with Ingroup Contact. Intercultural Contact served as the single predictor in Block 2. Again, the dependent variables were Perceived Discrimination and acculturation strategies (for the immigrants), and intercultural attitudes and acculturation expectations (for the Greeks).

In the Greek sample, Intercultural Contact uniquely contributed in the prediction of higher Multicultural Ideology ($\beta = .18$, $p < .001$, $\Delta R^2 = .030$), less Prejudice ($\beta = -.15$, $p = .002$, $\Delta R^2 = .021$), less negative Attitudes to Immigration ($\beta = -.13$, $p = .007$, $\Delta R^2 = .017$), as well as higher expectations for Marginalization of immigrants ($\beta = .17$, $p = .001$, $\Delta R^2 = .028$).

In the immigrant sample, the only significant effect of Intercultural Contact, after accounting for demographic factors and Ingroup Contact, was on Separation ($\beta = -.18$, $p = .048$, $\Delta R^2 = .024$). In all other dependent variables, although the pattern of relationships was in the expected direction, the coefficients of Intercultural Contact did not reach statistical significance.

A person-centred approach was considered appropriate to address the integration hypothesis, employing k-means clustering. Using a specification criterion of four clusters, the four expected acculturation profiles were identified for both Greeks and immigrants. However, their distribution differed significantly between the two groups, $\chi^2(3, N = 596) = 8.39$, $p = .039$. While Integration was most preferred among both Greeks (35.6%) and immigrants (38.1%), more Greeks (27.6%) than immigrants (17.7%) preferred Marginalization. The opposite was true for Separation (15.4% and 23.1%, respectively). Assimilation was ranked third in their preferences (21.4% and 21.1%, respectively).

Subsequent multivariate analyses of variance tested for differences across the acculturation profiles with respect to adaptation. In the Greek sample, acculturation expectations accounted for 13.3 per cent of the variance of intercultural adaptation, namely Multicultural Ideology ($\eta^2 = .06$), Prejudice ($\eta^2 = .12$) and Attitudes to Immigration ($\eta^2 = .06$).

Paired comparisons using the Scheffé criterion showed that individuals promoting Integration and Marginalization scored higher in Multicultural Ideology than those with a preference for Separation and Assimilation. Separation had the highest scores in Prejudice and negative Attitudes to Immigration, while Integration had the lowest.

In the immigrant sample, acculturation strategies explained 14.2 per cent of the variance of psychological adaptation, which was mainly due to Self-Esteem ($\eta^2 = .14$) and Psychological Problems ($\eta^2 = .09$), and 4.6 per cent of Sociocultural Adaptation. According to Scheffé contrasts, Integration scored the highest in Self-Esteem and Sociocultural Adaptation, and the lowest in Psychological Problems. Marginalization had the worst profile in terms of Psychological Problems (highest) and Self-Esteem (lowest). Individuals with a preference for Separation scored the lowest in Psychological Problems but also in Self-Esteem, while at the same time they were equally low in Sociocultural Adaptation. Assimilation was positioned at moderate levels. Finally, with respect to intercultural adaptation, immigrants adopting Marginalization and Separation reported more instances of Perceived Discrimination than those who preferred Integration and Assimilation ($\eta^2 = .05$).

5.3   Integrative Models of the Combined MIRIPS Hypotheses

We now summarize the variables involved in the three MIRIPS hypotheses in an integrative model that depicts mutual intercultural relations in Greece. Analyses were performed using AMOS 21.

In the Greek sample (Figure 9.1), three latent variables were created. The first latent variable is Security; its components directly correspond to the multiculturalism hypothesis and the key constructs of ITT. Cultural and Socioeconomic Security refer to symbolic and realistic threat, respectively; Intercultural Competence is the corresponding opposite of intergroup anxiety; and negative Immigration Attitudes serve as a proxy for negative stereotypes. Extending the contact hypothesis, it was assumed that high Intercultural Contact and low Identification with one's Ethnic group will be associated with a greater sense of Security which, in turn, may lead to more positive Intercultural Attitudes (as proposed in the Multiculturalism Hypothesis). The two components of this latent construct (Multicultural Ideology and Tolerance/Prejudice) are necessary preconditions for promoting Integration of immigrants in the society of settlement, the former referring to cultural diversity and the latter to (the lack of) social equality. The third latent factor accounts for the pattern of acculturation expectations, with high Integration and low Assimilation, Separation and Marginalization. This last path of hypothesized relations

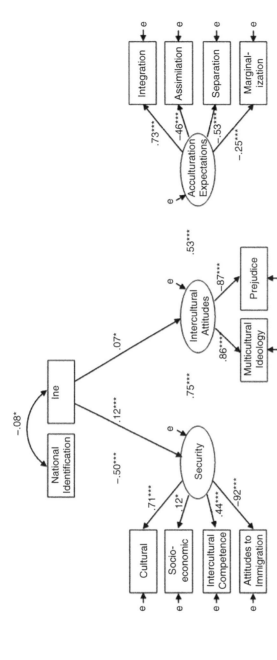

Figure 9.1. Structural equation model of the combined MIRIPS hypotheses for the Greek participants ($N = 449$).
Note: * $p < .05$; ** $p < .01$; *** $p < .001$. Values are standardized regression weights. Fit indices for the model:
CMIN = 132.67, DF = 42, $p < .001$; CMIN/DF = 3.15; CFI = .95; IFI = .95; TLI = .92; RMSEA = .069 (LO = .056, HI = .083); SRMR = .056.

(i.e., from intercultural attitudes to acculturation) is actually a modified version of the integration hypothesis, where the direction of prediction is reversed in this model.

As shown in Figure 9.1, the empirical data seem to provide adequate support for the hypothesized model. The explained variance reached 27.6 per cent for Security, 56.3 per cent for Intercultural Attitudes and 27.9 per cent for Acculturation Expectations. Following suggestions of the modification indices, a path was added from Intercultural Contact to Intercultural Attitudes. The independent variables (Greek Identification and Intercultural Contract) were allowed to correlate, which yielded a negative coefficient of low size. Finally, it should be noted that alternative models were tested (e.g., with Acculturation Expectations predicting Intercultural Attitudes or with different configuration of the observed Security components), but they produced worse fit or did not converge at all.

In the immigrant sample, again, three latent factors were formed, that is, Security, Acculturation and Adaptation. The first had only one observed variable (Cultural Security) in common with the respective latent construct in the Greek sample. In the case of immigrants, it also included low levels of Perceived Discrimination and Identification with both groups (i.e., the product of Ethnic by National Identity). According to the multiculturalism hypothesis, Security was expected to predict acculturation strategies favouring Immigration over Assimilation, Separation or Marginalization. Then, following the integration hypothesis, this latent acculturation factor may contribute to the adaptation of immigrants, in terms of higher Self-Esteem and Life Satisfaction, fewer Psychological Problems and better Sociocultural Adaptation. The empirical data provided good fit to the earlier model (Figure 9.2). Overall, security explained 67.4 per cent of acculturation strategies, and these, in turn, accounted for 28.4 per cent of immigrant adaptation.

Some interesting conclusions can be drawn from the alternative models that failed to reach acceptable fit. For example, the direct path from security to adaptation was not significant. More important, in contrast to the model for the Greek sample, there was no way to include Intercultural Contact predicting any of the three latent factors or their indicators, thus failing to accommodate the contact hypothesis in the model for the immigrant sample.

6   Discussion and Conclusions

In this chapter, we have reported evidence that is in full or partial support for the three MIRIPS hypotheses in Greece. This support in both the

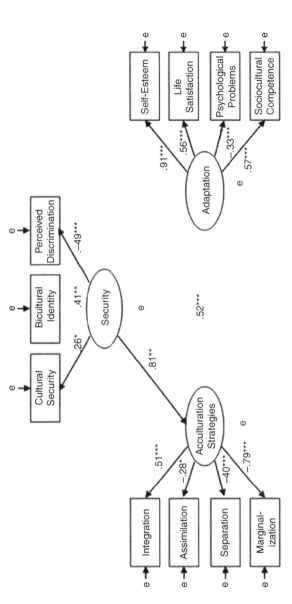

Figure 9.2. Structural equation model of the combined MIRIPS hypotheses for the immigrant participants ($N = 147$).
Note: * $p < .05$; ** $p < .01$; *** $p < .001$. Values are standardized regression weights. Fit indices for the model: CMIN = 52.19, DF = 39, $p = .077$; CMIN/DF = 1.30; CFI = .95; IFI = .95; TLI = .93; RMSEA = .054 (LO = .023, HI = .074); SRMR = .064.

Greek and immigrant samples provides evidence that the same principles are working in similar ways in both the non-dominant and dominant groups, thus confirming the 'mutual' perspective on intercultural relations. In addition to evaluating these three hypotheses, our approach was also informed by social psychological intergroup theories to test integrative models of intercultural relations.

The multiculturalism hypothesis was validated. Feeling secure about one's cultural identity and place in society contributes to more tolerant attitudes and the acceptance of diversity. This was especially true for Greeks (compared to immigrants) and for cultural (compared to socioeconomic) aspects of security. The inverse of this dimension is the link found between perceived threat and negative outgroup attitudes, which corresponds to the findings of meta-analyses (e.g., Riek, Mania & Gaertner, 2006).

The question arises: What constitutes security and threat? This yielded somewhat different answers from our two samples. For Greeks, in line with the Integrated Threat Theory (Stephan & Stephan, 2000), intergroup security consisted of feeling safe about one's cultural identity, living in a stable and predictable socioeconomic environment, being able to understand cultural differences in interpersonal interactions, and holding positive opinions of the consequences of immigration for the receiving country. Socioeconomic security was the weakest component of the four, probably because it refers to the societal, rather than to the personal level of analysis, and is therefore a more distant measure.

For immigrants, security included not only feeling safe about one's cultural identity, but also developing a bicultural identity and perceiving low levels of being discriminated against. So, there is more to security than feeling safe. It seems to be conceptually connected to pluralism and social inclusion, in spite of differences in the components of the construct between groups. This was illustrated in studies analyzing the 'incompatibility' between ethnic and national identities (Chryssochoou & Lyons, 2010) and the construction of immigrants' 'illegality' (Figgou, 2015).

In contrast to previous research, economic status failed to predict perceived security/threat. As Tajfel and Turner (1979) point out in their seminal paper on intergroup conflict, mere assignment to a social category is not enough to produce group differentiation; rather, individuals must have internalized group membership as an aspect of their self-concept. Education may act as such a lens that shapes perceptions of belonging and social comparisons. In our study, education did predict security as well as more positive intergroup attitudes. That is, security/threat does not rely solely on objective data of an economic nature; rather, subjective evaluations and context framing can fuel associations of different types of immigrants with different threats (Hellwig & Sinno, 2017).

In accordance with predictions stemming from both the multicultural-ism and contact hypotheses, low level of national identification and high level of intercultural contact were associated with increased sense of security for Greeks. In fact, the contact hypothesis was clearly confirmed from the point of view of the majority group. Not only did contact predict intercultural attitudes (i.e., more agreement with multicultural ideology and less prejudice), but also this relationship was partly explained through the mediation of security, as shown in the structural equation model. This result was expected because the effect of intergroup contact in reducing prejudice is a very robust finding in meta-analytic reviews (Pettigrew & Tropp, 2006). The mediating role of threat in the earlier relationship has also been established (Ward & Masgoret, 2006).

Unlike Greeks, however, for immigrants contact was not associated with security, acculturation strategies or adaptation. An explanation for this unexpected result is to be sought in the qualitative aspects of contact, which constitute Allport's (1954) optimal conditions for positive outcomes and which vary considerably between natives and immigrants. As members of a majority group, in terms of both size and power, Greeks are usually in the position to choose the type and frequency of intergroup contact. On the contrary, these intercultural contacts are less frequently under the control of minority group members. For immigrants, contact may or may not be voluntary, and status inequality or lack of institutional support are com-monplace in Greek society (Sapountzis, 2013). On the other hand, factors such as immigrant integration and culture learning may compensate for stressful intergroup interactions, as can be inferred by a longitudinal study of native and immigrant youth in Greek schools (Motti-Stefanidi et al., 2012). Thus, the aggregate of positive and negative experiences may result in a non-significant effect of contact on intercultural attitudes and adapta-tion. More concrete measures and context-specific information, preferably using qualitative methods, are required in order to better understand the nature, determinants and outcomes of intergroup contact from the per-spective of immigrants.

The integration hypothesis is probably one of the most frequently examined in acculturation research. The present study provides further support to the proposition that acculturation strategies are related to adaptation of immigrants (Berry, 1997, 2001). As was predicted, and in line with previous findings in Greece (Pavlopoulos et al., 2011), integra-tion yielded the most positive outcomes in both psychological and socio-cultural adaptation, while marginalization was clearly the least favourable strategy. Assimilation and separation were positioned in-between, with the former close to integration and the latter close to marginalization. This pattern of findings did not vary considerably between psychological and sociocultural adaptation, although differences were more pronounced in domains of the emotional and psychological adjustment rather than in the interpersonal and social functioning.

When the integration hypothesis is evaluated from the perspective of the majority group, the question of interest is somewhat different. In the acculturation model of Berry (2001), acculturation strategies of immigrants are predicted to lead to their adaptation. Social psychological approaches (e.g., Bourhis et al., 1997) also focus on the acculturation expectations of the members of the larger society as they derive from ideology and state policies. In our Greek sample, we identified multicultural ideology and prejudice as predictors of acculturation expectations, which provide the background beliefs on diversity and equity (Berry, 2016).

The most striking deviation of acculturation conceptualizations between immigrants and Greeks refers to marginalization. It is evident that, while for the understanding of immigrants this is a maladaptive strategy, it has a positive connotation for Greeks, as it was the second-most-preferred acculturation expectation, and it was positively associated with intercultural contact and multicultural ideology. Overall, the pattern of relationships of marginalization for the majority group resembles what Bourhis and his colleagues (1997) refer to as 'individualism'. It also confirms Berry's (2001) suggestion that different labelling is appropriate for acculturation strategies vs. expectations in order to avoid confusion. In our Greek sample, it seems that marginalization is conceived as a strategy that minimizes the (potentially threatening) cultural incompatibility between nationals and immigrants and focuses instead on the interpersonal aspects of contact in terms of citizenship rather than ethnicity (see also Chryssochoou & Lyons, 2010; Figgou, 2015).

On a more general note, the direction of associations in the models that we tested is not conclusive, which can be a twofold issue. One aspect is methodological and has to do with the limitations of a cross-sectional study to establish causality. The second is epistemological and refers to a researcher's discipline. Sociologists adopt a top-down approach, from the social level to psychological attributes. Thus, in their cross-national study Schlueter, Meuleman and Davidov (2013) found that immigrant integration policies significantly predicted perceived group threat. On the other hand, psychologists usually prefer a bottom-up approach, from the psychological to societal level of analysis. For example, in the dual process model of Satherley and Sibley (2016) dangerous and competitive worldviews formed key motives of group-based dominance and threat-driven social cohesion that led to less support for policies promoting immigration and trade from China to New Zealand. Whichever perspective is chosen, it is not possible to account for all relevant variables in a single research project, which holds for our study. For example, more detailed measures of perceived threat and socioeconomic status may have allowed for more elaborate hypotheses testing.

The generalizability of our findings is another issue that demands caution. It is not only the (non-random) sampling procedures that determine the external validity of the study. The rapidly changing landscape of immigration in Greece, which includes socioeconomic as well as geopolitical agents inside the country and in the wider region, challenges any attempt for reliable predictions.

The earlier considerations being acknowledged, they do not undermine the social relevance of the conclusions to be drawn from our data. On the contrary, informed opinions are more necessary than ever in this field of public discourse that is in danger to be taken over by populist politicians, xenophobic followers, far-right extremists and greedy opportunists.

References

Adamczyk, A. (2016). Albanian immigrants in Greece: From unwanted to tolerated? *Journal of Liberty and International Affairs*, *2*(1), 49–59.

Allport, G. W. (1954). *The Nature of Prejudice*. Reading, MA: Addison-Wesley.

Anagnostaki, L., Pavlopoulos, V., Obradović, J., Masten, A., & Motti-Stefanidi, F. (2016). Academic resilience of immigrant youth in Greek schools: Personal and family resources. *European Journal of Developmental Psychology*, *13*, 377–393. doi:10.1080/17405629.2016.1168738

Berry, J. W. (2001). A psychology of immigration. *Journal of Social Issues*, *57*(3), 615–631. doi:10.1111/0022-4537.00231

Berry, J. W. (2016). Diversity and equity. *Cross Cultural & Strategic Management*, *23*, 413–430. doi:10.1108/CCSM-03-2016-0085

Besevegis, E., & Pavlopoulos, V. (2008). Acculturation patterns and adaptation of immigrants in Greece. In M. Finklestein & K. Dent-Brown (Eds.), *Psychosocial Stress in Immigrants and in Members of Minority Groups as a Factor of Terrorist Behaviour* (pp. 23–34). Amsterdam: IOS Press. doi:10.3233/978-1-58603-872-4-23

Bourhis, R. Y., Moïse, L. C., Perreault, S., & Senécal, S. (1997). Towards an interactive acculturation model: A social psychological approach. *International Journal of Social Psychology*, *32*, 369–386. doi:10.1080/002075997400629

Cavounidis, J. (2013). Migration and the economic and social landscape of Greece. *South-Eastern Europe Journal of Economics*, *1*(1), 59–78.

Chryssochoou, X., & Lyons, E. (2010). Perceptions of (in)compatibility between identities and participation of ethnic minorities to the national polity. In A. Azzi, X. Chryssochoou, B. Klandermans & B. Simon (Eds.), *Identity* and Participation in Culturally Diverse Societies: A Multidisciplinary Perspective (pp. 69–88). Oxford: Wiley-Blackwell. doi:10.1002/9781444328158.ch4

European Commission (2015). *Standard Eurobarometer 84.* Available from http://ec.europa.eu/COMMFrontOffice/PublicOpinion/

Figgou, L. (2015). Constructions of 'illegal' immigration and entitlement to citizenship: Debating an immigration law in Greece. *Journal of Community & Applied Social Psychology, 26,* 150–163. doi:10.1002/casp.2242

Frontex (2016). *Risk analysis for 2016.* Warsaw: Frontex. doi:10.2819/26690

Hellenic Statistical Authority (2014). *2011 population and housing census.* Piraeus: Hellenic Statistical Authority. Available from www.statistics.gr/en/2011-census-pop-hous

Hellwig, T., & Sinno, A. (2017). Different groups, different threats: Public attitudes towards immigrants. *Journal of Ethnic and Migration Studies, 43*(3), 339–358. doi:10.1080/1369183X.2016.1202749

Iosifides, T., Lavrentiadou, M., Petracou, E., & Kontis, A. (2007). Forms of social capital and the incorporation of Albanian immigrants in Greece. *Journal of Ethnic and Migration Studies, 33,* 1343–1361. doi:10.1080/13691830701614247

McLaren, L. (2003). Anti-immigrant prejudice in Europe: Contact, threat perception, and preferences for the exclusion of migrants. *Social Forces, 81,* 909–936. doi:10.1353/sof.20030038

Motti-Stefanidi, F., & Asendorpf, J. (2012). Perceived discrimination of immigrant adolescents in Greece: How does group discrimination translate into personal discrimination? *European Psychologist, 17,* 93–104. doi:10.1027/1016-9040/a000116

Motti-Stefanidi, F., Asendorpf, J., & Masten, A. (2012). The adaptation and well-being of adolescent immigrants in Greek schools: A multilevel, longitudinal study of risks and resources. *Development and Psychopathology, 24,* 451–473. doi:10.1017/S0954579412000090

Motti-Stefanidi, F., Pavlopoulos, V., Obradović, J., Dalla, M., Takis, N., Papathanassiou, A., & Masten, A. S. (2008). Immigration as a risk factor for adolescent adaptation in Greek urban schools. *European Journal of Developmental Psychology, 5,* 235–261. doi:10.1080/17405620701556417

Motti-Stefanidi, F., Pavlopoulous, V., Obradović, J., & Masten A. S. (2008). Acculturation and adaptation of immigrant adolescents in Greek urban schools. *International Journal of Psychology, 43,* 45–58. doi:10.1080/00207590701804412

OECD & European Union (2015). *Indicators of immigrant integration 2015: Settling In.* Paris: OECD Publishing. doi:10.1787/9789264234024-en

Pavlopoulos, V., Dalla, M., Georganti, K., & Besevegis, E. (2011, July). *Building integration indices of immigrants in Greece: Definition, measurement and relations with sociodemographic factors.* Paper presented at the IACCP Regional Conference, Istanbul, Turkey. doi:10.13140/2.1.3895.0084

Pettigrew, T., & Tropp, L. (2006). A meta-analytic test of intergroup contact theory. *Journal of Personality and Social Psychology, 90,* 751–783. doi:10.1037/0022-3514.90.5.751

Riek, B., Mania, E., & Gaerner, S. (2006). Intergroup threat and outgroup attitudes: A meta-analytic review. *Personality and Social Psychology Review, 10*(4), 336–353. doi:10.1207/s15327957pspr1004_4

Sapountzis, A. (2013). Dominant group members talk about the acculturation of immigrants in Greece: Who is in charge of the acculturation process. *Hellenic Journal of Psychology*, *10*(1), 24–46.

Sapountzis, A., Figgou, L., Bozatzis, N., Gardikiotis, A., & Pantazis, P. (2013). 'Categories we share': Mobilising common in-groups in discourse on contemporary immigration in Greece. *Journal of Community & Applied Social Psychology*, *23*, 347–361. doi:10.1002/casp.2128

Satherley, N., & Sibley, C. (2016). A Dual Process Model of attitudes toward immigration: Predicting intergroup and international relations with China. *International Journal of Intercultural Relations*, *53*, 72–82. doi:10.1016/j.ijintrel.2016.05.008

Schlueter, E., Meuleman, B., & Davidov, E. (2013). Immigrant integration policies and perceived group threat: A multilevel study of 27 Western and Eastern European countries. *Social Science Research*, *42*, 670–682. doi:10.1016/j.ssresearch.2012.12.001

Stephan, W. G., & Stephan, C. W. (2000). An integrated threat theory of prejudice. In S. Oskamp (Ed.), *Reducing Prejudice and Discrimination* (pp. 23–45). Mahwah, NJ: Lawrence Erlbaum Associates.

Tajfel, H., & Turner, J. C. (1979). An integrative theory of intergroup conflict. In W. G. Austin & S. Worchel (Eds.), *The Social Psychology of Intergroup Relations* (pp. 33–48). Monterey, CA: Brooks-Cole.

Triandafyllidou, A. (2014). *Migration in Greece: Recent developments in 2014.* Athens: Hellenic Foundation for European & Foreign Policy. Available from www.eliamep.gr/wp-content/uploads/2014/10/Migration-in-Greece-Recent-Developments-2014_2.pdf

Tziovas, D. (Ed.). (2009). *Greek Diaspora and Migration since 1700: Society, Politics and Culture.* Farnham, UK: Ashgate.

Van Acker, K., & Vanbeselaere, N. (2011). Bringing together acculturation theory and intergroup contact theory: Predictors of Flemings' expectations of Turks' acculturation behavior. *International Journal of Intercultural Relations*, *35*, 334–345. doi:10.1016/j.ijintrel.2010.06.004

Ward, C., & Masgoret, A.-M. (2006). An integrative model of attitudes toward immigrants. *International Journal of Intercultural Relations*, *30*, 671–682. doi:10.1016/j.ijintrel.2006.06.002

10 Intercultural Relations in Italy

Cristiano Inguglia, Pasquale Musso and Alida Lo Coco
Università degli Studi di Palermo, Palermo, Italy

1 Introduction

Recent changes in migration flows are fast turning Italy into a multicultural society, characterized by a patchwork of people in search of new patterns of intercultural coexistence. Hence, the country provides an interesting perspective from which to analyze the processes underlying the changing nature of intercultural relations. Italy is below the midpoint on the diversity and integration indexes, and second from the bottom on the multiculturalism policy index.

2 Context of Intercultural Relations in Italy

Italy is becoming more and more ethnically and culturally diverse. In the last few years, the foreign-born population in the country has grown substantially while the native-born population has dramatically decreased. According to Cesareo (2016), the total number of legal immigrants who are permanent residents in Italy has increased from about 1,000,000 in 2001 to more than 5,000,000 in 2014. Such an enlargement is related to a greater frequency of migration flows directed especially to its southern regions like Sicily. Currently, a large proportion of immigrants come from Africa due to its geographical closeness, via countries like Libya and Tunisia.

2.1 Immigration

In the most recent years, this increase of migration flows is particularly due to changes in the socio-political geography of some North African and Middle Eastern countries (e.g., the Arab Spring, conflicts in Syria).

Consequently, Italy is part of the Mediterranean Migration Crisis, which is characterized by unprecedented numbers of people taking dangerous journeys across the Mediterranean to reach the Italian coasts. For instance, in 2014, at least 219,000 migrants and asylum seekers crossed the Mediterranean, around 60,000 more than the previous year (Human Rights Watch, 2015). According to the United Nations High Commissioner for Refugees (UNHCR, 2015), 89,500 crossed the Mediterranean in the first five months of 2015. Unfortunately, this crossing is often full of dangers and fatalities. In 2014, over 3,500 women, men and children were reported dead or missing (UNHCR, 2015).

These changes in migration are increasing the diverse character of Italy. Hence, the country provides an interesting perspective from which to analyze the processes underlying the changing nature of intercultural relations. Furthermore, in Italy there is a lack of scientific understanding of the psychological processes underlying intercultural relations, which is fundamental to designing effective settlement and integration policies. Such an understanding is still inadequate because the local studies focused on these topics are very limited in number (Dimitrova, 2011; Inguglia & Musso, 2015; Musso, Inguglia, Lo Coco, Albiero & Berry, 2016; Mancini & Bottura, 2014). Given this lack of previous research, the aim of this chapter is to expand the knowledge of the psychological variables related to the quality of intercultural relations in a context like Italy.

2.2   Policies in Italy

Within Europe, Italy is one of the most recent immigrant-receiving societies, with immigrants currently making up around 9% of the total population. In addition to the 5,000,000 legal immigrants, there are also about 130,000 people of foreign origins who have acquired Italian citizenship, as well as a large number of illegal immigrants that is estimated to be between 500,000 to 700,000 (Fondazione Ismu, 2016). The largest numbers of immigrants (59.5%) live in northern Italy, which is the most economically developed area; 25.4% live in the central regions and 15.1% live in the southern regions that are characterized by the highest rates of unemployment. The most numerous groups come from Romania (about 22%), Albania (about 10%), Morocco (about 9%), China (about 5.5%) and Ukraine (about 4.5%). Additionally, more than 20% of them are children and adolescents with a prevalence of second-generation (about 60%).

In 2007, Italy was one of the European countries with the best integration policies, according to Migrant Integration Policy Index.

Since then, the country has moved to a middle position in the ranking due to more restrictive policies (e.g., the 2009 Security Law). However, this has been attenuated by some new policies, such as opening public sector jobs to long-term residents. Nevertheless, considering eight key areas of life (health, political participation, labor market mobility, education, access to nationality, family reunion, permanent residence, anti-discrimination), the conditions of immigrants living in Italy remain only halfway favourable for integration (Migrant Integration Policy Index, 2015). Although some steps towards integration have been achieved, many steps still remain to be done. For instance, numerous long-settled immigrants have found jobs below the level of their qualification since they have not been able to access education and training. In addition, many immigrants of non-EU countries experience difficulties in becoming full Italian citizens due to the restrictive and bureaucratic paths (Migrant Integration Policy Index, 2015).

The road to inclusion of immigrants in Italy is still long and requires the completion of several steps (Cesareo, 2016). Among them are the increase of employment rates of immigrants through on-the-job training and guidance activities; the resolution of the problems related to the "over-qualification" of immigrants, which consists in the fact that immigrant workers are not able to find jobs matching their skills and expertise; the prevention of early school leaving by supporting intercultural education and providing training and professional support to school teachers and staff; and building a sense of trust among immigrants towards Italian public authorities, who must do more to counter ethnic and religious discrimination.

2.3   *Public Attitudes towards Immigrants and Immigration*

Along with the integration policies, one key aspect that affects the settlement of immigrants, as well as contributing to the quality of intercultural relations, is the attitudes of Italians towards immigrants and immigration. Although this topic will be analyzed in the next sections of this chapter with reference to our findings, we now present some general information about these attitudes reported by other studies.

According to Ambrosini (2013), the attitudes of Italians towards immigration are deeply contradictory, especially those of people living in the richer regions of the country. On the one hand, they are aware that Italy is becoming more and more multi-ethnic, in terms of the number of residents of other cultural backgrounds, participation in the labor market, transition to self-employment, mixed marriages and the origin of students in schools. On the other hand, they tend to deny this reality, refusing to accept the presence of immigrants in their country.

Kosic, Manetti and Sam (2005) notice a negative orientation of Italians towards immigrants and immigration flows. According to them, these hostile attitudes arose around the year 2000 against a background of a number of factors, such as the lack of clear immigration and settlement policies, the large presence of immigrants with irregular residence permits and the fact that immigrants are portrayed in the mass media and in political speeches as potential criminals and as being involved in a number of clandestine activities. Furthermore, a more recent survey (Eurobarometer, 2014) has pointed out that Italy is one of the EU countries that show the most negative attitudes towards immigration from outside the European Union.

Over the years, the unfriendly attitude of Italians towards immigrants has been directed towards various ethnic and national groups depending on specific social and historical circumstances. For instance, in the last two decades, prejudice against people coming from Romania was high, linked to some isolated violent crimes committed by Romanian immigrants (Caritas Italiana, 2008). However, in more recent years the prejudice seems to be mainly directed towards Muslim immigrants who are often erroneously linked to radicalism and labeled as potential terrorists. In confirmation of this, Italians were found to display the most unfavourable attitudes towards Muslims across different EU states (e.g., PEW Research Center, 2015).

The negative attitude towards immigration is witnessed by the rising popularity of right-wing political parties supporting policies of closing of the frontiers and refusing to extend citizenship to immigrant people. Such stances are represented, for instance, by the anti-immigrant party Lega Nord that has electoral strength in northern regions of Italy (i.e., Veneto, Lombardia). Politicians of Lega Nord often blame immigrants for crime, terrorism, the black market, stealing jobs from locals, trampling over Italian values and undermining social cohesion (Calavita, 2005).

Nevertheless, there are identifiable differences in attitudes towards immigrants and immigration among the Italian regions. Generally, the northern regions of the country are characterized by higher levels of hostile attitudes, whereas the southern regions are more friendly towards immigration. For instance, previous studies found that Italians living in Sicily report high levels of support for multiculturalism and positive attitudes towards immigration (Inguglia & Musso, 2013, 2015; Musso, Inguglia, Lo Coco et al., 2016).

3   Evaluation of the MIRIPS Hypotheses

The Italian MIRIPS project evaluated all three hypotheses. In addition, we were interested in investigating some related issues. In this section of the chapter, we outline the ways in which the three main hypotheses were operationalized, as well as the additional issues that were analyzed in our studies.

With regard to the multiculturalism hypothesis, we expected that individuals who feel secure in their place in society would be more accepting of people from different cultures and ethnic groups. In particular, we focused on members of dominant groups, predicting that their scores of perceived security would be positively associated with their levels of both multicultural ideology and tolerance. We also considered the opposite side of this hypothesis, predicting that when individuals are threatened, they will prefer separation. We also analyzed this issue among non-dominant group members and in relation to their psychosocial well-being, which will be discussed in the section dealing with the integration hypothesis.

With regard to the contact hypothesis, we expected that intergroup contact would be positively related to attitudes towards the out-groups in both non-dominant and dominant group members. In the case of non-dominant group members, we hypothesized that social contacts with Italian peers would be positively associated with a favourable attitude towards Italians and Italian culture. In the case of dominant group participants, we expected that social contacts with immigrant peers would be positively associated with tolerance and multiculturalism.

Finally, with regard to the integration hypothesis we expected that a high preference for integration would be associated with better psychosocial adjustment in non-dominant group members. We have tested this hypothesis in some studies by using both variable-oriented and person-oriented approaches (Inguglia & Musso, 2015; Inguglia, Musso, Lo Coco & Berry, 2016; Musso, Inguglia & Lo Coco, 2015). In the case of the variable-oriented approach, we analyzed the associations between acculturation strategies and the indicators of psychosocial well-being, such as self-esteem, life satisfaction, psychological problems and socio-cultural competence. In the person-oriented approach, we first identified some acculturation profiles, namely classifications of immigrants obtained by combining variables associated with the acculturation process, such as acculturation strategies, ethnic and national identities, ethnic and national social contacts, languages spoken. Then, we analyzed the differences between these acculturation profiles with regard to immigrants' well-being. In accordance with other studies using a similar approach

(Berry, Phinney, Sam & Vedder, 2006; Brown, Gibbons & Hughes, 2013), we expected to identify at least three acculturation profiles: one resembling integration, one resembling assimilation and one resembling separation. In both cases, we hypothesized that integration, or the acculturation profile resembling integration, would be positively associated with psychological well-being more than the other strategies or profiles.

For the dominant sample, we also used a person-oriented approach, by identifying acculturation expectation profiles through the combination of variables such as acculturation expectations, national identity and ethnic and national social contacts. Berry (2011) argued that in contexts characterized by a positive attitude towards multiculturalism, the structure of acculturation expectations will have a preference for multiculturalism at one end of the dimension, and the other expectations at the other end. Hence, we hypothesized that we would identify two profiles, one resembling multiculturalism and the other including a combination of melting pot, exclusion and segregation. Then, we analyzed the relationships between the acculturation expectation profiles and the psychological well-being, in terms of life satisfaction, self-esteem and psychological problems. Based on the consideration that multicultural acceptance is often associated with better psychological functioning (Inguglia & Musso, 2015; Verkuyten, 2009), we expected that the profile resembling multiculturalism would be associated with higher levels of both life satisfaction and self-esteem, and lower levels of psychological problems, than the other profile.

In addition to evaluating the three main hypotheses, we were interested in analyzing other issues that are also relevant in determining the quality of intercultural relations in Italy (Inguglia & Musso, 2015; Inguglia et al., 2016; Musso et al., 2015; Musso, Inguglia, Lo Coco et al., 2016). First, considering non-dominant group members, we analyzed the associations between perceived discrimination, separation (as acculturation strategy or profile) and psychosocial well-being (Inguglia et al., 2016; Musso et al., 2015). In one case, we based our work on the multiculturalism hypothesis proposing that the experience of discrimination is an indicator of threat that undermines individuals' sense of security and is associated with the preference for higher levels of interest in cultural maintenance and little interest in having relations with other cultures and people. In a second case, we investigated the moderating role of acculturation profiles in the relationships between perceived discrimination and psychosocial well-being. In line with previous research, we expected that the acculturation profile resembling separation would protect immigrants from the detrimental effects of perceived group discrimination (Armenta & Hunt, 2009; Umana-Taylor & Updegraff, 2007).

Second, we investigated the relationship between dominant group members' multicultural ideology and their attitude towards immigrants, considering also the mediating role of both tolerance and perceived consequences of immigration. On the basis of previous studies, we hypothesized that multicultural ideology would be positively associated with attitudes towards immigrants (Hui, Chen, Leung & Berry, 2015; Ward & Masgoret, 2008), although this association would be mediated by tolerance and the perceived consequences of immigration (Hui et al., 2015). In particular, we expected that the higher the levels of multicultural ideology and tolerance, the higher the levels of positive perceived consequences of immigration and more positive attitudes towards immigrants would be (Musso, Inguglia, Lo Coco et al., 2016).

4   Method

4.1   Samples

The Italian project focused on the study of adolescents (aged approximately from 14 to 18 years old) and emerging adults (approximately from 19 to 29 years old) from both non-dominant and dominant groups living in Italy. The rationale behind the choice to take into account two different life stages is related to the peculiar characteristics of adolescence and emerging adulthood, which permit the study of how the processes related to the quality of intercultural relations may change during the developmental changes youth undergo in the passage from adolescence to adulthood. Adolescence is a critical period for the formation of intercultural strategies, cultural identities and attitudes towards other cultures both in non-dominant and dominant groups (Inguglia & Musso, 2015; Musso et al., 2015; Sam & Berry, 2006). During adolescence, in fact, youth try to learn more about history, practices and beliefs of their own ethnocultural group (Musso, Inguglia & Lo Coco, 2016), as well as about those of the other groups living in their society. Moreover, the awareness of their ethnocultural belonging increases; consequently, the cultural dimension becomes very salient and affects the process of identity development and the relationships with people of other ethnocultural groups (Umaña-Taylor et al., 2014). Emerging adulthood is an interesting period for studying these issues (Musso, Inguglia, Lo Coco et al., 2016) because the acceptance of culturally diverse others is facilitated by a number of developmental strides, including new cognitive abilities and corresponding improvements in moral reasoning (Arnett, 2010; Gerson & Neilson, 2014). Such advances, along with the overcoming of adolescent identity crisis, allow emerging adults to better address the ideological concerns about cultural diversity and cultural belonging, as well as to understand and appreciate their own and others' cultural views and needs (Arnett, 2010).

The studies of non-dominant groups were focused mainly on people of Tunisian origin. They are one of the most interesting and understudied immigrant groups living in Sicily, the region in which the greater part of our studies were carried out. Tunisians are the second-largest immigrant group (about 18,000 persons) in Sicily and have a long history of exchanges with this region that began in the 1960s (Ben-Yehoyada, 2011). Tunisian and Sicilian groups are characterized by similarities and differences that are remarkable for the study of intercultural relations. On the one hand, Tunisia and Sicily are geographically close and are marked out by socio-cultural interactions that have often resulted in similar habits, for instance, with regard to food, architecture, family culture or values. On the other hand, there are differences between the two groups, particularly related to spoken languages, religions practiced and the legal status of Tunisian immigrants that may pose some real barriers to their effective integration (Musso, Inguglia & Lo Coco, 2016).

The dominant group sample was recruited from Italian adolescents and emerging adults who were born in Italy living in two different regions, one southern (Sicily) the other northern (Veneto)[1]. In particular, we chose Sicily because it is characterized by a relatively friendly immigration socio-political climate and by rather open immigration policies. Conversely, Veneto is characterized by a relatively unfriendly immigration socio-political climate, where the largest party is Lega Nord advocating closed immigration policies. The reason underlying this choice was to investigate the moderating role of socio-political context in the psychological processes affecting intercultural relations. Table 10.1 shows detailed information about the samples of our studies.

4.2   Procedure

We used two structured versions of the MIRIPS questionnaire, one for immigrant groups and one for the Italian sample. The scales were translated from English into Italian following the recommendations of the International Test Commission (2005). An independent teacher, whose native language was English and who was fluent in Italian, did a back translation. Discrepancies were resolved following the guidelines outlined

---

[1] We would like to thank professor Paolo Albiero of Padua University for leading the data collection in Veneto.

Table 10.1 *Samples recruited for the studies of the Italian section of the MIRIPS Project.*

Study	Dominant samples Participants' number (region of residence)	Non-dominant samples Participants' number and ethnicity (generation)	Age Means (range)	Gender Male (%)
Inguglia & Musso (2015)	129 (Sicily)	127 Tunisians (54 first-generation and 73 second-generation)	Italians: 15.92 (14 to 18) Tunisians: 15.64 (14 to 18)	Italians: 44.19% Tunisians: 49.61%
Musso et al. (2015)	–	348 Tunisians (all second-generation)	15.72 (14 to 18)	51.72%
Musso, Inguglia, Lo Coco et al. (2016)	204 (Sicily) 101 (Veneto)	–	Sicilians: 23.55 (18 to 29) Venetians: 23.04 (18 to 29)	Sicilians: 51.49% Venetians: 41.67%
Inguglia et al. (2016)	256 (Sicily)	188 Tunisians (77 first-generation and 111 second-generation)	Italians: 16.34 (13 to 18) Tunisians: 15.94 (13 to 18)	Italians: 42.19% Tunisians: 51.06%

Table 10.2 *Characteristics of the MIRIPS Questionnaire for non-dominant group members.*

Construct	Scale/Subscales	Number of Items	Cronbach's Alpha
Acculturation Attitudes	Integration	4	.69
	Separation	4	.65
	Assimilation	4	.76
	Marginalization	4	.63
Cultural Identity	Ethnic Identity	7	.82
	National Identity	3	.90
Social Contacts	Number of Ethnic Peer Contacts	1	–
	Frequency of Ethnic Peer Contacts	1	–
	Number of National Peer Contacts	1	–
	Frequency of National Peer Contacts	1	–
Psychological Well-being	Self-Esteem	10	.77
	Life Satisfaction	5	.83
	Psychological Problems	15	.88
Socio-cultural Competence	Difficulties in the Host Countries (Reverse)	20	.89
Perceived Discrimination	Perceived Discrimination	5	.81

Note: Reported values of Cronbach's alpha are equal to the average values extracted after considering the following studies: Inguglia & Musso (2015); Inguglia et al. (2016); Musso et al. (2015).

by Knight, Roosa and Umaña-Taylor (2009). Tables 10.2 and 10.3 show the main characteristics of the two versions of MIRIPS questionnaire.

All our studies were approved by the local ethics committees and were performed in accordance with the Italian Association of Psychology (2015) ethical principles for psychological research. We usually contacted participants in schools (adolescents) or universities (emerging adults), as well as in community centers. All participants (and their parents, in case of adolescents) were informed about the purpose of the research, the voluntariness of participation and the anonymity of responses through specific meetings. Questionnaires were single-administered with the support of cultural mediators when needed.

Table 10.3. *Characteristics of the MIRIPS Questionnaire for dominant group members.*

Construct	Scale/Subscales	Number of items	Cronbach's alpha
Acculturation	Multiculturalism	4	.73
Expectations	Segregation	4	.65
	Melting Pot	4	.64
	Exclusion	4	.62
Cultural Identity	National Identity	7	.87
Social Contacts	Number of Ethnic Peer Contacts	1	–
	Frequency of Ethnic Peer Contacts	1	–
	Number of National Peer Contacts	1	–
	Frequency of National Peer Contacts	1	–
Psychological Well-being	Self-Esteem	10	.81
	Life Satisfaction	5	.82
	Psychological Problems	15	.90
Multicultural Ideology (MCI)	MCI	10	.77
Perceived Security	Perceived Security	6	.60
Tolerance	Tolerance	11	.82
Perceived Consequences of Immigration (PCI)	PCI	11	.74
Attitude towards Immigrants	100-Point Feeling Thermometer	1 rating for each group	–

Note: Reported values of Cronbach's alpha are equal to the average values extracted after considering the following studies: Inguglia & Musso (2015); Inguglia et al. (2016); Musso, Inguglia, Lo Coco et al. (2016).

The analyses used both a variable-oriented and person-oriented approaches. The first approach focuses on the analysis of variables and assumes that they are inter-related similarly and linearly across all groups under consideration. Therefore, the variable-oriented approach supposes that the meaning and covariation of all variables is the same for all groups (Bergman & Trost, 2006). However, although this approach can be useful to reveal interesting information, immigrant and autochthonous groups also exhibit patterns of several interrelated dimensions that are not captured by unidimensional analyses. Hence, we also used a person-oriented approach that provides information concerning which combinations of factors are significant and prevalent, and how such combinations may change for different subgroups of individuals (Magnusson, 2003). In doing so, some of our studies were aimed at creating classifications of adolescents based on several dimensions related to intercultural strategies, as well as examining the multidimensional relationships among these patterns. For this purpose, we used empirical ways of classifying individuals, such as clustering methods, that permit a more integrative approach to acculturation data and a more realistic identification of profiles with respect to the acculturation outcomes (Brown et al., 2013; Schwartz & Zamboanga, 2008), as well as the expectations towards acculturation.

5   Results and Discussion

In this part of the chapter, we summarize our findings (see Table 10.4) with reference to the main hypotheses and the other relevant issues presented in the previous section.

5.1   Evaluating the Three MIRIPS Hypotheses

Multiculturalism hypothesis. Our studies provide support for this hypothesis, by showing that perceived security is positively associated with both multicultural ideology and tolerance (Inguglia et al., 2016). Thus, our findings highlight once more the importance of feelings of being secure for those living in plural society. People who feel confidence and security with

Table 10.4 *MIRIPS main hypotheses: Findings from Italian studies.*

Study	Multiculturalism Hypothesis	Contact Hypothesis	Integration Hypothesis
Inguglia & Musso (2015)	Not Tested	Not Tested	Mostly Supported
Musso et al. (2015)	Not Tested	Not Tested	Mostly Supported
Inguglia et al. (2016)	Supported	Supported	Supported

regard to their identity and their place in society tend to show greater acceptance and respect for others, as well as valuing diversity and equity across ethnocultural groups.

For the contact hypothesis, we found support in both dominant and non-dominant group members. With regard to dominant group adolescents, we found that the opportunity to be in contact with immigrant peers is positively associated with attitudes towards multiculturalism. For instance, the more Italian peers spend time with their Tunisian peers, the more they prefer that Tunisian adolescents maintain their heritage culture while adopting the Italian habits (Inguglia et al., 2016). Similarly, Tunisian adolescents who have a greater number of social contacts with Italian peers tend to show a favourable attitude towards having contact with Italian culture and people, in terms of high levels of integration. Hence, the more immigrant adolescents spend time in contact with Italian teens, the more they participate in Italian culture while maintaining also their own heritage culture.

For the integration hypothesis, it was mostly supported using both person-oriented and variable-oriented approaches. In particular, we performed two studies using the person-oriented approach to identify acculturation profiles in non-dominant-group adolescents (Inguglia & Musso, 2015; Musso et al., 2015). One study (Inguglia & Musso, 2015) involved a sample of Tunisian adolescents, both first- and second-generation immigrants. A cluster analysis on the scores of acculturation strategies, ethnic and national identities, and ethnic and national social contacts identified two acculturation profiles. The first is ethnic (39.52%), in which members were characterized by a strong preference towards separation as an acculturation strategy and by a predilection for maintaining social contacts with people of their own ethnic group. The second is integrated-national (60.48%), characterized by a preference for integration as an acculturation strategy, a strong identification with Italians and a preference for social contact with Italians.

Another study of the integration hypothesis (Musso et al., 2015) involved a sample of second-generation Tunisian adolescents. Using clustering methods with the scores of acculturation strategies, ethnic and national identities, ethnic and national languages, and ethnic and national social contacts, we identified three acculturation profiles: integrated (51.73%), ethnic (27.01%) and national (21.26%). The integrated profile was characterized by high levels of involvement in both Italian and Tunisian cultures in terms of language, identity and social contacts, as well as high levels of preference for the integration strategy, along with low preferences for assimilation and separation. The ethnic profile was defined by high levels of involvement only in Tunisian culture (in terms of ethnic identity, proficiency in the Arabic language and social contacts with Tunisian peers), along with high levels of separation. The national profile was characterized by high levels of involvement in Italian culture (in terms of national identity, proficiency in Italian language and social contacts with Italian peers), along with higher levels of assimilation than the other two profiles.

In both studies we found that adolescents who belong to acculturation profiles resembling integration reported higher levels of psychosocial well-being, in terms of self-esteem, life satisfaction and socio-cultural competence, than those of the ethnic profile resembling separation (Inguglia & Musso, 2015; Musso et al., 2015). Moreover, when using a variable-oriented approach, findings suggested that integration is positively associated with life satisfaction and self-esteem, while separation is negatively associated with self-esteem, and assimilation has no significant associations with psychological well-being (Inguglia et al., 2016). Thus, our findings are mostly consistent with the integration hypothesis, showing the importance of integration as compared to separation. Nevertheless, no relevant significant differences were found between integration and assimilation in terms of well-being, even if assimilation has lower associations with positive outcomes than integration. Hence, the results highlight the importance of integration for immigrant youth living in Italy, probably because this strategy supports the development of an harmonious bicultural identity that is important for the psychological functioning in this period of life (Musso, Inguglia & Lo Coco, 2016; Umana-Taylor et al., 2014).

We examined the acculturation expectations of the dominant group of adolescents, using the profile method. In line with our predictions, we found two acculturation expectation profiles. One is the multicultural profile (63.56%), characterized by a positive attitude towards multiculturalism and low levels of expectations for melting pot, segregation and exclusion (Inguglia & Musso, 2015). The other is the non-multicultural profile (36.34%), characterized by preferences for melting pot, segregation and exclusion as acculturation expectations, and a general negative attitude towards multiculturalism. These findings seem to confirm the unidimensional structure of acculturation expectations, with preference for multiculturalism anchoring one end of the dimension, and the preferences for melting pot, segregation and exclusion anchoring the other end. This pattern has been observed in contexts where there are positive attitudes towards integration, along with a rejection of the other three ways (Arends-Tóth & Van de Vijver, 2003; Berry, 2011). Such an explanation is appropriate for our research context because Sicily is characterized by high rates of openness towards cultural diversity, especially towards Tunisian people who live on the other side of Mediterranean Sea, very close to Sicily (Musso et al., 2015).

The evaluation of the integration hypothesis using the profile approach among the Italian sample showed that Italian adolescents who fit the multicultural profile display higher levels of self-esteem and life satisfaction when compared to their not-multicultural counterpart. This is in line with previous studies on similar topics (e.g., Verkuyten, 2009) which have observed that recognition and acceptance of cultural diversity appears to be associated with better self-esteem on the part of majority group members. Thus, the more people are open-minded to differences, the more they are satisfied with their own life and their own self.

5.2   Other Issues

With respect to the other issues that are related to the three main hypotheses, our findings provide some additional support for them. First, as expected, data showed that perceived discrimination is positively associated with the separation strategy, meaning that the more the immigrant youth feel threatened by acts of discrimination of the dominant-group members, the more they tend to value their original culture and, at the same time, to avoid interaction with other cultures and people (Inguglia et al., 2016). This is an example of 'reciprocity' in intercultural relations (Berry, Kalin & Taylor, 1977), who found that being rejected by others (by discrimination) is reciprocated by rejecting the source of the original rejection (by adopting the separation strategy). Furthermore, perceived discrimination was found to be negatively related to immigrant youth's psychosocial adjustment, but this relationship may be moderated by the acculturation profile to which immigrants belong (Musso et al., 2015). Research has shown that there are two forms of discrimination (Motti-Stefanidi & Asendorpf, 2012): perceived discrimination against one's ethnic group (perceived group discrimination) and perceived discrimination against the self (perceived personal discrimination). Given this distinction, in line with previous studies (Armenta & Hunt, 2009) we found that the acculturation profile resembling separation seems to protect adolescents' psychological adjustment from the effects of group discrimination, but not from the effects of personal discrimination; rather it can worsen them. In other words, when adolescents feel that the discrimination is directed against themselves rather than against their own ethnic group, the feeling of belonging to this group is not effective to protect them against the negative effects of the perception of discrimination on the psychological well-being.

Second, our data showed that, among Italian emerging adults, high levels of multicultural ideology are associated with positive attitudes towards non-dominant groups. We also found that tolerance and the perceived consequences of immigration play a mediating role in this association (Musso, Inguglia, Lo Coco et al., 2016). In other words, emerging adults' perception of cultural diversity as a resource for society seems to be related to both support for equal rights between ethnocultural groups and the perception of immigration as a positive phenomenon. These traits, in turn, are linked to more favourable views of the ethnocultural groups. These results are in line with the findings of previous studies on similar topics (Hui et al., 2015). However, we also found that the cultural context partially moderates these relationships. Both the direct effect of multicultural ideology on tolerance and the related indirect effects on attitudes towards immigration were stronger in emerging adults living in Veneto (northern Italy) than in those living in Sicily (southern Italy). Such results indicate that in contexts more friendly towards immigration, like Sicily, the levels of attitudes towards immigration are probably affected to a greater extent by general receptive socio-political perspectives than by personal variables, such as multicultural ideology. Instead, in contexts where there are more unfriendly policies towards immigration, the effect of personal variables, such as multicultural ideology, become more relevant.

6   Conclusion and Implications

From the analysis of our findings, we conclude that the three MIRIPS hypotheses are quite effective in predicting general trends of associations among variables. In sum, the three hypotheses were supported by the studies where they were evaluated. The multiculturalism hypothesis and the contact hypothesis were supported by Inguglia et al. (2016); and the integration hypothesis was supported by Inguglia and Musso (2015), by Musso et al. (2015) and by Inguglia et al. (2016). In no case was contrary evidence found.

However, these confirming relationships need to be examined with reference to the contextual features of the particular socio-cultural contexts in which intercultural relations occur. We also need to consider the mediating and moderating processes in these relationships. For instance, taking into account the features of the research context can help to better understand our results about the integration hypothesis. The long history of exchanges between Tunisian and Sicilian groups, along with the presence of remarkable similarities between these groups, may facilitate the possibility that Tunisians tend to show higher levels of integration with respect to the other acculturation strategies, and that integration is associated with positive outcomes. Moreover, the potential benefits of assimilation for immigrant youth that were highlighted in some of our studies (e.g., Inguglia & Musso, 2015) can be understood

226 Inguglia, Musso and Lo Coco

considering that Italy is a country of recent immigration in which a positive attitude towards the culture of the larger society is valued and considered a fundamental requirement for immigrants' inclusion. Finally, the findings about the negative outcomes associated with separation can be explained by taking into account the fact that Sicilians hold positive expectations towards the integration of immigrant people (Musso, Inguglia & Lo Coco, 2016). Hence, being separated can be perceived by the Sicilians as a refusal to accept Italian culture on the part of the Tunisians and may be associated with acts of discrimination against them. In turn, as predicted by the multiculturalism hypothesis, this may further promote the tendency of young immigrants to prefer the separation strategy or to develop an ethnic profile resembling separation; this pattern may have negative consequences for their psychological well-being, especially when the discrimination is perceived as directed against the person and not against the ethnocultural group. Moreover, our results lend support to the use of clustering methods as a way of including multiple indicators of acculturation, thereby gaining a more comprehensive understanding of the process. This is another direction for future research.

Although our findings provide support for the three MIRIPS hypotheses among adolescents and emerging adults living in Italy, they should be considered in light of some limitations of our studies. First, the data are cross-sectional and correlational, which hinders our ability to clearly establish the mediating processes. Thus, longitudinal research is needed to determine temporal ordering and causality among the variables. Second, the measures were all self-report and, as a consequence, they might lead to social desirability bias. Future studies should adopt mixed methods or experimental designs. Third, we focused only on people of Tunisian origin as the non-dominant group; this is because we consider them as one of the more interesting in our Sicilian research context. However, future research should also consider other immigrant groups living in Italy who can be characterized by different cultural features from those of the Tunisians. Finally, our research did not take into account the influence of family as well as the socio-political variables. Future research should investigate such variables in order to gain a deeper knowledge of the processes affecting mutual intercultural relations in adolescents and emerging adults.

Despite these limitations, our studies make a novel contribution to the literature because they extend the testing of the multiculturalism, contact and integration hypotheses in an understudied and important context such as Italy, using both variable-oriented and person-oriented approaches. Our conclusions are likely to be generalizable to other immigrants who live in contexts that are characterized simultaneously by strong ties with the heritage culture, quite high levels of integration and good relationships with the host society members.

Finally, the results of our studies should provide insights for decision-makers and practitioners to design effective social policies and programs to enhance the quality of intercultural relations among all the ethnocultural groups living in Italy (both non-dominant and dominant), promoting by this means their psychosocial well-being. With regard to non-dominant youth, it seems important to design intervention programs with at least two main goals. First, these programs should be aimed at pursuing the integration of immigrant youth by providing them with opportunities to maintain their culture of origin and, concurrently, to participate in the larger society and to have contacts with Italians. Second, the interventions should attempt to limit the perception of discrimination by the non-dominant group members since its effects could be detrimental for the psychological well-being of the immigrant youth. With regard to the dominant group, adolescents and emerging adults should be provided with more opportunities to develop a positive attitude towards multiculturalism and multicultural ideology, for instance, through intercultural education programs that try to enhance the sense of perceived security, as well as to reduce the sense of threat related to immigration and the presence of other ethnocultural groups in the host society.

To conclude, social policies and educational programs targeted to both non-dominant and dominant group members are needed to promote more opportunities for intercultural contacts between groups. However, in designing such opportunities it is important to consider the views of Allport (1954), who argued that in order to improve the quality of intergroup relations contact should take place only under certain conditions. In particular, contact should be voluntary, of equal status, and should be promoted by shared norms or by public policy. To date the previous insights are supported by empirical evidence coming from different studies from across the world, such as Berry (2013); Hui et al. (2015); Lebedeva & Tatarko (2013); Lebedeva, Tatarko & Berry (2016); Nguyen & Benet-Martínez (2013). This synthesis could be the basis for developing effective policies aimed to promote intercultural dialogue and psychological well-being of ethnocultural groups living in plural societies.

References

Allport, G. (1954). *The Nature of Prejudice*. Reading, MA: Addison-Wesley.
Ambrosini, M. (2013). Immigration in Italy: Between economic acceptance and political rejection. *Journal of International Migration and Integration*, *14*, 175–194.

Arends-Tóth, J., & Van de Vijver, F. J. (2003). Multiculturalism and accultura-tion: Views of Dutch and Turkish–Dutch. *European Journal of Social Psychology*, *33*, 249–266.

Armenta, B. E., & Hunt, J. S. (2009). Responding to societal devaluation: Effects of perceived personal and group discrimination on the ethnic group identifica-tion and personal self-esteem of Latino/Latina adolescents. *Group Processes & Intergroup Relations*, *12*, 23–39.

Arnett, J. J. (2010). *Adolescence and Emerging Adulthood: A Cultural Approach* (4th ed.). Upper Saddle River, NJ: Pearson Prentice Hall.

Ben-Yehoyada, N. (2011). The moral perils of Mediterraneanism: Second gen-eration immigrants practicing personhood between Sicily and Tunisia. *Journal of Modern Italian Studies*, *16*, 386–403.

Bergman, L. R., & Trost, K. (2006). The person-oriented versus the variable-oriented approach: Are they complementary, opposites, or exploring different worlds? *Merrill-Palmer Quarterly*, *52*, 601–632.

Berry, J. W. (2011). Integration and multiculturalism: Ways towards social solidarity. *Papers on Social Representations*, *20*, 1–21.

Berry, J. W. (2013). Intercultural relations in plural societies: Research derived from multiculturalism policy. *Acta de InvestigaciónPsicológica*, *3*, 1122–1135.

Berry, J. W., Phinney, J. S., Sam, D. L., & Vedder, P. (2006). Immigrant youth: Acculturation, identity and adaptation. *Applied Psychology: An International Review*, *55*, 303–332.

Brown, C. M., Gibbons, J. L., & Hughes, H. M. (2013). Acculturation clusters and life satisfaction. *Acta de InvestigaciónPsicológica*, *3*, 1108–1121.

Calavita, K. (2005). *Immigrants at the Margins: Law, Race, and Exclusion in Southern Europe*. Cambridge: Cambridge University Press.

Caritas Italiana (2008). *Romania. Immigrazione e lavoro in Italia. Statistiche, problemi e prospettive*. Rome: Edizioni Idos.

Cesareo V. (2016). *Twenty-First Italian Report on Migrations 2015*. Milan: McGraw-Hill Education.

Dimitrova, R. (2011). Children's social relationships in the Northern Italian school context: Evidence for the immigrant paradox. *Journal of Modern Italian Studies*, *16*, 478–491.

Eurobarometer (2014). *Standard Eurobarometer 82/Autumn 2014 – TNS opinion & social*. Retrieved from http://ec.europa.eu/public_opinion/archives/eb/eb82/eb82_publ_en.pdf.

FondazioneIsmu (2016). *Ventunesimorapportosullemigrazioni 2015*. Milan: FrancoAngeli.

Gerson, M. W., & Neilson, L. (2014). The importance of identity development, principled moral reasoning, and empathy as predictors of openness to diversity in emerging adults. *SAGE Open*, *4*, 1–11.

Hui, B. P. H., Chen, C. X., Leung, C. M., & Berry, J. W. (2015). Facilitating adaptation and intercultural contact: The role of bicultural integration and multicultural ideology in dominant and non-dominant groups. *International Journal of Intercultural Relations*, *45*, 70–84.

Human Rights Watch (2015). *The Mediterranean migration crisis. Why people flee, what the EU should do*. Retrieved at www.hrw.org/sites/default/files/report_pdf/eu0615_web.pdf.

Inguglia, C., & Musso, P. (2013). In-group favouritism and out-group derogation towards national groups: Age-related differences among Italian school children. *International Journal of Intercultural Relations*, *37*, 385–390. doi: 10.1016/j.ijintrel.2013.02.005.

Inguglia, C., & Musso, P. (2015). Intercultural profiles and adaptation among immigrant and autochthonous adolescents. *Europe's Journal of Psychology*, *11*, 79–99. doi: 10.5964/ejop.v11i1.872.

Inguglia, C., Musso, P., Lo Coco, A., & Berry, J. W. (2016). *Mutual Intercultural Relations in Italy*. Manuscript in preparation.

International Test Commission. (2005). *International Test Commission guidelines for translating and adapting tests*. Retrieved from www.intestcom.org/files/guideline_test_adaptation.pdf.

Italian Association of Psychology (2015). *Codice etico per la ricerca in psicologia* [Ethical code for psychological research]. Retrieved from www.aipass.org/node/26.

Knight, G. P., Roosa, M. W., & Umaña-Taylor, A. J. (2009). *Methodological Challenges in Studying Ethnic Minority or Economically Disadvantaged Populations*. Washington, DC: American Psychological Association.

Kosic, A., Manetti, L., & Sam, D. L. (2005). The role of majority attitudes towards out-group in the perception of the acculturation strategies. *International Journal of Intercultural Relations*, *29*, 273–288.

Lebedeva, N., & Tatarko, A. (2013). Multiculturalism and immigration in post-Soviet Russia. *European Psychologist*, *18*, 169–178.

Lebedeva, N., Tatarko, A., & Berry, J. W. (2016). Intercultural relations among migrants from Caucasus and Russians in Moscow. *International Journal of Intercultural Relations*, *52*, 27–38.

Magnusson, D. (2003). The person approach: Concepts, measurement models, and research strategy. *New Directions for Child and Adolescent Development*, *101*, 3–23.

Mancini, T., & Bottura, B. (2014). Acculturation processes and intercultural relations in peripheral and central domains among native Italian and migrant adolescents. An application of the Relative Acculturation Extended Model (RAEM). *International Journal of Intercultural Relations*, *40*, 49–63.

Migrant Integration Policy Index (2015). *Italy*. Retrieved from www.mipex.eu/italy.

Motti-Stefanidi, F., & Asendorpf, J. (2012). Perceived discrimination of immigrant adolescents in Greece: How does group discrimination translate into personal discrimination? *European Psychologist*, *17*, 93–104.

Musso, P., Inguglia, C., Lo Coco, A., Albiero, P., & Berry, J. W. (2016). Mediating and moderating processes in the relationship between multicultural ideology and attitudes towards immigrants in emerging adults. *International Journal of Psychology*. Advance online publication. doi:10.1002/ijop.12290.

Musso, P., Inguglia, C., & Lo Coco, A. (2015). Acculturation profiles and perceived discrimination: Associations with psychosocial well-being among Tunisian adolescents in Italy. *Social Inquiry into Wellbeing*, *1*, 76–90.

Musso, P., Inguglia, C., & Lo Coco, A. (2016). Relationships between ethnic identity, ethnic attitudes, and acculturative stress in Tunisian individuals in early and middle adolescence. *Journal of Early Adolescence.* Advance online publication. doi:10.1177/0272431616659557.

Nguyen, A. M. D., & Benet-Martínez, V. (2013). Biculturalism and adjustment: A meta-analysis. *Journal of Cross-Cultural Psychology, 44*, 122–159.

PEW Research Center (2015). *Faith in European project reviving.* Retrieved from www.pewglobal.org/2015/06/02/faith-in-european-project-reviving/.

Sam, D. L., & Berry, J. W. (Eds.). (2006). *The Cambridge Handbook of Acculturation Psychology.* Cambridge: Cambridge University Press.

Schwartz, S. J., & Zamboanga, B. L. (2008). Testing Berry's model of acculturation: A confirmatory latent class approach. *Cultural Diversity and Ethnic Minority Psychology, 14*, 275–285.

Umaña-Taylor, A. J., Quintana, S. M., Lee, R. M. et al. Ethnic and Racial Identity in the 21st Century Study Group (2014). Ethnic and racial identity during adolescence and into young adulthood: An integrated conceptualization. *Child Development, 85*, 21–39.

Umana-Taylor, A., & Updegraff, K. A. (2007). Latino adolescents' mental health: Exploring the interrelations among discrimination, ethnic identity, cultural orientation, self-esteem, and depressive symptoms. *Journal of Adolescence, 30*, 549–567.

United Nations High Commissioner for Refugees (2015). *UNHCR global trends. Forced displacement in 2014.* Retrieved from www.unhcr.org/556725 e69.pdf.

Verkuyten, M. (2009). Self-esteem and multiculturalism: An examination among ethnic minority and majority groups in the Netherlands. *Journal of Research in Personality, 43*, 419–427.

Ward, C., & Masgoret, A. M. (2008). Attitudes toward immigrants, immigration, and multiculturalism in New Zealand: A social psychological analysis. *International Migration Review, 42*, 227–248.

11   Intercultural Relations in Malta

Gordon Sammut and Mary Anne Lauri
University of Malta, Malta

1   Introduction

The study of intercultural relations in Malta is important because of its unique position between North Africa and Europe. While for centuries, it has served as a cross-roads between these continents, these movements have resulted in a society that is now relatively homogeneous. Malta is lowest on the ethnic diversity index and also low on the migrant integration index. It is not included in the multiculturalism policy index, but is estimated to be low as well. As a result, Malta may serve as special context in which to examine the three hypotheses.

2   Context of Intercultural Relations in Malta

Acculturation research in Malta is relatively new. Malta has a long history of colonization; Malta was colonized by the Phoenicians, the Romans, the Moors, the Normans, the Sicilians, the Spanish, the Order of St John, the French and lastly the British. All these powers left some indelible mark on the country, its culture and the habits of its citizens. In 1964, Malta gained independence from the United Kingdom and proceeded to declare itself a republic in 1974. Thirty years later, in 2004, Malta joined the European Union (EU) as a full member state. It joined the Schengen Zone in 2007 and the Eurozone soon after, in 2008.

Geographically, Malta lies around 80 kilometers south of Sicily and 284 kilometers north-east of Tunisia. Malta, or more accurately the Maltese islands, consists of an archipelago of three islands (Malta, Gozo and Comino), of which the island of Malta is the largest (246 km^2) with a population of 386,057 as per the last census (NSO, 2014). The combined population in Gozo (67 km^2) and Comino (3.5 km^2) is of 31,375. Its small size and population of less than half a million make Malta the most densely populated country in the EU (Eurostat, 2014).

As noted earlier, whilst the history of Malta is highly diverse, the culture currently embraced by the population is relatively homogenous, as evidenced in the last national census carried out in 2011, which coincided with the administration of our MIRIPS survey (NSO, 2014). Out of a total population of 417,432 inhabitants, only 20,289 are non-Maltese, representing 4.86% of total inhabitants.

The present state of intercultural relations in Malta reflects its recent history. Malta opened its borders to migrants upon EU accession. During the same period, Malta became a target destination for irregular migration from North Africa. British migrants constitute by far the largest group of non-Maltese inhabitants at 6,652, representing 33% of migrants. A further 5,563 inhabitants hail from various other EU countries. The total proportion of migrants from within the EU thus stands at just over 60% of total migrants. A total of 4,496 respondents to the census, representing a further 22% of immigrants, hail from unspecified countries. The census (NSO, 2014) does not identify the nationality of these immigrants. A clue, however, may be found in the percentage of the population that is versed in foreign languages. Amongst the population aged 10 and over (360,325), 3,948 report that they speak Arabic very well. It is fair to conclude, therefore, that the Arab community in Malta is rather sizeable, relative to the number of migrants hailing from other countries. Moreover, migration to Malta shows signs of settlement in the last census. Out of a total of 413,209 inhabitants aged 1 and over, only 4,178 (1%) resided abroad in the year preceding the census. This figure includes Maltese citizens who lived abroad. A further set of noteworthy statistics concerns the distribution of the non-Maltese population across various regions in Malta. Out of a total of 20,289 non-Maltese inhabitants, 4,262 reside in the neighboring villages of Sliema, St.Julians and Swieqi (21%), 3,023 (15%) reside in St Paul's Bay and a further 1,986 (10%) reside in Birżebbuġa. Almost half of the non-Maltese inhabitants (46%) are clustered in 5 regions out of a total of 54 identified in the census of Malta.

The most recent Eurobarometer (European Commission, 2015) shows that migration has risen to being the primary concern amongst European citizens. This is specifically the case in Malta. Maltese are second from last (just above Greece) in their view about accepting migrants. Scholars have noted how human beings are predisposed to distinguish between outgroup and ingroup. This categorical distinction leads to discrimination along social, ethnic and cultural lines (Tajfel & Turner, 1986; Haslam, Ellemers, Reicher, Reynolds & Schmitt, 2010).

In an encounter with culturally different others, human subjects are predisposed to deprecate others' views especially those who are perceived to be in some way inferior (Sammut & Sartawi, 2012). This intergroup attribution can potentially precipitate a spiral of conflict between ethnocultural groups (Sammut, Bezzina & Sartawi, 2015) that co-exist within the same society. In an age of calamitous warfare technology, the psychological underpinnings of intercultural contact have become a serious and justified concern (Moghaddam, 2008). As Farrell and Oliveri (2006) have argued, the predominant challenge facing contemporary plural societies remains that of turning cultural diversity into added value.

Addressing the challenge of diversity requires a coherent and concerted effort to map the states and strategies of intercultural contact between dominant and non-dominant groups. This challenge constitutes the central focus of the present volume. This chapter reports the findings of an inquiry into the mutual acculturation preferences amongst diverse ethnocultural groups in Malta.

The present study investigated intercultural relations amongst the dominant Maltese population and five non-dominant ethnocultural groups, namely Western European, Eastern European, South Asian, East Asian and Arab groups. We omitted a focus on the sub-Saharan African community due to the fact that at the time the study was undertaken, this community was heavily transient with migrants often leaving to continue their journey towards other European destinations at the first available opportunity. We recommend that this community be included in future acculturation research in Malta.

For the purposes of the present study, we started by looking at the various groups' acculturation preferences (strategies and expectations). We expected the dominant group to demonstrate a higher preference for a melting pot acculturation strategy than any of the other strategies. Previous acculturation research has demonstrated that this preference is salient amongst many dominant groups including those in European countries (Van Oudenhoven, Ward & Masgoret, 2006; Zick, Wagner, Van Dick & Petzel, 2001). Conversely, we expected non-dominant groups to demonstrate higher preferences for integration relative to the other acculturation strategies. This is in line with previous acculturation research concerning migrant communities (see Berry, Phinney, Sam & Vedder, 2006). We proceeded to study reciprocal attitudes between the various ethnocultural groups. We expected a predominance of warm attitudes, given the seemingly low level of intercultural discord in Malta. However, we also expected that the Arab group would be perceived less warmly than other groups. This is in line with previous findings concerning widespread Islamophobic attitudes levelled at Arabs in a number of European countries (Helbling, 2012). Following these contextual analyses, we proceeded to test the three MIRIPS hypotheses detailed in Chapter 1.

We evaluated all three MIRIPS hypotheses. Specifically, with respect to the Multiculturalism hypothesis, we hypothesized that Security would be positively correlated with Multicultural Ideology amongst both dominant and non-dominant groups. For the contact hypothesis, we hypothesized that Contact with other ethnocultural groups would be positively correlated with Multicultural Ideology. And for the Integration hypothesis, we hypothesized that Integration/Multiculturalism preferences would be positively correlated with Self-Esteem and Sociocultural Competence for both the non-dominant and dominant groups, respectively.

3   Method

3.1   Samples

The total number of respondents for the survey including dominant and non-dominant groups in Malta was 443. The first wave of the survey was administered to a random sample of 193 Maltese respondents, stratified by geographical region in Malta. Data gathering was undertaken in 2010 with randomly selected respondents from the General Election Register of Malta. The second wave of the survey targeting non-dominant groups utilized a convenience sampling strategy, due to the fact that no official data are available on the residence distribution of immigrants in Malta that could enable random sampling. The second wave of administration was carried out in 2011.

Fifty respondents from each of the targeted ethnocultural groups participated in this phase of the study from each of the following communities: Western European, Eastern European, South Asian, East Asian and Arab communities. The age of respondents ranged from 18 to 83 (M=38, SD=15.747); 260 respondents (59%) were female, whilst 183 (41%) were male. Respondents reported varying levels of education. Only 2.9% reported having stopped their formal education at primary level or lower. Conversely, 24.4% of respondents reported that they had completed part or all of secondary school. A further 44.7% had completed some post-secondary education, whilst 25.8% reported having completed a tertiary-level qualification. The remaining respondents failed to identify their educational attainment. With regard to religious beliefs, the largest religious orientation was Roman Catholic (43.1%). Catholicism remains the official religion of Malta, so its widespread distribution is not surprising. This was followed by those expressing no faith in a religious organization (23.9%), Muslim (11.3%), Orthodox Christian (8.1%), Hindu (4.3%), Protestant (4.1%) and Buddhist (1.4%). All respondents in the study (100%) confirmed that they have a mobile phone, a washing machine, a car and a computer at home. These possessions were construed as a measure of socioeconomic status.

4   Results

We started our analyses by looking at the four acculturation strategies and expectations (assimilation/melting pot; separation/segregation; marginalisation/exclusion; integration/multiculturalism) and their variability across both dominant and non-dominant groups. To assess acculturation strategies and expectations, we used the four acculturation scales in the MIRIPS questionnaire. We conducted one-way ANOVAs on each of these attitudes to determine whether there were any mean differences between the various samples. Where indicated, we ran Tukey's HSD post-hoc tests to determine which differences proved significant. Following this analysis, we proceeded to explore variability in the four acculturation attitudes in more depth by examining how these varied across the dichotomous dominant/non-dominant group conditions. We conducted a 2×4 mixed design ANOVA and a repeated measures ANOVA within groups to explore main effects and interaction effects across group conditions.

We then examined the Attitudes towards Ethnocultural Groups; we conducted a 2×6 mixed design ANOVA and a repeated measures ANOVA to explore differences in reciprocal Attitudes towards Ethnocultural Groups. We used the MIRIPS 100 point feeling thermometer, with 50 set as the mid-point between warm and cold attitudes towards the various ethnocultural groups investigated in the present inquiry.

To assess the multiculturalism hypothesis, we used the scales of: Security (incorporating elements of personal, cultural and economic security); Multicultural Ideology; Self-Esteem; and Sociocultural Competence (all from the MIRIPS questionnaire). We conducted one-way ANOVAs on each of the variables to determine whether any mean differences existed across ethnocultural groups. We then correlated these variables to evaluate the multiculturalism hypothesis. To assess the contact hypothesis, we used the number and the frequency of Social Contacts. We then correlated these Social Contacts with Multicultural Ideology Finally, we evaluated the Integration hypothesis by correlating the Integration/Multiculturalism acculturation preference (non-dominant

/dominant groups) with Self-Esteem and Sociocultural Competence. We adopted the 0.05 level of probability throughout our analyses.

Before reporting on the evaluations of the three hypotheses, we present findings on the distributions of the strategies and expectations.

With respect to the Integration/Multiculturalism preferences, we expected the non-dominant groups to express a clear preference for this acculturation form relative to other forms. We also expected the dominant Maltese group to rate this acculturation form less highly than other forms. The Multiculturalism/Integration strategy was rated more highly by all groups than all other acculturation preferences. However, the Maltese group demonstrated the lowest mean (M=14.95, SD=2.97), and a one-way ANOVA demonstrated this to be significantly different from the mean of all other groups except the East Asian group, $F(5, 408) = 17.83$, p<0.01, $\eta^2 = 0.179$ (W. European: M=16.46, SD=2.94; E. European: M=17.28, SD=1.09; S. Asian: M=18.38, SD=1.63; E. Asian: M=15.98, SD=3.19; Arab: M=17.45, SD=2.79). Tukey's HSD showed the difference between the Western European and the South Asian groups to be significant (p<0.01), as was the difference between the South Asian and the East Asian groups (p<0.01).

With respect to the assimilation / melting pot preferences, we expected the dominant group to demonstrate a significantly higher mean relative to non-dominant groups. The Maltese group (M=8.21, SD=2.48) and the Arab group (M=8.21, SD=2.54) demonstrated the highest mean on this measure, whilst the Eastern European group demonstrated the lowest (M=5.38, SD=0.86). A one-way ANOVA showed that the differences between groups were statistically significant, $F(5, 409) = 16.471$, p<0.01, $\eta^2 = 0.168$. Post-hoc tests showed that all differences between the Maltese and Arab groups with every other group were statistically significant except for that between the Arab and the East Asian group (M=6.67, SD=2.54). All other differences between groups were not statistically significant.

With respect to the Segregation/Separation preferences, we expected the Maltese group to demonstrate a high preference for this acculturation form relative to non-dominant groups. The Eastern European group demonstrated the lowest mean for separation (M=5.98, SD=1.49) relative to every other group. A one-way ANOVA showed this to be significantly different from all other groups, $F(5, 408) = 17.19$, p<0.01, $\eta^2 = 0.174$ (Maltese: M=9.80, SD=3.23; W. European: M=8.68, SD=2.77; S. Asian: M=11.06, SD=3.42; E. Asian: M=10.02, SD=3.39; Arab: M=9.17, SD=3.32). Post-hoc tests showed the difference between the Western European and the South Asian groups to be statistically significant.

Finally, with respect to the marginalization/exclusion preferences, we expected the dominant group to demonstrate a higher preference for this acculturation form than non-dominant groups. The Maltese group had the highest mean ($M=8.47$, $SD=2.72$) for this measure. A one-way ANOVA showed this to be significantly different from every other group except Western Europeans, $F(5, 408) = 40.36$, p<0.01, $\eta^2 = 0.331$ (W. European: $M=7.54$, $SD=2.55$; E. European: $M=4.00$, $SD=0.01$; S. Asian: $M=5.06$, $SD=1.57$; E. Asian: $M=7.00$, $SD=2.39$; Arab: $M=5.72$, $SD=2.36$). Tukey's HSD showed the differences between Western European and Eastern European (p<0.01) as well as South Asian (p<0.01) and Arab (p<0.05) were statistically significant. On the other hand, the differences between Eastern European and East Asian (p<0.01) and Arab (p<0.05) groups were statistically significant as was the difference between South Asian and East Asian groups (p<0.01). The difference between East Asian and Arab groups was not statistically significant.

Across our samples, we expected the dominant group to demonstrate a higher preference for the melting pot strategy over other forms, whilst the non-dominant groups were expected to demonstrate a higher preference for integration. The Integration/Multiculturalism strategy was rated more highly than any other acculturation strategy by all groups, as detailed earlier. We conducted a 2×4 mixed design ANOVA using the dichotomous variable dominant/non-dominant group to explore preferences for the various acculturation strategies. Results showed a significant main effect for acculturation strategies (Wilks' Lambda: 0.14, $F(3, 410)=836.77$, p<0.01) as well as a significant interaction effect (Wilks' Lambda: 0.72, $F(3, 410)=52.79$, p<0.01). This demonstrates a difference between the dominant/non-dominant group conditions for the various acculturation preferences, despite multiculturalism/integration being the most favored by all groups.

We conducted further analyses using a repeated measures ANOVA within groups design. This revealed that differences between preferences for the integration/multiculturalism strategy and the other three acculturation strategies were statistically significant for all groups (Table 11.1). Our expectations were thus partially confirmed. Specifically, however, our expectation of a high preference for the melting pot strategy amongst the dominant group was rejected. The Maltese dominant group expressed a significant preference for multiculturalism over other forms. Our expectations regarding high endorsement of integration amongst non-dominant groups were supported, in line with previous research findings. While the Maltese expressed a statistically significant preference for multiculturalism over other forms, the magnitude of this preference

Table 11.1. *Differences between preferences for the integration/ multiculturalism strategy and the other three acculturation strategies, using repeated measures ANOVA.*

Ethnocultural Group	Wilks' Lambda	F-Statistic
Maltese	0.23	(3, 190) = 215.46*
W. European	0.14	(3, 47) = 97.66*
E. European	0.10	(3, 47) = 2698.88*
S. Asian	0.24	(3, 47) = 640.56*
E. Asian	0.15	(3, 39) = 72.21*
Arab	0.10	(3, 26) = 76.56*

* $p<0.01$.

was significantly less than that expressed by non-dominant groups, as demonstrated in the interaction effect in the previous analysis.

We next examined the Attitudes towards Ethnocultural Groups. We expected the Arab group to be rated less warmly than other groups by the various other ethnocultural groups. Our expectations were confirmed for all groups except the Eastern European group (Table 11.2). The Maltese dominant group, along with the South Asian and the East Asian groups, rated only the Arab group in negative territory (i.e., cold attitudes) (Maltese: $M=29.9$, $SD=23.2$; S. Asian: $M=33.7$, $SD=25.8$; E. Asian: $M=46.5$, $SD=23.0$). They rated every other group in positive territory (i.e., warm attitudes). The Western European and Eastern European groups rated every other group in positive territory. The Western European group, however, also rated the Arab group lowest amongst the various groups ($M=54.60$, $SD=26.7$).

We conducted further analyses using a 2×6 mixed design ANOVA using the condition of dominant/non-dominant group to explore differences in inter-group attitudes amongst the six ethnocultural groups. The results showed a main effect for attitudes (Wilks' Lambda=0.31, F (5, 409)=180.67, p<0.01) as well as an interaction effect with the dominant/non-dominant group condition (Wilks' Lambda=0.65, F(5, 409) =43.20, p<0.01). We also conducted a repeated measures ANOVA within groups that showed statistically significant differences in inter-group attitudes for all groups (Table 11.3).

These intergroup attitudes show some degree of ethnocentrism, in that four of the seven groups rate their own group higher than they rate the other groups (all except East European, East Asian and Asian). Beyond this ingroup preference, there is a general consensus among the groups to rate the dominant Maltese group highest. Third, the ratings given to the

Table 11.2. *Attitudes towards ethnocultural groups, using 100-point thermometer.*

	Maltese	West Europeans	East Europeans	East Asian	Asian	Arab
Maltese	M=85.91	M=75.21	M=59.69	M=55.11	M=53.15	M=29.87
	(z=.32)	(z=.13)	(z= −.10)	(z= −.32)	(z= −.21)	(z= −.46)
	SD=14.72	SD=18.24	SD=22.85	SD=22.48	SD=23.55	SD=23.22
	(z=.83)	(z= 1.00)	(z= 1.12)	(z= 1.04)	(z= 1.06)	(z=.83)
West European	M=75.66	M=81.40	M=70.10	M=65.90	M=67.20	M=54.60
	(z= −.26)	(z=.47)	(z=.41)	(z=.18)	(z=.42)	(z=.42)
	SD=21.60	SD=16.54	SD=19.47	SD=21.56	SD=20.46	SD=26.74
	(z= 1.22)	(z=.91)	(z=.95)	(z= 1.0)	(z=.92)	(z=.96)
East European	M=85.58	M=67.60	M=66.00	M=78.40	M=56.80	M=65.60
	(z=.30)	(z= −.29)	(z=.21)	(z=.76)	(z= −.05)	(z=.81)
	SD=8.52	SD=16.97	SD=15.39	SD=11.84	SD=13.32	SD=17.16
	(z=.48)	(z=.93)	(z=.75)	(z=.55)	(z=.60)	(z=.62)
East Asian	M=60.12	M=59.38	M=55.23	M=54.30	M=72.21	M=46.51
	(z= −1.13)	(z= −.73)	(z= −.32)	(z= −.36)	(z=.65)	(z=.13)
	SD=20.89	SD=18.35	SD=17.56	SD=20.60	SD=22.13	SD=22.98
	(z= 1.18)	(z= 1.00)	(z =.86)	(z=.95)	(z= 1.00)	(z=.82)
Asian	M=76.80	M=72.00	M=60.60	M=73.90	M=53.00	M=33.70
	(z= −.19)	(z= −.05)	(z= −.06)	(z=.55)	(z= −.22)	(z= −.33)
	SD=14.83	SD=15.78	SD=15.96	SD=11.35	SD=20.10	SD=25.75
	(z=.84)	(z=.87)	(z=.78)	(z=.53)	(z=.90)	(z=.92)
Arab	M=76.03	M=72.24	M=65.00	M=64.14	M=62.41	M=79.48
	(z= −.23)	(z= −.03)	(z=.16)	(z=.10)	(z=.20)	(z= 1.31)
	SD=13.59	SD=14.61	SD=19.37	SD=18.62	SD=17.86	SD=17.13
	(z=.77)	(z=.80)	(z=.95)	(z=.86)	(z=.80)	(z=.61)

Arab group are the lowest of all groups (except by themselves and by the East Europeans).

With respect to the perception of Security, we expected all groups to report high levels of perceptions of their own security. A one-way ANOVA revealed statistically significant differences in the levels of security perceived by respondents, $F(5, 414) = 15.813$, p<0.01, $\eta^2 = 0.19$. The Arab group demonstrated the highest mean for this measure ($M=45.52$, $SD=5.05$). Tukey's HSD demonstrated this to be

Table 11.3. *Repeated Measures ANOVA for inter-group attitudes.*

Ethnocultural Group	Wilks' Lambda	F-Statistic
Maltese	0.17	(5, 188) = 188.21*
W. European	0.50	(5, 45) = 8.87*
E. European	0.18	(5, 45) = 41.3*
S. Asian	0.24	(5, 45) = 28.72*
E. Asian	0.48	(5, 38) = 8.28*
Arab	0.52	(5, 24) = 4.45*

* $p<0.01$

significantly different from all other groups except the Maltese (Maltese: $M=42.97$, $SD=5.57$, p=*ns*; W. European: $M=41.80$, $SD=5.51$, p<0.05; E. European: $M=38.98$, $SD=2.02$, p<0.01; S. Asian: $M=37.66$, $SD=4.29$, p<0.01; E. Asian: $M=40.63$, $SD=4.70$, p<0.01). Similarly, the differences between the Maltese group and all the other groups except the Arab group were significant (p<0.05). The difference between the Western European and the South Asian group, and the South Asian and the East Asian groups were also statistically significant (p<0.05).

With respect to multicultural ideology, we expected the Maltese group to demonstrate a lower mean on this measure than the other groups. A one-way ANOVA showed that the differences between groups were statistically significant, $F(5, 408) = 19.641$, p<0.01, $\eta^2 = 0.194$. Tukey's HSD showed that the mean for the Maltese group ($M=32.40$, $SD=4.77$) was significantly different from all other groups except for the Eastern European group (W. European: $M=36.20$, $SD=6.77$; E. European: $M=34.24$, $SD=1.60$; S. Asian: $M=38.14$, $SD=3.97$; E. Asian: $M=36.17$, $SD=4.23$; Arab: $M=38.28$, $SD=5.54$). The difference between the Arab group, who demonstrated the highest mean on this measure, and the Eastern European group, who demonstrated the lowest mean, was found to be significant by Tukey's HSD (p<0.01). The difference between the Eastern European group and the South Asian group was also significant (p<0.01).

With respect to social contacts, we asked respondents the number of co-ethnic and other ethnic friends they have, and the frequency of contact with these friends. The Maltese dominant group reported having mostly Maltese friends. Almost half of respondents (45.6%) have no friends who are not Maltese. Respondents further reported that they met their

Maltese friends more regularly than they did their other-ethnic friends. Over three-quarters (76.7%) of Maltese respondents reported meeting other-ethnic friends either rarely or never. The non-dominant groups reported a broader range of both Maltese and other-ethnicity friends as well as increased contact. The majority reported having a few Maltese friends (31.4%), a few co-ethnic friends (37.6%) and a few other friends of a different ethnic background (37.6%). Only 15.3% reported having no Maltese friends at all and almost a quarter (22.3%) reported having many Maltese friends. Moreover, the large majority of respondents reported meeting their Maltese friends either often or daily (59.4%). However, respondents nevertheless demonstrated a bias, like the Maltese, towards both the number of and level of contact with co-ethnic friends.

With respect to self-esteem, we expected the Maltese to demonstrate a higher mean on this measure than the non-dominant groups. In fact, the Maltese group showed the lowest mean (M=32.36, SD=3.14). A one-way ANOVA showed statistically significant differences between groups: $F(5, 409) = 70.46$, p<0.01, $\eta^2 = 0.463$. Tukey's HSD showed the differences between the Maltese group and all the other groups to be significant (W. European: M=40.34, SD=5.94; E. European: M=43.22, SD=0.93; S. Asian: M=36.06, SD=6.50; E. Asian: M=38.37, SD=5.32; Arab: M=39.17, SD=5.24). Moreover, the differences between the Eastern European group, who demonstrated the highest mean for this measure, and all other groups were statistically significant (p<0.01). The differences between the South Asian group and the Western European group as well as the Arab group were also significant (p<0.05).

With respect to sociocultural competence, we expected the Maltese to demonstrate a higher mean on this measure than other groups. In line with our expectations, the Maltese reported the highest mean on this measure (M=83.37, SD=11.26) and a one-way ANOVA showed that the differences between the Maltese and every other ethnocultural group were statistically significant: $F(5, 385) = 421.2$, p<0.01, $\eta^2 = 0.85$ (W. European: M=39.72, SD=14.1; E. European: M=39.76, SD=3.83; S. Asian: M=32.92, SD=9.63; E. Asian: M=33.74, SD=9.1; Arab: M=25.76, SD=7.87). Tukey's HSD showed statistically significant differences between the Western European and the South Asian group (p<0.05), the Eastern European and the South Asian group (p<0.05), the Western European and the Arab group (p<0.01) and the Eastern European and the Arab group (p<0.01).

We now turn to the evaluation of the three hypotheses.

Multiculturalism Hypothesis

We hypothesized that Security would be positively correlated with Multicultural Ideology for both dominant and non-dominant groups. Amongst the Maltese, security was *negatively* correlated with Multicultural Ideology ($r=-0.21$, $p<0.01$). For non-dominant groups, the correlation was not statistically significant ($r=-.09$, $p=ns$, $1-\beta=0.4$). Our first hypothesis was therefore not supported.

Contact Hypothesis

We hypothesized that Multicultural Ideology would be positively correlated with (i) number and (ii) frequency of contact with other-ethnic friends. Amongst members of the dominant group, Multicultural Ideology was correlated with both number ($r=0.24$, $p<0.01$) and frequency ($r=0.25$, $p<0.01$) of other-ethnic friends, as expected. For the non-dominant groups, however, Multicultural Ideology was *negatively* correlated with number ($r=-0.20$, $p<0.01$) and frequency ($r=-0.30$, $p<0.01$) of contact with Maltese friends and was not statistically significant with number ($r=-0.09$, $p=ns$, $1-\beta=0.4$) or frequency of other-ethnic friends ($r=-0.04$, $p=ns$, $1-\beta=0.2$). Our second hypothesis was therefore confirmed for the dominant group but not supported for non-dominant groups.

Integration Hypothesis

We hypothesized that the Integration/Multiculturalism acculturation preference would be positively correlated with (a) Self-esteem and (b) Sociocultural competence. Amongst the Maltese, the Multiculturalism acculturation preference was in fact *negatively* correlated with self-esteem ($r=-0.25$, $p<0.01$). The correlation for non-dominant groups was not statistically significant ($r=-0.05$, $p=ns$, $1-\beta=0.2$). The Multiculturalism acculturation preference was uncorrelated with sociocultural competence for the dominant group ($r=0.01$, $p=ns$, $1-\beta=0.99$). The integration acculturation preference, however, was *negatively* correlated with integration ($r=-0.27$, $p<0.01$) for non-dominant groups. Our third hypothesis was therefore not supported.

4   Discussion

The findings of the present inquiry present clear cause for concern with regard to the nature of intercultural relations in Malta. While our finding that integration is the preferred acculturation strategy amongst both dominant and non-dominant groups in Malta provides evidence of mutual acceptance, there is 'little' consolation. Effectively, the discrepancy between the dominant and non-dominant groups on this measure is worrying insofar as it spells a degree of resistance amongst the Maltese towards the integration of migrants in Malta. Whilst the Maltese dominant group expresses a preference for multiculturalism over other ways of acculturating, they do so significantly less than the other ethnocultural groups. At the same time, they also express relatively high preferences for melting pot as well as exclusion.

The integration of the Arab community is particularly concerning. Arab migration to European countries has increased dramatically due to widespread social unrest in a number of Arab countries in recent years. For the Maltese, the events in Libya leading to and following the displacement of Libyan leader Muammar Gaddafi played an acute role, as Malta became a target destination for asylum seekers fleeing the unrest from Libyan shores across the Mediterranean. Consequently, the proportion of migrants in Malta originating from Arab countries has increased. Whilst no formal statistics documenting the prevalence of Arab migrants in Malta are available, the proportion of fluent Arabic speakers in Malta suggests that this community is sizeable relative to other communities. The findings of the present study demonstrate that by and large Arabs are negatively regarded, that diverse ethnocultural groups in Malta converge in their antipathy towards Arabs, and that the Arab group is not faring well in terms of social well-being. We believe that this scenario provides fertile grounds for a spiral of conflict (Sammut, Bezzina & Sartawi, 2015) between the Arab community and the rest of the population, as Arab migrants struggle to secure a legitimate place for themselves in Maltese society. We recommend further research to investigate the grounds for this antipathy to determine whether the preferences for multiculturalism/ integration demonstrated by all groups are qualified with regard to Arabs.

With regard to the three MIRIPS hypotheses, the present study provides mixed findings. The multiculturalism hypothesis, suggesting that higher feelings of security are associated with increased acceptance of different others, was not supported. The more security the Maltese reported feeling, the *less* they were inclined to accept different others. We believe that these findings are sensible for the dominant Maltese group. Given that Malta has only recently opened up its borders to immigrants, those Maltese who are comfortable in Malta and who find it a reasonably secure place to live are also the ones most threatened by the presence of different others who stand to change the sense of comfort and security they presently enjoy as dominant group. The high endorsement rate for melting pot and exclusion acculturation expectations amongst the dominant group, once again, lends support to this interpretation. We further suggest that this sense of security is based in cultural norms and practices, considering that the Arab community along with the Maltese report significantly higher levels of security than other ethnocultural groups. Contrarily, those Maltese who are not equally positive about Malta and the status presently enjoyed by them as members of the dominant group (perhaps due to what they perceive as undue privileges granted to a proportion of their compatriots) perceive greater value in integrating different others. We believe that this endorsement of others' different ways may serve to mitigate a discomfort they experience with the present state of affairs, as well as a hope that integration of different others may ameliorate their present condition.

Similarly, we found no support in the present study for the contact hypothesis amongst non-dominant groups. Seemingly, the more non-dominant group members affiliate with the dominant Maltese, the less they subscribe to multicultural ideology. Contact, in this case, may be serving to rub off restrictive attitudes held amongst the Maltese on non-dominant group members. This is a form of acculturation that may serve the interests of those seeking to displace a stigmatized identity through assimilation with the larger society (Sammut, 2012). This could well be the case for the Arab community in Malta, who are aware of the negative attitudes levelled towards them. This interpretation is supported by the finding that, in the present study, the Maltese dominant group along with the Arab group reported high preferences for assimilation / melting pot compared to other groups. It is therefore reasonable to expect the Arab group in Malta, given the fact that this group is largely negatively regarded, will express equally high preferences for an assimilation / melting pot acculturation strategy as the dominant group. Some Arabs may perceive that they stand to lose a stigmatized identity through assimilation, which could be replaced by that pertaining to the dominant group. On the other hand, non-dominant group members who are not quite as ready to shun their own native identities and align themselves with the cultural practices of the homogeneous dominant group may, in their turn, disassociate themselves from local Maltese and seek fewer opportunities for contact. Clearly, the Arab group has the least reason to pursue this form of acculturation.

With regard to the dominant group, our findings support the contact hypothesis. Maltese respondents who report having non-Maltese friends and who report associating with them also report higher levels of multicultural ideology. One wonders whether, over time as opportunities for contact inevitably increase with certain immigrant communities taking root in Malta, levels of multicultural ideology amongst the dominant group may rise, thereby precipitating changes in the extent to which multiculturalism is preferred. This could potentially reverse the trend evidenced in the present findings concerning the multiculturalism hypothesis. Should this prove to be the case, the present findings concerning these hypotheses are also expected to change.

We believe that this explanation further accounts for our findings regarding the integration hypothesis. The prediction that preferences for integration/multiculturalism are associated with higher levels of personal and social well-being was not supported. In fact, we found that self-esteem is negatively correlated with a preference for multiculturalism amongst the dominant Maltese. Seemingly, Maltese individuals who experience relatively lower levels of self-esteem endorse multiculturalism more than those who report higher levels of self-esteem. We believe that this finding needs to be interpreted in light of the very recent history of migration in Malta. In particular, it is worth noting that Malta opened its borders following EU accession only a little more than a decade ago. This finding might be due to the fact that those Maltese individuals who command a good level of social and psychological well-being (Ward, 1996) in Malta presently do so by virtue of their inclusion in a relatively homogenous society, as noted at the outset. This situation may serve to bolster self-esteem amongst those who are accustomed to and who subscribe to Maltese ways, particularly amongst those who enjoy some privilege by virtue of their status as the dominant group. These individuals arguably have much less reason to incorporate elements from other cultures into their own society. The high rate of endorsement for melting pot as well as exclusion amongst the Maltese compared to these acculturation preferences amongst non-dominant groups lends support to this interpretation. On the other hand, those Maltese individuals who, for one reason or another, do not entirely fit in with this homogeneity may endorse multiculturalism to a greater extent in the hope that it will provide a welcome change to cultural homogeneity. Their ill fitment with their own dominant group is arguably reflected in their self-esteem. This explains the fact that those reporting lower levels of self-esteem endorse multiculturalism more strongly than those reporting higher levels of self-esteem. We think our interpretation of this finding is reasonable and warrants further study. It will be interesting to observe whether this trend reverses in future in the event that Malta becomes more heterogeneous over time as a result of European immigration.

With regard to non-dominant group members, the present findings show additional cause for concern. Non-dominant group members who report a higher preference for integration seem to be less, not more, socially adjusted. Arguably, their inclination towards integration proves to be an obstacle rather than a resource for achieving social well-being. This low level of sociocultural competence seems particularly acute for the Arab group. It seems, that an integrationist mindset amongst immigrants is actually counterproductive to their achieving social wellbeing. Migrants who seek to integrate in Malta do not fare well.

5   Conclusion and Implications

We strongly believe that the findings of the present study need to be considered in light of Malta's very brief history of immigration. The three MIRIPS hypotheses evaluated in the present inquiry were largely unsupported. We found security to be negatively correlated with multicultural ideology amongst the dominant group. We also found that a preference for multiculturalism is negatively correlated with self-esteem in the same group. We believe that the reason for this, as suggested earlier, lies in the fact that the same objective situation may be perceived very differently by different groups, depending on their respective social representations of the issue (Sammut & Howarth, 2014). We found that contact with different ethnocultural groups is correlated with multicultural ideology amongst the Maltese, but that contact is negatively correlated amongst non-dominant group members who associate with the Maltese. We also found that integration is correlated with low levels of social well-being amongst non-dominant group members.

We reiterate that these findings present cause for concern, particularly with regard to relations with the Arab community in Malta. A further concern relates to the fact that whilst positive, the findings concerning the contact hypothesis amongst the dominant group may be curtailed by the fact that migrants in Malta are concentrated in a very small number of localities. Indeed, almost half of Maltese respondents in this study reported having no friends who are not Maltese. This clearly impedes opportunities for contact and may serve to facilitate segregation at a societal level regardless of the acculturation preferences prevailing in the population. Clearly, the policy debate concerning multiculturalism versus assimilation (Jedwab, 2014; Kymlicka, 2012) is relevant for Malta. We believe that the Maltese case requires active social policy to transform cultural diversity into added value (Farrell & Oliveri, 2006), as this is seemingly not taking place of its own accord. We conclude by recommending that contact, particularly that between the dominant group and other non-dominant groups, especially Arabs, be actively promoted, since it seems to provide the only glimmer of hope to potentially negative and adversarial intercultural relations in Malta.

Acknowledgements

The authors would like to thank Professor Josef Lauri and Professor Colleen Ward for assistance with the project and contributions to earlier versions of the manuscript. The authors would like to thank the University of Malta Research Fund Committee for grants PSYRP03-01/02 which have funded this study.

References

Berry, J.W., Phinney, J.S., Sam, D.L., & Vedder, P. (2006). Immigrant youth, acculturation, identity, and adaptation. *Applied Psychology*, 55 (3), 303–332.

European Commission (2015). *Eurobarometer 83: Public Opinion in the European Union: First Results*. Retrieved September 28, 2015, from < http://ec.europa.eu/public_opinion/archives/eb/eb83/eb83_en.htm>.

Eurostat (2014). *Key Figures on the Enlargement Countries*. (014 edition) Luxembourg: Publications Office of the European Union.

Farrell, G., & Oliveri, F. (Eds.). (2006). *Achieving Social Cohesion in a Multicultural Europe: Concepts, Situation and Developments*. Trends in Social Cohesion, No. 18 (pp. 13–22). Strasbourg: Council of Europe.

Giddens, A. (1991). *Modernity and Self-Identity: Self and Society in the Late Modern Age*. Cambridge: Polity.

Haslam, S. A., Ellemers, N., Reicher, S. D., Reynolds, K. J., & Schmitt, M. T. (2010). The social identity perspective tomorrow: Opportunities and avenues for advance. In T. Postmes & N. R. Branscombe (Eds.), *Rediscovering Social Identity: Core Sources* (pp. 357–379). New York: Psychology Press.

Helbling, M. (Ed.). (2012). *Islamophobia in the West: Measuring and explaining individual attitudes*. Oxford: Routledge.

Jedwab, J. (Ed.)(2014). The Multiculturalism Question: Debating Identity in 21st-Century Canada. Montreal: McGill-Queen's University Press.

Kymlicka, W. (2012). *Multiculturalism: Success, Failure and the Future*. Washington: Transatlantic Council on Migration.

Moghaddam, F.M. (2008). *Multiculturalism and Intergroup Relations: Psychological Implications for Democracy in Global Context*. Washington, DC: American Psychological Association.

National Statistics Office (NSO) (2014). *Census of Population and Housing 2011: Final Report*. Valletta, Malta: National Statistics Office.

Sammut, G. (2012). The immigrants' point of view: Acculturation, social judgment, and the relative propensity to take the perspective of the other. *Culture & Psychology*, 18(2), 184–197.

Sammut, G., Bezzina, F., & Sartawi, M. (2015). The spiral of conflict: Naïve realism and the black sheep effect in attributions of knowledge and ignorance. *Peace and Conflict: Journal of Peace Psychology*, 21 (2), 289–294.

Sammut, G., & Howarth, C. (2014). Social representations. In T. Teo (Ed.), *Encyclopedia of Critical Psychology* (pp. 1799–1802). New York: Springer.

Sammut, G., & Sartawi, M. (2012). Perspective-taking and the attribution of ignorance. *Journal for the Theory of Social Behavior, 42*(2), 181–200.

Tajfel, H., & Turner, J. C. (1986). The social identity theory of intergroup behaviour. In S. Worchel & W. G. Austin (Eds.), *Psychology of intergroup relations* (2nd ed., pp. 7–24). Chicago: Nelson-Hall.

Van Oudenhoven, J.P., Ward, C., & Masgoret, A.-M. (2006). Patterns of relations between immigrants and host societies. *International Journal of Intercultural Relations, 30*(6), 637–651.

Ward, C. (1996). Acculturation. In D. Landis & R. Bhagat (Eds.), *Handbook of Intercultural Training* (2nd ed., pp. 124–147). Newbury Park: Sage.

Zick, A., Wagner, U., Van Dick, R., & Petzel, T. (2001). Acculturation and prejudice in Germany: Majority and minority perspectives. *Journal of Social Issues, 57*(3), 541–557.

12   Intercultural Relations in Portugal

Félix Neto and Joana Neto

Faculdade de Psicologia e de Ciências da Educação,
Universidade do Porto, Portugal

1   Introduction

Portugal provides a unique multicultural context for the examination of
mutual intercultural relations. While it is low on the diversity index, it is at
the top of the integration index; and it is near the middle on the policy
index. This pattern provides an important context for the study of acculturation and intercultural relations. However, until now there has been
a dearth of studies on mutual relations between majority and minority
members in Portugal. The present study evaluates all three MIRIPS
hypotheses.

2   Context of Intercultural Relations in Portugal

Intercultural relations have been taking place for centuries in Portugal
from its founding in the twelfth century until the present day. Given the
long history of emigration from Portugal (Godinho, 1978), and especially
the rapid increase of immigration flows in recent decades, understanding
the problems of intercultural relations in Portuguese society has become
very relevant. Portugal provides a unique natural laboratory for the study
of migration (Rocha-Trindade, 2014).

2.1   Immigration

Portugal is positioned in the south-western part of Europe on the Iberian
Peninsula. Its location and small size have produced a particular history of
intercultural contact: long Atlantic coastline; historical Christian mis-
sionary zeal; proximity to the north of Africa; commercial ambition and
adventurous spirit. All these factors early led the Portuguese into the

vocation of being sailors and the discoveries of new lands. These were the basic motivations why Portugal extended its influence and culture throughout other continents: namely, Africa, India, East and Southeast Asia and South America, principally between the fifteenth and eighteenth centuries. During the last century the migratory Portuguese experience has been marked by intense emigration, which has impacted the structure of this country. However, the favourable economic conditions linked with its entry into the European Union in 1986 led to increased demand for immigrant labour and this country also became a receiver society for international migratory flows. That is, Portugal became at the same time a country of origin and a destination for migration flows.

However, international financial problems changed that trend, and Portugal has returned to its traditional emigration profiles. In fact, Portugal presented a negative net migration in the mid-1970s, continuing this tendency between 1982 and 1992, and again after 2011. The high levels of emigration and the decline in immigration to Portugal have produced a negative net migration since 2011 (Observatório da Emigração, 2015). In both 2013 and 2014, the total number of Portuguese emigrants to countries of settlement exceeded 110,000. There were only five years with higher emigration values across the twentieth and twenty-first centuries – 1969 to 1973. In 2015, Portuguese migrants across the world numbered more than 2.3 million (Observatório da Emigração, 2015), which corresponds to about 20 per cent of the population living in Portugal.

Emigration from this country has had a long tradition, and it continues to be important, but Portugal is also a country of immigration. From the 1970s onwards, after the April 1974 revolution and accession to the European Union in the mid-1980s, Portugal has become a destination country. The overwhelming majority of immigrants came from countries with which Portugal had historic relations (e.g., Cape Verde, Angola, Brazil, Mozambique, São Tomé e Príncipe, Guinea-Bissau). Since the 1990s, there has been a cultural and linguistic diversity of immigrant origins, a new period of the migrant experience beginning with the arrival of East Europeans (e.g., Ukrainians, Moldavians, Russians, Romanians) and Asiatic citizens (e.g., Chinese).

There has been large return migration of Portuguese people during the last four decades. According to the National Statistics Institute (INE, 2012) about 1.5 million Portuguese people who lived in Portugal in 2011 had resided abroad at least for one year and returned to Portugal. The most represented countries among this returned population were France (26.3%) and Angola (15.2%), followed by Mozambique (7.8%), Germany (7.6%), Switzerland (7.2%), Venezuela (4.5%), and Brazil

(4.5%). These were traditionally countries of settlement for Portuguese emigrants, and the return migration from African countries was mostly associated with the process of decolonization. In fact, the highest number of returned people to Portugal occurred during the 1970s (1971–1980, 31.6%) from ex-colonies as a result of decolonization. A second wave of return migration took place in the 1980s (19.6%) and 1990s (21.9%), in great part linked to traditional migration (e.g., work migration). Despite the extent of the return migration, empirical investigation on this flow is scanty (Silva et al., 1984; Neto, 2016).

Diverse ethnocultural groups now comprise the current immigrant population. According the 2011 Census (INE, 2012), 394,496 foreign citizen lived in Portugal, corresponding to 3.7 per cent of the total population of 10,562,178. The growth of the immigrant population has basically been from the 1990s onwards, when there were only approximately 100,000 immigrants. The figures show about a 400 per cent increase in the two following decades. Brazilian immigrants (28%) were the most numerous, with Cape-Verdeans (10%) occupying the second, and Ukrainians (9%) in third place. The following were Angolans (6.8%), Romanians (6.2%), and Guineans (4.1%). Immigrants from PALOP (African countries with Portuguese as official language) represented 24 per cent of the total foreigners, which corresponds to the same number of EU foreigners (24%). The majority of foreign residents were women (52.3%). The foreign population lived predominantly in the littoral; more than half were located in the area of Lisbon (51.6%), and in the Algarve (13.2%), followed by the Centre (13.9%), and North (13.1%). Regarding economic activity, 61.1 per cent of the foreign population was economically active (compared to 47% in the native Portuguese population). The majority of foreigners worked mostly in four main areas: agriculture, manufacturing industry, building and civil engineering, and services. Residents of European origin were employed mainly in the professional and service sectors; most Brazilians were employed in the service sector; whereas the majority of Africans were employed in the industrial and construction sectors (INE, 2012).

2.2   Policies

As a country of immigration and of emigration and with a long history of contact with other cultures, the Portuguese people have become tolerant of cultural diversity and among whom positive interethnic attitudes prevail (Neto, 2009b). In regard to interethnic relationships, Neto also pointed out that in Portugal the situation was stable during the preceding 20 years, which prevented intercultural problems or conflicts.

Adolescents from immigrant backgrounds tend to report very few personal acts of discrimination from native Portuguese (Neto, 2006). A survey (Lages & Policarpo, 2003) showed a rather strong difference in attitudes with respect to immigration policy (i.e., prospective immigrants) and immigrant policy (i.e., immigrants already living in the country). Slightly more than 70 per cent of Portuguese over the age of 17 wanted to avoid having more immigrants come to Portugal. At the same time a high percentage (97.2%) were of the opinion that immigrants should have the same rights that Portuguese immigrants have in other countries. Ninety-three percent were in favour of the right of family reunification for immigrants, and 84 per cent wanted to facilitate the gaining of citizenship by immigrants. Moreover, most of the respondents were of the opinion that living alongside immigrants promotes mutual understanding.

As noted in the introduction, among countries in the MIRIPS project, Portugal places low on the diversity index, but high on the integration index, and is in the middle on the policy index. The trend in the placement of Portugal on the policy index shows that the score for Portugal rose from 1.0 in 1980 to 2.0 in 1990, and to 3.5 in 2010. These scores reveal two aspects: (a) Portugal has supported some level of multiculturalism policies over the last three decades; and (b) the last decade has seen a strengthening of multiculturalism policies in Portugal. Portugal's ranking in the three indexes seems consonant with a country where multiculturalism and pluralism are greatly valued. These indices reflect the evolution of integration policies "from a *laissez-faire* policy in the 1980s to reluctant assimilationist policies in the early 1990s and to a more pluralist approach from the late 1990s to the present" (Malheiros & Horta, 2008, p. 108).

While multiculturalism is highly accepted, ethnic hierarchy is also evident as some ethnocultural groups are assessed more positively than others. When Portuguese adolescents rated 17 ethnocultural groups (Neto, 2009b), the top place was occupied by Brazilians, followed by Timorese and French. African countries with Portuguese as their official language occupied intermediate places (Angolans, Cape-Verdeans, Guineans, Mozambicans, and San Tomeans). Gypsies had the lowest acceptance rating.

A specific characteristic of immigrants in this country is that the majority of them come from Portuguese-speaking countries. These are above all former colonies where Portugal has influenced the local culture, the religion, and the judicial and educational systems. It might be much easier for them to adapt to settling in Portugal than it is for immigrants who have a larger cultural distance (cf. Galchenko & Van de Vijver, 2007). Thus, in some ways the majority of the immigrant population in Portugal is more homogeneous than the immigrant populations in many other Western countries; moreover, due to the remnants of the colonial history in their countries of origin one may suppose that the acculturation process conducive to a swift integration in Portuguese society started long before the actual move to Portugal.

In summary, Portugal is an atypical country, being (a) both an emigration and an immigration country, (b) a country with the majority of immigrants whose cultural distance to the Portuguese culture is relatively small, and (c) a country whose nationals evidence positive and protective attitudes towards immigrant people.

3   Evaluation of the MIRIPS Hypotheses

This research in Portugal evaluates all three hypotheses.

The multiculturalism hypothesis proposes that confidence in one's identity underlies the possibility of accepting "others". This acceptance comprises valuing cultural diversity and intercultural contact, being tolerant, the reduction of discrimination, accepting immigrants and ethnocultural groups in society. In contrast, when one's identity is threatened, individuals will develop hostility and prejudice.

The multiculturalism hypothesis has been previously examined in Portugal. This research showed support for the multiculturalism hypothesis: when adolescents felt that their place was secure in their own plural society, they were both tolerant of, and more welcoming to, immigrants (Neto, 2009b).

In the present research we use the construct of multicultural ideology to assess the acceptance of multiculturalism. This construct includes the core characteristics of multiculturalism: cultural maintenance, intergroup contact, and willingness to engage in mutual exchange. In this study, we examine whether multicultural ideology is associated with the acceptance of those who differ from us.

The contact hypothesis (Allport, 1954) proposes that intercultural contacts often lead to more positive intercultural relations. This link has been evidenced in different settings, usually under certain conditions (e.g., equal status of the groups in situation, cooperation rather than competition, common goals, and authority support). Intergroup friendships are likely to meet several of these conditions (Gieling et al., 2014). Research has shown that contact in neighbourhood and social settings leads to more positive attitudes towards minority members (Voci & Hewstone, 2003; Ward & Masgoret, 2008). Pettigrew and Tropp (2006) performed a meta-analysis, providing general support for the contact hypothesis: intergroup contact generally relates negatively to prejudice in both majority and minority members.

In the current study, we explore whether positive intergroup attitudes among immigrants and among members of the majority society are associated with intercultural contact. As indicators of intergroup attitudes we will consider tolerance, perceived consequences of immigration, and attitudes towards ethnocultural groups.

The integration hypothesis argues that the integration strategy is more beneficial for psychological adaptation and sociocultural adaptation than the assimilation, separation and particularly the marginalization strategy. This hypothesis has been supported by many studies (e.g., Berry, Phinney, Sam & Vedder, 2006; Brown, Gibbons & Hughes, 2013). In Portugal, Neto (2010a) found that the integration strategy was significantly and positively related to psychological adaptation and socio-cultural adaptation among young immigrants from Angola, Cape Verde, Guinea-Bissau, India, Mozambique, São-Tomé and East Timor.

Intercultural expectations of majority groups have been much less studied than intercultural strategies of immigrants. Only a few studies have approached the relationship between the intercultural expectations of the majority members and their own adaptation (e.g., Hui et al., 2015; Lebedeva et al., 2016). In Germany, for example, the integration expec-tation was the most adaptive one (Schmitz & Berry, 2009). Hui et al. (2015) showed that Hong Kong residents who held higher integration expectations with respect to migrants had higher scores on psychological adaptation than those who had lower integration expectations.

A third form of adaptation, in addition to psychological adaptation and sociocultural adaptation, concerns the degree to which people are able to establish harmonious intercultural relations with others, including low levels of prejudice and discrimination (intercultural adaptation). In the current research, we explore whether the integration strategy (for immigrants) and the multiculturalism expectation (by Portuguese) have more benefits for the three forms of adaptation of immigrants and non-immigrants than the other intercultural strategies and expectations.

4   Method

4.1   Samples

Two samples were used in this study (see Table 12.1). The first sample consisted of 1505 participants who described themselves as members of minority groups, and who had two minority group parents. The six min-ority groups constituted the top six immigrant groups living in Portugal (i.e., Angolans, Brazilians, Cape-Verdeans, Guineans, Romanians, and Ukrainians). Their mean age was 37 years ($SD = 10.4$). There were 806

Table 12.1. *Socio-demographic characteristics of the samples of immigrants and native Portuguese.*

	Immigrants (N = 1505)	Native Portuguese (N = 348)
Mean age (SD)	37.04 (10.42)	30.18 (10.73)
Gender		
Male	806 (53.5%)	138 (39.7%)
Female	695 (46.2%)	210 (60.3%)
Not answered	4 (.3%)	
Nationality		
Angola	252 (16.7%)	–
Brazil	258 (17.1%)	–
Cape Verde	283 (18.8%)	–
Guinea-Bissau	280 (18.6)	–
Romania	214 (14.2%)	–
Ukraine	218 (14.5%)	–
Portugal	–	348 (100%)
Mean years in Portugal (SD)	15.90 (9.51)	–
Marital status		
Married	859 (57.1%)	41 (11.8%)
Not married	619 (41.1%)	301 (86.5%)
Not answered	27 (1.8%)	6 (1.7%)
Level of education		
Less than secondary school	547 (36.4%)	24 (6.9%)
Secondary school	494 (32.8%)	87 (25.0%)
Tertiary education	425 (28.2%)	236 (67.9%)
Not answered	39 (2.6%)	1 (.3%)
Work		
Unskilled work	461 (30.6%)	20 (5.7%)
Skilled work	480 (31.6%)	28 (8.0%)
Managerial work	134 (8.4%)	20 (5.7%)
Professional work	100 (6.6%)	42 (12.1%)
Without work	246 (16.4%)	225 (64.6%)
Not answered	84 (5.6%)	14 (3.7%)
Religion		
No religion	197 (13.1%)	107 (30.7%)
Roman Catholic	753 (50.0%)	203 (58.3%)
Protestant	76 (5.0%)	1 8.3%)
Orthodox Christian	366 (24.3%)	14 (4.0%)
Muslim	45 (3.0%)	–
Other	39 (2.6%)	17 (4.9%)
Not answered	29 (1.9%)	6 (1.7%)

men, 695 women, and 4 did not indicate their gender. Most of the sample were married. The mean length of their residence was 15.9 years (*SD* = 9.5). Among immigrants, 36.4 per cent had not completed secondary school, 32.8 per cent had completed secondary school, 28.2 per cent attended or had completed university, and 2.6 per cent did not provide information on their level of education. Almost two-thirds of the immigrants were employed in unskilled/skilled work, and half of them identified as Roman Catholics.

The second sample consisted of 348 native Portuguese participants who described themselves as Portuguese and had parents of Portuguese origin. Their mean age was 30.2 years (SD = 10.8). There were 138 men, and 210 women. Most of the sample was not married. About two-thirds attended or had completed university and did not work. The majority identified as Roman Catholics. Although socio-demographic characteristics such as age, gender, marital status, level of education and work differed in the two samples, this was not relevant, as we are not directly comparing both samples.

Participants were recruited in the Lisbon metropolitan area. We used a convenience sample, recruited through snowball sampling using personal contacts as well as community groups. Drawing a convenience sample is suitable in cross-cultural research when the researcher does not have access to an accurate list of the entire population, as is the case of migrants in Portugal (Lonner & Berry, 1986). Participants completed the questionnaire supervised by research assistants. Identical instructions were given to all participants. The participants were informed that their responses would be kept confidential and used solely for research purposes. All participants were unpaid volunteers. Completion of the questionnaire required about 40 minutes.

4.2   Measures

This research used some scales from the MIRIPS project. These scales had been translated into Portuguese and adapted for use in Portugal in previous international projects (International Comparative Study of Ethnocultural Youth -ICSEY- Berry et al., 2006; Neto, 2002, 2006, 2010b; and International Study of Attitudes Towards Immigration and Settlement -ISATIS- Berry & Kalin, 1995; Neto, 2009b). For this study, participants answered on a 5-point scale: 1 – *strongly disagree*; 2 – *disagree*; 3 – *not sure/neutral*; 4 – *agree*; 5 – *strongly agree*.

The following scales were used (see Table 12.2): intercultural strategies of migrants; intercultural expectations of native Portuguese; multicultural ideology; intercultural contacts; tolerance; perceived consequences of immigration; attitudes towards ethnocultural groups; perceived discrimination; psychological adaptation; and sociocultural adaptation.

Table 12.2. *Means, standard deviations, and reliability coefficients of the measures for the samples of immigrants (N = 1505) and native Portuguese (N = 348)*

	M	SD	Number of items	Cronbach's α
	Immigrant			
Assimilation	2.29	.91	4	.77
Integration	3.82	.86	4	.68
Separation	2.35	.98	4	.66
Marginalization	1.99	.85	4	.79
Multicultural ideology	3.32	.59	10	.63
Tolerance	3.72	.59	11	.66
Intercultural contacts	3.77	.87	2	.78
Perceived cons. of immigration	3.26	.73	11	.76
Attitudes towards Portuguese	8.41	2.57	1	–
Perceived discrimination	2.15	1.09	5	.90
Sociocultural adaptation	3.74	.82	20	.92
Satisfaction with life	3.45	.91	5	.86
Self-esteem	3.83	.72	10	.72
Psychological problems	2.41	.79	15	.91
	Native Portuguese			
Melting pot	1.93	.73	4	.70
Multiculturalism	4.15	.77	4	.73
Segregation	2.05	.67	4	.60
Exclusion	1.73	.75	4	.73
Multicultural ideology	3.68	.61	10	.76
Tolerance	3.94	.66	11	.83
Intercultural contacts	2.44	1.11	2	.89
Perceived cons. of immigration	3.44	.67	11	.82
Attitudes towards immigrants	5.99	1.88	17	.96
Perceived discrimination	1.69	.83	5	.89
Sociocultural adaptation	3.87	.82	20	.94
Satisfaction with life	3.62	.80	5	.87
Self-esteem	3.97	.70	10	.88
Psychological problems	2.42	.73	15	.93

Attitudes towards specific ethnocultural groups were assessed: immigrants were asked to rate Portuguese; native Portuguese participants were asked to rate 17 groups, including Angolans, Brazilians, Chinese, and Cape Verdeans, etc.

Psychological adaptation was assessed using three scales: Satisfaction with Life Scale (SWLS, Diener, Emmons, Larsen & Griffin, 1985; Neto, 1993, 1995), Rosenberg Self-Esteem Scale (RSES; Rosenberg, 1965; Neto, 1996) and Psychological Problems Scale (Berry et al., 2006; Neto, 2009a). A composite score for psychological adaptation was computed by averaging scores for life satisfaction, self-esteem, and psychological problems, as has been previously done (e.g., Neto, 2012; Hui et al., 2015).

Demographic information. In addition, respondents were requested to supply information on age, gender, place of birth, place of birth of both parents, age at arrival in Portugal (if born abroad), level of education, and occupation.

5   Results

Prior to testing the hypotheses, preliminary analyses were conducted in order to examine the psychometric properties of the scales and test whether the constructs of life satisfaction, self-esteem and psychological problems could be used as indicators of psychological adaptation. Descriptive statistics and reliability coefficients of the scales used in this study are presented in Table 12.2. Cronbach alphas were estimated to check the reliability of the scales containing multiple items. The Cronbach alpha reliability coefficients for the scales showed acceptable internal consistency in immigrant and native Portuguese samples.

To test the *multiculturalism hypothesis*, we used the concept and scale of perceived discrimination, which is the opposite to feelings of security. As a first step, hierarchical multiple regressions were conducted in both groups. Prior to performing the regression analyses, collinearity diagnostics were analysed to ensure that the variance inflation factor did not exceed 10. This will be done in all the next multiple regressions which will be conducted. To control for possible confounding effects, age and gender were entered in the first block and separation/segregation and marginalization/exclusion in the second block. For immigrants, the regression model showed that 6 per cent of the total variance in perceived discrimination could be explained by the independent variables, $F(4, 1477) = 25.55$ $p <. 001$. Perceived discrimination was predicted by separation ($\beta =.06$, $p <.05$) and marginalization ($\beta =.21$, $p <.001$). For native Portuguese, the regression model showed that 24 per cent of the total variance in perceived discrimination could be explained by the independent variables, $F(4, 331) = 27.59$, $p <. 001$. Perceived discrimination was predicted by gender (men; $\beta =-.18$, $p <.001$), segregation ($\beta =.21$, $p <.001$) and exclusion ($\beta =.29$, $p <.001$).

Furthermore, we examined whether perceived discrimination was predicted by tolerance and multicultural ideology. For immigrants, the regression model showed that 4 per cent of the total variance in perceived discrimination could be explained by the independent variables, $F(4, 1458) = 13.41$ $p <.001$. Perceived discrimination was predicted by tolerance (β =–.20, p <.001). For native Portuguese, the regression model showed that 14 per cent of the total variance in perceived discrimination could be explained by the independent variables, $F(4, 321)$ = 12.57, p <. 001. Perceived discrimination was predicted by gender (men; β = –.17, p <.001), tolerance (β = –.19, p <.001) and multicultural ideology (β = –.13, p <.001).

The nature of the construct of multicultural ideology was further explored. Mean scores of immigrants on the MCI (M = 3.32, SD =.59) and of native Portuguese (M = 3.68, SD =.61) were significantly above the scale midpoint of 3, suggesting a positive attitude in both samples. For immigrants, multicultural ideology was positively associated with tolerance (r =.36, p <.001), perceived consequences of immigration (r =.57, p <.001), and attitudes towards Portuguese (r =.30; p <.001). For native Portuguese a similar pattern of correlations was found. Multicultural ideology was positively associated with tolerance (r =.61, p <.001), perceived consequences of immigration (r =.58, p <.001), and attitudes towards immigrants (r =.26; p <.001).

Hierarchical multiple regressions were performed to predict multicultural ideology. To control for possible confounding effects of age and gender, they were also entered in the first block. Ethnic tolerance, perceived consequences of immigration and attitudes towards ethnocultural groups were entered in the second block. For the immigrant sample, the regression model showed that 38 per cent of the total variance in multicultural ideology could be explained by the independent variables, $F(5, 1435)$ = 174.97, p <.001 (Table 12.3). The effect of age and gender were not significant, p >.05. Multicultural ideology was predicted by high ethnic tolerance, positive perceived consequences of immigration and attitudes towards Portuguese. For native Portuguese the regression analysis showed that 51 per cent of the total variance in multicultural ideology could be explained by the independent variables, $F(5, 319)$ = 64.81, p <.001. The effects of age and gender were not significant, p >.05. Multicultural ideology was predicted by higher ethnic tolerance and positive perceived consequences of immigration.

To evaluate the *contact hypothesis*, hierarchical multiple regressions were also performed to predict intercultural contact. To control for possible confounding effects of age and gender, they were entered in the first block. Perceived discrimination among immigrants, tolerance, perceived consequences of immigration and attitudes towards immigrants among native Portuguese were entered in the second block. For immigrants, intercultural contact was not predicted by perceived discrimination, $F(3, 1476)$ = 1.58, p >.05. For native Portuguese, the

Table 12.3. *Hierarchical regression models predicting multicultural ideology among immigrants and native Portuguese.*

Variables	Block 1 β	Block 2 β
		Immigrants
Age	.00	.02
Gender	−.01	.02
Tolerance		.24***
Perceived consequences of immigration		.47***
Attitudes towards Portuguese		.08***
R^2	.00	.38
Adjusted R^2	.00	.38
F change	.11	291.60***
		Native Portuguese
Age	.04	.06
Gender	.04	−.07
Tolerance		.51***
Perceived consequences of immigration		.28***
Attitudes towards immigrants		.01
R^2	.00	.51
Adjusted R^2	-.00	.50
F change	.45	107.35***

* $p <.05$; ** $p <.01$; ***$p <.001$.

regression showed that 4 per cent of the total variance in intercultural contact could be explained by independent variables, $F(5, 292) = 2.43$, $p <.05$. Intercultural contact was predicted by higher tolerance ($\beta =.22$, $p <.001$). These findings partially support the contact hypothesis.

To evaluate the *integration hypothesis*, we first tested whether the constructs of satisfaction with life, self-esteem and psychological problems could be used as indicators of psychological adaptation by means of principal component analyses were performed. For immigrants, this resulted in one factor (eigenvalue greater than 1 as criteria), accounting for 49.39 per cent of the variance. For the native Portuguese, the results also showed one factor (eigenvalue greater than 1 as criteria), accounting for 58.95 per cent of the variance.

One-sample t-tests showed that average scores for integration ($M = 3.82$) and multiculturalism ($M = 4.15$) were significantly higher than the midpoint (3) of the scales ($p <.001$). Also, average scores for assimilation/melting pot, separation/segregation, and marginalization/exclusion were significantly lower than the midpoint of the scale (all p's <.001).

Table 12.4. *Correlations between intercultural strategies/ expectations of immigrants and of native Portuguese and adaptation.*

	Psychological adaptation	Sociocultural adaptation
Immigrants Strategies		
Integration	.37***	.11***
Assimilation	−.44***	−.33***
Separation	−.28***	−.26***
Marginalization	−.44***	−.34***
Native Portuguese Expectations		
Multiculturalism	.14*	.17**
Melting pot	−.19***	−.24***
Segregation	−.12*	−.22***
Exclusion	−.24***	−.31***

$*p < .05; **p < .01; ***p < .001.$

An inspection of these average scores showed two groupings among immigrants and native Portuguese: integration/multiculturalism was clearly on the preferred side, while assimilation/melting pot, separation/segregation, and marginalization/exclusion were not preferred.

As expected for immigrants, the integration strategy was positively correlated with psychological adaptation and sociocultural adaptation, while assimilation, separation, and marginalization were negatively associated with both kinds of adaptation (see Table 12.4). For non-immigrants, the multiculturalism expectation was positively correlated with psychological adaptation and sociocultural adaptation, while melting pot, segregation, and exclusion expectations were negatively associated with both kinds of adaptation. These findings support the integration hypothesis.

Hierarchical multiple regressions were performed to predict intercultural adaptation (see Table 12.5). To control for the possible confounding effects of age and gender, they were entered in the first block. The four intercultural/expectation strategies were entered in the second block. For immigrants, the regression showed that 25 per cent of the total variance in multicultural ideology could be explained by independent variables, $F(6, 1466) = 81.66, p < .001$. Multicultural ideology was predicted by higher integration and by lower assimilation, separation and marginalization. For native Portuguese, the regression showed that 32 per cent of the total variance in multicultural ideology could be explained by

Table 12.5. *Hierarchical regression models predicting multicultural ideology and tolerance among immigrants and native Portuguese.*

	Multicultural ideology		Tolerance	
Variables	Block 1 β	Block 2 β	Block 1 β	Block 2 β
	Immigrants			
Age	.01	.03	−.05*	−.02
Gender	−.01	.00	−.01	.01
Integration		.20***		.16***
Assimilation		−.23***		−.18***
Separation		−.06*		−.11***
Marginalization		−.17***		−.30***
R^2	.01	.25	.00	.34
Adjusted R^2	.00	.25	.00	.34
F change	.11	81.66***	2.07	187.79***
	Native Portuguese			
Age	.04	.05	.01	.02
Gender	.04	−.01	.18**	.14**
Multiculturalism		.24***		.22***
Melting pot		−.29***		−.24
Separation		−.15*		−.23***
Exclusion		−.02		−.01
R^2	.00	.32	.03	.35
Adjusted R^2	−.00	.31	.03	.33
F change	.45	25.19***	5.31**	38.82***

*p <.05; ** p <.01; ***p <.001.

independent variables, $F(6, 331) = 25.19$, p <.001. Multicultural ideology was predicted by higher multiculturalism and by lower melting pot and segregation.

We have considered tolerance, in addition to multicultural ideology, as an indicator of intercultural adaptation. For immigrants, the regression showed that 34 per cent of the total variance in tolerance could be explained by independent variables, $F(6, 1459) = 126,32$, p <.001. Tolerance was predicted by higher integration and by lower assimilation, separation and marginalization. For native Portuguese, the regression showed that 35 per cent of the total variance in tolerance could be explained by independent variables, $F(6, 328) = 28.47$, p <.001. Tolerance was predicted by higher multiculturalism and by lower melting pot expectations and segregation. These findings with respect to psychological, sociocultural and intercultural adaptation all support the integration hypothesis.

6   Discussion

This research investigated reciprocal intercultural relations between majority-Portuguese members group and immigrants. We made predictions based mostly on three hypotheses (multicultural, contact and integration hypotheses) which have been derived from research on intercultural relations in Canada and internationally. These predictions were tested separately, using data from two samples: the six numerically largest immigrant groups living in Portugal and the native Portuguese. Overall, the empirical evidence found in this research on mutual intergroup relations in Portugal showed evidence in support all three hypotheses.

First, with respect to the distribution of intercultural strategies and expectations, this research displayed a high degree of reciprocity in the strategies/expectations preferred by immigrants and members of the society at large. Both groups chose integration/ multiculturalism as the most preferred strategies, followed by separation/segregation, assimilation/melting pot and the least preferred strategy/expectation was marginalization/exclusion. In addition to showing mutuality, these findings also reflect positive intercultural relations in Portugal. If immigrants desire to integrate, and national populations desire to incorporate immigrants in their society by way of multiculturalism, then the acculturation orientations are consensual (Bourhis et al., 1997) and social harmony is likely to be enhanced. This mutual consistency may prevent conflict at the levels of the larger society, and it is consonant with previous findings among adolescents (Neto, 2009b).

The multiculturalism hypothesis was supported. This hypothesis predicts that when immigrants are threatened by acts of discrimination, they will prefer separation and marginalization strategies. This was observed in the current study using perceived discrimination as the obverse to feelings of security about peoples' cultural identity and place in society. Furthermore, this view was expanded to intercultural expectations.

The multiculturalism hypothesis also predicts that security (in the present study, its opposite, discrimination) will be associated with more acceptance of others in the society (in this case, higher multicultural ideology and tolerance). Our findings showed that perceived discrimination was predicted among immigrants by low levels of tolerance, and among native Portuguese by low levels of both tolerance and multicultural ideology.

Positive intergroup attitudes such as tolerance, perceived consequences of immigration, and attitudes towards ethnocultural groups also emerged as significant predictors of multicultural ideology.

Therefore, multicultural ideology seems to be associated with the overall acceptance of others.

The contact hypothesis was partially supported. Perceived discrimination was not significantly related to intercultural contact among immigrants; however, positive intergroup attitudes predicted intercultural contact for native Portuguese. Tolerance appeared as a significant predictor, but the explained variance was relatively low. The low percent of the total variance found in intercultural contact hypothesis can be due to our measure of intercultural friendships. Future research should use other measures such as self-disclosure with out-group friends.

With respect to the integration hypothesis, preference for the integration strategy (among immigrants) and the multiculturalism expectation (among Portuguese) were positively and strongly associated with better psychological and sociocultural adaptation. In contrast, the other three strategies were negatively associated with both forms of adaptation. We also found that in the native Portuguese sample the multiculturalism expectation was positively related to their psychological adaptation and sociocultural adaptation. And again, in contrast, the other three expectations were negatively associated with these adaptations. We also tested the integration hypothesis using the outcome of intercultural adaptation. More integration/multiculturalism and less assimilation/melting pot emerged as significant predictors of multicultural ideology and of tolerance.

Thus, this research supported the integration hypothesis for migrants, as well as for members of society at large. For both populations, integration/multiculturalism is the strategy associated with the best psychological, sociocultural and intercultural outcomes. Overall, the results of this Portuguese MIRIPS study support the view that there are advantages of the integration strategy for the adaptation of migrants (Berry et al., 2006; Neto et al., 2005; Nguyen & Benet-Martinez, 2013). This research also expands these results to the expectation of multiculturalism held by members of the society of settlement. A possible explanation for these findings has been advanced by Berry (2013, p. 667): "those who are doubly engaged with both cultures receive support and resources from both, and are competent in dealing with both cultures".

Our findings should be considered in light of the research limitations. First, both samples were ones of convenience. Migrants and native Portuguese were recruited through the snowball technique, which limits their representativeness. Second, the research included self-reports only. Third, reliability estimates of a few scales were below .70. Fourth, the findings of this research are correlational and therefore do not yield any evidence of causality. Finally, given the space limitations we did not control for nationality, socio-economic status, and some socio-demographic variables that may influence the relations among the variables considered.

This chapter outlined the multicultural ways of living together in Portugal. Both current empirical results and the place of Portugal on international indexes indicate that this country advocates and achieves the multicultural vision.

These results have important implications for policy and practice internationally, as well as in Portugal. Current work combined the research traditions of acculturation and ethnic relations into one study, seeking to contribute to a new way of approaching intercultural relations. If the findings of the current research are also found in other cultural settings, then general principles might be taken into consideration in order to develop broadly applicable policies.

The research has also practical implications. For example, given that integration is associated with the best psycho-social adjustment of minority members and of members of society at large, it is relevant to find out how this beneficial acculturation strategy might be promoted and facilitated. In both samples, multicultural ideology and intercultural contact are predicted by tolerance. That is, tolerance might influence attitudes towards multiculturalism and contact with outgroups. Such mutual relationships have been largely neglected (Tip et al., 2012). Practitioners should promote tolerance: for example, by providing immigrants and native Portuguese with opportunities to interact in a cooperative setting. Tolerance may be a means to cope with conflicting views, as people engaged in "heterogeneous associations are more likely to be tolerant towards other groups" (Rapp & Freitag, 2015, p. 1046). Hence, the contribution of this research is not only theoretical but also practical.

References

Allport, G. W. (1954). *The Nature of Prejudice*. Reading, MA: Addison-Wesley.

Berry, J. W. (2013). Research on multiculturalism in Canada. *International Journal of Intercultural Relations, 37*, 663–675.

Berry, J. W., & Kalin, R. (1995). Multicultural and ethnic attitudes in Canada: An overview of the 1991 national survey. *Canadian Journal of Behavioural and Science, 27*, 301–320.

Berry, J. W., Phinney, J. S., Sam, D.L., & Vedder, P. (Eds.) (2006). *Immigrant Youth in Cultural Transition: Acculturation, Identity and Adaptation across National Contexts*. Mahwah: Lawrence Erlbaum Associates.

Bourhis, R., Moise, C., Perrault, S., & Senecal, S. (1997). Towards an interactive acculturation model: A social psychological approach. *International Journal of Psychology, 32*, 369–386.

Brown, C. M., Gibbons, J. L., & Hughes, H. M. (2013). Acculturation clusters and life satisfaction. *Acta de Investigación Psicológica, 3*, 1108–1121.

Diener, E. R., Emmons, R. Larsen, R., & Griffin, S. (1985). The satisfaction with life scale. *Journal of Personality Assessment, 49*(1),71–75.

Galchenko, I., & Van de Vijver, F. J. R. (2007). The role of perceived distance in the acculturation of exchange students in Russia. *International Journal of Intercultural Relations, 31*, 181–197.

Gieling, M., Thijs, J., & Verkuyten, M. (2014). Dutch adolescents' tolerance of Muslim immigrants: The role of assimilation ideology, intergroup contact, and national identification. *Journal of Applied Social Psychology, 44*, 155–165.

Godinho, M. (1978). L'émigration portugaise: Histoire d'une constante structurale. *Revista de História Económica e Social, 1*, 5–32.

Hui, B., Chen, S., Leung, C., & Berry, J. W. (2015). Facilitating adaptation and intercultural contact: The role of integration and multicultural ideology in dominant and non-dominant groups. *International Journal of Intercultural Relations, 45*, 70–84.

INE (2012). *A população estrangeira em Porugal- 2011*. Lisbon: Instituto Nacional de Estatística.

Lages, M., & Policarpo, V. (2003) *Atitudes e valores perante a imigração [Attitudes and values vis-à-vis immigration]*. Lisbon: ACIME.

Lebedeva, N., Tatarko, A., & Berry, J. W. (2016). Intercultural reactions among migrants from Caucasus and Russians in Moscow. *International Journal of Intercultural Relations, 52*, 27–38.

Lonner, W. J., & Berry, J. (1986). Sampling and surveying. In W. J. Lonner & J. W. Berry (Eds.), *Field Methods in Cross-Cultural Research* (pp. 85–110). London: Sage.

Malheiros, J., & Horta, A. P. (2008). Citizenship and integration policies in Portugal: An overview of recent immigration to Portugal. *Canadian Diversity, 6*(4), 107–110.

Neto, F. (1993). Satisfaction with life scale: Psychometric properties in an adolescent sample. *Journal of Youth and Adolescence, 22*, 125–134.

Neto, F. (1995). Predictors of satisfaction with life among second generation immigrants. *Social Indictors Research, 35*, 93–116.

Neto, F. (1996). Correlates of social blushing. *Personality and Individual Differences, 20*, 365–373.

Neto, F. (2002). Acculturation strategies among adolescents from immigrant families in Portugal. *International Journal of Intercultural Relations, 26*, 17–38.

Neto, F. (2006). Psycho-social predictors of perceived discrimination among adolescents of immigrant background: A Portuguese study. *Journal of Ethnic and Migration Studies, 32*, 89–109.

Neto, F. (2009a). Predictors of mental health among adolescents from immigrant families in Portugal. *Journal of Family Psychology, 23*, 375–385.

Neto, F. (2009b). Are attitudes of young Portuguese towards immigration also hardening? A comparison between 1999 and 2006. In A. Garie K. Mylonas, *Quod erat demonstrandum: From Herodotus' ethnographioc journeys to cross-cultural research* (pp. 255–264). Athens: Pedio Books Publishing. Published for International Association of Cross-Cultural Psychology.

Neto, F. (2010a). *Portugal intercultural: Aculturação e adaptação de jovens de origem imigrante*. Porto: Livpsic.

Neto, F. (2010b). Re-acculturation attitudes among adolescents from returned Portuguese immigrant families. *International Journal of Intercultural Relations*, *34*, 221–232.

Neto, F. (2012). Re-acculturation and adaptation among adolescents from returned Portuguese immigrant families. *Journal of Applied Social Psychology*, *42*, 133–150.

Neto, F. (2016). Predictors of loneliness among Portuguese youths from returned migrant families. *Social Indicators Research*, *126*, 425–441.

Neto, F., Barros, J., & Schmitz, P. G. (2005). Acculturation attitudes and adaptation among Portuguese immigrants in Germany: Integration or separation. *Psychology and Developing Societies*, *17*, 19–32.

Nguyen, A. M., & Benet-Martinez, V. (2013). Biculturalilsm and adjustment: A meta-analysis. *Journal of Cross-Cultural Psychology*, *44*, 122–159.

Observatório da Emigração (2015), *Portuguese Emigration Factbook 2015*, Lisbon, Observatório da Emigração, CIES-IUL, ISCTE-IUL. doi: 10.15847/ CIESOEMFB2015.

Pettigrew, T. F., & Tropp, L. R. (2006). A meta-analytic test of intergroup contact theory. *Journal of Personality and Social Psychology*, *90*, 751–783.

Rapp, C., & Freitag, M. (2015). Teaching tolerance? Associational diversity and tolerance formation. *Political Studies*, *63*, 1031–1051.

Rocha-Trindade, M. B. (2014). *Das migrações à interculturalidade*. Porto: Edições Afrontamento.

Rosenberg, M. (1965). *Society and the Adolescent Self-Image*. Princeton, NJ: Princeton University Press.

Schmitz, P. G., & Berry, J. W. (2009). Structure of acculturation attitudes and their relationships with personality and psychological adaptation: A study with immigrant and national samples in Germany. In K. Boehnke (Ed.), Proceedings of IACCP Congress (Bremen-on line).

Silva, M. et al. (1984). *Retorno, emigração e desenvolvimento regional em Portugal*. Lisbon: Instituto de Estudos para o Desenvolvimento.

Tip, L., Zagefka, H., González, R., Brown, R., Cinniralla, M., & Na, X. (2012). Is support for multiculturalism threatened by ... threat itself? *International Journal of Intercultural Relations*, *36*, 22–30.

Voci, A., & Hewstone, M. (2003). Intergroup contact and prejudice toward immigrants in Italy: The mediational role of anxiety and the moderation role of group salience. *Group Processes and Intergroup Relations*, *6*, 37–52.

Ward, C., & Masgoret, A. M. (2008). Attitudes toward immigrants, immigration, and multiculturalism in New Zealand: A social psychological analysis. *International Migration Review*, *42*, 222–243.

13   Intercultural Relations in Spain

Hector Grad[1]

Universidad Autonoma de Madrid, Madrid, Spain

1   Introduction

The study of intercultural relations is especially interesting in Spain due to the combination of existing large regional, cultural and linguistic diversity within the country, and with a wave of increasing immigration, which has recently multiplied the foreign-born population by a factor of six. Although research shows relatively positive attitudes of the autochthonous population towards immigration and ethnocultural diversity, there are also some hints about a gap between the discourse supporting multiculturalism and the actual demands of unilateral adaptation of immigrants to the host culture (i.e., expectations of assimilation; Solanes, 2009). Spain is relatively high on the diversity and policy indexes, but is in the middle of the integration index.

In this context, immigration from Ecuador shifted from being a tiny group to be the third-largest immigrant group (after Morocco and Romania). Ecuadoreans, like immigrants from other former colonies, share language and cultural characteristics (for instance, majority of Catholic religion and traditions), and enjoy legal advantages in their access to Spanish legal residence and citizenship. Against this background of relatively favourable conditions, potential difficulties in the mutual acculturation with the population of the larger society may be especially interesting and justify a close look at their intercultural relations.

[1] This chapter was written during a stay at the Graduate Center, City University of New York, with funding of the Program for academic mobility to foreign higher education and research centers (2015-PRX15/00445) of the Spanish Ministry of Education, Culture and Sports (Spain). The research was partially supported by the Spanish National Plan of RD&I of the Ministry of Education in the framework of the project "National identity, ideologies about cultural diversity, and integration of immigrants" (Project SEJ2006-09662/PSIC) and a small R+D grant of the Universidad Autonoma de Madrid for the fieldwork.

2   The Context of Intercultural Relations in Spain

2.1   Sources of Cultural Diversity

Due to its historical and contemporary development, Spanish society has a great regional, cultural and linguistic diversity. In the political domain, Spanish nationalism was unable to impose itself as the single hegemonic national ideology, or to overcome various regional demands by building an ideal nation-state (Linz, 1973, 1993). Spain is currently configured as a plurinational state where a central Spanish nationalism coexists and interacts with a number of regional nationalisms. Therefore, a central national Spanish identity coexists with other significant national identities in different regions (Grad, 2001, 2011; Grad & Martín Rojo, 2003). After the restoration of democracy, the 1978 Constitution reflected this country's national diversity and established a quasi-federal structure, granting administrative autonomy to 17 regions (called "autonomous regions"). The Constitution acknowledged the existence of 'historical nationalities' in the Basque Country, Catalonia, Galicia, and the co-officiality of the Spanish language with Catalan, Basque and Galician, which are spoken in the autonomous regions. Hence Catalonia, Valencia, Mallorca, Basque Country and Galicia, whose languages were formerly considered dialects and their use restricted to informal situations, are nowadays bilingual regions. In keeping with this change, the educational system was decentralized, and the regional administrations decide 45–35 per cent of the curriculum.

The cultural diversity of Spanish society was increased by several waves of internal and foreign migration. The first modern wave was the internal migration from rural to northern and central urban areas since the late nineteenth century due to industrialization. Furthermore, economic and political hardships like the Civil War pushed migration waves of emigration to America and Northern European countries until the 1970s. Economic development, the restoration of democracy, and the access to the European Union reversed these trends. According to the National Statistics Institute (INE, 2016a, 2016b), the foreign-born population grew from 631,546 persons (1.7% of total population) in 1981 to 1,173,767 (2.9%) in 1998, then to 4,391,484 (10.0%) in 2015, to reach 6,759,780 (14.3%) in 2012. During this time, the annual average net inflow of immigrants was close to 500,000 people, making Spain the second-largest recipient of immigrants in absolute terms among the 30 countries of the Organization for Economic Cooperation and Development (OECD), behind the United States. In consequence, Spanish society underwent a deep socio-demographic and cultural transformation in the last two decades, shifting the society from a producer of emigration to one of immigration, and becoming a highly diverse society. In consequence, Spain shifted from being the seventh most ethnically diverse in 1985 to being the second most diverse of the OECD countries, only behind Canada (Ethnic Fractionalization Index, Patsiurko, Campbell & Hall, 2012).

The origin of the immigrant population has changed over time. Morocco has remained the main country of origin since the 1980s, with a rise in numbers from around 200,000 in 1998 to over 775,000 in 2015. During the same period, Romanian immigration rose from around 3000 - per year to become almost as high as the Moroccan immigration in 2015. In this general context of rising immigration, those from Ecuador rose from around 5000 in 2008, to over 420,000 in 2015 (INE, 2016a and b).

In spite of this rapid increase in the ethno-cultural diversity of Spanish society, and the deep economic crisis and rising unemployment rates, social surveys depict Spanish society as holding tolerant (or at least ambivalent) attitudes towards immigration and cultural diversity. With small variation over time, Eurobarometers (for instance, TNS Opinion & Social, 2016) show that about 50 per cent of the Spanish population has positive feelings (vs. about 40% with negative feelings) towards immigration from outside the EU. These figures are far more favourable towards immigration than the EU total figures (35% vs. 58% in correspondence). The Special Eurobarometer 380 (TNS Opinion & Social, 2012) renders Spain as the third EU country most supporting that "legal immigrants [from outside the EU] should have the same rights as the own national citizens" (84% of agreement), behind Sweden (93%) and the Netherlands (85%), and is right above the figure for the whole European Union (68%). Furthermore, the main nation-wide survey of the Spanish adult population on racism and xenophobia shows small variations in the attitudes towards immigration and cultural diversity in comparison to survey waves before the economic crisis (Cea D'Ancona & Valles Martínez, 2008, 2011, 2015; see Cea D'Ancona, 2015, for a review).

The survey report (Cea D'Ancona & Valles Martínez, 2015) found that 79 per cent supports the immigrants' right to family reunification, 88 per cent supports the right to receive unemployment subsidies, 65 per cent supports the right to vote in local elections, 57 per cent supports the right to vote in national elections, and 68 per cent the right to obtain Spanish citizenship to immigrants living in stable and regular ways. Regarding the regularization of immigrants lacking legal permit of residence, 15 per cent supported the regularization to all immigrants with no conditions, 21 per cent requiring years of residence (with or without a job), 39 per cent only to those having jobs (with no relation to length of residence) and 15 per cent supported the returning of immigrants to countries of origin. Conversely, 49 per cent of interviewees disagreed with an expression of xenophobia like the expulsion of long-term unemployed immigrants in contrast to 37 per cent agreeing with this option.

In some contrast to this rather positive picture, support of the priority of Spaniards before immigrants in access to public health, the selection of children's school, and access to jobs increased during the first years of the economic crisis but has decreased since 2010. During this same period, the value of diversity for Spanish society in race/skin colors, religions, cultures and countries steadily increased. Nevertheless, the opinion about the contribution of immigrants to enrich Spanish culture is clearly divided: 47 per cent agreed vs. 45 per cent disagreed on this contribution.

The survey included a direct question about the preferred acculturation of immigrants. The answers showed 8 per cent support for a full assimilation option ("Immigrants should adapt to Spanish culture and customs forgetting their own") and 47 per cent for a more socially desirable expression of the same option ("Immigrants should maintain only aspects of their culture and customs that do not disturb the rest of Spaniards"), while only 43 per cent preferred an integration option ("Even if they learn our culture and customs, it is good that immigrants also maintain theirs").

Reflecting Spanish social policies and attitudes towards cultural diversity, as noted in the introduction, Spain scores high on the diversity and policy indexes, and moderately on the integration index (Huddleston et al., 2015; Multiculturalism Policy Index, 2010). Summing up, Spanish society combines a clear openness to immigration and ethnocultural diversity, but with strong assimilation expectations.

2.2   Ecuadorean Immigrants in Spain

This study focuses on Ecuadorian immigrants to Spain. Ecuadorian immigration began to grow significantly at the end of the twentieth century, mainly pushed by the financial and social crisis in Ecuador (1998–2002). Immigration to Spain was pulled by the growth of the Spanish economy, demanding a cheap labor force for construction, agriculture and services industries, the sharing of Spanish language and Catholic beliefs, the ease of legal entry and residence and immigration for Latin American (and other former colonies), and the dynamism of social networks of Ecuadorean migrants in Spain (Ramirez & Ramirez, 2005).

According to Jokisch and Pribilsky (2002), this migrant flow was geographically, ethnically and socioeconomically diverse. While previous immigration came from the Otavalo and Loja regions (including Saraguro indigenous people), the current flow included mestizo and white populations from every province and a variety of backgrounds ranging from the rural and urban working poor to relatively well-off Quiteños.

Another feature of Ecuadorean migration to Spain was the rapid formation of a transnational community. Ecuadoreans maintained social and economic connections with their home communities, continued to practice their cultural traditions and mostly planned to return within a few years. Transnational communication was enhanced by simultaneous broadcasting of radio programs at both countries. Another transnational link arose from the emergence of a renowned immigrants' organization, the Spanish-Ecuadorean Association Rumiñahui, which became an important advocacy group for Ecuadorean migrants in Spain as well as in Ecuador (Jokisch and Pribilsky, 2002, pp. 88–89).

The legal framework facilitated the incorporation of these immigrants into Spanish society. Until 2003, Ecuadoreans were not required to obtain a tourist visa for entry to Spain if the stay was less than three months. As a result, at the beginning of the immigration wave, many Ecuadoreans entered Spain with visa waiver, then extended their stay beyond that period, and regularized their legal status by getting a work contract, settling down or having a residence amnesty (Jokisch, 2014; Jokisch & Pribilsky, 2002). Furthermore, the Spanish immigration law[2] allowed foreign residents from former colonies (Latin America and the Philippines) to apply for Spanish citizenship after two years of authorized residence. In consequence, the number of Ecuadorean immigrants with Spanish citizenship began to grow with little delay after the immigration wave. The proportion of immigrants from Ecuador with Spanish citizenship grew from 1.5 per cent in 2005 to 38 per cent in 2012 and to 61 per cent in 2015 (INE, 2016b).

The EPOERE survey of Ecuadorean population in Spain (Iglesias Martínez et al., 2015)[3] showed that 54 per cent of the interviewees had Spanish citizenship, 25 per cent permanent residence, 14 per cent

---

[2] Organic Law 4/2000 of January 11, 2000, on Rights and Freedoms of Aliens in Spain and their Social Integration.

[3] The Survey to the Population of Ecuadorean Origin with Residence in Spain (EPOERE – Encuesta a la Población de Origen Ecuatoriano Residente en España) included a representative survey of Ecuadorean residents from 16 years on and a following focus group in each of four Spanish regions (Barcelona, Madrid, Murcia and the Mediterranean Coast) which comprise 70% of the Ecuadorean population in Spain (Iglesias Martínez et al., 2015, p. 17).

temporal residence, and only 2.9 per cent lack authorized residence These figures suggest that most Ecuadorean immigrants enjoy legal and administrative security and access to education and social welfare services. The Spanish citizenship implies legal equality with the autochthonous population including the right to vote in Spain, avoiding administrative troubles when travelling to Ecuador and back, and freedom of movement in the Schengen space of the European Union. This legal status facilitates settling down in Spanish society, protection against potential discrimination, and development of dual identities.

Regarding the acculturation processes, the EPOERE focus groups (Iglesias Martínez et al., 2015) disclosed ambivalent feelings towards integration in Spain. On the one hand, the immigrants perceived strong stereotypes, prejudices and discrimination against Ecuadorean and, in general, Latin American people. In the survey, almost half of the interviewees reported being object of discrimination at job and street contexts (48% and 47%), which was expressed verbally (80%) or in accusations of taking jobs from natives (25%) or being cause of the crisis (19%). They also reported adaptation problems because of cultural and value differences. For instance, they claimed that interpersonal politeness was more formal, distant and hierarchical, that male chauvinism was stronger, and that, in school contexts, and teacher authority and prestige were higher in Ecuador. In spite of the shared language, regional variations of Spanish use were construed as sources of differentiation and derogation of immigrants.

On the other side, the immigrants acknowledged the welcoming attitude of the host population and appreciated the opportunities of achievement in Spain. Furthermore, in their frequent visits to their homeland, immigrants realized they had become different to their fellows there because of their acculturation in Spain. They remain identified with their country of origin, its traditions and history but, at the same time, became aware of their change due to the stay in Spain, where they acquired cultural and identity features of their host country. This perception weakened the intentions to return especially among the younger Ecuadorean, who were more likely to reject this possibility. Facing this question, moving to a third (European or North American) country was a more desirable option for them.

Survey and focus groups pointed to a significant generation gap in the intentions to return, the sense of belonging and the Ecuadorean national identity as well as in expectations towards Spanish society. Older immigrants showed stronger identification with Ecuador and its culture than younger immigrants, who were mainly socialized in Spain and had a living experience more similar to their Spanish fellows (for instance in the lack of job stability) than to their parents.

MIRIPS will help us to illuminate the acculturation of Ecuadorean immigrants in Spain as well as the complexity and ambivalence of the inter-ethnic relations between the Ecuadorean and Spanish-born population in the context of a fast immigration process.

2.3   *Evaluation of the MIRIPS Hypotheses in Spain*

The three MIRIPS hypotheses are evaluated by examining the mutual relations between Ecuadorean immigrants and the Spanish-born population. Since Ecuador is a former Spanish colony[4], the choice of this immigrant target group has several implications for the evaluation of the MIRIPS hypotheses. First, postcolonial literature (Césaire, 1955; Fanon, 1952, 1961; Memmi, 1957; Said, 1978; Spivak, 1988) has shown that current intercultural relations would reflect enduring social, cultural and psychological effects of the historical colonial domination on both the colonized and the colonizer people; these do not disappear with formal decolonization. Quijano (2000b)[5] labeled them as "coloniality", embracing hierarchies of power (in relations of domination and subalternization), knowledge (in Eurocentric beliefs and colonial intergroup difference) and also psychological domains (in mutual beliefs and identity).

In consequence, such coloniality would affect the acculturation processes of people from colonies living in the metropolis in paradoxical ways. On one side, the history of interaction between native and colonizer cultures brought some degree of cultural hybridization in colonized countries. Therefore, their culture would be closer to the colonizing culture than the culture of other immigrant groups. For instance, Ecuadorean immigrants in Spain share language and Catholic beliefs with the Spanish-born population. In principle, these shared characteristics could work as social capital facilitating their integration. The cultural distance between the immigrants and the larger society is reduced, and the shared history and culture could facilitate more positive attitudes in the larger society towards these groups.

On the other side, colonialism produces a racialized stratification (Quijano, 2000a) in which these potential assets are devalued, assigning a subordinate status to people from colonies. For instance, linguistic varieties and practices of Ecuadoreans, and Latin American immigrants

---

[4] Ecuador got independence from Spain at the beginning of the nineteenth Century.
[5] Castro-Gómez & Grosfoguel (2007), Mignolo (2002, 2007), Lugones (2007), Maldonado-Torres (2007, 2007), and Walsh (2009) elaborated on epistemological, relation to modernity, gender, self, and intercultural aspects of coloniality.

generally, are assessed applying the standard of "true" Spanish native speakers which labels their speaking as less "correct" and prestigious than the vernacular speaking (Márquez Reiter & Martín Rojo, 2014). Immigrant children are subject in the Spanish educational system to linguistic correction, and, on occasions, they are even sent to language enrichment classes along with speakers of other languages (Martín Rojo, 2010, pp. 229–235).

As a result of both these trends, coloniality produces ambivalent attitudes and an intermediate position in the ethnic stratification of immigrants from colonies at their metropolis. Sharing history and culture with the majority population could be a relative advantage in relation to other immigrant groups, but this potential advantage is challenged by a colonial criteria imposing social and cultural subordination to colonized people in the colonizing society. We expect to find such effects in the verification of MIRIPS hypotheses in Spain.

The awareness of this ethnic stratification led to another feature of the Spanish application of MIRIPS. Building on the research which has shown the variation in the intergroup and acculturation beliefs of the larger society depends on the target immigrant group (Hagendoorn & Hraba, 1987; López-Rodríguez et al., 2014a, 2014b; Montreuil & Bourhis, 2001, 2004; Navas & Rojas, 2010; Strabac and Listhung 2008), the Spanish MIRIPS questionnaire was worded referring to the specific target ethnocultural group (Ecuadorean immigrants and culture) instead of referring to the general categories like "immigrants" or "immigrant culture".

Furthermore, the Spanish study was directed towards populations with actual contact and intercultural experience. To accomplish this goal, samples of both populations were drawn from the same neighborhood. This matching design also allows the partial control of external variables which may affect the possibility and content of mutual relationships, such as differences in SES, education and ghettoization.

3 Method

The questionnaire was used in individual interviews at public social spaces (streets, squares), centers for Ecuadorean immigrants' information, and local Ecuadorean immigrants' organizations of the selected neighborhoods.

3.1 Samples

Samples of Spanish-born and Ecuadorean-born populations were drawn from the same neighborhood, in the six Madrid districts with the highest relative frequency of Ecuadorean population (greater than 4% of the total

Table 13.1. *Spanish samples' size by birthplace, age and gender.*

Age		20–35		36–50		>50		Total
Gender		M	F	M	F	M	F	
Birth	Ecuador	40	40	44	40	21	20	**205**
place	Spain	40	40	40	40	20	20	**200**
Total		**80**	**80**	**84**	**80**	**41**	**40**	**405**

population). The matched samples (N=200 each) were balanced by gender and three age groups (20–35, 36–50, and over 50 years old). Table 13.1 shows the samples according to Birthplace, Age and Gender.

Due to the sample design, there is no significant difference in gender composition and mean age (50% vs. 49% female; 40.4 vs. 39.9 years) between the Spanish and the Ecuadorean sample.

3.2   Variables and Instruments

The MIRIPS questionnaire was translated into Spanish, and the translation was cross-verified by two researchers who were trained in intercultural relations. Translation discrepancies were solved by discussion between these researchers.[6]

Due to fieldwork constraints, several MIRIPS scales were skipped or shortened. For instance, the sharing of Spanish language by the two populations made the language scale unnecessary. Other scales were shortened: Security was shortened from 13 to 6 items, and Multicultural Ideology was shortened from 10 to 6 items. The Marginalization/ Exclusion scale was not used due to the difficulty of understanding the double negative.[7]

All the items of the questionnaire for the majority population about the minority group were worded specifically to refer to the Ecuadorean ethnocultural group (i.e., referred to "Ecuadorean immigrants", or "Ecuadorean culture").

3.3   Data Analysis

MIRIPS hypotheses were simultaneously tested by Structural Equation Modelling in each sample. In these analyses, Perceived Security,

---

[6] Thanks to Isabel Nuñez for her contribution in the translation of the questionnaire.
[7] The final scales are available from the chapter author.

Perceived Discrimination, Integration/Multiculturalism acculturation strategy and Sociocultural Competence (which was worded as difficulties in the host culture, and reversed)were measured by their general indexes; Intercultural Adaptation was estimated by Multicultural Ideology and Tolerance/Prejudice indexes; and Psychological Adaptation was estimated by Psychological Problems, Self-Esteem, and Life Satisfaction indexes. Furthermore, since the Contact Hypothesis states that intercultural contact would predict higher intercultural adaptation, the number and frequency of Social Contacts were operationalized by reference to the participants' relevant ethnocultural ingroup and outgroup.

4 Results

4.1 Structure and Reliability of MIRIPS scales

The structure and reliability of MIRIPS scales were tested in each of the ethnocultural groups to verify their cross-cultural validity in the Spanish abridged questionnaire.[8] The analyses supported, in general, the cross-cultural structure of scales and disclosed a few unreliable items in Perceived Security, Acculturation strategies, and Tolerance/Prejudice scales.[9] The mean, standard deviation, reliability and intergroup contrasts of MIRIPS variables are summarized in Table 13.2.

In the Perceived Security scale, the items "Learning other languages makes us forget our own cultural traditions" (SEC3) and "I am concerned about losing my cultural identity" (SEC4) presented total means of 4.51 and 4.03 (after reversion) in a 5-point answer scale with no significant intergroup difference, and emerged as a separated factor in both ethnocultural groups. These findings may suggest that language and identity do not represent a cultural security concern in the Spanish samples, and therefore these items were dropped in further analyses of this scale. Moreover, the expected distinction between Integration, Assimilation and Separation strategies of acculturation was only found in the older Ecuadorean immigrants. In the more recent immigrants and the Spanish-born sample, a single bipolar factor with Integration/Multiculturalism and Separation/Segregation as opposite poles (and Assimilation/Melting Pot close to this pole) was found. In the Tolerance/Prejudice scale, the item "If employers only want to hire certain groups of people, that's their business" (TP3) emerged as unreliable in both samples and was dropped in further analyses of this scale.

---

[8] These specific analyses are available from the chapter author.
[9] Analyses of sub-scales are omitted when the general score is used.

Table 13.2. *Means, standard deviations, reliability coefficients, and intergroup contrasts of MIRIPS scales of Spanish-born and Ecuadorean Immigrant samples.*

Scale	items	TOTAL				Spanish				Ecuadorean			
		N	Mean	SD	α	N	Mean	SD	α	N	Mean	SD	α
Gender:% Female	1	405	49.4%			200	50.0%			205	48.8%		
Age	1	405	40.1	12.02		200	40.4	13.66		205	39.9	10.20	
Social Contacts: Quantity													
Ethnocultural ingroup	1	396	4.54***	.86	–	195	4.74	.69	–	201	4.34	.96	–
Ethnocultural outgroup	1	398	2.76***	1.53	–	195	1.72	1.20	–	203	3.76	1.09	–
Social Contacts: Frequency													
Ethnocultural ingroup	1	384	3.88***	.83	–	190	4.07	.65	–	194	3.69	.94	–
Ethnocultural outgroup	1	253	3.11	1.06	–	63	2.90	1.27	–	190	3.18	.98	–
Perceived Security	4	402	2.25***	.98	.70	199	2.61	.97	.64	203	1.90	.86	.68
Perceived Discrimination	5	404	1.83***	.84	.79	199	1.66	.75	.84	205	2.00	.88	.76
Acculturation attitudes/ expectations													
Integration/ Multicultural	3	394	4.43***	.82	.85	191	4.24	.92	.85	203	4.62	.66	.84
Separation/Segregation	3	392	1.65	.92	.72	192	1.62	.80	.63	200	1.68	1.03	.77
Assimilation/ Melting pot	3	388	1.49**	.82	.65	190	1.60	.85	.63	198	1.38	.77	.68
Multicultural Ideology	6	402	3.88	.77	.61	199	3.89	.87	.75	203	3.87	.67	.38

Tolerance/Prejudice	8	405	4.36	.66	.72	200	4.33	.70	.79	205	4.39	.62	.65
Perceived Consequences of Immigration	5	405	4.16***	.87	.76	200	4.01	.97	.83	205	4.30	.73	.62
Sociocultural Competence	20	403	4.60***	.47	.91	200	4.49	.48	.90	203	4.71	.44	.89
Self-Esteem	4	403	4.31***	.76	.76	199	4.16	.76	.79	204	4.44	.74	.71
Life Satisfaction	5	403	3.65***	.88	.86	199	3.47	.82	.83	204	3.82	.90	.88
Psychological Health	15	403	1.82	.65	.93	199	1.86	.63	.93	204	1.78	.66	.92

Notes: ***$p<.001$ **$p<.01$.

Finally, the Multicultural Ideology scale emerged as unreliable (Cronbach's alpha = .38) in the Ecuadorean-born sample.

4.2   *Intergroup Comparison of MIRIPS Intercultural Variables*

Reflecting a shared collectivist orientation (Hofstede, 2001), Spanish and Ecuadorean-born participants reported high levels of ingroup sociability, having a greater number and frequency of Social Contacts with their ethnocultural ingroup. Beyond this trend, Spanish-born participants reported more friends and frequency of ingroup contacts than Ecuadorean-born (for instance, means of 4.74 vs. 4.34, $t(394)$ = 4.80, $p<.001$, reflecting "many" vs. "some" friends), and Ecuadorean-born participants had far more friends and frequency of intercultural contacts with Spanish people than Spanish-born participants with Ecuadorean immigrants. Ecuadorean immigrants reported "some" Spanish friends while Spanish-born participants reported an average of "one" Ecuadorean friend, with 69 per cent reporting no Ecuadorean friend at all (the means were 3.76 vs. 1.72, $t(396)$ = 17.82, $p<.001$).

Both samples reported, on average, low levels of Perceived Security and Discrimination. As expected, Spanish-born participants perceived higher security and lower discrimination than Ecuadorean immigrants (2.61 vs. 1.90, $t(400)$ = 7.73, $p<.001$; 1.66 vs. 2.00, $t(402)$ = 4.16, $p<.001$ in correspondence).

Regarding acculturation strategies, Multicultural expectations and Integration attitudes were the preferred strategy for Spanish and Ecuadorean participants. The support for this strategy was very high, and significantly stronger in the Ecuadorean group (4.62 vs. 4.24, $t(392)$ = 4.74, $p<.001$). On the other side, monocultural strategies were rejected in both samples, with no difference in Separation/Segregation (1.62 and 1.68, $t(390)$ = .55, *n.s.*), but stronger rejection of Assimilation by the Ecuadoreans than the rejection of Melting pot by the Spanish sample (1.38 vs. 1.60, $t(386)$ = 2.64, $p<.01$).

A similar trend was found in Intercultural Adaptation because both samples showed support, with no significant intergroup difference, for Multicultural Ideology and Tolerance (means 3.89 and 3.87, $t(400)$ = .23, *n.s.*; 4.33 and 4.39, $t(403)$ = .86, *n.s.*, for Spain and Ecuador in correspondence). Also, both samples perceived Consequences of Immigration as very positive, though this perception was significantly stronger in the Ecuadorean participants (mean: 4.30 vs. 4.01 in the Spanish-born sample, $t(403)$ = 3.43, $p<.001$).

Regarding Sociocultural and Psychological Adaptation, first, both samples showed high levels of Sociocultural Competence. In this context, Ecuadorean immigrants reported higher of competence in host cultural customs and practices (means: 4.71 vs. 4.49 in the Spanish-born sample, t (401) = 4.63, $p<.001$). Second, Ecuadorean immigrants also reported better Psychological Adaptation than Spanish-born participants, since their Self-Esteem and Life Satisfaction were higher on average (4.44 vs. 4.16, $t(401)$ = 3.71, $p<.001$; 3.82 vs. 3.47, $t(401)$ = 4.08, $p<.001$, in correspondence), with no significant intergroup difference in Psychological Health (1.78 vs. 1.86, $t(400)$ = 1.13, $n.s.$).

Summing up, these figures reflect the relational orientation of Spanish culture. The deep economic crisis impaired economic and personal security, but these factors did not affect the benevolent attitude, the weak discrimination, and the perception of positive consequences of immigration, the support for Integration/Multicultural strategies of acculturation and Multicultural Ideology, nor the relative sociocultural and psychological well-being of Spanish-born and Ecuadorean immigrants in Spain

4.3   Assessing Intercultural Relations

Our initial theoretical SEM for testing the three MIRIPS hypotheses is represented in Figure 13.1:

1. The upper left side of the model represents the Multiculturalism Hypothesis: Higher perceptions of Security and lower perceptions of Discrimination will predict
    a. Higher support for Integration/Multicultural acculturation strategy and
    b. Higher Intercultural Adaptation (reflected in higher Multicultural Ideology and Tolerance).
2. The lower left side represents the Contact Hypothesis: More Intercultural Contacts will predict
    a. Higher support for Integration/Multicultural acculturation strategy as well as
    b. Higher Intercultural Adaptation (both Multicultural Ideology and Tolerance).
3. The right side of the model represents the Integration Hypothesis: The preference of Integration/Multicultural strategy will predict
    a. Higher Psychological Adaptation (reflected in Life Satisfaction, Self-Esteem and Psychological Health) and
    b. Higher Sociocultural Adaptation (Competence).

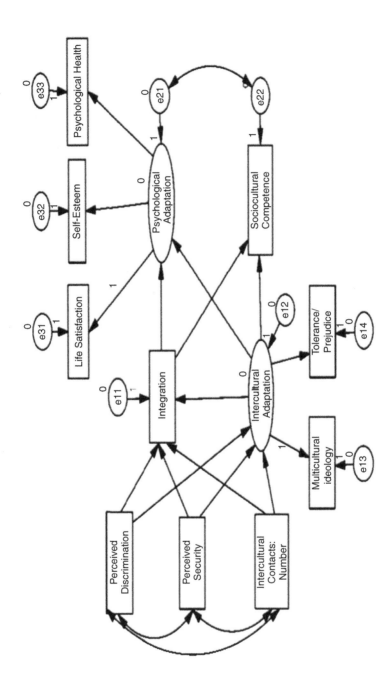

Figure 13.1: Theoretical complete model for MIRIPS hypotheses.

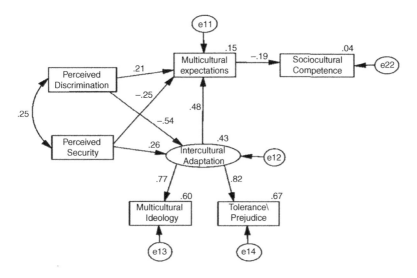

Figure 13.2: Final model for MIRIPS hypotheses for Spanish-born sample.
Note: $\chi^2(6) = 13.58$, $p<.05$; CFI = .96, TLI = .91, RMSEA = .08; All coefficients are $p<.001$ except for Multicultural expectations-Sociocultural Competence ($p<.01$) and Perceived discrimination-Multicultural expectations ($p<.05$).

The complete model showed poor fit to the data in both samples ($\chi^2(25) = 84.86$, $p<.001$; CFI = .84, TLI = .72, RMSEA = .12 for Spanish-born; $\chi^2(26) = 72.19$, $p<.001$; CFI = .74, TLI = .55, RMSEA = .10 for Ecuadorean immigrants). A better goodness of fit was achieved with more parsimonious specifications which are presented in Figures 13.2 and 13.3.

The final SEM of both groups presents acceptable fit to the data (RMSEA<.08, CFI and TLI>.90). In both solutions, Intercultural Adaptation was reliable measured by Multicultural Ideology and Tolerance/Prejudice, and there were significant paths to the prediction of Sociocultural Competence. Nevertheless, the paths to the prediction of the Psychological Adaptation were unreliable and, therefore, this construct was dropped from the final models.

For the Spanish-born sample (Figure 13.2), firstly, Perceived Security and Discrimination predicted Intercultural Adaptation Multicultural expectations in line with the Multiculturalism Hypothesis. Higher Perceived Security and lower Perceived Discrimination predicted higher Intercultural Adaptation. Secondly,

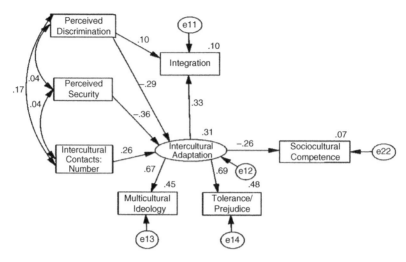

Figure 13.3: Final model for MIRIPS hypotheses for Ecuadorean immigrants sample.
Note: $\chi^2(6) = 18.98$, $p<.05$; CFI = .92, TLI = .83, RMSEA = .07; All coefficients are $p<.001$ except for Intercultural Adaptation–Sociocultural Competence ($p<.01$), Intercultural Contacts–Intercultural Adaptation ($p<.05$) and Perceived Discrimination–Integration (*n.s.*).

both perceptions had direct contributions to Multicultural expectations of acculturation of towards Ecuadorean immigrants. However, contrary to the hypothesis, higher Multicultural expectations were directly related to lower Perceived Security and higher Perceived Discrimination (though this was a weak path). The expected effect on Multicultural expectations was conveyed through the mediation of Intercultural Adaptation. Thirdly, Multicultural expectations of acculturation were also positively predicted by Multicultural Ideology and Tolerance. This path allowed indirect contributions of Perceived Security and Discrimination to Multicultural expectations, mediated by Intercultural Adaptation. These effects superseded their direct contribution, rendering a positive contribution of Security and a negative contribution of Discrimination to Multicultural expectations. In this way, the Multiculturalism Hypothesis was verified also in reference to the Multicultural expectations of acculturation. Furthermore, the Contact Hypothesis received no support because the number of Intercultural Social Contacts did not predict Intercultural Adaptation in this group. Lastly, the Integration Hypothesis was clearly supported because higher Multicultural expectations predicted higher Sociocultural Competence.

For the Ecuadorean immigrant sample (Figure 13.3), the model was more complex. The model did not support the Multicultural hypothesis regarding the acculturation strategy, and only partially supported this hypothesis regarding Intercultural Adaptation. Firstly, Perceived Security and Discrimination did not significantly predict Integration attitudes of acculturation directly, but only through the mediation of Intercultural Adaptation, which consistently reinforced Integration attitudes. Secondly, lower Perceived Discrimination predicted higher Intercultural Adaptation as expected. Nevertheless, thirdly, participants with lower Perceived Security tended to report better Intercultural Adaptation, contrary to the hypothesis expectations. On the other hand, the Contact Hypothesis was supported because more Intercultural Social Contacts predicted higher Intercultural Adaptation in this group. Finally, the Integration Hypothesis was not supported because Sociocultural Competence was not significantly predicted by the Integration attitudes of acculturation but by Intercultural Adaptation. Nonetheless, higher Intercultural Adaptation predicted lower (not higher) Sociocultural Competence. Perhaps those immigrants supporting Multicultural Ideology and Tolerance feel less motivated to develop Sociocultural Competence.

5   Discussion

The intergroup comparison of MIRIPS variables in the Spanish and Ecuadorean immigrant groups in Spain showed that in spite of the relative recency of immigration, the deep economic crisis and unemployment rates in the last decade, these groups share support for multicultural ideology, tolerance, the perception of positive consequences for immigration, and the preference of integrative strategies of acculturation. Reflecting the uncertainty of immigrant status, our findings point out that security and discrimination concerns affect the immigrant groups more than the Spanish-born ones. The benevolent attitude of the Spanish population towards immigration and cultural diversity does not preclude an uneven profile of mutual social contacts, which, beyond the majority-minority group size, would reflect the coloniality of the ethnic hierarchy in intergroup relations in Spain.

The SEM analyses of MIRIPS in Spain found significant support for the Multiculturalism Hypothesis, mainly regarding Intercultural Adaptation (measured by Multicultural Ideology and Tolerance/Prejudice). Perceived Security and Perceived Discrimination made a reliable contribution to the Intercultural Adaptation in the Spanish-born and the Ecuadorean immigrant group. Our analyses also showed the contribution of Intercultural Adaptation to reinforce the Integration/ Multicultural strategy/expectation in both populations. In turn, this relation uncovered an indirect contribution of the perceptions of Security and Discrimination to the acculturation strategy through the mediation of the Intercultural Adaptation. This indirect path emerged as the most consistent support of the Multiculturalism Hypothesis. On the other hand, the expected direct contribution of the perceptions of Security and Discrimination to this acculturation strategy was ambiguous, weak, and mainly present in the Spanish-born group.

The Contact Hypothesis was supported only in the immigrant group since Intercultural Social Contacts, measured as the number of friends of the ethnocultural outgroup, did not predict Intercultural Adaptation nor Multicultural expectation in the Spanish-born group. Having more Spanish friends is related to the Multicultural Ideology and Tolerance of Ecuadorean immigrants, but having Ecuadorean friends does not affect this Intercultural Adaptation or the Multicultural expectations of acculturation in the Spanish-born group.

The Integration Hypothesis found support only regarding Sociocultural Competence and only in the Spanish sample. Psychological Adaptation was neither predicted by the Intercultural Adaptation nor the strategy of acculturation in this study. Finally, Sociocultural Competence was not related to the acculturation strategy but to the Intercultural Adaptation in the Ecuadorean immigrant group.

It is apparent that the evaluation of the MIRIPS hypotheses in Spain was conditioned by the coloniality of relations between the autochthonous and immigrant groups studied. The sharing of language, religion and other cultural practices led to smaller cultural diversity (in contrast to other possible immigrant groups), and may explain the Multicultural expectations towards the Ecuadorean immigrants in the host population (in contrast to Melting Pot expectations found by Cea D'Ancona & Valles Martínez, 2015), but it does not ensure tolerance of even this diversity, nor of smooth intercultural relations, or of common mechanisms in the building of acculturation strategies, psychological well-being and socio-cultural adaptation.

6   Conclusions and Implications

The evaluation of MIRIPS hypotheses in the autochthonous and Ecuadorean immigrant populations shows general support for the Multicultural Hypothesis predicting Intercultural Adaptation and underscores the mediation role of this variable in the prediction of Integration/ Multicultural strategies of acculturation in Spain. The expected direct prediction of these strategies of acculturation by the perceptions of Security and Discrimination is ambiguous, weak, and supported only in the majority group.

This test also sheds light on the differential functioning of Contact and Integration hypotheses. Intercultural Contacts are only relevant to Intercultural Adaptation and only in the immigrant group. Further research may verify whether this unexpected finding is the consequence of a different relevance of these contacts for the host population, of its limited knowledge of the migrant population, or of having referred to a specific ethnocultural group instead of asking about immigrants in general. Psychological adaptation was not affected by intercultural variables in any group of this study, while Sociocultural Competence is predicted, as expected, by Multicultural expectations of acculturation in the Spanish-born group but by Intercultural Adaptation in the Ecuadorean immigrants. This study focuses on the Integration/ Multicultural strategies. However, the MIRIPS hypotheses should be tested also with respect to the other strategies of acculturation in both ethnocultural populations.

Our analyses suggest the desirability of further tests of the majority-minority and cross-cultural functioning of MIRIPS hypotheses. Moreover, our results underscore the need to pay attention to the Multicultural Ideology and Tolerance attitudes, whose contributions emerge as more consistent than those of the perceptions of Security and Discrimination or Intercultural Social Contacts, as reliable sources of both the support to Integration/Multicultural strategies of acculturation and the development of Sociocultural Adaptation. These relations suggest the importance of investing in basic and applied research about the sources of Intercultural Adaptation. They also have straightforward implications for intercultural, social, psychological, educational and sociocultural interventions. The questioning of the beliefs about national groups and identities and decolonizing intercultural relations should be among these research and intervention paths.

References

Castro-Gómez, S., & Grosfoguel, R. (Eds.). (2007). *El giro decolonial. Reflexiones para una diversidad epistémica más allá del capitalismo global [The decolonial turn: Reflections for an epistemic diversity beyond the global capitalism]*. Bogotá: Siglo del Hombre Editores.

Cea D'Ancona, M. Á. (2015). Immigration as a Threat: Explaining the changing pattern of xenophobia in Spain. *International Migration & Integration, 17*, 569–591. doi: 10.1007/s12134-015-0415-3.

Cea D'Ancona, M. Á., & Valles, M. S. (2008). Evolución del racismo y la xenofobia en España (Informe 2008). Madrid: OBERAXE, Ministerio de Trabajo e Inmigración.

Cea D'Ancona, M. Á. y Valles Martínez, M. S. (2011) *Evolución del racismo y la xenofobia en España (Informe 2011) [Evolution of racism and xenophobia in Spain (Report 2011)]*, Madrid. OBERAXE. Ministerio de Trabajo e Inmigración.

Cea D'Ancona, M. Á., & Valles Martínez, M. S. (2015). *Evolución del racismo, la xenofobia y otras formas conexas de intolerancia en España (Informe-Encuesta 2014) [Evolution of racism, xenophobia, and other connected related forms of intolerance in Spain (Report-Survey 2014)]*. Madrid: OBERAXE, Ministerio de Empleo y Seguridad Social.

Césaire, A. (1955). *Discours sur le colonialisme [Discourse on colonialism]*. Paris and Dakar: Présence Africaine.

Fanon, F. (1952/1967). *Black Skin, White Masks* (Translation by Charles Lam Markmann). New York: Grove.

Fanon, F. (1961/2004). *The Wretched of the Earth* (Translation by Richard Philcox). New York: Grove.

Grad, H. M. (2001). Los significados de la identidad nacional como valor personal. In M. Ros y V.V. Gouveia (Coords.), *Psicología social de los valores humanos: Desarrollos teóricos, metodológicos y aplicados* (pp. 265–284). Madrid: Biblioteca Nueva.

Grad, H. M. (2011). National identity and cultural ideology: A cross-cultural discourse analysis of ethnic and civic factors. Paper delivered at Regional Conference of the International Association for Cross-Cultural Psychology. Istanbul, Turkey, June 30 –July 3, 2011.

Grad, H. M., & Martín Rojo, L. (2003). 'Civic' and 'ethnic' nationalist discourses in Spanish parliamentary debates. *Journal of Language and Politics, 2* (Special Issue on parliamentary discourse), 31–70.

Grosfoguel, R. (2007). The epistemic decolonial turn. *Cultural Studies, 21* (2), 211–223.

Hagendoorn, L., & Hraba, J. (1987). Social distance toward Holland's minorities: Discrimination against and among ethnic outgroups. *Ethnic and Racial Studies, 10*, 120–133.

Hofstede, G. (2001). *Culture's Consequences Comparing Values, Behaviors, Institutions, and Organizations across Nations* (2nd ed.). Thousand Oaks, CA: Sage.

Huddleston, T., Bilgili, O.; Joki, A.-L., & Vankova, Z. (2015). Migrant Integration Policy Index 2015. Barcelona/Brussels: Barcelona Centre for International Affairs (CIDOB) & Migration Policy Group (MPG). Retrieved from www.mipex.eu.

Iglesias Martínez, J., Moreno Márquez, G., Fernández García, M., Oleaga Páramo, J. A., & Vega de la Cuadra, F. (2015). *La población de origen ecuatoriano en España. Características, necesidades y expectativas en tiempo de crisis – 2015.* Madrid: Embajada de Ecuador en España, Instituto Universitario de Estudios sobre Migraciones (Universidad de Comillas) & Observatorio Vasco de Inmigración Ikuspegi (Universidad del País Vasco).

INE (2016a). Census 1981. Population – National total: Population by country of birth and sex. Madrid: Instituto Nacional de Estadística. Retrieved from www .ine.es/dynt3/inebase/en/index.htm?type=pcaxis&path=/t20/e243/e01/a1981/ &file=pcaxis.

INE (2016b). Main series of population since 1998 – National total: Population (Spaniards/Foreigners) by country of birth, sex and year. Madrid: Instituto Nacional de Estadística. Retrieved from www.ine.es/jaxi/tabla.do?path=/t20/e2 45/p08/l1/&file=01006.px&type=pcaxis&L=1.

Jokisch, B. (2014). Ecuador: From Mass Emigration to Return Migration? *Migration Information Source*, The Online Journal of the Migration Policy Institute, Washington D.C. Retrieved from www.migrationpolicy.org/article/e cuador-mass-emigration-return-migration.

Jokisch, B. D., & Pribilsky, J. (2002). The panic to leave: Economic crisis and the "new emigration" from Ecuador. *International Migration*, *40*, 75–102.

Linz, J. J. (1973). Early state-building and late peripheral nationalisms against the state: The case of Spain. In S.N. Eisenstadt & S. Rokkan (Eds.), *Building States and Nations: Models, Analyses and Data across Three Worlds* (pp. 32–116). Beverly Hills: SAGE.

Linz, J. J. (1993). Los nacionalismos en España. Una perspectiva comparada. In E. D'Auria & J. Casassas (Coords.), *El estado moderno en Italia y España. Ponencias del Simposio Internacional "Organización del estado moderno y contemporáneo en Italia y España"* (pp. 79–87). Barcelona: Universitat de Barcelona & Consiglio Nazionale delle Richerche.

López-Rodríguez, L., Navas, M., Cuadrado, I., Coutant, D., & Worchel, S. (2014b). The majority's perceptions about adaptation to the host society of different immigrant groups: The distinct role of warmth and threat. *International Journal of Intercultural Relations*, *40*, 34–48. doi: http://dx.doi.org/10 .1016/j.ijintrel.2014.02.001 .

López-Rodríguez, l., Zagefka, H., Navas, M., & Cuadrado, M. (2014a). Explaining majority members' acculturation preferences for minority members: A mediation model. *International Journal of Intercultural Relations*, *38*, 36–46.

Lugones, M. (2007). Heterosexualism and the colonial/modern gender system. *Hypatia*, *22* (1), 186–209.

Maldonado-Torres, N. (2004). The topology of being and the geopolitics of knowledge: Modernity, empire, coloniality. *City*, *8* (1), 29–56.

Maldonado-Torres, N. (2007). On the coloniality of being. *Cultural Studies*, *21*(2), 240–270. doi: 10.1080/09502380601162548.

Márquez Reiter, R. M., & Martín Rojo, L. (2014). The dynamics of (im)mobility: (In)Transient capitals and linguistic ideologies among Latin American migrants in London and Madrid. In R. M. Márquez Reiter & L. Martín Rojo (Eds.), *A Sociolinguistics of Diaspora: Latino Practices, Identities, and Ideologies* (pp. 83–101). New York: Routledge.

Martín Rojo, L. (2010). Managing linguistic diversity in a traditionally mono-lingual area. In L. Martín Rojo (Ed.), *Constructing Inequality in Multilingual Classrooms* (Ch. 7, pp. 221–260). Berlin: Mouton de Gruyter.

Memmi, A. (1957). *Portrait du colonisé, précédé par Portrait du colonisateur* [The colonized and the colonizer]. Paris: Gallimard.

Mignolo, W. (2002). The geopolitics of knowledge and the colonial difference. *South Atlantic Quarterly, 101*, 57–96.

Mignolo, W. (2007). Delinking: The rhetoric of modernity, the logic of coloniality, and the grammar of de-coloniality. *Cultural Studies, 21*(2),449–514. doi: 10.1080/09502380601162647.

Montreuil, A., & Bourhis, R. Y. (2001). Majority acculturation orientations towards "valued" and "devalued" immigrants. *Journal of Cross-cultural Psychology, 32*, 698–719.

Montreuil, A., & Bourhis, R. Y. (2004). Acculturation orientations of competing host communities toward valued and devalued immigrants. *International Journal of Intercultural Relations. 28*, 507–532.

Multiculturalism Policy Index (2010). Retrieved from www.queensu.ca/mcp/.

Navas Luque, M., & Rojas Tejada, A. J. (Coords.). (2010). *Aplicación del Modelo Ampliado de Aculturación Relativa (MAAR) a nuevos colectivos de inmigrantes en Andalucía: rumanos y ecuatorianos.* Seville: Junta de Andalucia.

Patsiurko, N., Campbell, J. L., & Hall, J. A. (2012). Measuring cultural diversity: ethnic, linguistic and religious fractionalization in the OECD. *Ethnic and Racial Studies, 35* (2), 195–217. doi: http://dx.doi.org/10.1080/01419870.2011 .579136

Quijano, A. (2000a). Colonialidad y clasificación social. *Journal of World Systems Research* (Colorado), VI (2, Fall/Winter), 342–388. [Special Issue by G. Arrighi & W. L. Goldfrank (Eds.), *Festschrift For Immanuel Wallerstein*]

Quijano, A. (2000b). Coloniality of Power, Eurocentrism, and Latin America. *Nepentla: Views from the South, 1* (3), 533–580.

Ramírez, F., & Ramírez, J. P. (2005). La estampida migratoria ecuatoriana: Crisis, redes transnacionales y repertorios de acción migratoria. Quito (Ecuador): Centros de Investigaciones CIUDAD- UNESCO-ABYA YALA-ALISEI.

Said, F. (1978). *Orientalism.* London: Pantheon.

Strabac, Z., & Listhung, O. (2008). Anti-Muslim prejudice in Europe. *Social Science Research, 37*, 268–286.

Solanes Corella, A. (2009). La respuesta internacional al desafio de las migraciones: el caso de la Unión Europea [The international answer to migrations' challenge: The case of the European Union]. In A. M. Marcos del Cano (Ed.), *Inmigración, multiculturalidad y derechos humanos* (pp. 291–324). Valencia: Tirant lo Blanch.

Spivak, G. C. (1988). *In Other Worlds: Essays in Cultural Politics.* New York: Routledge.

TNS Opinion & Social (2012). Special Eurobarometer 380 – Wave EB76.4. Awareness of home affairs. Brussels: European Commission, Directorate-General for Communication (DG COMM "Research and Speechwriting" Unit).

TNS Opinion & Social (2016, May). Standard Eurobarometer 85 – Wave EB85.2. Brussels: European Commission, Directorate-General for Communication.

Walsh, C. (2009). *Interculturalidad, Estado, Sociedad. Luchas (de)coloniales de nuestra época [Interculturality, state, society. Current (de)colonial struggles].* Quito: Universidad Andina Simón Bolívar / Abya-Yala Editores.

14   Intercultural Relations in India

Ramesh C. Mishra, Shabana Bano* and
Rama Charan Tripathi***
* Banaras Hindu University, Varanasi, India
** University of Allahabad, India

1   Introduction

The MIRIPS study in India examines the intercultural relations between two groups: the Hindu majority and the Muslim minority. The tag of 'minority' in the case of Muslims in India is a recent appellation that followed the deepening of the discourse on the nation-state, driven largely by the Eurocentric paradigm (Mukherjee, 2010), which sees nations as ethnically bounded and nation-states as exercising sovereignty over a territory. We seek to examine the conditions and processes that lead members of these two groups in India to make choices for creating spaces that are mutually shared or seemingly appropriated. India is moderately high on the diversity index, moderate on the integration index but very high on the policy index.

2   Context of Intercultural Relations in India

India is one of the few nation states in the world which qualifies to be called a 'civilizational state' (alongside China). Indian history is associated with the origin of many great civilizations (e.g., Harappan, Indus Valley, Vedic) and the birth of many religions of the world. India also faced recurrent foreign invasions over many centuries, such as from the Greeks, the Arabs, the Turks and the Mongols. From the twelfth to about the eighteenth century, a large part of India remained under the rule of the Muslim invaders from Central Asia. The British kept it colonized for almost two centuries after that. These political and social upheavals, despite being upsetting experiences for its people, have added to the cultural diversity of India.

India is not limited to a single ethnic, religious or language group. The majority of Indian population (about 80%) is Hindu. Muslims are the largest minority group (13.4%), followed by Christians (2.3%), Sikhs (1.9%), Buddhists (0.8%) and other religious groups (1%). The Adivasi

People (indigenous groups, many of whom believe in traditional faith systems) constitute about 8.6 per cent of the total population.

Indian society has a caste-based hierarchical social structure. Although seriously questioned today, it still is the mainstay of political discourses in the country. Caste and its practice of endogamy also characterize the other religious groups in India (e.g., Islam and Christianity). The major social categories most often used for intergroup differentiation in India are religion and caste. Although both have been the focus of studies on intercultural relations, the category of religion has figured more prominently in studies because religion was central to the partition of India in 1947 and has been a major factor in intergroup violence since then.

2.1   Demography

Based on their numbers and their representation in positions of power, Hindus clearly represent the majority group. Other religious groups, including Muslims, are treated as a religious minority by the National Commission for Minorities. The mix of population based on religion is not the same for different regions of the country. For example, Muslims are numerically the majority community in Jammu and Kashmir, and Christians in the three North Eastern States.

Since the minority groups are integral to the cultural mosaic of India, their status is very different from that of such groups in some other parts of the world. Many Western nations have become multicultural by design to accommodate the inflow of migrants from different cultures. Intercultural relations in India have evolved over a long period of time. The cultures that came in had a base here, and they developed synchronically with Hinduism and other cultures. Questions relating to 'entitlements' do not get raised in India, as people belonging to the minority groups have always shared with the dominant group their rights to all resources. The questions raised by members of various minority groups relate more to equity, fairness and social justice. Thus, the dynamics of relationship that obtain in India between the minority and majority groups are based on different terms compared to Western nations.

Intercultural relations in India also differ in terms of the nature of the self that forms the core of social identities. A distinction has been made between group identities that have within their core an 'independent' or an 'interdependent' self (Markus & Kitayama, 1991) or 'relational' self (Chen, Boucher & Kraus, 2011). Asian cultures are largely characterized by interdependent and relational selves, which require adjusting to the needs of the others in the group to which one belongs. These selves involve 'social proximity', whereas the 'independent' self involves the process of 'distancing'.

The degree to which membership of a group is based on ascription or on achievement and the degree of permeability of group boundaries is another distinguishing feature of societies. Groups formed on the basis of ascription have less permeable boundaries than those formed on the basis of achievement. In India, both personal and social identities are constructed in terms of relationships as well as ascriptions. They are permeable and impermeable in different domains (Tripathi, in press).

Psychological studies show that, in culture-contact situations, smaller groups engage not only in 'negotiation of identities', but also in 'invention of new identities' (Berry, 1981; Mishra et al., 1996). People's definition of themselves in relation to others depends much on how their social and cultural identities have been formed in the course of interaction with the members of other groups, which has implications for a conflict arising between personal and social identities.

It is not our contention that intercultural relations in India are stable and face no challenges. In fact, understanding of the micro-level dynamics of intercultural relations in India is made complex because it requires taking into consideration the historical context in which these relations have evolved, along with the present social and political contexts.

2.2   Interactions among Religious Groups

It is argued that the processes and dynamics of group relationship in India may not be understood in terms of the course that intergroup relationships have followed in other societies. This is because the bearers of the cultures of India have not only maintained their cultures, but they have also adapted liberally to other cultures. There has been a lot of 'give and take' between cultures. In this process, other cultures, which entered India, also have undergone transformation in significant ways. Tripathi and Mishra (2016) suggest that cultures within India have experienced processes of *inculturation* (entering cultures imbibing indigenous elements), *interculturation* (cultures entering into a mutual give and take relationship) and *multiculturation* (people belonging to diverse cultures valuing practices and beliefs of other cultures and supporting their free expression). While the inculturation process has worked in India with smaller groups, such as the Adivasi (Sagayaraj, 2013), in the larger religious groups (e.g., the Muslims), changes have come about through the process of interculturation. Depending on the nature of groups who share cultural spaces, the process has also taken the form of multiculturation. Here, the elements coming from different cultures have become 'integrated' or 'synthesized' to produce a new kind of syncretic or 'composite' culture (Chandra & Mahajan, 2007).

In 'composite culture', the cultural elements, qualities and shades of interacting cultures are represented like the colorful threads interwoven in a piece of cloth. This is also referred to as *Tana-Bana* culture. The term refers to the production of silk in which threads of different colors and shades are intermixed to create a splendorous, unified and whole fabric. At the social level, it symbolizes the interwoven, coexisting and interdependent nature of the life of Muslims (weavers) and Hindus (traders) in the production and sale of silk for which Varanasi is known worldwide. Another metaphor popularly used for such syncretic culture that has come out of intercultural interactions and exchanges between Hindus and Muslims is *Ganga-Jamuni* culture. The term refers to two sacred rivers of India, which originate from different points, flow through different routes carrying water of white and bluish shades, but meet along their journey at a point from where they flow together as one stream with the water getting a new tinge. In a study by Tripathi et al., (2009), composite cultural ideology was preferred by the majority (74%) of participants in North India over a monocultural or secular/multicultural ideology.

2.3   *Intercultural Relations between Hindus and Muslims*

India has been a culturally plural, but largely homogenous, society for a long time. It has never been a witness to wars based on religions or faiths. Most religions entered India a long time back. Jews entered India more than 2500 years ago, and they have all along felt highly secure (Lentin, 2016; Weil, 2006). Christians came up India in the First Century, and there has been hardly any evidence of intolerance against them. The first mosque of Muslims in the world came to in India around 629 CE, and there was no protest against it. Some Muslim rulers built temples of Hindu Gods and gave maintenance grants to a large number of temples. Thus pluralistic cultural belief has been embedded in the psyche and lives of the Indian people for ages. Mutuality in relations has been the rule in India.

The relationship between the Hindu and Muslim communities in India cannot be seen from the lens of 'migrant' versus 'receiving cultures'. It is difficult to call Islam a 'migrant culture' after its presence in this region for more than a millennium. Hindus and Muslims have contributed equally to literature, music, sculpture, art forms and other aspects of Indian culture and life. Both groups have continued to show mutual respect and acceptance for each other's cultural practices and languages. As late as 1857, Hindus and Muslims came together to fight in India's first war of independence against the British in the name of a Muslim king.

The incidents of conflicts and episodes of violence between the Hindus and Muslims in India have increased in recent years. This pattern of relationship in modern times is often traced back to the policy of divide and rule of the British (Tambiah, 1997). The shared memories of the partition riots in 1947, in which more than half a million people were killed, also continue to affect the relationship of Hindus and Muslims. The political climate of India, driven largely by the politics of identity, has done everything to maintain the divide; in fact, to widen it for political gains.

The question which needs to be raised here is: "How is it that, in the context of past cordial relationship and an Indian Constitution that swears by secularism, the conflict between the two groups has deepened?" The answer may be found in some studies, which show that multicultural and secular ideologies are not associated with reconciliation, but more with retaliatory responses in the face of provocative communal situations (Tripathi et al., 2009). The changed perception of Muslims as having a low social status in the country they had ruled for over 600 years appears to be another explanatory factor. In several studies, Muslims have been found consistently high with respect to fraternalistic relative deprivation (Tripathi, Ghosh & Kumar, 2014). Following the Sachar Committee Report, which pointed out the poor status of Muslims in terms of education and employment, Muslims now have started laying claims to reservations in educational institutions and jobs like those given to many caste groups and Adivasi communities. This is another important factor influencing their relationship with Hindus (Tripathi, 2005). Hindus, on the other hand, perceive a danger of losing power to Muslims again and openly voice the fear that their growing population and political influence may lead to another partition of India.

3   Evaluation of the MIRIPS Hypotheses in India

The focus of this chapter is on the relationship between the Hindu and Muslim groups, which is more conflict-ridden relative to the other groups. The conflict between these groups in recent years has also been fuelled by the evidence that has surfaced relating to involvement of some Muslims in terrorist activities in some states of India. Even though sporadic, such events have led to suspicion, distrust, name calling and creation of gulf between the two groups. To better understand these issues, the project in India has examined all three hypotheses.

3.1   Previous Research

Studies of Hindu-Muslim relations in India have used a variety of theoretical perspectives, such as the theory of social identity (Mishra & Bano, 2003; Bano & Mishra, 2009), theory of relative deprivation (Tripathi & Srivastava, 1981), norm violation theory (DeRidder & Tripathi, 1992) and socialization theories, which see schooling as an important agent of socialization (Bano & Mishra, 2006, 2014). In almost all studies carried out in India, Muslims have been consistently found to report a high feeling of relative deprivation in the economic, political and social domains. This shows that they feel marginalized. However, they do not carry as negative attitudes towards Hindus as the Hindus carry towards them (Tripathi, Ghosh & Kumar, 2014). Their feelings of marginalization are more due to relative deprivation felt in the economic domain than in social or political domains (Tripathi & Srivastava, 1981). It is likely that the relatively positive attitudes of Muslim may be due to their feeling that they are living in India by the grace of the Hindus after their demand for a separate homeland was accepted by the British, and Pakistan was created. Hindus try to drive home this point whenever there is any communal strife.

The limited number of studies carried out with respect to the intercultural strategies of Hindu and Muslim groups suggest that both groups have firm roots in the national culture, and both want to live with each other in a state of peaceful 'coexistence'. The type of schooling is an important factor in determining their preferences. Tripathi and Mishra (2006) found that attending a monocultural school led to a relatively stronger preference for separation and marginalization strategies in the case of Hindus, but not in the case of Muslims. Bano and Mishra (2011) found Muslim adolescents showing a stronger preference for integration, co-existence and assimilation intercultural strategies than Hindu adolescents.

3.2   Theoretical Issues

It is important to note that the relationships between these groups is complex and is far from linear compared to nations that are relatively young and have started receiving migrants from other cultures recently. Since Hindus and Muslims have lived together for a long time and participated in the wider national life with full 'entitlement' to land and resources, one would expect them to prefer integration in various domains. On the other hand, the desire of the Muslims to maintain their heritage culture, their desire to secure power (political, economic and social) and competition for control of resources *vis-à-vis* Hindus may be expected to lead them to develop a separation attitude. As stated earlier, Hindus harbour the fear of another partition of the nation due to the rising population of Muslims. Therefore, they too may develop a preference for separation attitude.

Intercultural relations play out differently in electoral democracies in which political parties play 'vote bank' politics. Minority groups in such situations often feel that they stand to gain more by keeping away from the majority group and by maintaining their separate identities. Under these circumstances, the propensity to seek assimilation on either side is likely to be low. The preamble to the Indian Constitution explicitly asserts that India is a secular nation. This hands-off attitude of the state leaves both religious groups free to live their respective cultural and religious lives. Under such a situation, one may expect that the preference of either group for assimilation or marginalization will be weak.

Previous studies have pointed to a fifth intercultural strategy, called *coexistence* (Mishra et al., 1996; Tripathi & Mishra, 2016), which is widely used by people in India when dealing with other cultures (Sinha, 1988). This draws from the Indian kind of secularism referred to as *sarva dharm sambhaav* (equal respect for all religions). While the integration strategy involves a deliberate choice of areas in which individuals and groups want to collaborate or accept change, the coexistence strategy shuns any kind of evaluation. In coexistence, the elements of two cultures not only exist side by side, but members of those cultures keep the doors and windows of their cultures open to allow for the winds of other cultures to blow in. What we have referred to earlier as *Tana-Bana* or *Ganga-Jamuni* culture is an example of this. We propose that within the Indian context, the members of the Hindu and Muslim groups may prefer to use this intercultural strategy of coexistence over other intercultural strategies.

Although there have been long-term contacts between the Hindu and Muslim groups, the preferred intercultural strategies of groups may not be the strategies preferred by all the group members. There are likely to be individual differences in the level of their contacts as well as the domains (e.g., school, workplace, cultural events) in which the contact happens. The Indian Constitution provides for equal rights to all of its citizens, be they Hindu or Muslim, but personal life situations do influence people's security perceptions. As discussed earlier, Muslims generally suffer from feelings of 'relative deprivation' particularly in the economic domain. In view of this, we contend that Hindus and Muslims will differ with respect to their security perceptions.

In this study, the three propositions of the MIRIPS hypotheses were evaluated in the context of relations of Hindu and Muslim groups in India. The main objectives of the study, thus, were:

(1) To examine the mutual intercultural relations and adaptations of the Hindu and Muslim groups in terms of their security, social contact and intercultural strategies.

(2) To explore the relationship of intercultural strategies (both attitudes and expectations) with psychological and social well-being in Hindu and Muslim groups.

(3) To determine how well security and contact predict intercultural strategies, and the three forms of adaptation (psychological, socio-cultural and intercultural) and the well-being of members of the Hindu and Muslim groups.

4   Method

4.1   Samples

The study was carried out in Varanasi. Situated in the northern part of India, Varanasi is one of the holiest cities and a pilgrimage destination for Hindus. The city takes great pride in its multi-cultural ethos. About 28 per cent of its population is Muslim, roughly twice the national average for Muslims. There are more than a thousand Hindu temples and about 300 mosques. It is also seen as a centre of learning as it has four universities. The city is famous for its silk industry in which both the Hindu and Muslim groups work closely.

A non-probability sample of Hindu (N = 107) and Muslim (N = 107) respondents was taken. Both groups had 28 per cent female respondents and covered a wide age range (i.e., 20–60 years, Mean = 34.2, SD = 12.6). The mean years of education were 15.4 and 15.3 for Hindu and Muslim samples, respectively. In both the groups, about 35 per cent of the participants had low socio-economic status. Muslim participants had lived in the city for a longer period (Mean = 53.4 years) than the Hindu participants (Mean = 36.2 years).

4.2.   Measures

We used instruments that were developed for the MIRIPS project. One exception was the inclusion of a scale to measure the 'coexistence' intercultural strategy and expectations (Mishra et al., 1996). Specifically, we assessed participants on the measures of ethnic/religious identity, security (cultural, economic and social), multicultural ideology, intercultural attitudes and expectations (i.e., integration, coexistence, assimilation, separation, marginalization), perceived discrimination, self-esteem, tolerance/prejudice, psychological problems and socio-cultural competence. Most of the items required respondents to give ratings on a 5-point response scale. In some scales, the MIRIPS items were reworded to refer specifically to the Hindu and Muslim groups. The scales were translated and back-translated into Hindi and Urdu languages for use with the Hindu and Muslim participants, respectively. Data collection was done by a Hindu and a Muslim investigator. Both of them were trained in the process of interviewing.

Besides the earlier measures, a new measure of 'mutual acceptance' was created by aggregating scores of the participants on 'tolerance/prejudice' and 'attitude towards outgroup' because the two measures had a positive correlation. Similarly, measures of 'outgroup contact' and 'ingroup contact' were created based on the aggregated scores obtained on five measures: 'closeness to ingroup/outgroup'; 'interaction with ingroup/outgroup members at school'; 'interaction with ingroup/outgroup members out of school'; 'interaction with ingroup/outgroup play mates'; and 'reciprocity'. All the measures had coefficient alphas greater than .60, except for assimilation and marginalization attitudes and expectations, in which case the alphas ranged between .54 and .59.

The factor structure of measures was generally similar to ones found in other MIRIPS studies. Slight differences were noted for self-esteem, multicultural ideology, tolerance/prejudice and social competence measures. Certain items were deleted, which enhanced the internal homogeneity of the measures. The factor structures were not markedly different for the Hindu and Muslim groups.

5   Results

Analyses were carried out to examine the three MIRIPS hypotheses. Some other results of interest in the context of mutuality of Hindu-Muslim relations are also reported. Our preliminary analyses showed no gender difference on any of the measures except for marginalization expectations (male > female). Hence, the analyses were done on the overall sample of Hindu and Muslim respondents.

5.1   Descriptive Statistics

Table 14.1 presents the mean score for the Hindu and Muslim groups on various measures.

Table 14.1. *Mean score of Hindu and Muslim groups on various measures.*

Measures	Score-range	Groups Hindus (N = 107)	Muslims (N = 107)	*t*-value
Assimilation strategy	3–15	4.29 (2.32)	4.53 (1.99)	0.82
Integration strategy	3–15	10.65 (3.16)	13.15 (2.24)	6.60**
Co existence strategy	3–15	11.47 (3.23)	12.68 (2.41)	3.10**
Separation strategy	3–15	8.93 (4.00)	7.05 (3.09)	3.80**
Marginalization strategy	3–15	4.49 (2.16)	4.82 (2.56)	1.0
Assimilation expectation	3–15	5.24 (2.81)	4.83 (2.42)	1.12
Integration expectation	3–15	11.77 (2.80)	12.22 (2.49)	1.22
Co existence expectation	3–15	12.57 (2.58)	13.07 (2.19)	1.52
Separation expectation	3–15	7.61 (3.67)	6.43 (2.43)	2.78**
Marginalization expectation	3–15	4.62 (2.42)	4.65 (2.27)	0.08
Ingroup contact	30–150	87.38 (29.89)	66.27 (23.75)	5.71**
Outgroup contact	0–150	21.08 (14.23)	41.67 (24.27)	7.57**
Cultural security	5–25	17.63 (3.38)	18.60 (4.19)	1.86
Economic security	4–20	10.51 (3.28)	10.26 (2.89)	0.59
Social security	4–20	10.93 (2.93)	10.76 (3.23)	0.39
Perceived discrimination	5–25	12.00 (5.86)	9.02 (5.60)	3.80**
Multicultural Ideology	10–50	36.14 (4.68)	37.18 (3.64)	1.82
Mutual acceptance	4–120	66.28 (24.01)	88.04 (19.53)	7.27**
Self-esteem	10–50	40.31 (6.73)	39.51 (6.47)	0.88
Life satisfaction	5–25	18.67 (3.37)	19.14 (3.34)	1.01
Psychological problems	15–75	25.71 (9.03)	27.73 (11.85)	1.40
Social competency	20–100	87.83 (12.80)	88.43 (12.05)	0.35

Note: Values given in parentheses are the SDs., **p<.01.

With respect to intercultural strategies, Hindus showed preference for coexistence, followed by for integration, separation, marginalization and assimilation. Muslims preferred integration, which was followed by their preference for coexistence, separation, marginalization and assimilation. Compared to Hindus, Muslims displayed stronger preferences for integration and coexistence. Hindus, in contrast, displayed a significantly stronger preference for separation than Muslims.

For expectations about how the other group should relate, Hindus and Muslims did not differ with respect to integration and coexistence, but Hindus showed a higher separation expectation than the Muslims. Interestingly, Hindus, though they are the dominant group in society, perceived more discrimination than did the Muslims. Muslims reported less ingroup contact and greater mutual acceptance than the Hindus. Differences on the measures of security, multicultural ideology, self-esteem, life satisfaction, psychological problems and social competence were not found to be significant between the two groups.

5.2   Correlations among Variables

The differences found between Hindus and Muslims could be better understood by examining how the measures of intercultural strategies and expectations were associated with other variables within the two groups. We, therefore, first looked at the zero order correlations of intercultural strategies and expectations with other measures, separately for the two groups. We checked and found that none of the measures was influenced by social desirability.

Intercultural strategies and expectations correlated with other measures within and across the two groups differently. We now examine these correlations in the context of the multiculturalism, contact and integration hypotheses.

5.2.1   Multiculturalism Hypothesis

This hypothesis predicted that security (and its converse, perceived discrimination) would be related to the acceptance (rejection) of others in society (mutual acceptance and tolerance) and to the strategies that seek engagement with others (integration and assimilation, as well as co-existence). Evidence for these expectations will be discussed in section 5.3. For now, we examine the patterns of correlations among the intercultural strategies and expectations and some other variables in the study.

First in the Hindu sample, the *integration* strategy correlated, as expected, positively with cultural security (.44) and negatively with perceived discrimination (–.46). It also correlated in the expected direction with measures of the acceptance of others: outgroup contact (.41); and multicultural ideology (.20). The *co-existence* strategy also correlated positively with cultural security (.39) and negatively with perceived discrimination (–.38), and had positive correlations with outgroup contact (.40) and mutual acceptance (.21) in the expected direction. The *assimilation* strategy did not correlate with security, nor with perceived discrimination, but correlated positively with mutual acceptance (.24) and outgroup contact (.26). The *separation* strategy correlated negatively with cultural security (–.27) and positively with perceived discrimination (.39). It also correlated negatively with outgroup contact (–.53) and mutual acceptance (–.42). *Marginalisation* did not correlate with security, nor with perceived discrimination, or any of the intercultural variables. This overall pattern of correlations between intercultural strategies and the other variables provides some evidence in support of the multiculturalism hypothesis.

In the case of Muslims, the *integration* strategy did not correlate with security, but did so with perceived discrimination (–.20). *Co existence* also did not correlate with security, but did so with perceived discrimination (–.25). It also correlated with outgroup contact (.22) and multicultural ideology (.18). *Separation* correlated negatively with cultural security (–.19) and with outgroup contact (–.39). Finally, *marginalization* did not correlate with any of the intercultural variables. This pattern of correlations in the Muslim sample, although less substantial than for the Hindu sample, also provides some evidence in support of the multiculturalism hypothesis.

For intercultural expectations in the Hindu sample, the *integration* expectation correlated positively with cultural security (.24), outgroup contact (.22) and multicultural ideology (.25), and negatively with perceived discrimination (–.25). The *co existence* expectation correlated positively with cultural security (.34) and outgroup contact (.34). The *assimilation* expectation correlated negatively with cultural security (–.24), but not with any of the other intercultural variables. The *separation* expectation correlated positively with perceived discrimination (.30), and negatively with outgroup contact (–.39) and mutual acceptance (–.21). Finally, *marginalization* correlated negatively with cultural security (–.21) and multicultural ideology (–.19). Again, this pattern of correlations with expectations suggests modest support for the multiculturalism hypothesis.

In the Muslim sample, the *integration* expectation correlated positively with cultural security (.20) and mutual acceptance (.24). The *co-existence* expectation correlated positively with outgroup contact (.24). *Assimilation* correlated positively with ingroup contact (.28) and negatively with multicultural ideology (–.21). *Separation* correlated negatively with cultural security (–.23) and outgroup contact (–.30), but, contrary to expectation, it correlated positively with economic security (.24). Finally, the *marginalization* expectation correlated negatively with cultural and social security (–.19, and –.31), and positively with perceived discrimination(.33). This pattern once again suggests some support for the multiculturalism hypothesis.

5.2.2   Contact Hypothesis
This hypothesis proposes that intercultural contact and sharing would be associated with greater mutual acceptance. In both Hindu and Muslim samples, more outgroup contact was associated with greater mutual acceptance (.31 and .28, respectively). In the Muslim sample, outgroup

contact was associated both with co existence strategies (.22) and expectations (.24), and negatively with the separation strategy (−.39) and the separation expectation (−.30).

5.2.3   Integration Hypothesis

This hypothesis predicted that individuals showing preference for integration attitudes would show higher levels of well-being in both psychological and social domains. We expected similar relationships in the case of individuals with a preference for coexistence attitudes, also. In the case of Hindus, we found that the integration expectation was associated with lower feelings of discrimination (−.46) and higher multicultural ideology (.20), but these were not related to their psychological adaptation and well-being. Similar findings were obtained for the co existence strategy. Hindus who preferred the coexistence strategy perceived less discrimination (−.38) and showed greater mutual acceptance (.21), but the coexistence strategy did not correlate with psychological adaptation or with social competence. However, the marginalization expectation of Hindus did associate with the feelings of low cultural security (−.21), lack of acceptance of multicultural ideology (−.19) and poor social adaptation, which was reflected in its negative correlations with life satisfaction (−.21) and social competence (−.32).

In the case of Muslims, integration and coexistence attitudes were associated with raised self-esteem (.22 and .34, respectively), whereas marginalization attitude was associated with increased psychological problems (.26) and poor social competence (−.33). The separation attitude was positively associated with life satisfaction (.30). In general, the integration hypothesis based on zero-order correlations found support in the case of Muslims only for certain measures of psychological adaptation and well-being.

5.3   *Predicting Intercultural Strategies and Adaptation*

In order to address the third objective of the study, we used the MRA separately for the Hindu and Muslim groups. We first used cultural, social and economic security as predictors of integration, coexistence and assimilation strategies, and multicultural ideology and mutual acceptance (which included tolerance). Next, we used ingroup and outgroup contact as predictors of multicultural ideology, mutual acceptance as well as integration, coexistence and assimilation attitudes. Lastly, we predicted psychological problems and social competence employing integration, coexistence, assimilation, separation and marginalization strategies as predictors. Results presented next report only significant beta weights along with adjusted R^2 values.

5.3.1   Security as Predictor of Intercultural Attitudes and Intercultural Adaptation

In the Hindu group, only cultural security turned out to be a significant predictor of integration (Beta =.43, R^2 =.17) and of coexistence (Beta =.41, R^2 =.14), but not any of the intercultural adaptation measures except for social security, which raised the mutual acceptance (Beta =.25, R^2 =.05). In the Muslim group, cultural security predicted integration attitude (Beta =.21, R^2 =.04) and multicultural ideology (Beta =.21, R^2 =.04), but none of the adaptation or well-being measures. Economic security had no role in the case of either group. The variance explained by security measures in various criterion variables ranged between 4 and 17 per cent.

5.3.2   Contact as a Predictor of Intercultural Attitudes and Intercultural Adaptation

In the Hindu sample, outgroup contact brought about positive change in the strategies of integration (Beta =.45, R^2 =.17), co-existence (Beta =.44, R^2 =.17) and assimilation (Beta =.27, R^2 =.05). Outgoup contact also led to more mutual acceptance (Beta =.32, R^2 =.08). In the case of Muslims, it played a similar role in predicting the coexistence strategy (Beta =.22, R^2 =.03) and mutual acceptance (Beta=.25; R^2 =.08). It had a larger effect size in the case of Hindus than in Muslims. Ingroup contact did not predict any of the adaptation variables in the Hindu or Muslim samples. As in the case of the security measures, the total variance explained by contact variables ranged between 3 and 17 per cent.

5.3.3   Intercultural Strategies and Expectations as Predictors of Intercultural Adaptation and Well-Being

In the Hindu sample, only the assimilation strategy was associated with increased psychological problems (Beta =.32, R^2 =.14); other intercultural strategies played no role in the prediction of psychological or social well-being. The assimilation expectation too added to psychological problems in a similar manner (Beta =.26), but explained very little variance (R^2 =.02). Marginalization expectation reduced levels of social competence for Hindus (Beta = −.38, R^2 =.07). In the Muslim sample, social competence was predicted significantly (R^2=.16) by integration (Beta = −.33), and marginalization (Beta = −.33); both were expected to bring down social competence. On the contrary, coexistence attitude had a positive regression coefficient (Beta =.28) leading to raised social competence. In comparison to intercultural strategies, assimilation (Beta = −.42) and coexistence expectations (Beta= −.24) were expected to lead to reduced social competence (Total R^2 =.29).

For Muslims, the marginalization strategy significantly predicted psychological problems (Beta =.24), although the variance explained was only about 5 per cent. Marginalization expectation did better (Beta =.29; R^2 =.16). Both were expected to add to psychological problems.

6   Discussion

What do we learn from the earlier findings about the mutual relationship of Hindu and Muslim groups in the diverse cultural context of India? Speaking generally, the Muslims of Varanasi appeared more positive about their intercultural relationship than did Hindus. It is quite possible that this relationship may not be true for other parts of India. In the following sections, we will discuss our results in relation to the three hypotheses.

6.1   Multiculturalism Hypothesis

The multiculturalism hypothesis proposes that individuals and groups that feel secure will have more positive intercultural attitudes, and a preference for integration and assimilation attitudes. In our case, a distinctive preference for integration and coexistence was indeed found in the case of both Hindus and Muslims, but not for assimilation which, in fact, was least preferred by both the groups. In the context of the composite cultural ethos of Varanasi, assimilation may not only be non-normative, but also threatening. Integration and coexistence strategies, as expected, related positively with cultural security and also with multicultural ideology in Hindus, but these strategies did not link up with cultural security to enhance social and psychological adaptation and well-being.

The integration strategy and cultural security played a more important role in the case of Muslims. The findings indicated that integration and cultural security positively related with multicultural ideology, although both had no role in the prediction of intercultural adaptation or well-being. Social and economic security too did not play any role in the promotion of psychological and social well-being. This was surprising as security is generally seen as a major concern of this minority group. Economic or social security is not much of a concern for Varanasi

Muslims, because a very large number of them work in family business and are fully embedded in their social networks. But cultural security is their concern. Any sort of cultural change threatens their cultural identity. It gets threatened when Muslim children attend vernacular multicultural or English-medium schools or are put in other similar situations. Cultural security acts as a buffering device to protect them from such cultural stressors. This was reflected in their experiencing fewer psychological problems, less discrimination and in developing competencies, which allowed them to get along better with others in the society.

6.2   *The Contact Hypothesis*

The contact hypothesis highlights the role of contact with members of the other group more than with ingroup members. It proposes that such contacts in different spheres of life are likely to develop greater understanding, positive relationships and appreciation of each other. Our findings indicated that greater contact with Muslims did make Hindus prefer integration and coexistence intercultural strategies more. Similarly, in the case of Muslims, outgroup contact predicted the coexistence strategy, but not integration. Muslims, in fact, were more emphatic than Hindus in their preference for coexistence. Muslim adolescents were also found to prefer the coexistence strategy in another study (Bano & Mishra, 2011). This made sense in the context of the locale of the study. Contact between Hindus and Muslims in Varanasi takes place almost routinely. Both Hindus and Muslims feel culturally secure. It shows up in a variety of social exchanges between them, but more prominently in religious festivals in which members of both groups participate. Varanasi, perhaps, is the only place where an event that may be considered highly sacrilegious involving the marriage of a Hindu icon, Lat Bhairava, with Ghazi Miyan, a Muslim saint, is allowed to take place annually with gaiety (Chalier-Visuvalingam & Visuvalingam, 1993).

6.3   *The Integration Hypothesis*

The integration hypothesis needs to be examined alongside our proposal for the importance of the coexistence strategy. Both integration and coexistence turned out to be the preferred intercultural strategies of Hindu and Muslim groups to guide their relations. This may not be surprising. Multiculturalism in the form of secularism may be India's state policy, but pluralism lies at the core of Indian culture. However, multicultural ideology, at least in the case of Hindus, did correlate positively with both the integration strategy and expectation. In the case of both integration and coexistence, the two cultures seek to align with each other. In the former case, there is a degree of asymmetry in relationships, but none in the case of the latter. We may point out that coexistence does not allow for a complete blending of cultural elements, but only for their interweaving in a manner such that the various cultural strands are both together and stand apart at the same time.

In this context, the relevant question to ask will be whether the relationship of integration with adaptation and well-being variables played out in a similar fashion or differently in comparison to the coexistence strategy. The answer is that it played out somewhat differently. Integration and coexistence did correlate negatively with perceived discrimination in both Hindu and Muslim groups, more strongly in Hindu than in the Muslim group. This suggested that the engagement of the members of smaller groups with the larger society made them feel socially included and, therefore, less discriminated against.

The other hypothesis, which expected that integration as well as coexistence strategies would promote psychological well-being and social competence, did not find support in either sample. This suggests that there is a need to understand other factors that may influence the dynamic of adaptation and well-being. This becomes clear in the light of another finding. In the Hindu group, the use of the integration and coexistence intercultural strategies led to enhanced cultural security, greater outgroup contact and more mutual acceptance, but these did not predict psychological, sociocultural or intercultural adaptation.

The separation strategy, which was preferred over assimilation, threatened cultural security, reduced outgroup contact and mutual acceptance, and related to a higher level of perceived discrimination. This was the case for separation expectations also. In some research (e.g., Berry & Hou, 2016), separation did not differ from integration in promoting the well-being of immigrants to Canada.

The marginalization strategy never looked like a viable option in the pluricultural context of India. The findings showed that it worked as predicted. In Hindus, marginalization led to enhancement of psychological problems and reduction of social competence, suggesting that this strategy interferes with psychological and social well-being. In the case of Muslims too, the marginalization expectation threatened people's cultural security and reduced acceptance of multicultural ideology and the level of social competence.

Another interesting finding is the positive association of assimilation with psychological problems. Indian history is replete with examples of Hindus being converted to Islam during the reign of some Muslim rulers, or made to pay taxes for maintaining their Hindu religious affiliation.

Such collective memories along with sporadic instances of religious conversion in recent years may be responsible for the development of not only a negative attitude towards assimilation but also its negative consequences. In view of the numerical strength of Muslims in India and also with the rise in the assertion of Islamic identity all over the world, one would not expect assimilation to be a dominant intercultural strategy in the case of Muslims. But strategies and expectations do not have a one-to-one relationship. Assimilation expectations, where they were present, appeared to have implications for psychological and social well-being. This explains why psychological problems are higher with the assimilation expectations in the case of Hindus. Greater ingroup contact noticed in this case has implications for non-acceptance of multicultural ideology and low social competence, which interferes with successful living and working with members of the other groups in the society.

What needs to be especially noted is that the variables operated differently for the Hindu and Muslim groups. For example, the assimilation strategy, which predicted greater psychological problems for the Hindus, did not do so for the Muslims. Similarly, the integration and coexistence intercultural strategies, which predicted social competence in the Muslim group, did not do so in the case of Hindus. There are other adaptation and well-being measures for which the predictors for the Hindu and Muslim groups were either different, or they worked differently (i.e., positive in one case and negative in another). Exceptions to this kind of result were the variables of cultural security (which promoted the integration strategy in the case of both the groups) and outgroup contact (which led to greater degree of mutual acceptance in both the groups). These similarities attest to the importance of having mutual intercultural relationships in such a complex socio-cultural context as India. The differences, however, require unpacking them in order to explain psychological adaptation and social well-being of members of the Hindu and Muslim groups.

6.4   General Comments

In recent years, the increasing incidents of violence against Hindus and liberal Muslims in some states of India have posed new challenges to the intercultural relations between the two groups. Varanasi presents us with an example of a cultural setting where the relationship of Hindus and Muslims is more of 'interdependence'. Therefore, the generality of these findings requires caution. We hope that another MIRIPS study that we are doing in Mumbai (where relationships between groups are more at formal and professional level), and in Jammu and Kashmir (where the Muslims are numerically dominant), will allow us to address some of the issues concerning the complex relationship of the Hindu and Muslim groups and develop a more nuanced understanding of the relationship.

6.5   Conclusions

Broadly speaking, the findings support the general premises of the MIRIPS study with respect to security, contact and integration principles, but emphasize the need for their contextual understanding. Integration does not result in the kind of positive outcomes in terms of the relationship of groups, including their psychological and social well-being, as has been found in studies in Europe, Canada and Australia. However, the opposite phenomena (marginalization and perceived discrimination) have opposite relationships with well-being in both samples. The predictors of well-being also differ between the Hindu and Muslim groups, but such differences may be expected in other societies also. We believe that the intercultural relationship model used in the MIRIPS project, which is rooted in the principles of multiculturalism, may be in need of slight tweaking in cultures that have sought to build a nation-state around their plural cultures and have to contend with a variety of sub-nationalisms, as in the case of India.

References

Bano, S., & Mishra, R. C. (2006). The effect of schooling on the development of social identity and prejudice in Hindu and Muslim children. *Indian Journal of Community Psychology, 2* (2), 168–182.

Bano, S., & Mishra, R. C. (2009). Social identity and inter-group perception of Hindu and Muslim adolescents. *Journal of Psychosocial Research, 4* (2), 417–425.

Bano, S., & Mishra, R.C. (2011). Intercultural strategy of Muslim and Hindu adolescents in traditional and modern schools. In P. Singh, P. Bain, C. Leong, G. Misra & Y. Ohtsubo (Eds.), *Individual, Group and Cultural Processes in Changing Societies* (pp. 219–230). New Delhi: MacMillan.

Bano, S., & Mishra, R.C. (2014). Social identity and prejudice in Hindu and Muslim adolescents of traditional and modern schools. *Journal of Psychosocial Research, 9* (2), 299–307.

Berry, J.W. (1981). Social and cultural change. In H.C. Triandis & R. Brislin (Eds.), *Handbook of Cross-Cultural Psychology* (Vol. 5, pp. 211–279). Boston: Allyn & Bacon.

Berry, J.W., & Hou, F. (2016). Acculturation and wellbeing among immigrants to Canada. *Canadian Psychology: Special Issue on Immigrants and Refugees in Canada, 57* (4), 254–264.

Chandra, B., & Mahajan, S. (2007). *Composite Culture in Multicultural Society.* New Delhi: Pearson Longman.

Charlier-Visuvalingam, E., & Visuvalingam, S. (1993). Between Mecca and Banaras: Towards an acculturation model of Hindu-Muslim relations. *Islam and the Modern Age, 24* (1), 20–69.

Chen, S., Boucher, H., & Kraus, M. W. (2011). The relational self: Emerging theory and evidence. In S. J. Schwartz, K. Luyckx & V. L. Vignoles (Eds.), *Handbook of Identity Theory and Research* (pp. 149–175). Dordrecht: Springer Science+Business Media.

DeRidder, R., & Tripathi, Rama Charan (1992). *Norm Violation and Intergroup Relations*. Oxford: Clarendon Press.

Lentin, S. (2016). Indian Jews: The little known minority community has a rich heritage. *India News*, 16 June.

Markus, H., & Kitayama, S. (1991). Culture and the self: Implications for cognition, emotion, and motivation. *Psychological Review*, 98 (2), 224–253.

Mishra, R.C., & Bano, S. (2003). Ethnic identity and bias in Hindu and Muslim children. *Social Science International*, 19 (1), 52–64.

Mishra, R.C., Sinha, D., & Berry, J.W. (1996). *Ecology, Acculturation and Psychological Adaptation: A Study of Adivasis in Bihar*. New Delhi: SAGE.

Mukherjee, P.N. (2010). Civic-secular and ethnic nationalisms as bases of the nation-state: Multiculturalism at the crossroads? *Asian Ethnicity*, 11 (1), 1–23.

Sagayaraj, A. (2013). Christianity in India: A focus on inculturation. *Research Papers of the Anthropological Institute*, 1 (2), 114–142.

Sinha, D. (1988). Basic Indian values and behavior dispositions in the context of national development: An appraisal. In D. Sinha & H.S.R. Kao (Eds.), *Social Values and Development: Asian Perspectives* (pp. 31–55). New Delhi: SAGE.

Tambiah, S. (1997). *Levelling Crowds: Ethnonationalist Conflicts and Collective Violence in South Asia*. New Delhi: Vistaar Publications.

Tripathi, Rama Charan (2005). Hindu social identities and imagined past: The faceoff between Ram Temple and "Martyred" mosque at Ayodhya. *Psychological Studies*, 50 (2–3), 102–110.

Tripathi, Rama Charan (in press). Unity of the individual and the collective. In G. Misra (Ed.), *The Sixth ICSSR Survey of Research in Psychology*. New Delhi: Pearson.

Tripathi, Rama Charan, Ghosh, E.S.K., & Kumar, R. (2014). The Hindu-Musim divide: Building sustainable bridges. In Rama Charan Tripathi & Y. Sinha (Eds.), *Psychology, Development and Social Policy in India* (pp. 257–284). New Delhi: Springer.

Tripathi, Rama Charan, Kumar, R., Siddiqui, R., Mishra, R.C., & Bano, S. (2009). *Ideological frames and reactions to norm violations*. Paper presented at the VIIIth Biennial conference of Asian Association of Social Psychology, New Delhi, December, 11–14.

Tripathi, Rama Charan, & Mishra, R. C. (2006). *Contextual factors in intergroup relations in Indian society*. Paper presented at the XVI International Congress of Cross-Cultural Psychology, Spetses, Greece, July 11–15.

Tripathi, Rama Charan, & Mishra, R.C. (2016). Acculturation in South Asia. In D. Sam & J.W. Berry (Eds.), *The Cambridge Handbook of Acculturation Psychology* (2nd ed., pp. 337–354). Cambridge: Cambridge University Press.

Tripathi, Rama Charan, & Srivastava, R. (1981). Relative deprivation and intergroup attitudes. *European Journal of Social Psychology*, 11 (3), 313–318.

Weil, S. (2006). Indian Judaic tradition. In S. Mittal & G. Thursby (Eds.), *Religions in South Asia* (pp. 169–183). London: Palgrave.

15   Intercultural Relations in Hong Kong

Algae K. Y. Au
Hong Kong Polytechnic University, Hong Kong

Bryant P. H. Hui
University of Cambridge, U.K.

Sylvia Xiaohua Chen
Hong Kong Polytechnic University, Hong Kong

1   Introduction

The study of the mutual views of Mainland Chinese immigrants and Hong Kong Chinese residents on immigration is an interesting and important topic in intercultural relations research. This is partly because of the territory's long colonial history; during this period, British cultural influences were introduced. More recently (1997), Hong Kong came under increasing influence from Mainland China. Thus, acculturation and intercultural relations are complex, and in transition. On the diversity index, Hong Kong is low; its place on the other indexes cannot be estimated at present.

2   Context of Intercultural Relations in Hong Kong

Historically, from before World War Two to the present, the influx of immigrants from China to Hong Kong has never ceased. About 93.6 per cent of Hong Kong population are ethnic Chinese (Census and Statistics Department, 2012), and many of them are in fact descendants of Mainland Chinese immigrants (Chief Secretary for Administration's Office, 2015). Socially, despite the geographical proximity, there are wide socio-cultural discrepancies between Hong Kong and Mainland China (e.g., Chen, Benet-Martínez, & Bond, 2008). Hong Kong, as a former British colony and a metropolis, embraces Western values, whereas Socialist values are upheld in Mainland China. Despite their shared ethnicity, the two places differ in their language systems. Hong Kong Chinese residents use traditional Chinese characters and speak Cantonese, while most Mainland Chinese use simplified Chinese characters and speak Mandarin.

Demographically, Mainland Chinese immigrants are the single largest immigrant group in Hong Kong. Increased contact between Hong Kong and the Mainland for the past few decades has facilitated cross-boundary marriages. In 2014, cross-boundary marriages made up 36.7 per cent of locally registered marriages (Census and Statistics Department, 2015a). Growing cross-boundary marriages also lead to an increasing demand for One-Way Permits (OWP) from Mainland spouses and dependent children to reunite with their family in Hong Kong. Apart from the OWP scheme, Mainland Chinese can also apply to reside in Hong Kong in the capacity of talents, professionals and investors, through other specific immigration schemes (Immigration Department, 2016). With a daily quota of 150, the OWP scheme alone has brought in around 828,000 Mainland Chinese immigrants, from the 1997 handover to mid-2014 (Chief Secretary for Administration's Office, 2015), approximately 11.4 per cent of the total 7.24 million Hong Kong population in mid-2014 (Census and Statistics Department, 2016). It is believed that Mainland Chinese immigrants will continue to be the Hong Kong's main source of population growth (Chief Secretary for Administration's Office, 2015), and a major force in shaping its demographic composition in the future.

Politically, since the transfer of its sovereignty in 1997, Hong Kong has transformed from a British colony to a Special Administrative Region of China. Under the "one country two systems" constitutional framework, Hong Kong, while being a part of China, is also supposed to retain its distinct political system, and maintain a high degree of autonomy. However, with the Chinese Central Government's increasing involvement in and control of Hong Kong issues, the implementation of "one country two systems" is constantly the focus of political debate.

In view of the special political situation of Hong Kong, immigration from Mainland China to Hong Kong represents a unique intra-country migration phenomenon that is rarely found in other societies. In this distinctive context, the multicultural ideology and acculturation attitudes held by both Hong Kong Chinese residents and Mainland Chinese immigrants, the intercultural relations between them, and the adaptation issues arising from intra-country migration, are all due for examination (e.g., Hui, Chen, Leung, & Berry, 2015). In this chapter, we will examine the three hypotheses of Mutual Intercultural Relations in Plural Society (MIRIPS) project: the multiculturalism hypothesis, contact hypothesis and integration hypothesis (Berry 2013a) in this Mainland-Hong Kong intra-country migration context.

3   Evaluation of the Hypotheses

According to the multiculturalism hypothesis, security in one's identity is a psychological prerequisite for mutual acceptance. In contrast, when one's identity is threatened, rejection will occur (Berry, Kalin, & Taylor, 1977). In short, security will lead to mutually positive intercultural adaptation. Security consists of three components: cultural security, economic security and personal security. Mutual acceptance includes multicultural ideology and tolerance. According to Berry (2006), multicultural ideology refers to the general support of cultural diversity and equity in the society, whereas tolerance denotes an attitude towards social equality, encompassing ethnic tolerance and social egalitarianism. For the dominant group, acceptance may also include attitudes towards immigration, including the perceived size of current population of the area and the perceived consequences of immigration.

In the Hong Kong context, anti-Mainland sentiment has gradually emerged in society recently. The discontent arises from political and social causes, such as conflicts over political issues, unruly behaviours of some Mainland Chinese visitors, rampant cross-boundary parallel trading, and the large influx of immigrants from the Mainland. In particular, Mainland Chinese immigrants may be perceived as cultural, economic and personal threats to Hong Kong Chinese residents. Mainland Chinese immigrants are often accused of competing for local resources, increasing unemployment and creating social instability (Chiu, Choi, & Ting, 2005). As one of the most densely populated cities in the world, Hong Kong's capacity to accommodate more immigrants is in doubt. However, as a city that relies on human capital as its greatest asset, immigrants may help replenish the decreasing labour force due to low fertility rate and ageing population. Therefore, a sense of security or threat is important to Hong Kong Chinese residents' perception of the current population of Hong Kong and the consequences of immigration that can bring to the city.

For Mainland Chinese, migration to Hong Kong has never been an easy decision. As they are not allowed to have dual citizenship, all Mainland Chinese have to give up their *Hukou* (household) registration, which is the government's record of citizens' granted official residency, and all associated rights at their hometown before moving to Hong Kong (GovHK, 2016). *Hukou* substantially impacts a Mainlander's livelihood in every possible aspect, including the rights to education, healthcare, housing and employment. Therefore, it takes great determination for a Mainlander to give up the *Hukou* for a better life in Hong Kong. However, when they finally reside, many of them face difficulties in the new environment, especially in language, work and housing (Home Affair Department and Immigration Department, 2016). Cultural, economic and personal threats from language, work and housing difficulties in turn affect their endorsement of multiculturalism and tolerance. Therefore, when it comes to the issue of Mainland Chinese immigration, security may be particularly relevant to the mutual acceptance among both Hong Kong Chinese residents and Mainland Chinese immigrants.

With respect to the multiculturalism hypothesis, based on previous research and the current situation of Hong Kong, we expect that security would positively predict positive intercultural adaptation (multicultural ideology and tolerance) for both Hong Kong Chinese residents and Mainland Chinese immigrants. For Hong Kong Chinese residents, security would further negatively predict perceived current population and perceived consequences of immigration.

According to the contact hypothesis, contact and sharing can promote mutual acceptance, provided that the contact is between groups of equal social and economic status, the contact is voluntary, and the contact is supported by society through norms and laws (Allport, 1954).

Due to the geographical closeness of Hong Kong and Mainland China, advancement of technology, and the ease of travel, intergroup contact between Hong Kong Chinese residents and Mainland Chinese is common (Chen et al., 2016). For Hong Kong Chinese residents, travelling to the Mainland and making friends with Mainland Chinese may enhance their understanding of Mainland culture and increase tolerance. For Mainland Chinese immigrants, travelling around Hong Kong and building friendship with locals may also increase their knowledge of local culture and reduce their perceived discrimination.

Based on previous research and the current situation of Hong Kong, we expect that intergroup contact would positively predict tolerance among Hong Kong Chinese residents, and negatively predict perceived discrimination among Mainland Chinese immigrants.

According to the integration hypothesis, individuals who are engaged in both their heritage culture and the host culture have more positive adaptation outcomes. For the immigrant group, adaptation outcomes generally involve both psychological and sociocultural adaptations when they acculturate in a new culture. For the dominant group, the main adaptation outcome of their acculturation expectations is psychological adaptation, as they may need to psychologically adjust themselves in a changing cultural context. However, sociocultural adaptation is less relevant to the dominant group, as they are assumed to be able to manage their daily life in a place that they have been residing for a long period of time.

Taken together, we expect that the integration strategy would positively predict both psychological and sociocultural adaptations for Mainland Chinese immigrants. We also predict that the integration expectation would positively predict psychological adaptation among Hong Kong Chinese residents.

In sum, the following hypotheses were formulated:

Multiculturalism hypothesis: Security positively predicts acceptance. Specifically: Hypothesis 1a. Security would positively predict positive intercultural adaptation (i.e., multicultural ideology and tolerance) among Mainland Chinese immigrants. Hypothesis 1b. Security would positively predict the intercultural adaptation (i.e., multicultural ideology, tolerance and perceived consequences of immigration), and negatively predict perceived number of immigrants as being "too many" among Hong Kong Chinese residents.

Contact hypothesis: Intergroup contact positively predicts intercultural adaptation. Specifically: Hypothesis 2a. Contact with Hong Kong Chinese residents would negatively predict perceived discrimination among Mainland Chinese immigrants. Hypothesis 2b. Contact with Mainland Chinese would positively predict tolerance among Hong Kong Chinese residents.

Integration hypothesis: Integration strategy/expectation positively predicts adaptation. Specifically: Hypothesis 3a. Integration strategy would positively predict psychological and sociocultural adaptations among Mainland Chinese immigrants. Hypothesis 3b. Integration expectation would positively predict psychological adaptation among Hong Kong Chinese residents.

4 Method

4.1 Samples

We recruited two samples: Mainland Chinese immigrants and Hong Kong Chinese residents. The immigrant sample consisted of 182 adults (149 females; M_{age} = 41.64, SD = 11.14, age ranged 22–79), who were born and lived in Mainland China before. The gender ratio and age range of this sample roughly resemble the characteristics of Mainland Chinese immigrants to Hong Kong in past and recent surveys (Home Affairs Department, 2013).

The Hong Kong Chinese resident sample consisted of 181 adults (106 females; M_{age} = 44.98, SD = 14.41, age range 20–82). The demographic quota was set based on official statistics of age ranges and gender ratio of Hong Kong Chinese residents (Census and Statistics Department, 2011). Then participants were randomly sampled within each stratum.

4.2 Measures

The measures used were mainly the ones in the MIRIPS questionnaire. In some items, we replaced "ethnic" and "national" with "Mainland

Chinese/Mainland Chinese immigrant/Mandarin" and "Hong Kong Chinese resident/Cantonese", respectively.

Mainland Chinese Immigrant Sample

Cantonese ability. The scale for Cantonese proficiency measured participants' abilities to understand, speak and write in Cantonese. The reliability coefficient in the present study was .94.

Security. The scale for security tapped participants' cultural, economic and personal security. The reliability coefficient of overall security was .42 after removing seven items that had negative item-total correlations (cultural security: α = .54 after removing three items; economic security: α = .50 after removing two items; personal security: α = .70 after removing two items). Due to the modest reliability of the scale, the results should be interpreted with caution.

Acculturation strategies. Based on the Acculturation Attitudes Scale, four acculturation strategies adopted by immigrants were assessed: integration, separation, marginalization and assimilation. The Cronbach's alphas in the present study were .70, .48, .44 and .52 for integration, separation, marginalization and assimilation, respectively.

Travel. An item was used to tap the frequency of travelling within Hong Kong in the past five years.

Friendship with Hong Kong Chinese residents. This was measured by evaluating the quantity and frequency of contact with Hong Kong friends. Then the scores of quantity and frequency items were averaged (α = .80).

Multicultural ideology. The Multicultural Ideology Scale was used to measure participants' endorsement of the view that cultural diversity and multiculturalism are good for the society at large and its individual members (α = .64, after four items with negative item-total correlations were removed).

Tolerance. The Tolerance Scale measured the degree of acceptance of individuals or groups that are culturally or racially different from oneself (α = .70).

Psychological adaptation. Psychological adaptation was measured with three scales: Satisfaction with Life Scale (SWLS; α = .89), Rosenberg Self-Esteem Scale (RSES; α = .79) and the Scale for Psychological Problems (α = .93). A composite score for psychological adaptation was derived by averaging the standardized scores for self-esteem, life satisfaction and psychological problems (reversed).

Sociocultural adaptation. This scale focuses on skills required to manage social situations in a new cultural environment and was employed to tap sociocultural adaptation (α = .92).

Perceived discrimination. The Perceived Discrimination Scale was used for Mainland Chinese immigrants only, assessing perceived frequency of feeling unaccepted, being treated unfairly or negatively or being teased, and so on, because of one's ethnicity ($\alpha = .84$).

Hong Kong Chinese Resident Sample

Mandarin ability. The scale for Mandarin proficiency measured participants' abilities to understand, speak and write in Mandarin. The reliability coefficient in the present study was .94.

Security. Same as for the Mainland Chinese immigrant sample. The alpha of overall security was .42 after removing seven items due to negative item-total correlations (cultural security: $\alpha = .37$ after removing three items; economic security: $\alpha = .48$ after removing two items; personal security: $\alpha = .63$ after removing two items). Results in relation to this variable should be interpreted with caution because of the modest reliability.

Acculturation expectations. Same as acculturation strategies, but Hong Kong Chinese residents' acculturation expectations for Mainland Chinese immigrants were assessed. The Cronbach's alphas in the present study were .64 and .51 (after removing one item), .59, and .54 for integration, separation, marginalization and assimilation, respectively.

Travel. An item was used to tap the frequency of travelling within Mainland China in the past five years.

Friendship with Mainland Chinese. This was measured by evaluating the quantity and frequency of contact with Mainland friends ($\alpha = .78$).

Multicultural ideology. Same as the previous one ($\alpha = .48$, after one item with negative item-total correlation was removed).

Tolerance. Same as the previous one ($\alpha = .65$).

Perceived current population. An item was used to tap the perception of number of current population.

Perceived consequences of immigration. The scale for perceived consequences of immigration was employed to measure the positive consequences produced by Mainland Chinese immigrants ($\alpha = .73$ after removing one item with negative item-total correlation).

Psychological adaptation. Same as for the Mainland Chinese immigrant sample ($\alpha = .88$, .80 and .93 for the SWLS, RSES, and the Scale for Psychological Problems, respectively).

5   Results

Descriptive statistics, including means, standard deviations, reliability coefficients and correlation coefficients for the Mainland Chinese immigrant sample and Hong Kong Chinese resident sample, are shown in Tables 15.1 and 15.2, respectively. We next presented our correlation

Table 15.1. *Means, standard deviations, reliability coefficients and intercorrelations for the measures in Mainland Chinese immigrant sample (n = 182).*

	Mean	SD	2	3	4	5	6	7	8	9	10	11	12	13	14	15	16	17	18	19
1 Age	41.64	11.14	.03	-.35***	-.08	-.03	.18*	.18	.17	-.01	.14	.12	.21**	-.18*	-.11	-.18*	-.19**	-.05	-.09	.18*
2 Gender	—	—	—	-.30***	.23**	.11	-.06	-.17*	-.07	.10	-.10	-.07	.14	.18*	-.04	.08	.16*	.05	.08	.01
3 Education	3.88	1.90		—	-.23**	.06	-.01	.18*	.19**	.08	-.10	-.09	-.28***	.09	.07	.18*	.19**	.19*	.05	-.14
4 CA	3.62	1.02			.94	-.02	-.09	-.06	-.10	-.01	-.12	-.10	-.04	.15*	.22**	.06	.15*	.05	.16*	-.30***
5 CS	3.46	0.99				.54	-.37***	.08	.56***	.32***	-.37***	-.07	-.13	.10	.07	.24***	.46***	.25***	.05	-.08
6 ES	2.56	1.07					.50	.18	.22**	-.22**	.14	.01	.18*	-.04	-.13	-.05	-.23**	-.19*	-.03	-.05
7 PS	2.66	1.10						.70	.79***	.13	-.10	-.10	.05	.07	.07	.17*	.10	.26***	.21**	-.08
8 OS	2.97	0.68							.42	.25***	-.25***	-.07	.00	.10	.04	.27***	.31***	.27***	.17*	-.13
9 INT	3.70	0.79								.70	-.19**	-.04	-.01	.05	.16	.27***	.45***	.44***	.23**	-.11
10 SEP	2.42	0.71									.48	.54***	.25***	-.06	-.05	-.25***	-.32***	-.27***	-.10	.15*
11 MAR	2.27	0.74										.44	.21**	-.12	.06	-.06	-.10	-.15*	-.18*	.06
12 ASS	2.12	0.66											.52	-.16*	-.14	-.27***	-.27***	-.01	.00	.23**
13 THK	2.78	1.41												—	.14	.21**	.23**	.02	.07	-.30***
14 FHKCR	3.18	1.01													.84	.17*	.18*	.09	.06	-.32***
15 MI	3.34	0.43														.64	.47***	.33***	.07	-.27***
16 Tolerance	3.63	0.58															.70	.35***	.18*	-.25***
17 PA	0.00	0.77																.81	.40***	-.17*
18 SA	4.28	0.55																	.92	-.06
19 PD	2.52	0.89																		.84

Note: CA = Cantonese ability; CS = cultural security; ES = economic security; PS = personal security; OS = overall security; INT = integration; SEP = separation; MAR = marginalization; ASS = assimilation; THK = travel in Hong Kong; FHKCR = friendship with Hong Kong Chinese residents; MI = multicultural ideology; PA = psychological adaptation; SA = sociocultural adaptation; PD = perceived discrimination. The reliability coefficients are found along the diagonal line.

* p <.05, ** p <.01, *** p <.001.

Table 15.2. Means, standard deviations, reliability coefficients and intercorrelations for the measures in Hong Kong Chinese resident sample (n = 181).

	Mean	SD	1	2	3	4	5	6	7	8	9	10	11	12	13	14	15	16	17	18	19
1 Age	44.98	14.41	—	-.00	-.63***	-.15*	-.03	.01	-.04	-.03	-.12	.20	.22	.14	-.11	-.03	-.21**	.11	-.22**	.10	-.06
2 Gender	—	—		—	-.19*	-.06	-.02	-.03	-.11	-.09	.33	-.05	-.07	.01	-.03	.01	.03	.01	.10	.01	-.05
3 Education	4.77	2.09			—	.23*	.07	.03	.14	.13	.12	.17*	-.24**	-.19*	.18*	-.01	.20**	.03	.13	-.09	.11
4 MA	3.15	1.17				.94	-.00	.03	.15*	.10	.11	.01	-.13	-.03	.28***	.29***	.23***	.21**	-.09	.10	.01
5 CS	3.59	0.87					.37	-.24**	.16*	.47***	.13	-.19**	-.15	-.12	.12	.04	.20**	.19*	-.08	.03	.19*
6 ES	2.31	0.94						.48	.28***	.59***	-.21**	.10	.11	.10	-.19**	-.08	-.15*	-.06	-.20**	.08	.09
7 PS	2.98	0.95							.63	.79**	-.01	-.25**	-.19**	-.03	-.09	.04	.08	.02	-.05	.18*	.34***
8 OS	2.96	0.57								.42	-.05	-.18*	-.12	-.02	.01	.00	.06	.08	-.18*	.17*	.34***
9 INT	3.91	0.68									.64	-.29***	-.34***	-.18*	.28***	.20**	.29***	.29***	.14	-.07	.23**
10 SEP	2.36	0.76										.51	.59***	.30***	-.13	-.12	-.35***	-.17*	-.24**	-.04	-.22**
11 MAR	2.13	0.74											.59	.33**	-.12	-.16*	-.36***	-.25***	-.19**	-.18*	-.20**
12 ASS	2.35	0.67												.54	-.12	-.04	-.28***	-.13	-.12	-.03	-.10
13 TMC	3.13	1.32													—	.27***	.18*	.02	.09	-.03	.13
14 FMC	2.75	1.05														.78	.16*	.24**	.01	.07	.17*
15 MI	3.48	0.45															.48	.46***	.03	.18*	.16*
16 Tolerance	3.57	0.53																.65	.08	.28***	.14
17 PCP	4.12	0.90																	—	-.15*	-.00
18 PCI	3.02	0.56																		.73	.25***
19 PA	0.00	0.74																			.82

Note: MA = Mandarin ability; CS = cultural security; ES = economic security; PS = personal security; OS = overall security; INT = integration; SEP = separation; MAR = marginalization; ASS = assimilation; TMC = travel in Mainland China; FMC = friendship with Mainland Chinese; MI = multicultural ideology; PCP = perceived current population; PCI = perceived consequences of immigration; PA = psychological adaptation. The reliability coefficients are found along the diagonal line.

*p <.05, **p <.01, ***p <.001.

and hierarchical multiple regression analyses in separate sections, one for each of the three hypotheses that we tested.

Multiculturalism Hypothesis

Mainland Chinese immigrants Sample. Correlation analyses showed that cultural security was positively associated with multicultural ideology, $r = .24$, $p < .001$, and tolerance, $r = .46$, $p < .001$; personal security was positively correlated with multicultural ideology, $r = .17$, $p = .022$; and overall security was positively linked with multicultural ideology, $r = .27$, $p < .001$, and tolerance, $r = .31$, $p < .001$. These results provided initial support for Hypothesis 1a. Inconsistent with our prediction, however, economic security was negatively associated with tolerance, $r = -.23$, $p = .001$.

To further test the predictive power of security, we conducted a series of hierarchical multiple regressions, controlling for the possible confounding effects of age, gender, education level and Cantonese ability. As shown in Table 15.3, cultural security significantly predicted multicultural ideology, $\beta = .22$, $p = .002$, and tolerance, $\beta = .43$, $p < .001$, respectively, after controlling for the demographic variables. The predictors explained 12 per cent and 30 per cent of the total variance in multicultural ideology, $F(5, 175) = 4.61$, $p < .001$, and tolerance, $F(5, 175) = 15.10$, $p < .001$, respectively. Personal security significantly predicted multicultural ideology, $\beta = .17$, $p = .026$, after controlling for the demographic variables, and the regression model explained 10 per cent of the total variance in multicultural ideology, $F(5, 175) = 3.66$, $p = .004$. Similarly, after controlling for demographic variables, overall security significantly predicted multicultural ideology, $\beta = .27$, $p < .001$, and tolerance, $\beta = .30$, $p < .001$, respectively (see Table 15.4). All predictors explained 14 per cent and 21 per cent of the total variance in multicultural ideology, $F(5, 175) = 5.49$, $p < .001$, and tolerance, $F(5, 175) = 9.31$, $p < .001$, respectively. Economic security, however, negatively predicted tolerance, $\beta = -.20$, $p = .006$, after controlling for the demographic variables, and the whole model explained 16 per cent of total variance in tolerance, $F(5, 175) = 6.73$, $p < .001$ (see Table 15.3). Taken together, the results generally supported Hypothesis 1a except that of economic security.

Hong Kong Chinese resident sample. Cultural security was positively associated with multicultural ideology, $r = .20$, $p = .007$, and tolerance, $r = .19$, $p = .011$; economic security was negatively associated with perceived number of current population in Hong Kong, $r = -.20$, $p = .006$; personal security was positively correlated with perceived consequences of immigration, $r = .18$, $p = .013$; and overall security was negatively associated with perceived number of current population,

Table 15.3. *Hierarchical regression models for different types of security and other variables predicting multicultural ideology and tolerance in Mainland Chinese immigrant sample.*

Variables	Multicultural ideology		Tolerance		Tolerance		Multicultural ideology	
	Block 1 β	Block 2 β	Block 1 β	Block 2 β	Block 1 β	Block 2 β	Block 1 β	Block 2 β
Age	-.11	-.11	-.10	-.10	-.10	-.06	-.11	-.12
Gender (1 = male, 2 = female)	.12	.09	.21**	.14*	.21**	.20**	.12	.14
Education	.20*	.17*	.26**	.22	.26**	.26**	.20*	.17*
Cantonese ability	.07	.08	.16*	.17*	.16*	.14	.07	.07
Cultural security		.22**		.43***				
Economic security						-.20**		
Personal security								.17*
R^2	.07	.12	.12	.30	.12	.16	.07	.10
ΔR^2	.07	.05	.12	.18	.12	.04	.07	.03
Fchange	3.24*	9.49**	6.24***	44.43***	6.24***	7.75**	3.24*	5.06*

*p < .05, **p < .01, ***p < .001.

Table 15.4. *Hierarchical regression models for overall security and other variables predicting multicultural ideology and tolerance in Mainland Chinese immigrant sample.*

Variables	Multicultural ideology		Tolerance	
	Block 1 β	Block 2 β	Block 1 β	Block 2 β
Age	−.11	−.13	−.10	−.12
Gender (1 = male, 2 = female)	.12	.12	.21**	.20**
Education	.20*	.13	.26**	.19*
Cantonese ability	.07	.08	.16*	.17*
Overall security		.27***		.30***
R^2	.07	.14	.12	.21
ΔR^2	.07	.07	.12	.09
Fchange	3.24*	13.58***	6.24***	19.06***

$*p$ <.05, $**p$ <.01, $***p$ <.001.

$r = -.18$, $p = .015$, but positively correlated with perceived consequences of immigration, $r = .17$, p <.026. These correlational results basically supported Hypothesis 1b except that economic security was negatively associated with multicultural ideology, $r = -.15$, $p = .045$.

Likewise, as shown in Table 15.5, we conducted a series of hierarchical multiple regressions, controlling for the potential confounding effects of age, gender, education level and Mandarin ability. Cultural security significantly predicted multicultural ideology, $\beta = .19$, $p = .007$, and tolerance, $\beta = .19$, $p = .008$, respectively, after controlling for the demographic variables. The predictors explained 13 per cent and 10 per cent of the total variance in multicultural ideology, $F(5, 175) = 5.01$, p <.001, and tolerance, $F(5, 175) = 3.78$, $p = .003$, respectively. Economic security significantly predicted perceived number of current population, $\beta = -.20$, $p = .006$, after controlling for demographic variables, and the whole model explained 11 per cent of the total variance in perceived current population, $F(5, 175) = 4.18$, $p = .001$. Similarly, personal security significantly predicted perceived consequences of immigration, $\beta = .20$, $p = .009$, after controlling for the same confounding variables. All predictors explained 7 per cent of the total variance in perceived consequences of immigration, $F(5, 175) = 2.41$, $p = .038$. Lastly, as shown in Table 15.6, overall security significantly predicted perceived consequences of immigration, $\beta = .18$, $p = .018$, and perceived current population, $\beta = -.18$, $p = .015$, respectively. All predictors explained 6 per cent and 10 per cent of the total variance in perceived

Table 15.5. *Hierarchical regression models for different types of security and other variables predicting multicultural ideology, tolerance, perceived current population and perceived consequences of immigration in Hong Kong Chinese resident sample.*

Variables	Multicultural ideology		Tolerance		PCP		PCI	
	Block 1 β	Block 2 β	Block 1 β	Block 2 β	Block 1 β	Block 2 β	Block 1 β	Block 2 β
Age	-.13	-.13	-.16	-.16	-.20*	-.19*	.06	.05
Gender (1 = male, 2 = female)	.05	.05	-.01	-.01	.08	.08	.00	.02
Education	.08	.07	-.13	-.14	.04	.05	-.09	-.11
Mandarin ability	.19*	.19**	.22**	.22**	.12	.12	.13	.11
Cultural security		.19**		.19**				
Economic security						-.20**		
Personal security								.20**
R^2	.09	.13	.06	.10	.07	.11	.03	.07
ΔR^2	.09	.04	.06	.04	.07	.04	.03	.04
Fchange	4.27**	7.34***	2.82*	7.25**	3.21*	7.59**	1.25	6.91**

Note: PCP = perceived current population; PCI = perceived consequences of immigration.

*p <.05, **p <.01, ***p <.001.

Table 15.6. *Hierarchical regression models for overall security and other variables predicting perceived consequences of immigration and current population in Hong Kong Chinese resident sample.*

Variables	PCI		PCP	
	Block 1 β	Block 2 β	Block 1 β	Block 2 β
Age	.06	.05	− .20*	− .19*
Gender (1 = male, 2 = female)	.00	.01	.08	.08
Education	− .09	− .11	.04	.07
Mandarin ability	.13	.12	− .12	− .11
Overall security		.18*		− .18*
R^2	.03	.06	.07	.10
ΔR^2	.03	.03	.07	.03
Fchange	1.25	5.73*	3.21*	6.02*

Note: PCI = perceived consequences of immigration; PCP = perceived current population.
*p <.05.

consequences of immigration, $F(5, 175) = 2.17$, $p = .050$, and perceived current population, $F(5, 175) = 3.85$, $p = .002$, respectively. All these results supported Hypothesis 1b.

Contact Hypothesis

Mainland Chinese immigrant sample. Correlation analysis showed that friendship with Hong Kong Chinese residents was negatively associated with perceived discrimination, $r = -.32$, p <.001, which is consistent with Hypothesis 2a. Next, in a regression model, friendship with Hong Kong Chinese residents significantly predicted perceived discrimination, $\beta = -.21$, $p = .003$, after controlling for age, gender, education level, Cantonese ability, and the frequency of travelling around Hong Kong (see Table 15.7). The whole model explained 24 per cent of the total variance in perceived discrimination, $F(6, 174) = 9.08$, p <.001.

Hong Kong Chinese resident sample.
Friendship with Mainland Chinese immigrants was positively associated with tolerance, $r = .23$, $p = .001$. To further test Hypothesis 2b, we regressed tolerance on age, gender, education level, Mandarin ability, and the frequency of travelling around Mainland China. As shown in Table 15.7, friendship with Mainland Chinese immigrants significantly predicted tolerance, $\beta = .20$, $p = .010$, after controlling for other

Table 15.7. *Hierarchical regression models for friendship and other variables predicting perceived discrimination and tolerance in Mainland Chinese immigrant sample and Hong Kong Chinese resident sample, respectively.*

| Variables | Mainland Chinese immigrants | | Hong Kong Chinese residents | |
| | Perceived discrimination | | Tolerance | |
	Block 1 β	Block 2 β	Block 1 β	Block 2 β
Age	.09	.05	−.16	−.15
Gender (1 = male, 2 = female)	.03	.05	−.01	−.01
Education	−.18*	−.13	−.13	−.09
Cantonese ability	−.35***	−.27***		
Mandarin ability			.22**	.18*
Travel in Hong Kong		−.21**		
Travel in Mainland China				−.09
Friendship (Hong Kong Chinese residents)		−.21**		
Friendship (Mainland Chinese)				.20**
R^2	.15	.24	.06	.10
ΔR^2	.15	.09	.06	.04
Fchange	7.61***	10.41***	2.82*	3.56*

*p <.05, **p <.01, ***p <.001.

predictors, and the whole model explained 10 per cent of the total variance in tolerance, $F(6, 174) = 3.12, p = .006$.

Integration Hypothesis

Mainland Chinese immigrant sample.
Correlation results showed that integration strategy was positively associated with psychological adaptation, $r = .44, p <.001$, and sociocultural adaptation, $r = .23, p = .001$, providing initial support for Hypothesis 3a. Hierarchical multiple regression was conducted to predict psychological adaptation. To control for the possible confounding effects of age, gender, education level, and Cantonese ability, they were entered in the first block. The second block contained strategies of separation, marginalization, and assimilation, as well as our variable of interest, integration. As shown in Table 15.8, integration strategy significantly predicted psychological adaptation, $\beta = .39, p <.001$, after controlling for other

Table 15.8. *Hierarchical regression models for integration and other variables predicting psychological and sociocultural adaptation in Mainland Chinese immigrant sample and psychological adaptation in Hong Kong Chinese resident sample.*

	Mainland Chinese immigrants				Hong Kong Chinese residents	
	Psychological adaptation		Sociocultural adaptation		Psychological adaptation	
Variables	Block 1 β	Block 2 β	Block 1 β	Block 2 β	Block 1 β	Block 2 β
Age	.05	.04	−.04	−.05	.00	.04
Gender (1 = male, 2 = female)	.11	.03	.07	.03	−.03	−.05
Education	.26**	.21*	.10	.07	.12	.08
Cantonese ability	.09	.08	.17*	.17*		
Mandarin ability					−.02	−.03
Integration		.39***		.24**		.17*
Separation		−.16*		.09		−.14
Marginalization		−.03		−.19*		−.06
Assimilation		.09		.05		.00
R^2	.06	.26	.04	.12	.01	.08
ΔR^2	.06	.20	.04	.08	.01	.09
Fchange	2.67*	11.75***	1.96	3.83**	0.63	3.58**

*p < .05, **p < .01, ***p < .001.

variables. The regression model explained 26 per cent of the total variance in psychological adaptation, $F(8, 172) = 7.54$, $p < .001$. In a regression model with identical predictors, sociocultural adaptation was significantly predicted by integration strategy, $\beta = .24$, $p = .001$. The model as a whole explained 12 per cent of the total variance in sociocultural adaptation, $F(8, 172) = 2.96$, $p = .004$. All results consistently supported Hypothesis 3a.

Hong Kong Chinese resident sample.
The integration expectation was positively correlated with psychological adaptation, $r = .23$, $p = .002$. To further test Hypothesis 3b, in a regression model, integration expectation significantly predicted psychological adaptation, $\beta = .17$, $p = .033$, after controlling for age, gender, education level, Mandarin ability and expectations of separation, marginalization and assimilation (see Table 15.8). The overall model explained 8 per cent of the total variance in psychological adaptation, $F(8, 172) = 2.12$, $p = .036$.

6   Discussion

By and large, the three MIRIPS hypotheses were supported in the context of Hong Kong, indicating the validity of these hypotheses in an intra-country migration context.

The multiculturalism hypothesis was generally supported in both dominant and immigrant groups. For the Hong Kong Chinese resident group, cultural security positively predicted both multicultural ideology and tolerance, economic security negatively predicted perceived number of current population, personal security positively predicted perceived consequences of immigration and overall security negatively predicted perceived number of current population while it positively predicted perceived consequences of immigration. For the Mainland Chinese immigrant group, cultural and overall security positively predicted both multicultural ideology and tolerance, and personal security positively predicted multicultural ideology.

However, one unanticipated finding for the multiculturalism hypothesis is that economic security negatively predicted tolerance among Mainland Chinese immigrants. A possible explanation is that along with the rapid economic development in China, some affluent Mainland Chinese migrated to Hong Kong not for economic improvement, but for other reasons, such as better education for their children, or a more metropolitan lifestyle. These rich Mainland Chinese immigrants are the beneficiaries of the political and economic systems of Mainland China, in which social equality, ethnic tolerance and social egalitarianism are less emphasized. Therefore, the more economically secure the Mainland Chinese immigrants feel, the less tolerant they become. On the other hand, those hard-up Mainland Chinese immigrants are more likely to embrace tolerance, as they may see social equality, ethnic tolerance and social egalitarianism as important factors for the improvement of their economic status in the new context.

The contact hypothesis was consistently supported in the Hong Kong Chinese resident group, in which friendship with Mainlanders positively predicted tolerance. The hypothesis was fully supported in the Mainland Chinese immigrant group, in which both travelling around Hong Kong and friendship with Hong Kong people negatively predicted perceived discrimination.

The integration hypothesis was fully supported in both dominant and immigrant groups. For the Hong Kong Chinese resident group, integration expectation positively predicted psychological adaptation. For the Mainland Chinese immigrant group, integration strategy positively predicted both psychological and sociocultural adaptations, separation strategy negatively predicted psychological adaptation and marginalization negatively predicted sociocultural adaptation.

According to Berry and colleagues (1977), there are three different meanings of multiculturalism: demographic fact, multicultural policy and multicultural ideology. Demographically, Hong Kong has a multicultural population composition (Census and Statistics Department, 2012). On the policy level, the Hong Kong government has been actively advocating multiculturalism by providing support services for the Mainland Chinese new arrivals (Home Affairs Department, 2015), and the legislation of Race Discrimination Ordinance (Equal Opportunities Commission, 2016).

However, the government's effort in promoting Mainland culture in the community has not been successful in gaining support from the general public. For example, the plan to implement the "Moral and National Education Subject" in school had to be withdrawn due to the strong opposition from the public (Information Services Department, 2012). Moreover, the proposal for the introduction of simplified Chinese characters to students has also received strong objection from intellectuals, educators and parents (Yau, 2016). Previous research showed that the support of the continuity of a certain group may threaten the majority position of local people (Berry, 2013b). Therefore, the Hong Kong government's active promotion of Mainland culture may backfire, as it may be perceived as a cultural threat to Hong Kong Chinese residents. As the findings of the present study reveal, when

Hong Kong Chinese residents' cultural security is under threat, their endorsement of multicultural ideology and tolerance decrease.

Due to the rapid economic development of Mainland China for the past two decades, the economic gap between Hong Kong and Mainland has narrowed. Many believe that Hong Kong is gradually losing its competitive edge to other Mainland cities. The loss in economic security may intensify Hong Kong Chinese residents' perceived competition from Mainland Chinese immigrants. As shown in our findings, when Hong Kong Chinese residents' economic security is under threat, their perceived number of current immigrant population increases. The findings are consistent with previous research on threat and crowdedness, that when people's sense of self is being threatened, their perception of crowdedness increases (Paulus, 1988). At first glance, it seems to be just a matter of fact that the influx of immigrants would inevitably increase the population density. However, density only refers to an objective description of physical condition, while crowdedness is a subjective experience of the density-related situation so that much depends on how people perceive it (Stokols, 1972). Therefore, economic security is an important factor that influences Hong Kong Chinese residents' perception of current population, which in turn affects their attitudes towards immigration.

In terms of personal safety, Hong Kong ranked first in safety and security in the world (Legatum Institute, 2015). As our findings reveal, personal safety is crucial to perceived consequences of immigration. Therefore, maintaining Hong Kong as a safe and secure city is essential for Hong Kong Chinese residents to have a more positive view of the consequences of immigrants. Furthermore, because overall security predicts Hong Kong Chinese residents' positive attitudes towards immigration, government should address the various security needs of Hong Kong Chinese residents when immigration policy is implemented.

For Mainland Chinese immigrants, our results generally converged to show cultural, personal and overall security as crucial to mutual acceptance, except for the interesting finding that economic security negatively predicted tolerance. Recently, there is a trend for wealthy Mainland Chinese to migrate overseas, with the United States, Canada and Australia as the top three destinations (Hurun Report, 2014). However, as our findings imply, the more economically secure the Mainland Chinese immigrants are, the less tolerant they become; this is an attitude in striking contrast with their destined immigration countries in which intercultural mutual acceptance is embraced (Banting & Kymlicka, 2006). In view of the growing number of wealthy Mainland Chinese immigrants, the impact of mismatched intercultural attitudes on the receiving countries should not be overlooked. Nevertheless, as our find-ings are only drawn from the Mainland–Hong Kong intra-country migra-tion context, research in other inter-country migration contexts is needed before any conclusion can be made.

Findings from our study converged to support the integration strategy and expectation as the most adaptive acculturation attitude among Mainland Chinese immigrants and Hong Kong Chinese residents, respectively; this supports the validity of the integration hypothesis in the Mainland–Hong Kong intra-country migration context. Moreover, con-tact theory is supported among both groups, indicating that mutual acceptance can be enhanced through equal, voluntary and supported intercultural contacts, despite the sociocultural discrepancies between them.

The special political situation of Hong Kong has made it a unique milieu for the examination of acculturation and intercultural relations in an intra-country migration context. Despite the geographic proximity, shared ethnicity and similar linguistic systems between the Mainland and Hong Kong, our findings show that the three MIRIPS hypotheses are generally supported in this intra-country migration context. Our findings are consistent with previous research that both intra-country and inter-country migrants face similar acculturation challenges and achieve optimal acculturation outcomes with integration strategy (Gui, Berry & Zheng, 2012). Among most other research that focuses on inter-country migration, our findings have provided unique evidence for the MIRIPS hypotheses. However, as the study of acculturation and intercultural relations in intra-country migration contexts is relatively scarce, more research in this new direction is needed. For example, the MIRIPS hypotheses can be tested in Macau, a former Portuguese overseas terri-tory, which became another special administrative region of China since 1999. On the other hand, while a large number of Mainland Chinese have migrated to Hong Kong, there are also a number of Hong Kong people who reside on the Mainland. The study of acculturation and intercultural relations of these Hong Kong people may provide different perspectives for our understanding of intercultural relations in an intra-country migra-tion context.

Hong Kong, with over 7.24 million people crammed in a tiny city of $1,104 \text{ km}^2$, has been listed one of the most densely populated cities in the world (Census and Statistics Department, 2015b). To prepare for the large influx of Mainland Chinese immigrants in the near future, accul-turation and intercultural relations are definitely a pressing issue. From a wider perspective, with increased mobility of people around the world and ever-changing contexts of migration, acculturation and intercultural relations will also continue to be an important topic that needs constant examination.

References

Allport, G. W. (1954). *The Nature of Prejudice.* Reading, MA: Addison-Wesley.

Banting, K., & Kymlicka, W. (2006–2012). *The multiculturalism policy index.* Retrieved from www.queensu.ca/mcp/.

Berry, J. W. (2006). Mutual attitudes among immigrants and ethno-cultural groups in Canada. *International Journal of Intercultural Relations,* 30, 719–734.

Berry, J. W. (2013a). Mutual intercultural relations in plural societies (MIRIPS). Retrieved from www.victoria.ac.nz/cacr/research/mirips/MIRIPSprojectdescri ption-August-2013.pdf.

Berry, J. W. (2013b). Research on multiculturalism in Canada. *International Journal of Intercultural Relations,* 37, 663–675.

Berry, J. W., Kalin, R., & Taylor, D. M. (1977). *Multiculturalism and ethnic attitudes in Canada.* Ottawa: Ministry of Supply and Services.

Census and Statistics Department. (2011). *2011 population census.* Retrieved from www.census2011.gov.hk/en/main-table.html.

Census and Statistics Department. (2012). *Thematic report: Ethnic minorities.* Retrieved from www.statistics.gov.hk/pub/B11200622012XXXXB0100.pdf.

Census and Statistics Department. (2015a). *Hong Kong annual digest of statistics 2015.* Retrieved from www.statistics.gov.hk/pub/B10100032015AN15B0100.pdf.

Census and Statistics Department. (2015b). *Hong Kong: The facts.* Retrieved from www.gov.hk/en/about/abouthk/factsheets/docs/population.pdf.

Census and Statistics Department. (2016). *Population estimates.* Retrieved from www .censtatd.gov.hk/hkstat/sub/sp150.jsp?tableID=002&ID=0&productType=8.

Chen, S. X., Benet-Martínez, V., & Bond, M. H. (2008). Bicultural identity, bilingualism, and psychological adjustment in multicultural societies: Immigration-based and globalization-based acculturation. *Journal of Personality,* 76, 803–838.

Chen, S. X., Lam, B. C. P., Hui, B. P. H., Ng, J. C. K., Mak, W. W. S., Guan, Y., Buchtel, E. E., Tang, W., & Lau, V. C. Y. (2016). Conceptualizing psychological processes in response to globalization: Components, antecedents, and consequences of global orientation. *Journal of Personality and Social Psychology,* 11, 302–331.

Chief Secretary for Administration's Office. (2015). *Population policy: Strategies and initiatives.* Retrieved from www.hkpopulation.gov.hk/public_engagement/ pdf/PPbooklet2015_ENG.pdf.

Chiu, S. W., Choi, S. Y., & Ting, K. F. (2005). Getting ahead in the capitalist paradise: Migration from China and socioeconomic attainment in colonial Hong Kong. *International Migration Review,* 39, 203–227.

Equal Opportunities Commission. (2016). *Race Discrimination.* Retrieved from www.eoc.org.hk/eoc/graphicsfolder/showcontent.aspx?content=race%20dis crimination%20ordinance%20and%20i.

GovHK. (2016). *Nationality Law of the People's Republic of China.* Retrieved from www.gov.hk/en/residents/immigration/chinese/law.htm.

Gui, Y., Berry, J. W., & Zheng, Y. (2012). Migrant worker acculturation in China. *International Journal of Intercultural Relations*, 36, 598–610.

Home Affairs Department. (2013). *Home Affairs Department and Immigration Department statistics on new arrivals from the Mainland*. Retrieved from www .had.gov.hk/file manager/tc/documents/public services/services for new arrivals from the mainland/report 2013q1.pdf.

Home Affairs Department. (2015). *Support services for new arrivals from the Mainland and ethnic minorities*. Retrieved from www.had.gov.hk/en/public_ser vices/services_for_new_arrivals_from_the_mainland/index.htm.

Home Affair Department and Immigration Department. (2016). *Statistics on new arrivals from the Mainland (fourth quarter of 2015)*. Retrieved from www .had.gov.hk/file_manager/tc/documents/public_services/services_for_new_arri vals_from_the_mainland/report_2015q4.pdf.

Hui, B. P. H., Chen, S. X., Leung, C. M., & Berry, J. (2015). Facilitating adaptation and intercultural contact: The role of bicultural integration and multicultural ideology in dominant and non-dominant groups. *International Journal of Intercultural Relations*, 45, 70–84.

Hurun Report. (2014). 2014 Immigrant investor white paper. Retrieved from ht tp://up.hurun.net/Hufiles/201504/20150427162545633.pdf.

Immigration Department. (2016). *Introduction of admission schemes for talent, professionals and entrepreneurs*. Retrieved from www.immd.gov.hk/eng/ useful_information/admission-schemes-talents-professionals-entrepreneurs .html.

Information Services Department. (2012). *Policy change set for immediate imple-mentation*. Retrieved from http://archive.news.gov.hk/en/categories/school_ work/html/2012/09/20120910_153910.shtml.

Legatum Institute. (2015). *The Legatum prosperity index: 2015*. Retrieved from h ttps://lif.blob.core.windows.net/lif/docs/default-source/publications/2015-legatum-prosperity-index-pdf.pdf?sfvrsn=2.

Paulus, P. (1988). *Prison Crowding: A Psychological Perspective*. New York, NY: Springer-Verlag.

Stokols, D. (1972). On the distinction between density and crowding: Some implications for future research. *Psychological Review*, 79, 275–277.

Yau, C. (2016, March 3). Character assassination? Hong Kong's furore over simplified Chinese. *South China Morning Post*. Retrieved from www.scmp .com/news/hong-kong/education-community/article/1920406/character-assassination-hong-kongs-furore-over.

16   Intercultural Relations in Australia

Justine Dandy
Edith Cowan University, Australia

Kevin Dunn
Western Sydney University, Australia

Jolanda Jetten
University of Queensland, Australia

Yin Paradies
Deakin University, Australia

Lena Robinson
Central Queensland University, Australia

Tahereh Ziaian
University of South Australia, Australia

1   Introduction

Australia was culturally diverse prior to European settlement. The original inhabitants, Indigenous Australians, comprised diverse cultures and language groups with separate territories, laws and systems (Dudgeon, Wright, Paradies, Garvey & Walker, 2014). Colonisation and subsequent immigration increased this diversity, to the point where Australia is now moderately high on the ethnic diversity index. It is near the top of the migrant integration index, and at the top of the multiculturalism policy index.

2   Context of Intercultural Relations in Australia

At the time of British colonisation it is estimated that there were over 500 Aboriginal clan groups, with more than 250 distinct language groups, who had inhabited the continent for at least 40,000 years (Dudgeon et al.,

2014). Presently, approximately 2.5 per cent of the Australian population identify as Indigenous (Aboriginal and/or Torres Strait Islander). Australia was colonised by the British in 1788; currently Australians with British ancestry are the largest ethnocultural group. Nonetheless, Australia is a settler society with a significant proportion of the population born in other parts of the world.

2.1   Immigration

Australian immigration policy has tended to promote population and/or economic growth, commencing with significant migration from Asia in the mid-nineteenth century, and expanding to include settlers from Southern Europe, in particular, after the Second World War. This has resulted in a nation in which 28 per cent of residents was born overseas (Australian Bureau of Statistics [ABS], 2016), an additional 20 per cent has at least one parent who was born overseas and over 200 world languages are spoken (in addition to Indigenous languages). According to the 2011 Census, the top five countries of origin for those born overseas were the United Kingdom, New Zealand, China, India and Italy. In addition, since Federation in 1901 at least 750,000 refugees have settled in Australia (Refugee Council of Australia [RCOA], 2012) with persons from Indochina, particularly Vietnam, settling in large numbers from the 1970s onwards. In 2014–2015, the main countries of origin for persons granted residency under the Humanitarian Programme (refugees) were, in order: Iraq, Syria, Burma, Afghanistan and the Democratic Republic of the Congo.

2.2   Policy

In the first century after British colonisation, relations with Indigenous Australians were characterised by invasion, land appropriation, massacres, displacement, neglect, disease transmission and forced labour. From the early twentieth century, attempts were made to protect surviving Indigenous peoples (reduced from 300,000 to only 80,000) through segregation on government reserves and missions run by diverse religious denominations. A policy of assimilation was adopted in the mid-twentieth century, wherein Indigenous people of 'mixed-descent' were expected to adopt White Australian culture at the expense of their own. From the 1970s, growing Indigenous activism has led to the self-determination era, which peaked during the early 21st century but still persists into the present. This era is one in which Indigenous people have considerable control over their involvement and integration into Australian society, with the expectation that this will lead to social and health outcomes that steadily improve to match those of other Australians over time.

Notwithstanding the Asian migration during the Australian 'gold rush' of the mid to late nineteenth century, early Australian immigration policy was designed to limit the racial and ethnic backgrounds of new settlers to persons of white, preferably British, ancestry (The Immigration Restriction Act, 1901; Jupp, 2002). However, even in the early days of Federation, there was concern about the long-term viability of a nation comprising "a small isolated people, very far from their original homeland" (Jupp, 2002, p.10). Thus, after World War 2 a more substantial – but still highly controlled – immigration program was introduced. Since the 1970s, this has been increasingly open to immigrants from diverse linguistic, ethnic and racial backgrounds, after the government announced that immigration decisions would not be racially or religiously discriminatory (Jupp, 2002).

In 1978, the government adopted a policy of multiculturalism in order to address issues related to the increasing diversity of the Australian population through immigration. Prior to this, the approach had been one of assimilation, which was seen to have detrimental effects on immigrants' sense of belonging and integration into the broader community and resulted in many returning home. Assimilation was not working, and multiculturalism (cultural pluralism), in which cultural diversity was encouraged and immigrants were entitled to maintain language and culture, was seen as more socially just (Collins, 2003; Soutphommasane, 2012). The policy of multiculturalism remains in place today, albeit with some revisions in which the responsibilities of Australian citizens are emphasised.

In recent years there has been debate about the success of multiculturalism, with claims that some minority groups are not 'fitting in', and we have witnessed a rise in conservative Australian nationalism, particularly during the years of the Howard Coalition government (Dandy, 2010; Soutphommasane, 2012). It is also evident that many Australians experience racism, particularly those who are: from more visible minority groups (Dunn, Forrest, Pe-Pua, Hynes & Maeder-Han, 2009); Muslim (Dunn, Klocker & Salabay, 2007; Human Rights and Equal Opportunity Commission [HREOC], 2004; Markus, 2016); Aboriginal or Torres Strait Islander Australian (Markus, 2016; Paradies, 2016); South Sudanese (Markus, 2016); or from recently arrived immigrant groups (Mansouri, Jenkins, Morgan & Tauk, 2009). Nonetheless, there is little evidence to suggest that Australian multiculturalism has 'failed'. In particular, (1) there is a very high (68%) uptake of citizenship among migrants and refugees, 20 percent higher than the OECD average (DIAC, 2011); (2) on indicators of well-being, social conflict and tolerance Australia compares very favourably with other nations (OECD, 2016; Wilkinson & Pickett, 2010); (3) Australians report high levels of life satisfaction, sense of belonging and pride in Australia and the Australian way of life[1] (Markus, 2015; 2016).

2.3   *Previous Australian Research*

There is a paucity of Australian research that has addressed the MIRIPS hypotheses, and there has been no national study examining intercultural relations using the mutual acculturation framework. Nonetheless, past research has consistently demonstrated a link between perceptions of security and attitudes to outgroups[2] among Australians, which relates to the multiculturalism/security hypothesis. For example, in previous research for the International Study of Attitudes to Immigration and Settlement (Berry, 2006), which was the precursor to MIRIPS, we found that security was positively correlated with endorsement of multicultural ideology, social equality beliefs and the perceived consequences of immigration and diversity (Dandy & Pe-Pua, 2010). In addition, security was negatively correlated with immigration prohibition and level: respondents who were more secure were less likely to agree that certain groups should be prohibited from immigrating to Australia and that the current level of immigration is too high. In sum, respondents who reported feeling more personally, economically and culturally secure had more favourable attitudes towards immigration and diversity, and were more tolerant. These relationships were the same within each of the dominant (majority) and non-dominant (minority) subgroups in the sample. However, internal consistency of scores on our measure of security was relatively low ($\alpha = 0.46$), and more research was needed to explore the proposed sub-components of security and their relationships with each other, and with attitudes, in the Australian context.

As noted in Chapter 1, threat has been conceptualised as the opposite to security in integrated threat theory (Stephan & Stephan, 2000; Stephan, Renfro, Esses, Stephan & Martin, 2005). A number of different outgroups have been the focus of Australian intercultural research,

---

[1] Levels of life satisfaction and identification with Australia appear to be lower among recently arrived migrants (2001–2015) than among the Australian-born, although still moderate to high.
[2] Outgroups can be defined as groups which are ethnoculturally and/or religiously distinct from the respondent. When majority members' attitudes are assessed, these typically include immigrants, and ethnic and religious minorities.

including refugees (Schweitzer, Perkoulidis, Krome, Ludlow & Ryan, 2005), asylum seekers (McKay, Thomas & Kneebone, 2012), Muslims (White, Duck & Newcombe, 2012) and international students (Mak, Brown & Wadey, 2013). In those studies in which the effects of different types of threat have been compared, realistic threat (concerns about employment, and economic and political power) is often shown to be the strongest individual predictor of attitudes (e.g., Schweitzer, Perkoulidis, Krome, Ludlow & Ryan, 2005). Australians who feel that their access to jobs, education and other resources are threatened, are concerned about their personal financial situation (Bilodeau & Fadol, 2011), or feel that they are less well-off than others (Jetten, Mols & Postmes, 2015) are more likely to hold negative attitudes towards members of other ethnocultural or religious groups.

With respect to the contact hypothesis, several Australian studies have examined the role of contact in intergroup relations. Specifically, researchers have investigated the impact of intercultural contact on knowledge, attitudes/prejudice and stereotypes. Nesdale and Todd (1998, 2000) examined contact between international and local students in residence halls at an Australian university. In their first study, in which they examined contact in residence halls with different ratios of international-local students, they found that intercultural contact was highest for groups in a numerical minority and that contact generalised (favourably) to on-campus behaviour, enhanced intercultural knowledge and acceptance of outgroups. Their second study involved an intervention, a residential-hall program designed to enhance intercultural contact (Nesdale & Todd, 2000). The program had significant effects on cultural stereotypes, cultural knowledge and cultural openness but primarily for Australian students. The authors concluded that this was due, at least in part, to Australian students coming from a lower starting point on these dimensions; most international students approach their study-abroad experience with more knowledge about the host culture and greater openness and interest in intercultural interaction than their 'local' counterparts.

More recently, Ata, Bastian and Lusher (2009) and Bastian, Lusher and Ata (2012) examined contact (specifically friendship) between Muslim and non-Muslim Australians. The results of their studies, conducted with secondary school students, provide general support for the contact hypothesis: non-Muslim students who had a close Muslim friend were lower in perceived social distance to Muslims, sought increased contact with other Muslims and evaluated Muslims, in general, more positively than did those without a Muslim friend. Similarly, in a study of attitudes to international students among domestic (majority Australian) students, Mak et al. (2013) found that more contact quantity and quality predicted positive attitudes, with quality being the stronger predictor. The positive effects of contact quality on intercultural attitudes were further demonstrated in a study of international students' attitudes towards local students (Tawagi & Mak, 2015). Finally, one Australian study has extended the contact hypothesis to explore the effects of contact valence on attitudes. With a combined sample of nearly 1500 Australians (students and community members) across multiple datasets, Barlow et al. (2012) found not only that contact was related to prejudice towards Black Australians, Muslim Australians and asylum seekers, but also that negative contact was a more powerful predictor of racist attitudes than was positive contact a predictor of favourable attitudes.

There is even less Australian research on the relationship between acculturation strategy and psychological and/or sociocultural well-being (the integration hypothesis). A handful of studies have shown that immigrants who choose integration have better outcomes in terms of adaptation (Sam, Vedder, Ward & Horenczyk, 2006) and well-being (e.g., Zheng, Sang & Wang, 2004). However, past findings have been mixed and there is a lack of recent data. Moreover, much of the past research has focused on non-dominant – specifically immigrant – groups and neglected the perspectives of majority Australians and Indigenous Australians. Early work by Berry (1970) found an association between marginalisation and psychosomatic stress among Indigenous Australians, but this study was conducted more than 40 years ago.

3   Method

We do not utilise a single dataset that addresses the MIRIPS hypotheses but integrate the findings from our existing work, as they relate to the key themes underlying the hypotheses. Our findings are based on data derived from national and city-based attitude surveys, as well as qualitative data from in-depth interviews with Australians from migrant (India and China) and refugee backgrounds.

A summary of our samples is provided in Table 16.1.

Life in Australia survey: This study was part of a larger survey examining participants' perceptions of their life in Australia and their views of Australian society more generally (Jetten, Mols, Spears & Postmes, 2012)

A professional research company (Taverner Research based in Sydney) collected the data. Participants were sampled from the company's

Table 16.1. *Summary of sample characteristics of our datasets.*

Dataset name	Year	Method of data collection	Total sample	Gender distribution (% men;% women)	Mean age (SD)	Ethno-cultural composition
Life in Australia survey	2014	Online survey	621	47.5; 52.5	40.90 (12.78)	76.9% White Caucasian; 15.8% Asian; 1.4% Middle Eastern; 8% Aboriginal and/ or Torres Strait Islander; 3.9% 'other'
Challenging Racism project	2001–2008	Telephone survey	12512	42; 58	41.35 (21.74)	76.5% born in Australia; 23.5% born overseas; 0.8% Aboriginal and/or Torres Strait Islander; 3.9% 'other'
Ordinariness of Australian Muslims	2011 & 2013	Face-to-face & telephone survey	585	44; 56	32.54 (12.58)	Sydney residents who identified as Muslim
MIRIPS Australia pilot	2015–2016	In-depth interviews	39	38; 62	44.47 (14.46)	20 migrants from Chinese and Indian backgrounds; 19 refugees;
ICSEY Project (Australian data)	2003	Paper surveys in schools	456	39:61	15.22 (1.60)	Immigrant youth from Chinese, Filippino and Vietnamese backgrounds

research panel, which covered all Australian states and territories. Security is here operationalized as financial personal security. Three items were included to measure this construct: *Relative to others in your country, how would you classify your own wealth?* (ranging from 1 = very poor to 7 = very wealthy), *Are you unhappy or happy with your current wealth?* (ranging from 1 = very unhappy to 7 = very happy) and *How would you classify your own wealth?* (ranging from 1 = very poor to 7 = very wealthy). The alpha for these three items was .89.

Negative Attitudes towards Minorities was measured in two ways. First, we included a *general opposition to immigration* measure including 6 items assessing both realistic threat perceptions (e.g., *Immigrants take resources and employment opportunities away from Australians*) and symbolic threat perceptions (e.g., *The cultural practises of immigrants threaten the Australian way of life*). Responses were recorded on 7-point scales ranging from 1 = *Strongly disagree* to 7 = *Strongly agree*. Participants did not differentiate between realistic and symbolic threat, and we combined the items to form one scale, α = .95.

Negative attitudes were also assessed in relation to specific immigrant groups to Australia. In particular, participants were asked for 12 immigrant groups —British, Greek, Chinese, New Zealanders, Indians, Japanese, Afghanis, Vietnamese, Refugees arriving by boat, Ex-Yugoslavians (Croats, Serbs, Bosnians), Africans (e.g., Sudanese, Kenyans, Somalis), and Middle Easterners (e.g., Iraqis, Iranians) – *To what extent do you agree that Australian government should reduce immigration quotas for the following groups of prospective immigrants?* (responses range from 1 = strong reduction to 7 = strong increase).

The *Challenging Racism Project* (2011) National Dataset contains 43 survey items, including questions assessing racial attitudes, social distance items (level of concern if a close friend or family member married a person of specific background), experiences of racism, frequency of interethnic mixing, demographic questions and geographical identifiers. Pro-diversity attitudes were measured with the following item: *It is a good thing for a society to be made up of people from different cultures*; and assimilationist attitudes were assessed using: *Australia is weakened by people of different ethnic origins sticking to their old ways*. These items are similar to items in the Multicultural Ideology Scale used in MIRIPS. Responses were made using a 5-point Likert response format of: strongly disagree; disagree; neither disagree nor agree; agree; and strongly agree. The 12,512 interviews were conducted via telephone by the Social Research Centre and the Hunter Valley Research Foundation's call centre. Queensland and NSW data were collected in 2001, Victoria in 2006, South Australia and Australian Capital

Territory in 2007 and Northern Territory, Tasmania and Western Australia in 2008.

The *Ordinariness of Australian Muslims* survey was a community sample from Sydney Muslims in 2011 and 2013 (Dunn, Atie, Mapedzahama, Ozalp & Aydogan, 2015). The survey incorporated a range of well-established survey questions utilised in Australia for over two decades to test personal attitudes and experiences. The surveys also incorporated novel questions aimed at generating a broader picture of the everyday life of Australian Muslims, testing for civic participation, cross-cultural contact and participation in the labour force.

The *MIRIPS Pilot study* with Australians from immigrant and refugee backgrounds was conducted to pilot revisions of the MIRIPS instrument for use in a national survey. There were 39 participants (15 male and 24 female) who were recruited through personal networks and by third parties (e.g., multicultural and ethnic organisations, local council). Twenty participants had migrated to Australia under the Skilled and Family Reunion Programme (10 from Indian and 10 from Chinese backgrounds), and 19 participants had settled in Australia as part of the Humanitarian Programme (refugees). The latter came from a number of countries of origin, including Afghanistan, Bhutan, Nepal, Sri Lanka, Egypt, Poland and Sudan. All participants were from a CaLD (Culturally and Linguistically Diverse) background and had been living in Australia for a minimum of two years (range = 2 to 45 years, M = 11.33 years, SD = 9. 04). Participants were residents of Adelaide (n=15), Canberra (n=8) and Perth (n=16).

The International Comparative Study of Ethnocultural Youth (ICSEY) project[3] (Berry, Phinney, Sam & Vedder, 2006) employed samples from three immigrant communities in Australia (Chinese, Filipino and Vietnamese; N= 456) and members of the larger society (N=155). Acculturation profiles were created in the project as a whole by incorporating the four acculturation attitudes (towards integration, assimilation, separation and marginalisation) and the two dimensions ('ethnic' and 'national') on three variables (identities, language and friends). Two measures of adaptation were used in the study. Psychological adaptation included the variables of self-esteem, life satisfaction and (lower) psychological problems. Sociocultural adaptation included school adjustment and (lower) behaviour problems.

---

[3] ICSEY stands for The International Comparative Study of Ethnocultural Youth and is the acronym for a research project on young immigrants in a number of societies of settlement. The Australian data were collected by Rogelia Pe-Pua, Rosanna Rooney and David Sang, and key findings are summarized here with permission.

4   Results

4.1   *Multiculturalism Hypothesis*

Our data, obtained through the *Life in Australia Survey*, provide support for the multiculturalism hypothesis. See Table 16.2 for Means, Standard Deviations and correlations. In particular, these findings revealed that personal financial security was negatively related to general opposition to immigration, $r = -.12$, $p = .003$. There was considerable variation, however, in the strength of the correlations between personal financial security and negative attitudes as measured by endorsing a reduction of immigrant quotas. In particular, correlations between personal financial security and endorsing a reduction of immigrant quotas were more strongly negative for non-Western immigrants (e.g., Vietnamese, $r = .26$, $p < .001$; refugees

Table 16.2. *Means, standard deviations and correlation coefficients for security and immigration attitudes from the Life in Australia survey.*

Negative attitudes	*M* and *SD*	Correlation with financial personal security
	1 = Strongly disagree to 7 = Strongly agree	
General opposition to immigration	4.16 (1.74)	$r = -.12$, $p = .003$
	Mean endorsement that immigration quotas should be "strongly reduced" (1) to "strongly increased" (7)	
British	4.20 (1.25)	$r = .14$, $p < .001$
New Zealanders	4.02 (1.31)	$r = .17$, $p < .001$
Greek	3.97 (1.15)	$r = .16$, $p < .001$
Japanese	3.82 (1.47)	$r = .22$, $p < .001$
Vietnamese	3.56 (1.49)	$r = .26$, $p < .001$
Ex-Yugoslavians (Croats, Serbs, Bosnians)	3.54 (1.48)	$r = .27$, $p < .001$
Chinese	3.49 (1.52)	$r = .22$, $p < .001$
Africans (e.g., Sudanese, Kenyans, Somalis)	3.33 (1.65)	$r = .26$, $p < .001$
Afghanis	3.24 (1.64)	$r = .27$, $p < .001$
Indians	3.22 (1.55)	$r = .28$, $p < .001$
Middle Easterners (e.g., Iraqis, Iranians)	3.11 (1.74)	$r = .28$, $p < .001$
Refugees arriving by boat	3.10 (1.96)	$r = .26$, $p < .001$

arriving by boat, $r = .21$, $p < .001$; ex-Yugoslavians, $r = .22$, $p < .001$; Africans, $r = .26$, $p < .001$; Middle Easterners, $r = .28$, $p < .001$), than they were for Western or Caucasian immigrants (e.g., British, $r = .14$, $p < .001$; New Zealanders, $r = .17$, $p < .001$). General endorsement that the quota should be reduced was also higher for non-Western than for Western immigrant groups. Mean endorsement that immigration quotas should be reduced or increased is listed from the highest to the lowest endorsement that quotas should be increased.

Findings from the *Challenging Racism Project* national dataset also shed light on the relationship between multiculturalism (security) and attitudes towards others in Australia. Table 16.3 shows the relationship between the experience of racism (racist name calling), which we use to operationalise the concept of a sense of threat, and attitudes about diversity (as an indicator of respect for others and discriminatory attitudes). The data show that the experience of racism is associated with a less strong endorsement of the virtue of cultural diversity. Among those who had "hardly ever or never" experienced racist name calling, 88 percent saw cultural diversity as a positive for society, whereas among those who had experienced racist name calling, this figure dropped to almost 80 per cent (significantly different at $p < .0001$). Support for assimilationist thinking was stronger among those who had often experienced racist name calling, whereas the proportion of pro- and anti-assimilationist opinion was similar for those who had hardly ever or never experienced such racism. Cultural threat, as indicated by the experience of racism, was associated with a greater likelihood of a negative view about cultural diversity and unreconciled difference.

4.2   Contact Hypothesis

Drawing upon the national *Challenging Racism Project* (2011) dataset, we were able to examine the role of intercultural contact, by investigating the link with dispositions on diversity and intercultural acceptance (see Table 16.4). There is a clear positive association between pro-diversity attitudes and intercultural mixing, and a negative association between assimilationist thinking and mixing. For example, among those who often partake of intercultural mixing in social spheres, 90 per cent were positive about the virtues of cultural diversity. However, support for diversity was only at 80 per cent for those who hardly ever had such contact. Just over half of those without such intercultural contact held to the assimilationist view that Australia was weakened by unreconciled cultural difference, whereas only a third of those with high levels of intercultural mixing held to that view. The national dataset affirms that in Australia, intercultural

Table 16.3. *Attitudes towards diversity by experience of racism in the form of name calling or similar insult from the national Challenging Racism Project.*

		Called names or similarly insulted because of ethnicity								
		Often or very often		Sometimes		Hardly ever or never		Total		p
		N	%	N	%	N	%	N	%	
Pro-diversity	Agree	297	79.4	1040	86.2	9486	87.7	10823	87.3	.000
	Neither	24	6.4	88	7.3	652	6	764	6.2	
	Disagree	53	6.6	78	6.5	678	6.3	809	6.5	
	Total	374	100	1206	100	10816	87.3	12396	100	
Assimilationist	Agree	190	51.5	512	42.8	4423	41.4	5125	41.8	.001
	Neither	50	13.6	163	13.6	1660	15.5	1873	15.3	
	Disagree	129	35	520	43.5	4604	43.1	5253	42.9	
	Total	369	100	1195	100	10687	100	12251	100	

Note: p values refer to significant differences from chi-square analyses.

Table 16.4. *Attitudes towards diversity, by the level of intercultural mixing in social life from the national Challenging Racism Project*

		Level of intercultural mixing in social life								
		Often or very often		Sometimes		Hardly ever or never		Total		p
		N	%	N	%	N	%	N	%	
Pro-diversity	Agree	5537	90.4	3222	87.6	2037	79.8	10796	87.4	.000
	Neither	279	4.6	247	6.7	236	9.2	762	6.2	
	Disagree	310	5.1	210	5.7	280	11	800	6.5	
	Total	6126	100	3679	100	2553	100	12358	100	
Assimilationist	Agree	2166	35.8	1554	42.8	1393	54.8	5113	41.9	.000
	Neither	987	16.3	569	15.7	312	12.3	1868	15.3	
	Disagree	2892	47.8	1504	41.5	838	33	5234	42.8	
	Total	6045	100	3627	100	2543	100	12215	100	

Note: p values refer to significant differences from chi-square analyses.

contact (under the right conditions) is associated with more positive attitudes and intercultural acceptance.

We were also able to examine forms of civic engagement against levels of cultural mixing, using data from the *Ordinariness of Australian Muslims'* survey (Dunn et al., 2015; see Table 16.5). This particular set of cross tabulations assesses the relation between intercultural mixing in social life, which is one of the least compulsory spheres of mixing

Table 16.5. *Civic engagement, by the level of intercultural mixing in social life among Sydney Muslims, from the Ordinariness of Australian Muslims survey.*

		Often or very often		Sometimes		Hardly ever or never		Total		p
Civic engagement over last 12 months		N	%	N	%	N	%	N	%	
Voted in the last	Yes	267	70.1	104	69.8	31	67.4	402	69.8	.932
state election	No	114	29.9	45	30.2	15	32.6	174	30.2	
	Total	381	100	149	100	46	100	576	100	
Volunteered for	Yes	58	15.2	17	11.5	4	8.5	79	13.7	.302
a sporting	No	324	84.8	131	88.5	43	91.5	498	86.3	
association	Total	382	100	148	100	47	100	577	100	
Volunteered for	Yes	146	38.1	48	32.7	17	36.2	211	36.6	.504
a faith-based	No	237	61.9	99	67.3	30	63.8	366	63.4	
association	Total	383	100	147	100	47	100	577	100	
Involved in an	Yes	19	5	3	2	0	0	22	3.8	.102
Australian	No	364	95	146	98	47	100	557	96.2	
political party	Total	383	100	149	100	47	100	579	100	
Fundraised	Yes	201	52.6	68	45.9	15	31.9	284	49.2	.018
	No	181	47.4	80	54.1	32	68.1	293	50.8	
	Total	382	100	148	100	47	100	577	100	
Made a charitable	Yes	321	83.8	115	77.7	31	66	467	80.8	.007
donation	No	62	16.2	33	22.3	16	34	111	19.2	
	Total	383	100	148	100	47	100	578	100	
Involved in	Yes	111	29	35	23.5	13	27.7	159	27.5	.444
organising or	No	272	71	114	76.5	34	72.3	420	72.5	
signed a petition	Total	383	100	149	100	47	100	579	100	
Involved in an	Yes	41	10.7	7	4.7	2	4.3	50	8.6	.046
organised protest	No	342	89.3	142	95.3	45	95.7	529	91.4	
	Total	383	100	149	100	47	100	579	100	
Made a complaint	Yes	69	34	26	26	9	23.7	104	30.5	.228
about a product	No	134	66	74	74	29	76.3	237	69.5	
or service	Total	203	100	100	100	38	100	341	100	
Make an effort	Yes	119	59.2	51	52	13	34.2	183	54.3	.016
to buy Australian-	No	82	40.8	47	48	25	65.8	154	45.7	
made products*	Total	201	100	98	100	38	100	337	100	

* Not within a 12 month period, but generally.

(compared to the workplace or education; see Table 16.4). Those Muslims who had higher levels of intercultural mixing in social spheres had higher rates of involvement in party politics, political protests and prioritising Australia-made products, as well as fundraising. For example, prioritising the purchase of Australian-made products was more likely among those with higher intercultural mixing (59%) than those with some mixing (52%) and those with hardly any mixing (34%). Thus, for this sample, intercultural contact was positively related to civic engagement more broadly.

Our in-depth interviews with Australians from immigrant and refugee backgrounds (*MIRIPS Australia Pilot* study) also provide some insight into the relationship between intercultural contact and attitudes. The majority of interviewees expressed a strong desire for, and engaged in, intercultural mixing, although some noted a lack of genuine or deeper intercultural interaction with majority Australians (*"I don't have many Aussie friends just apart from work, we just hi, hello', that's about it"; "I still think the relationship is very much; one box is Aboriginal, one box is the dominant Australian culture, one box is migrants and the other box is refugees"*). They saw making friends outside of their ethnocultural group as a critical feature of integrating and developing a sense of belonging to the local and/or national community, as well as to combat the social isolation that many new migrants experience (*"I find it is very important because it can be very isolating and I also find that it depends on the individual, if you do not make the effort to go out and socialise, it's not going to come knocking at your door"*). The majority also expressed a strong belief in the role of contact for enhancing mutual understanding, tolerance and acceptance of others. When asked about the benefits of intercultural contact, one participant, a refugee from Sudan, said: *"Understanding, peace, you have a greater understanding of a different variety of things. And you can learn things from each other. You can learn so many different things"*.

It was evident that those participants who indicated they had a more diverse social network (these were the majority of the sample) were more content and settled in their new life in Australia, although this was also a function of the length of residency. In addition, and highlighting the bidirectional nature of the relationship between contact and attitudes, those participants who described themselves as being more culturally open and aware prior to settling in Australia were more likely to report friendships and interactions with members of other cultural groups. This was particularly common among migrants from India, who described intercultural mixing as a normal feature of daily life in big cities like Mumbai. Some interviewees also described positive interactions with Aboriginal and Torres Strait Islander Australians that had led to more positive attitudes towards these groups and a greater understanding of their current situation. In contrast, those interviewees who reported negative interactions tended to avoid future interactions (although this did not necessarily result in negative attitudes but something more akin to intergroup anxiety). However, most interviewees reported very few inter-actions with Aboriginal or Torres Strait Islander Australians.

4.3   Integration Hypothesis

Research on the integration hypothesis in Australia was carried out within the International Ethnocultural Youth Project (see Berry et al., 2006). Four acculturation profiles were found, using acculturation attitudes and three other variables: ethnic and national identities, language and friends. In the study as a whole, profile membership was highest for integration (36.4%) and lower for the other three profiles: assimilation 18.7 per cent; separation, 22.5 per cent, and marginalisation, 22.4 per cent. The Australian profiles varied from those found in the study as a whole. In the Australia immigrant sample, profile membership was: integration 51.1 per cent; assimilation, 24.9 per cent; separation 8.5 per cent; and marginalisation 15.6 per cent. That is, memberships in the integration and assimilation profiles were higher in Australia, and separation and marginalisation were lower than for the study as a whole. In general, scores of Australian immigrant youth on measures of psycho-logical and sociocultural adaptation did not differ in any important ways from the mean of all immigrants in the study.

With respect to the integration hypothesis, the differences across accul-turation profiles in the Australian immigrant sample showed that those in the integration profile had better psychological and sociocultural adapta-tion than those in the other three profiles, which corresponds to the pattern in the international study as a whole. A more detailed analysis by Abu-Rayya and Sam (2017) of the relationship between integration (called 'bi-culturalism' in their re-analysis) and the adaptation variables showed positive correlations with self-esteem (.26), life-satisfaction (.17), psychological problems (.02), school adjustment (.12) and behavioural problems (–.06). That is, there is a pattern of positive correlations between being engaged in both cultures and their psychological and sociocultural adaptation. This corresponds well with the findings with respect to the integration hypothesis in the international study as a whole: self-esteem (.20); life satisfaction (.19); psychological problems (–.07); school adjustment (. 21); and behavioural problems (–.07).

5   Discussion and Conclusion

Drawing upon multiple datasets from the past 10 years, as well as pre-viously published research, we found some support for the MIRIPS hypotheses in Australia. The evidence is strongest for the roles of security/ threat and contact in attitudes to outgroups (or prejudice). Australians who feel more secure (or less threatened) have more favourable attitudes to outgroups. In past research this effect appeared to be most strong for perceived competition for resources as a form of threat or insecurity (realistic threat), although our respondents to the Life in Australia survey did not distinguish between realistic and symbolic threat and a combined measure was used. Further investigation of the proposed threat types (symbolic and realistic) and the sub-components of the related construct of security (cultural, economic and personal) is needed, as well as additional analysis of their effects on intercultural attitudes and behaviour in the Australian context. It is also evident that more research involving community samples is required: our samples are among the few which do not rely on university students as participants and education has been found to be a significant predictor of discriminatory attitudes (Ang, Brand, Noble & Wilding, 2002).

There is some evidence to support the contact hypothesis in Australia, both from our data and the findings of other researchers. Intercultural contact, under the right conditions, is associated with more favourable attitudes towards different 'others'. There are, however, few recent Australian studies in which the effects of contact have been comprehensively investigated, and again there has been a reliance on university student samples. Considerable international research has been devoted to the contact hypothesis (e.g., Swart, Hewstone, Christ & Voci, 2011) and much is now known about underlying mechanisms, directionality and the relationship between contact and other variables. These processes and relationships need to be investigated in the Australian context. In addition, it is important to conduct more applied research to identify ways to enhance opportunities for meaningful and positive contact between majority and minority groups – including Aboriginal and Torres Strait Islander Australians – because it is clear that such intercultural interaction is less common in Australia than is contact among minority groups (Ang et al., 2002; Dandy & Pe-Pua, 2013).

It is also apparent that more Australian research on the integration hypothesis is necessary: very little is known about the impact of the various acculturation strategies on well-being among refugees and immigrants in Australia. Whilst most indicators suggest that there are good outcomes for the majority of refugees and immigrants who settle in Australia, there is evidence of social exclusion and marginalisation for some individuals and/or groups (Hatoss, 2012), as well as discrimination (Colic-Peisker & Tilbury, 2007; Markus, 2016). Data from the international youth project showed that more young people from Chinese,

Filipino and Vietnamese backgrounds preferred an integration strategy compared with strategies of assimilation, separation and marginalisation. Moreover, there was a positive association between a preference for integration and psychological and sociocultural adaptation. However, this was a relatively small sample and only three ethnocultural groups were studied. Clearly there is a need for current and comprehensive investigations of Australians' preferred acculturation strategies and expectations, and their impacts on psychological and socio-cultural adaptation. This work should include Aboriginal and Torres Strait Islander Australians, whose perspectives have been largely overlooked in past research.

In conclusion, preliminary evidence relevant to the mutual acculturation framework and the three key hypotheses suggests the pattern of relationships in Australia is consistent with that observed in other national contexts. However, more research is required and in particular, there is a pressing need for a comprehensive national study in which these relationships are investigated more fully. Australia has been described as a successful example of the multicultural 'experiment' (Borowski, 2000). The disparate datasets we have assembled here support this assertion of success. Our data reveal that security, in all its facets, assures and reinforces support for mutual intercultural relations. Our data are less clear on how acculturation strategies may be linked to well-being and adaptation, but most intercultural contact in Australia appears to be associated with positive effects on intercultural attitudes and behaviours.

References

Abu-Rayya, H.M., & Sam, D.L. (2017). Is integration the best way to acculturate? A re-examination of the bicultural-adaptation relationship in the "ICSEY-data set" using the bilineal method. *Journal of Cross-Cultural Psychology, 48* (3), 287–293.

Ang, I., Brand, E., Noble, G., & Wilding, D. (2002). *Living Diversity: Australia's multicultural future. Artarmon, NSW:* Special Broadcasting Service.

Ata, A., Bastian, B., & Lusher, D. (2009). Intergroup contact in context: The mediating role of social norms and group-based perceptions on the contact–prejudice link. *International Journal of Intercultural Relations, 33*(6), 498–506.

Australian Bureau of Statistics [ABS]. (2016). *Migration Australia, 2014–2015.* Cat. 3412.0. Canberra: ABS, Australian Government. Retrieved July 25, 2016 from www.abs.gov.au/ausstats/abs@.nsf/mf/3412.0.

Barlow, F. K., Paolini, S., Pedersen, A., Hornsey, M. J., Radke, H. R., Harwood, J., Rubin, M., & Sibley, C.G. (2012). The contact caveat: Negative contact predicts increased prejudice more than positive contact predicts reduced prejudice. *Personality and Social Psychology Bulletin, 38*(12),1629–1643.

Bastian, B., Lusher, D., & Ata, A. (2012). Contact, evaluation and social distance: Differentiating majority and minority effects. *International Journal of Intercultural Relations, 36*(1), 100–107.

Berry, J.W. (1970). Marginality, stress and ethnic identification in an acculturated Aboriginal community. *Journal of Cross-Cultural Psychology, 1,* 239–252.

Berry, J.W. (2006). Mutual attitudes among immigrants and ethnocultural groups in Canada. *International Journal of Intercultural Relations, 30,* 719–734.

Berry, J.W., Phinney, J.S., Sam, D.L., Vedder, P. (Eds.). (2006). *Immigrant Youth in Cultural Transition. Acculturation, Identity, and Adaptation across National Contexts.* Mahwah: Lawrence Erlbaum Associates.

Bilodeau, A., & Fadol, N. (2011). The roots of contemporary attitudes toward immigration in Australia: Contextual and individual-level influences. *Ethnic and Racial Studies, 34,* 1088–1109.

Borowski, A. (2000). Creating a virtuous society: Immigration and Australia's policies of multiculturalism. *Journal of Social Policy, 29,* 459–475.

Challenging Racism Project (2011). *Challenging Racism – Findings, Challenging Racism: The Anti-Racism Research Project,* accessed 31st March 2011, last updated 22nd February, 2011: www.westernsydney.edu.au/challengingra cism/challenging_racism_project/our_research/our_research_-_originally_me thodology.

Colic-Peisker, V., & Tilbury, F. (2007). Integration into the Australian labour market: The experience of three "visibly" different groups of recently arrived refugees. *International Migration, 45,* 59–85.

Collins, J. (2003). *Immigration and immigrant settlement in Australia*: Political Responses, discourses and new challenges. Malmö, Sweden: School of International Migration and Ethnic Relations.

Dandy, J. (2010). 'F*&! Off we're full': Managing cultural diversity: Competing discourses in Australian multiculturalism. In *Cultural Diversity: Issues, Challenges and Perspectives.* Hauppauge, NY: Nova Science Publishers.

Dandy, J., & Pe-Pua, R. (2010). Attitudes to multiculturalism, immigration and cultural diversity: Comparison of dominant and non-dominant groups in three Australian states. *International Journal of Intercultural Relations, 34,* 34–46.

Dandy, J., & Pe-Pua, R. (2013). Beyond mutual acculturation: Intergroup relations among immigrants, Anglo-Australians and Indigenous Australians. *Zeitschrift für Psychologie/Journal of Psychology, 22,* 232–241.

Department of Immigration and Citizenship (DIAC). (2011). *The People of Australia: Australia's Multicultural Policy.* Canberra: Department of Immigration and Citizenship.

Dudgeon, P., Wright, M., Paradies, Y., Garvey, D., & Walker, I. (2014). Aboriginal social, cultural and historical contexts. In P. Dudgeon, H. Milroy, and R. Walker (Eds.), *Working Together: Aboriginal and Torres Strait Islander Mental Health and Wellbeing Principles and Practices* (2nd ed., pp. 3–24). Canberra: Commonwealth of Australia.

Dunn, K.M., Atie R., Mapedzahama, V., Ozalp, M., & Aydogan, A.F. (2015). *The Resilience and Ordinariness of Australian Muslims: Attitudes and Experiences of Muslims Report,* Western Sydney University and the Islamic Sciences and Research Academy, Sydney.

Dunn, K. M., Forrest, J., Pe-Pua, R., Hynes, M., & Maeder-Han, K. (2009). Cities of race hatred? The spheres of racism and anti-racism in contemporary Australian cities. *Cosmopolitan Civil Societies Journal*, *1*, 1–14.

Dunn, K., Klocker, N., & Salabay, T. (2007). Contemporary racism and Islamaphobia in Australia. *Ethnicities*, *7*, 564–589.

Hatoss, A. (2012). Where are you from? Identity construction and experiences of "othering" in the narratives of Sudanese refugee-background Australians. *Discourse & Society*, *23*, 47–68.

Human Rights and Equal Opportunity Commission [HREOC]. (2004). *Ismaᵓ – Listen: national consultation on eliminating prejudice against Arab and Muslim Australians*. Sydney: HREOC, Commonwealth of Australia.

Jetten, J., Mols, F., & Postmes, T. (2015). Relative deprivation and relative wealth enhances anti-immigrant sentiments: The v-curve re-examined. *PLoS ONE*, *10*(10), e0139156.

Jetten, J., Mols, F., Spears, R., & Postmes, T. (2012). *How Economic Prosperity Hardens Attitudes towards Minorities*. Canberra: Australia Research Council Discovery Grant Research Project.

Jupp, J. (2002). *From White Australia to Woomera: The Story of Australian Immigration*. Cambridge: Cambridge University Press.

Mak, A. S., Brown, P. M., & Wadey, D. (2013). Contact and attitudes toward international students in Australia: Intergroup anxiety and intercultural communication emotions as mediators. *Journal of Cross-Cultural Psychology*, *45*(3), 491–504.

Mansouri, F., Jenkins, L., Morgan, L., & Taouk, M. (2009). *The impact of racism on the health and wellbeing of young Australians*. The Institute for Citizenship and Globalisation, Faculty of Arts and Education, Deakin University, Australia. Report commissioned by the Foundation for Young Australians.

Markus, A. (2015). Mapping Social Cohesion. The Scanlon Foundation Surveys 2015. Caulfield, VIC: Monash University. Melbourne.

Markus, A. (2016). Australians Today. The Australia@2015 Scanlon Foundation Survey. Caulfield, VIC: Monash University. Melbourne.

McKay, F. H., Thomas, S. L., & Kneebone, S. (2012). 'It would be okay if they came through the proper channels': Community perceptions and attitudes toward asylum seekers in Australia. *Journal of Refugee Studies*, *25*(1), 113–133.

Nesdale, D., & Todd, P. (1998). Intergroup ratio and the contact hypothesis. *Journal of Applied Social Psychology*, *28*, 1196–1217.

Nesdale, D., & Todd, P. (2000). Effect of contact on intercultural acceptance: A field study. *International Journal of Intercultural Relations*, *24*, 341–360.

Organisation for Economic Co-operation and Development (OECD). (2016). *Society at a Glance. Better Life Index, Australia*. Retrieved July 10, from www.oecdbetterlifeindex.org/countries/australia/.

Paradies, Y. (2016). Colonisation, racism and indigenous health. *Journal of Population Research*, *33*(1), 83–96.

Refugee Council of Australia (RCOA). (2012). Refugee Council of Australia. (2012). *History of Australia's Refugee Program*. Retrieved from www.refugeecouncil.org.au/getfacts/seekingsafety/refugee-humanitarian-program/.

Sam, D.L., Vedder, P., Ward, C., & Horenczyk, G. (2006). Psychological and sociocultural adaptation of immigrant youth. In J.W. Berry, J. S. Phinney, D. L. Sam & Vedder, P. (Eds.). *Immigrant Youth in Cultural Transition* (pp. 117–142). Mahwah, NJ: Lawrence Erlbaum Associates.

Schweitzer, R., Perkoulidis, S., Krome, S., Ludlow, C., & Ryan, M. (2005). Attitudes towards refugees: The dark side of prejudice in Australia. *Australian Journal of Psychology, 57*(3), 170–179.

Soutphommaasane, T. (2012). *Don't Go Back to Where You Came From. Why Multiculturalism Works*. Sydney: NewSouth Publishing, University of New South Wales.

Stephan, W.G., Renfro, C.L., Esses, V.M., Stephan, C.W., & Martin, T. (2005). The effects of feeling threatened on attitudes toward immigrants. *International Journal of Intercultural Relations, 29*, 1–19.

Stephan, W.G., & Stephan, C.W. (2000). An integrated threat theory of prejudice. In S. Oskamp (Ed.), *Reducing Prejudice and Discrimination* (pp. 23–46). Hillsdale NJ: Lawrence Erlbaum.

Swart, H., Hewstone, M., Christ, O., & Voci, A. (2011). Affective mediators of intergroup contact: A three-wave longitudinal study in South Africa. *Journal of Personality and Social Psychology, 101*, 1221–1238.

Tawagi, A.L., & Mak, A. S. (2015). Cultural inclusiveness contributing to international students' intercultural attitudes: Mediating role of intergroup contact variables. *Journal of Community and Applied Social Psychology, 25*, 340–354.

White, C., Duck, J. M., & Newcombe, P. A. (2012). The impact of media reliance on the role of perceived threat in predicting tolerance of Muslim cultural practice. *Journal of Applied Social Psychology, 42*(12), 3051–3082.

Wilkinson, R., & Pickett, K. (2010). *The Spirit Level: Why Equality Is Better for Everyone*. London: Penguin Books.

Zheng, X., Sang, D., & Wang, L. (2004). Acculturation and subjective well-being of Chinese students in Australia. *Journal of Happiness Studies, 5*, 57–72.

17 Intercultural Relations in Canada

Saba Safdar, * *Yongxia Gui,* ** *Robert C. Annis,* ***
Ryan Gibson * *and John W. Berry* ****
* *University of Guelph, Canada*
** *Henan University of Economics and Law, China*
*** *Brandon University, Canada*
**** *Queen's University, Canada & National Research*
University, Higher School of Economics, Russia

1   Introduction

Intercultural relations and acculturation in Canada are complex phenomena, involving many groups, such as Indigenous Peoples, immigrants and refugees, ethnocultural groups and sojourners (Noels & Berry, 2016). In this chapter, we report on two studies, one with international students and the other with foreign workers. In both cases, we also include samples from the larger Canadian population with whom they are in contact. The international student study is presented first, followed by the worker study. A general discussion follows the presentation of both studies. With respect to the place of Canada on the three indexes, Canada places highest on the diversity index, near the top on the integration index and second on the policy index.

2   Context of Intercultural Relations in Canada

2.1   Demography

Canada has been a culturally plural society since before its formal establishment as a nation-state in 1867. Indigenous Peoples settled over 10,000 years ago. Around 500 years ago, Europeans arrived, followed by Africans, Asians and South Americans. As a result of contact among these groups, many acculturation phenomena have a long history in Canada.

Over these years, Canada has become a diverse and pluralistic modern society. The self-declared ethnic origin is highly diverse, with over 10 million indicating that they are Canadian, and another 12 groups with over 1 million: English, French, Scottish, Irish, German, Italian, Chinese, Aboriginal, Ukrainian, Indo-Pakistani, Dutch and Polish (Gibson, Racher & Annis, 2016). Aboriginal Peoples account for 3.8 percent of the population.

Canada has a high level of immigration with approximately one-fifth of its population of 35 million born outside the country. The percentage of immigrant settlement varies widely by region and city.

2.2   Policy

Immigration. In the 1950s, the federal government's immigration policy had been to meet the country's needs in the natural resource and industrial sectors; the policy later shifted towards acceptance of professionally educated workers. In the 1960s, Canada halted its previous preferential treatment of British, French and American citizens (Canada Immigration Act, 1952; see Citizenship and Immigration Canada, 2000) and implemented immigration policies that did not officially discriminate on the basis of ethnicity, color or religion.

Under its current immigration policy (Immigration and Refugee Protection Act, 2002), Canada seeks to take in around 1 percent of the population each year (around 300,000 people). These include applicants in the economic class (professionals and skilled workers and their immediate families), refugees (for those who meet Geneva Convention or other, mainly humanitarian, criteria) and those who come under the family reunification program (family members of permanent residents). There is also a provincial nominee programme which can be used to attract and admit both skilled and unskilled workers and foreign investors to provinces that need such workers (see Carter, Morrish & Amoyaw, 2008; Citizenship and Immigration Canada 2003).

Multiculturalism. The fundamental purpose of Canada's Multiculturalism Act (1971/1988) is to increase intergroup harmony and the mutual acceptance of all groups in the country; this goal is termed the "group acceptance" element of the policy (Berry, 2013). The policy also seeks to avoid assimilation by encouraging all cultural groups to maintain and develop themselves as distinctive groups within Canadian society; this element has been referred to as the "cultural" focus of the policy (Berry, 1997). The policy argues that cultural maintenance and development by itself is not sufficient to lead to mutual acceptance: "intergroup contact and sharing" is also required and has been referred to as the "social" focus of the policy. Full participation in Canadian society cannot be achieved if some common languages are not learned; thus the "learning of official languages" (English and French) is also encouraged by the policy (for an overview of research on multiculturalism in Canada, Berry, 2006; 2013).

3   Study 1: International Students

The first study examines the intercultural relations of international students and students who are members of the larger Canadian society. In 2013, Canada hosted about 300,000 international students, which is around 5 percent of international students globally (CIC, 2014). Canada is the world's seventh-most-popular destination for international students (CIC, 2014). International students in Canada come from 194 countries but the top five sending countries are China, India, South Korea, Saudi Arabia and France. These five countries represent more than half of the Canadian international students (CIC, 2014). Although there has been an 84 percent increase in the number of international students in Canada from 2003 to 2013, there is a coordinated national attempt to increase their numbers in the coming years. In 2014, the Canadian government released the first International Education Strategy (IES) outlining the importance of international education to Canada and ways to attract more international students. By 2020, it is expected to increase the number of international students to 450,000 (CIC, 2014). Attracting more international students has been regarded as a national priority and associated with economic and cultural prosperity (CIC, 2014). It has been projected that as international expenditures increase, more than 85,000 new jobs will be created, contributing $10 billion to the Canadian economy (Canada's IES, 2014). Additionally, international students contribute to Canadian social development by increasing and supporting the diversity of Canadian institutions (CIC, 2014).

Considering the earlier objectives and projections and also the finding that about 50 percent of international students are interested in staying long term in Canada (i.e., gaining Canadian permanent residency upon graduation; CIC, 2014), it is of considerable importance to examine their challenges and well-being. This includes academic experience and socio-psychological adjustment. Integration and orientation of these students are of particular importance to ensure that the right kinds of support services exist to enable them to succeed and develop a sense of connectedness to Canadian society. It has been reported that the majority of international students in Canada (i.e., 90%) were either satisfied or very satisfied with their academic experience in Canada (CBIE, 2014).

Additionally, 74 percent of students reported that they perceive Canada as a tolerant and non-discriminatory society (CBIE, 2014). However, more than half of international students surveyed in the study (N = 3,000) reported that they have no Canadian friends. Students identified various barriers for lack of integration including low attendance of Canadian students at on-campus diversity events and activities, which are heavily advertised for and attended by international students (CBIE, 2014). This is consistent with previous literature finding many challenges that international students encounter, including the experience of acculturative stress related to forming friendship with local students, perception of discrimination, feelings of loneliness and academic concerns (Chavajay & Skowronek, 2008; Safdar & Berno, 2016). Low integration of international students with domestic students has been also reported in the United States (Gareis, 2012), U.K. (The Huffington Post U.K., 2013, as cited in CBIE, 2014) and Australia (Gresham & Clayton, 2011, as cited in CBIE, 2014).

3.1   Method

In Study 1, we evaluated two of the three MIRIPS hypotheses (multiculturalism and integration). Two groups of students participated in the study: international students who are from China; and Canadian born and raised students. All students completed an online survey. The international students were recruited from several universities across Canada (except Quebec); Canadian students were recruited from an undergraduate course at a mid-size university and received a credit for their participation. More than 140 students completed the survey.

Some data were deleted based on results of the Social Desirability scale, missing information and age. The international student sample ($n=57$): 49 percent were female; ages ranged from 19 to 32 (M= 26.0, SD=3.0); they had lived in Canada on average 13.4 months (SD=17.1). The Canadian sample was reduced by selection in order to match as closely as possible the number, age and gender composition of the international student sample. There were 68 Canadian students: 54 percent were female; aged from 19 to 31 (M=21.9, SD=2.1).

Demographic variables included age, gender and length of time living in Canada and English Proficiency (for international students). The main MIRIPS variables were used with both samples. However, contact items were administered only to international students. The Social Desirability Scale was used to assess if respondents had a deliberate inflation of self-descriptions, and their data were not used. This resulted in deletion of 3 Canadian participants and 8 International students.

3.2   Results

Demographic variables included age, gender and length of time living in Canada and English Proficiency (for international students). The reliability of the scales in the Canadian sample ranged from .59 to .90 (with one outlier of .31 for Exclusion), and from .63 to .96 (with one outlier of .53 for Assimilation) in the international student sample.

Results for international students show that they preferred integration (mean of 4.4 on the 5-point scale) over separation (2.3) or marginalization (1.8) (Because assimilation had a low alpha (.53) with the international students, it was not used in the results.) Not surprisingly, international students had a higher ethnic identity (4.4) than a Canadian national identity (2.2). They had a higher level of ethnic contact (4.0) than Canadian contact (2.4) and had a high level of Tolerance (4.0).

Correlations were examined for relationships between variables that address the three hypotheses. For demographic variables, the correlations show that with more time international students spent in Canada, they were more proficient in English (.33), had more contact with Canadians (.42), had a higher preference for Integration (.30) and were more accepting of others (they had higher scores on Integration [.30] and Tolerance [.32] than for other strategies). There were no significant correlations between the time they spent in Canada and either psychological adaptation or sociocultural competence. However, English Proficiency significantly and positively correlated with Depression (.39).

Correlations supported the *multiculturalism hypothesis*: Perceived Discrimination (as an indicator of threat or negative security) had a significant negative correlation with Tolerance (−.37). Perceived Discrimination also had significant correlations with Acculturation Strategies: positive with Separation (.32) and Marginalization (.45) and negative with Integration (−.48). The other measure of security (Perceived Consequences of Immigration) had a positive correlation with Integration (.46) and negative correlations with Separation (−.38) and Marginalization (−.21).

Correlations between contact measures and tolerance were not significant, providing no support for the *contact hypothesis*. Correlations partially supported the *integration hypothesis*: Integration had significant positive correlations with Sociocultural Competence (.40) and with Tolerance (.57). However, there was only one significant relationship with an adaptation measure (Self-esteem, .25). Since the meaning of integration also involves both co-ethnic and national contacts, there were significant

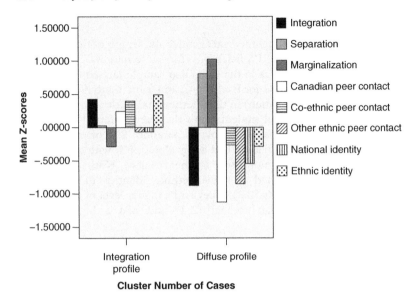

Figure 17.1. Cluster analysis for international students.

correlations between co-ethnic contacts and Self-esteem (.27), Life satisfaction (.24), Anxiety (–.25) and Depression (–.22). There were also non-
significant correlations in the expected direction with Canadian contacts:
.20, .23, –.15 and –.10, respectively.

To further examine these hypotheses, we conducted cluster analyses,
using standardized scores, and the k-means method to generate acculturation strategy clusters, for international students and Canadian students separately (see Figure 17.1). For international students, variables
included in the analysis were Acculturation Strategies (Integration,
Separation and Marginalization), Peer Contacts (Canadian, co-ethnic
and other-ethnic) and Cultural Identity (national and ethnic). Based on
the interpretability of the result, two clusters were identified (5 cases were
excluded from cluster analysis since there were missing values on Peer
Contact): *integration* cluster (*n*=36) and *diffuse* cluster (*n*=16).
The *integration* cluster was defined by a high preference for the integration
strategy, while the *diffuse* cluster combined characteristics of both the
marginalization and separation strategies. As shown in Figure 17.1,
those in the *integration* cluster scored higher than average on the integration strategy, much lower than the average score on marginalization and
a small deviation from average on separation. They scored higher than

Table 17.1. t-*test comparisons across international students' cluster membership.*

	Integration Cluster (*n*=36)	Diffuse Cluster (*n*=16)	*t*	*p* (1-tailed)
Time being in Canada	17.7(20.3)	6.1(3.3)	3.35	0.001
English proficiency	3.9(0.5)	3.5(0.6)	2.68	0.005
Perceived discrimination	1.8(0.6)	2.4(0.8)	2.84	0.004
Perceived consequences of immigration	3.7(0.4)	3.5(0.6)	1.25	0.108
Self-esteem	3.8(0.5)	3.7(0.6)	0.43	0.335
Life satisfaction	3.5(0.8)	3.4(0.6)	0.37	0.357
PS_anxiety	2.3(0.7)	2.3(0.7)	0.19	0.426
PS_depression	2.1(0.5)	2.2(0.6)	0.66	0.255
Sociocultural competence	3.3(0.5)	2.7(0.9)	2.47	0.012
Tolerance	4.1(0.4)	3.6(0.7)	2.66	0.008

average on Canadian Contact, and Co-Ethnic Contact (which taken together are indicators of integration) and on Ethnic Identity (but not on National Identity). For the *diffuse* cluster, international students scored high on both Separation and Marginalization, and low on Integration; they also scored lower than average on all Peer Contact measures and on both Cultural Identity scales.

Table 17.1 shows the differences between students in the two clusters by comparing them with one tailed *t*-test. *Integration* cluster students were those who had spent more time in Canada, and were more proficient in English. With respect to the multiculturalism hypothesis, *Integration* cluster students scored lower on Perceived discrimination than those in the *Diffuse* cluster. With respect to the integration hypothesis, those in the *Integration* cluster had a higher score on Sociocultural Competence, but there were no differences on Psychological Adaptation. They also had better intercultural adaptation, scoring higher on Tolerance.

With respect to the *multiculturalism hypothesis*, Canadian students' scores on Cultural Security and Perceived Consequences of Immigration had significant negative correlations with their expectation of the Melting Pot (−.61 and −.62, respectively). There were also significant positive correlations between cultural security and all scales measuring their acceptance of others: Multicultural Ideology (.76) and

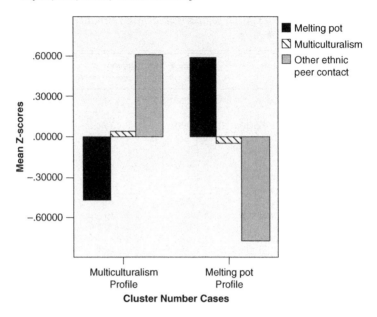

Figure 17. 2. Cluster analysis for Canadian students.

Tolerance (.58). For the *integration hypothesis*, correlations supported this hypothesis with a significant relationship between the Multiculturalism expectation and three psychological adaptation scales: Self-esteem (.41), Anxiety (–.28) and Depression (–.27); however there was no relationship with Life Satisfaction.

Cluster analysis was also carried out with the Canadian student sample, using the k-means method and standardized scores with the variables of Multiculturalism, Melting Pot and other ethnic Peer Contact. Figure 17.2 shows the two clusters *of Multiculturalism* (n=38) and *Melting Pot* (n=30). The variable of National Identity and Canadian Peer Contact were not included in the cluster analysis since Canadian students had very high scores on these variables, yielding a ceiling effect. Canadian students who were in the multiculturalism cluster had a higher than average score on the Multiculturalism expectation and a lower score on Melting Pot; they also had a higher than average score on Other Ethnic Peer Contact. Those in the melting pot cluster scored higher on Melting Pot and lower on Multiculturalism; they also reported lower than average Other Ethnic Peer Contacts.

Table 17.2. t-*test comparisons across Canadian students' cluster membership.*

	Multiculturalism cluster (38)	Melting pot cluster (30)	t	p (1-tailed)
Cultural security	4.2(0.5)	3.9(0.7)	2.14	0.018
Perceived consequences of immigration	3.7(0.5)	3.3(0.6)	2.96	0.002
National identity	4.9(0.3)	4.7(0.6)	1.35	0.092
Canadian contacts	4.6(0.6)	4.2(0.7)	2.26	0.014
Self-esteem	4.1(0.7)	4.0(0.6)	0.72	0.238
Life satisfaction	3.7(0.7)	3.4(0.9)	1.69	0.048
Anxiety	2.6(0.8)	2.7(0.7)	0.18	0.431
Depression	2.3(0.8)	2.4(0.7)	0.53	0.298
Multicultural ideology	4.1(0.5)	3.5(0.7)	3.67	0.001
Tolerance	4.5(0.5)	4.0(0.7)	3.41	0.001

Comparing the other variables between these two clusters using a one-tailed *t*-test, we can evaluate the multiculturalism and integration hypotheses. For the *multiculturalism hypothesis*, Canadian students in the multiculturalism cluster had higher Cultural Security and Perceived consequences of immigration scores. For the *integration hypothesis*, Canadian students in the multiculturalism cluster had a significantly higher score on Life Satisfaction and had significantly better intercultural adaptation (higher scores on Multicultural Ideology and Tolerance); they had more Canadian peer contact, but there were no differences on the other measures of psychological well-being (Self-esteem, Anxiety and Depression).

3.3   Discussion

Based on the Likert scale scores (which range from 1 to 5), our results indicate that International students perceive a low level of discrimination (score of 1.9 on Perceived Discrimination) and they endorse Integration as a way to live in Canada (mean of 4.4 out of 5). Canadians students feel secure in their cultural identity (4.0 on Cultural Security) and endorse Multiculturalism (4.2). There is an apparent high degree of acceptance of people with different ethnicity in the two samples. This overall satisfaction with Canadian experience has been reported by other authors. For example, in a qualitative study in Canada, Scott, Safdar, Desai Trilokekar and El Masri (2015) found that international students report low discrimination and are highly engaged with services at their university campuses.

However, although there is a high mean level of acceptance of others in these two samples, both correlational and cluster analyses revealed significant individual differences within the samples. Cluster analysis provided evidence that international students were divided into an *integration* cluster and a *diffuse* cluster: Canadian students were divided into a *multiculturalism* cluster and a *melting pot* cluster.

Comparisons between two clusters for both the international students and Canadian students support the *multiculturalism hypothesis.* International students in the *integration* cluster were those who perceived less discrimination, and they also had a higher score on Tolerance. Our findings confirm earlier research that when there is little perception of discrimination, newcomers are more likely to endorse the integration strategy (Berry et al., 2006), while threatening an individual's or group's identity is likely to lead to hostility (Berry, 2013). Canadian students in the *multiculturalism* cluster were those who had higher Cultural Security, and scored higher on Multicultural Ideology, Tolerance, and Perceived Consequences of Immigration. Consistent with previous findings, the more secure the Canadian students felt, the higher was their acceptance of others (such as Tolerance; see Lebedeva & Tatarko, 2013), and the more positive were their attitudes towards immigrants (see Ward & Masgoret, 2008).

Support for the *integration hypothesis* was also provided by the cluster analysis. For international students, those in the *integration* cluster had higher Sociocultural Competence scores than students in the *diffuse* cluster. This result is consistent with Ward and Kennedy's (1994) research with sojourners in New Zealand; they found that the greatest amount of social difficulty was experienced by respondents who endorsed a separatist orientation, and the least by those who endorsed the assimilation and integration. For Canadian students, those in the *multiculturalism* cluster had higher Life Satisfaction than those in the *melting pot* cluster. This finding could indicate that Canadian students who support the national policy of multiculturalism feel in harmony with the larger society and are feeling good about living in Canada. In comparisons to other psychological adaptation measures, none reached significance; however, there were no contradictory findings. Overall, the results indicate that for international students, *integration* is the better acculturation strategy, while being *diffuse* (combining a preference for separation and marginalization) is a worse strategy. This finding is consistent with much previous research with immigrant samples (reviewed by Berry, 1997; Nguyen & Benet-Martinez, 2013, Safdar, Choung, & Lewis, 2013).

It is also consistent with the findings that assimilation (Safdar, Lay & Struthers, 2003) or positive attitudes towards new culture acquisition (Safdar, Struthers & van Oudenhoven, 2009) are positively related to sociocultural adaptation.

Our results indicate some similarities between international and Canadian students in terms of the *multiculturalism* and *integration* hypotheses. That is, those who are secure in their culture and identity are more tolerant towards others, and those who endorse integration or multiculturalism have better psychological or sociocultural adaptation. This shared pattern of findings provides a research basis for promoting positive intercultural relations in Canada through integration and multiculturalism. If they had differed, it would be difficult to engage in a common program to achieve mutual adaptation and acceptance between international and domestic students. We suggest providing increased opportunities for international and domestic students to be exposed to each other's norms and values, and thereby to develop a mutual appreciation of their respective cultures. Additionally, as international students become more confident with their language and communication proficiency, they will likely gain more assurance to integrate into Canadian society. Our findings are not only consistent with much previous research (e.g., CBIE, 2014), they also enhance the existing literature because no study, to our knowledge, has conducted comparative analyses examining these hypotheses with both international and domestic students.

Limitations. There are some limitations to our research. First, our sample was a sample of convenience rather than a representative sample of students. Second, our international student sample was heterogeneous: they included both graduate and undergraduate students, and those who were studying English before entering university. These students thus had different experiences according to different courses, different universities and different cities within Canada, all of which could be reflected in their attitudes towards Canadian society. Future research should devote more effort to obtaining a more representative and more homogeneous student sample. Despite these limitations, we believe our study contributes to understanding the intercultural relations and adaptation of both international and domestic university students in Canada.

4   Study 2: Foreign Workers

The second Canadian study focused its attention on a group of foreign workers living in Brandon, Manitoba. Brandon is the second-largest city in the province, with a population of 44,885 in 2011 (Statistics Canada,

2013). The city is the major retail and government service center for the surrounding predominantly rural agricultural communities. The economic base of the city also includes a number of significant agricultural manufacturing and processing industries.

In the decades prior to 2001, Brandon's experience with immigration was quite limited. However, in the ensuing decade Brandon received unprecedented levels of immigration, lower than only the capital city of Winnipeg in total new permanent resident arrivals (Manitoba Labour and Immigration, 2010). Indeed, recent immigration has transformed the city. Over the past decade, the city has moved from a stable population and rather homogenous cultural composition, to a city with a growing population and dramatically increasing cultural diversity. During this period the city, along with many of its community-based organizations and service providers, worked hard to embrace the concept of Brandon as a 'Welcoming Community' and developed collaborative, proactive, and progressive development strategies with the aim of smoothing out this transition process and of truly being a welcoming community (Gibson, Bucklaschuk & Annis, 2017).

The participants in this study were drawn from approximately 1700 international workers at a recently opened and newly designed massive meat processing plant. The company began a foreign recruitment campaign in 2001 to hire temporary foreign workers from Mexico. Following this initial international campaign, the recruitment of foreign workers continued in China, Colombia, El Salvador, Mauritius, and the Ukraine. By 2009, approximately 1,700 foreign workers (representing approximately 70 percent of all workers) had been hired to work at the plant (Economic Development Brandon, 2010a).

The Temporary Foreign Worker Program, under which these new plant workers entered Canada, is regulated and managed by two federal government departments: Citizenship and Immigration Canada, and Human Resources and Skills Development Canada. It is designed to facilitate the hiring of foreign labour on a temporary basis for specific sectors experiencing labour shortages. Under this program, foreign workers are allowed a maximum of twenty-four months of employment in Canada. However, newly developed provincial policy in Manitoba permitted temporary foreign workers to also apply to its Provincial Nominee Program prior to the expiration of their work permit, affording these temporary foreign workers the opportunity to apply for permanent residency. If the application for Provincial Nominee status is approved, then temporary foreign workers immediately gain the right of mobility and permanent residency, and can also begin the process of applying for family reunification to bring their immediate family members to

Brandon (Citizenship and Immigration Canada, 2003; Moss, Bucklashuk & Annis, 2010).

Given that nearly 75 percent of temporary foreign workers at the plant have received permanent resident status, referring to this group as 'temporary' causes some confusion and in large measure has proved to be a misnomer over the years. Specifically, for the purposes of this study, although foreign workers arrive through the Temporary Foreign Worker program it would be better, and more apt, to refer to these individuals as 'transitional' foreign workers since their migration experiences in Brandon represent a transition from temporary to permanent resident. For the City of Brandon, it is also upon this basis that long-term planning for community services delivery can and does take place (Bucklaschuk, Moss & Annis, 2009).

The research was therefore influenced by two recent policy changes: the creation of the Provincial Nominee Program; and a new national and provincial focus on promoting immigration to non-metropolitan areas of Canada. Interest in immigration to non-metropolitan areas of Canada gained momentum in the mid-2000s, particularly after a national think tank hosted by the Canadian Rural Revitalization Foundation and the Rural Development Institute of Brandon University (cf. Silvius & Annis, 2005). This attention generated a series of rural immigration case studies, policy recommendations, and new research questions (cf. Beshiri & He, 2009; Silvius & Annis, 2007; Carter, Morrish & Amoyaw, 2008; Gibson, Bucklaschuk & Annis, 2017). At the same time, the federal government commissioned an investigation into welcoming communities in small centres by the National Working Group on Small Centres Strategies. In their terms, "A welcoming community has a strong desire to receive newcomers and to create an environment in which they will feel at home. A welcoming community ensures newcomers are able to participate fully in all aspects of community life. A welcoming community ensures newcomers have access to a full range of services and programs and can find meaningful employment opportunities" (National Working Group on Small Centre Strategies. 2007: p. 65). The present study is carried out partly to evaluate these initiatives, and partly to evaluate two of the three MIRIPS hypotheses: multiculturalism and integration.

4.1. Method

In partnership with the Temporary Foreign Worker Dialogue Group, the MIRIPS questionnaire along with additional questions pertaining to facets of Brandon as a welcoming community was used with both migrant workers and with long-term residents of Brandon. There were: 138

Canadian long-term resident and 189 new resident (93 from Latin America, and 96 from China) participants in the study. The length of residence were 27.9, 1.8 and 2.3 years respectively. The percentages of males were 30, 76 and 60 percent respectively. Although there is a gender imbalance in each sample, the means of variables by gender in each sample did not vary.

Participants were recruited through three strategies: a promotional flyer distributed in the community by Dialogue Group members, information booths at the local shopping mall and at the meat processing plant, and word of mouth. The MIRIPS questionnaire was administered as an interview and conducted in English, Mandarin, and Spanish. All interviews were conducted from February to April 2009. A $25 gift card was provided to all respondents who completed to the MIRIPS questionnaire to encourage participation in the study.

4.2   Results

As part of the survey of the community, questions were asked about Brandon as a 'welcoming community'. This information provides some evidence about the context of intercultural relations in the community. Brandon was judged to be welcoming by over 90 percent of Latin American and Chinese new residents, and by over 80 percent of Canadian long-term residents. It is also considered to be 'a good place to live' by 100 percent of the Latin American and 71 percent of the Chinese workers, and by 99 percent of the long-term residents. However, between 11 percent and 17 percent of the Latin American sample, and between 23 percent and 35 percent of the Chinese sample experienced difficulties in such things as obtaining housing, finding foods they enjoy, dealing with the climate, and communicating with people of other ethnic groups in Brandon.

Most MIRIPS variables were assessed in all three samples. Acculturation strategies and expectations had the following mean scores: for integration 4.47, 4.70, and 4.28 for the long-term resident, the Latin American and the Chinese worker samples respectively. For assimilation strategy, the means were 1.66, 1.96 and 1.94 for the long-term resident, the Latin American and the Chinese worker respectively; and for separation, they were 1.78, 1.53 and 2.38 respectively. Marginalization was not assessed. There were no significant variations across the three samples in these acculturation strategies and expectations. However, there was a tendency for the Chinese sample to prefer Separation, compared to the other two samples.

The Security scale had mean scores of 3.48, 3.66 and 3.27 for the long-term resident, the Latin American and the Chinese worker samples respectively. Perceived discrimination scores were 1.49, 2.13 and 1.93 for the three samples respectively. There were no significant differences across the three samples on either measure. However, there was a tendency for Perceived Discrimination to be higher in the two immigrant samples.

Multicultural ideology, tolerance and perceived (negative) consequence of immigration were all considered to be measures of the general notion of 'acceptance of others'. Scores on multicultural ideology were: 4.19, 4.19 and 3.58 for the long-term resident, the Latin American and the Chinese worker, respectively. Score for tolerance were 4.35, 4.41 and 4.01 for the three samples respectively. Scores for perceived (negative) consequences of immigration were: 1.85, 1.89 and 2.45 for the three samples, respectively. There were no significant differences on these three variables across the three samples. However, there was a tendency for the Chinese sample to be less in favour of Multiculturalism, to be less Tolerant, and to perceive more negative Consequences of Immigration.

Well-being was assessed by four variables: Self-Esteem had means of 4.52, 4.71 and 3.57 for the long-term resident, the Latin American and the Chinese worker, respectively. Life Satisfaction scores were 4.27, 4.41 and 3.84 for the three samples respectively. Psychological Problems scores were 2.12, 1.73 and 2.04 for the three samples, respectively; and scores on Sociocultural Competence were 4.55, 4.35 and 3.82 respectively. There were no significant differences across the three samples on these four variables. However, there was a tendency for the Chinese sample to have lower Self-Esteem, Life Satisfaction, and Sociocultural Competence.

In this study, we evaluated two of the three MIRIPS hypotheses: Multiculturalism and Integration. For the multiculturalism hypothesis, we expected that the acceptance of others (high multicultural ideology and tolerance, and low perceived negative consequences of immigration) will be positively associated with Security, and negatively associated with Perceived Discrimination. For the integration hypothesis, we expected that the four measures of Well-being will be positively associated with a preference for the Integration strategy. The evaluation of these two hypotheses was done by carrying out a Principal Component Factor Analysis. For each sample, a two-factor solution was indicated. In the long-term Canadian resident sample, the total percentage accounted for was 42 percent. It was 38 percent in each of the Latin American and Chinese samples. The factor structure is provided in Table 17.3.

Table 17.3. *Factor structure in the three samples in Brandon Worker Study.*

Variables	Canadian Long-Term Factor I	Canadian Long-Term Factor II	Latin America Factor I	Latin America Factor II	Chinese Factor I	Chinese Factor II
SE	.80		.40			.59
LS	.80		.76			.59
PP	−.75		−.63			−.68
SC	.68		.63			.79
PD	−.40			[.24]		−.66
MCI		.86		−.66	.55	
TOL		.79		−.48	.79	
PCI	−.79		−.59		−.74	
SEC		.52	.43		.42	
INT	.42		.53		.62	
ASS		−.56		.71	[−.17]	
SEP	−.43		−.59		[−.33]	
ID-E	[.13]			−.54	[−.30]	
ID-N	.33		.54	.47		[−.38]

SE = Self-esteem; LS = Life satisfaction; PP = Psychological problems; SC = Sociocultural competence; PD = Perceived discrimination; MCI = Multicultural ideology; TOL = Tolerance; PCI = Perceived consequences of immigration; SEC = Security; INT = Integration; ASS = Assimilation; SEP = Separation;

In two of the three samples, the three variables of multicultural ideology, tolerance and perceived consequences of immigration form one factor, which we call *Acceptance of Others* (in the Latin American sample, Perceived Consequences of Immigration does not load on this factor). The loadings of these three variables were between .79 and .86 for the long-term resident sample, between .48 and .66 for the Latin American sample, and between .55 and .79 for the Chinese sample. In addition to these variables, we assessed both ethnic and national cultural identities. In the long-term resident sample, these identities did not load on the acceptance factor. However, in the Latin American sample, ethnic identity loaded negatively, and national identity loaded positively on this factor. In the Chinese sample, there was a similar pattern, but it was not significant.

The most direct evidence bearing on the *multiculturalism hypothesis* is that Security loads on the factor that represents the *acceptance of others*. In all three samples, Security loads positively on this acceptance factor: .52, .43 and .42 respectively. That is, feeling secure is related to the acceptance of others, supporting the multiculturalism hypothesis. With respect to the *integration hypothesis*, the four measures of well-being all loaded on the second factor, which we call *adaptation*. These adaptation variables loaded between .68 and .80 in the long-term resident sample, between .40 and .76 in the Latin American sample, and between .59 and .79 in the Chinese sample. In two of the three samples, the preference for integration loaded on this adaptation factor: .42 in the long-term resident sample; .53 in the Latin American sample; however, in the Chinese sample, integration loaded .63 on the acceptance factor, but not on the adaptation factor. These loadings of integration on the adaptation factor in two of the three samples support the integration hypothesis.

In addition, we examined the loadings of a preference for assimilation and separation on this adaptation factor. There were no significant loadings for assimilation in any sample on this factor. However, for separation, there were negative loadings (of −.43, −.59 and −.33 respectively). That is, when individuals prefer segregation (in the long-term resident sample) and separation (in the two immigrant samples), they experience lower levels of adaptation.

Another way to evaluate the integration hypothesis is to examine the role of the experience of discrimination as a form of threat to wellbeing. Perceived discrimination is related to lower adaptation, in two of the three samples: long-term residents (−.40) and Chinese (−.66).

4.3   Discussion

The transitional foreign worker samples employed in this study represent something of a departure from the usual MIRIPS research sample group. Formally, the workers interviewed entered Canada as temporary foreign workers (TFW) with a two-year limit on their stay in Canada. In this regard, it could be argued that this sample has more in common and hence corresponds more with the long-standing programme of research in Europe with guest workers (*gastarbeiters*) who have come mainly from Morocco and Turkey (Sabatier, Phalet & Titzman, 2016).

These guest workers come with the expectation that they will not be staying in their host country on a permanent basis. Rather, after a period of time they will return home to their own country either because they wish to do so or because legally they must do so. For these groups, the host country is really a country of opportunity rather than of ongoing commitment for work purposes. In such circumstances, when there is little prospect that these guest workers will stay and settle into European society, it is reasonable to expect that they may not prefer to integrate or assimilate while there (Sabatier et al., 2016).

However, as has been argued here, there is a level of incongruity in categorizing these workers as temporary workers. In the Brandon, most of the workers come with a desire to stay, but can only formally apply to do so after they lived in the city for some time. However, during the time period that the workers apply for residency, it is not a forgone conclusion that they would be successful in their application. Hence for these "transitional" foreign workers, there may be some ambiguity of attachment to country of origin and possible long-term commitment to the country of current employment. Because of this period of indeterminate immigration status, it seems reasonable to expect that the "transitional" foreign workers in the Brandon sample may not develop strong preferences to integrate or assimilate for a period of time after arrival and fall somewhere on a continuum between the results found for TFW and landed immigrant groups. This possibility is supported by findings that immigrants to Canada usually shift from a preference for separation or marginalisation soon after arrival, to a preference for integration (and to a lesser extent, to assimilation) with longer residence in Canada (Berry & Hou, 2016) and internationally (Berry, et al, 2006; Ho, 1995).

The transitional workers' preference for integration was just over the midpoint of the scale, and their preference for assimilation was very low. This moderate preference for integration is well below the more usual finding for immigrants in Canada, where integration is routinely highly preferred (Noels & Berry, 2016). Similarly, the expectation in the long-term sample that these transitional workers should integrate is moderate while the expectation that they should assimilate into a melting pot is very low. Despite these relatively low preferences for integration and assimilation, the preference for separation and segregation were also relatively low. So, while these findings are in keeping with most other research on the way people prefer to engage in intercultural relations (that is a preference for integration), the levels are muted.

With respect to the multiculturalism hypothesis, the shared loading of feelings of security on the same factor as the acceptance of others provides support: when both long-term residents, and migrant workers feel mutually secure, they also hold positive attitudes towards others in their community. When the converse relationship is examined by the loading of perceived discrimination on the acceptance-of-others factor, only the long-term resident sample shows any relationship.

With respect to the integration hypothesis, a preference of this 'double engagement' way of living together in the new and evolving community setting of Brandon is clearly associated with a higher level of well-being. This is despite the rather low mean preference for integration; the power of this way still reveals itself even in this new and atypical situation of the experience of migrant workers. In contrast, for the two other strategies and expectations in this study, assimilation did not load on adaptation, but separation did load negatively.

Overall, the findings in this study of workers provide support for the two hypotheses: feeling secure (and not experiencing discrimination) are associated with the acceptance of others; and being doubly engaged in both the ethnic community and the larger society are associated with higher levels of adaptation and well-being. There is no claim possible that these associations are causal relationships. However, the patterns show that these experiences during acculturation form a complex set of inter-relationships that correspond to the general pattern found in the literature. The finding that these patterns are generally shared between the long-term residents and the immigrants supports a claim of mutuality. If these patterns had revealed opposing relationships, then no general programme to promote acceptance and well-being in the community as a whole would be possible. However, the search for mutual intercultural relationships in Brandon appears to have been successful.

5   General Discussion

These two studies extend the documentation available from previous studies of acculturation in Canada. By examining these two special 'sojourner' samples (see Safdar & Berno, 2016), we can test the generality of previous research with immigrants and refugees (Kirmayer et al. 2011; Noels & Berry, 2016).

With respect to the multiculturalism hypothesis, in much research security has consistently positively predicted tolerance and multicultural ideology since this relationship was first established in the 1970s (Berry et al., 1977). Conversely, the experience of discrimination has been a major negative predictor of a preference for integration and adaptation both in Canada (Berry & Sabatier, 2010) and internationally (Schmitt & Branscombe et al., 2014). The support for this hypothesis in these two studies adds to the growing evidence base for this hypothesis.

With respect to the integration hypothesis, the general pattern found previously with immigrants is for integration to be preferred, and for this preference to be associated with better psychological and social adaptation. For example, the study by Berry and Hou (2016) with a large sample of immigrants in Canada found that most had a double 'sense of belonging' to Canada and to their country of origin (i.e., preferred the integration strategy), and that these respondents had a higher scores on life-satisfaction and mental health than those with other preferred ways of acculturating). The support for this hypothesis in these two studies adds further to the growing evidence base for this hypothesis.

References

Berry, J. W. (1997). Immigration, acculturation and adaptation. *Applied Psychology: An International Review, 46*(1): 5–34.

Berry, J.W. (2003). Conceptual approaches to acculturation. In K. Chun, P. Balls-Organista & G. Marin (Eds.), *Acculturation: Advances in Theory, Measurement and Application* (pp. 17–37). Washington: APA Books.

Berry, J. W. (2006). Mutual attitudes among immigrants and ethnocultural groups in Canada. *International Journal of Intercultural Relations, 30* (6), 719–734. doi: 10.1016/j.ijintrel.2006.06.004.

Berry, J.W. (2013). Research on multiculturalism in Canada. *International Journal of Intercultural Relations, 37*: 663–675.

Berry, J.W., & Hou, F. (2016). Immigrant acculturation and wellbeing in Canada. *Canadian Psychology, 57*, 254–264.

Berry, J.W., Kalin, R., & Taylor, D. (1977). *Multiculturalism and Ethnic Attitudes in Canada*. Ottawa, ON: Supply & Services.

Berry, J. W., Phinney, J. S., Sam, D. L., & Vedder, P. (2006). Immigrant youth: Acculturation, identity, and adaptation. *Applied Psychology: An International Review, 55*(3): 303–332.

Beshiri, R., & He, J. (2009). *Immigrants to Rural Canada: 2006 (Rural and Small Town Canada Analysis Bulletin)*. Ottawa: Statistics Canada.

Bucklaschuk, J., Moss, A., & Annis, R. (2009). Temporary may not always be temporary: The impact of "transitional" foreign workers in increasing diversity in Brandon, Manitoba. *Our Diverse Cities, 6*, 64–70.

Canada's International Education Strategy (IES, 2014). *Harnessing Our Knowledge Advantage to Drive Innovation and Prosperity*. Ottawa: DFATD. Retrieved from: http://international.gc.ca/global-markets-marches-mondiaux/assets/pdfs/overview-apercu-eng.pdf.

Carter, T., Morrish, M., & Amoyaw, B. (2008). Attracting immigrants to smaller urban and rural communities: Lessons learned from the Manitoba Provincial Nominee Program. *Journal of International Migration and Integration, 9*(2), 161–183.

CBIE (Canadian Bureau for International Education, 2014). *A World of Learning: Canada's Performance and Potential in International Education*. ISSN: 2292–1966.

Chavajay, P., & Skowronek, J. (2008). Aspects of acculturation stress among international students attending a university in the USA. *Psychological Reports, 103*: 827–835.

Citizenship and Immigration Canada. (2000). *Glossary: International student*. Retrieved from www.cic.gc.ca/english/helpcentre/glossary.asp#foreign_student.

Citizenship and Immigration Canada (2003). Canada-Manitoba Immigration Agreement. Ottawa: Citizenship and Immigration Canada. Available online at www.cic.gc.ca/english/department/laws-policy/agreements/manitoba/can-man-2003.asp.

Citizenship and Immigration Canada. (2014). *International students with a valid permit on December 31st by gender and age, 1994 to 2013.* Retrieved from www.cic .gc.ca/english/pdf/2013-Facts-Temporary.pdf.

Citizenship and Immigration Canada. (2015). *International students by top 50 countries of citizenship and sign year, 2004 to 2013.* Retrieved from http://open .canada.ca/data/en/dataset/052642bb-3fd9-4828-b608-c81dff7e539c.

Economic Development Brandon. (2010). Maple Leaf overview. Accessed on 5 October 2011 from www.city.brandon.mb.ca/main.nsf/Pages+By+ID/648.

Gareis, E. (2012). Intercultural friendship: Effects of home and host region. *Journal of International and Intercultural Communication, 5* (4), 309–328. DOI: 10.1080/17513057.2012.691525.

Gibson, R., Bucklaschuk, J., & Annis, R. (2017). Fostering a welcoming prairie city through community partnerships: Brandon, Manitoba's response to temporary foreign workers. In G. Bonifacio & J. Drolet (Eds.), *Canadian Perspectives on Immigration in Small Cities. International Perspectives on Migration* (pp. 35–53). Springer.

Gibson, R., Racher, F., & Annis, R. (2016). Negotiating the culture of care. In A. Vollman, E. Anderson & J. McFarlene (Eds.), *Canadian Community as Partner* (pp. 154–176). Philadelphia: Lippincott, Williams, and Wilkins.

Ho, E. (1995). Chinese or New Zealander? Differential paths of adaptation of Hong Kong Chinese adolescents in New Zealand. *New Zealand Population Review, 21.* 27–49.

Kirmayer, L. J., Narasiah, L., Munoz, M., Rashid, M., Ryder, A. G., Guzder, J., & Pottie, K. (2011). Common mental health problems in immigrants and refugees: General approach in primary care. *Canadian Medical Association Journal, 183*(12), 959–967.

Lebedeva, N. M., & Tatarko, A.N. (2013). Multiculturalism and immigration in post-Soviet Russia. *European Psychologist, 18:* 169–178.

Manitoba Labour and Immigration. *Manitoba Immigration Facts: 2009 Statistical Report.* Winnipeg: Manitoba Labour and Immigration, 2010.

Moss, A., Bucklaschuk, J., & Annis, R. (2010). Small places, big changes: Temporary migration, immigration, and family reunification. *Canadian Issues,* 33–36.

National Working Group on Small Centre Strategies. (2007). *Attracting and retaining immigrants: A tool box of ideas for smaller centres* (2nd ed.). Accessed 14 August 2008. P.65, https://work.alberta.ca/documents/attracting-and-retaining-immigrants-toolbox.pdf.

Noels, K., & Berry, J.W. (2016). Acculturation in Canada.). In D.L. Sam & J.W. Berry (Eds.), *Cambridge handbook of acculturation psychology* (2nd ed.) (pp. 199–226). Cambridge: Cambridge University Press.

Nguyen, A.-M. D., & Benet-Martinez, V. (2013). Biculturalism and adjustment: A meta analysis. *Journal of Cross-Cultural Psychology, 44:* 122–159.

Redfield, R., Linton, R., & Herskovits, M. J. (1936). Memorandum for the study of acculturation. *American Anthropologist, 38* (1), 149–152.

Sabatier, C., Phalet, K., & Titzmann, P. (2016). Acculturation in Western Europe. In D.L. Sam & J.W. Berry (Eds.). *The Cambridge Handbook of Acculturation Psychology* (2nd ed.) (pp. 417–438). Cambridge: Cambridge University Press.

Safdar, S., & Berno, T. (2016). Sojourners: The experience of expatriates, students, and tourists (Chapter 10). In D.L. Sam & J.W. Berry (Eds.). *The Cambridge Handbook of Acculturation Psychology* (2nd edition) (pp. 173–195) Cambridge: Cambridge University Press.

Safdar, S., Choung, K., & Lewis, J.R. (2013). A review of the MIDA model and other contemporary acculturation models (213–230). In E. Tartakovsky (Ed.), *Immigration: Policies, Challenges and Impact*. Hauppauge, NY: Nova Science Publisher.

Safdar, S., Lay, C., & Struthers, W. (2003). The process of acculturation and basic goals: Testing a Multidimensional Individual Difference Acculturation Model with Iranian immigrants in Canada. *Applied Psychology: An International Review, 52*(4): 555–579.

Safdar, S., Struthers, W., & van Oudenhoven, J. P. (2009). Acculturation of Iranians in the United States, the United Kingdom, and the Netherlands. *Journal of Cross-Cultural Psychology, 40* (3): 468–491.

Schmitt, M, Branscombe, N. et al. (2014). The Consequences of Perceived Discrimination for Psychological Well-Being: A Meta-Analytic Review. *Psychological Bulletin, 140* (4), 921–948.

Scott, C., Safdar, S., Desai Trilokekar, R., & El Masri, A. (2015). International Students as 'Ideal Immigrants' in Canada: A disconnect between policy makers' assumptions and the lived experiences of international students. *Comparative and International Education, 43*(3). Available at: http://ir.lib.uwo.ca/cie-eci/vol43/iss3/5.

Silvius, R., & Annis, R. (2007). Reflections on rural immigration experience in Manitoba's diverse rural communities. *Our Diverse Cities, 3*, 126–133.

Silvius, R., & Annis, R. (2005). *Immigration and Rural Canada: Research and Practice*, CRRF-RDI National Think Tank. Brandon: Rural Development Institute, Brandon University.

Statistics Canada (2013). Brandon, Manitoba (code 4607062). Census profile, 2011 census (Catalogue no. 98-316-WXE). Ottawa: Statistics Canada

Ward, C., & Kennedy, A. (1994). Acculturation Strategies, psychological adjustment, and sociocultural competence during cross-cultural transitions. *International Journal of Intercultural Relations, 18* (3): 329–343.

Ward, C., & Masgoret, A.-M. (2008). Attitudes toward immigrants, immigration and multiculturalism in New Zealand: A social psychological analysis. *International Migration Review 42*: 222–243.

18 Evaluation of the Hypotheses and Conclusions

John W. Berry

Queen's University, Canada, and Higher School of Economics, Russian Federation

18.1 Introduction

The first goal of the MIRIPS project is to evaluate whether there is support for the three hypotheses (multiculturalism, contact and integration) in the various societies. The second goal is to examine whether support is present in both the dominant national and non-dominant ethnic groups; is there evidence of *mutual* views about how to engage in intercultural relations in the society? The third goal is to discover if there is a pattern of findings in the evaluation of the three hypotheses that is related to the contextual features of the societies, especially in relation to the three indexes (diversity, integration, and policy), and to historical and political factors. The fourth goal is to determine whether support found for the hypotheses constitutes a basis for a claim that they are universal principles of intercultural relations, and hence may serve as a possible basis for proposing the development of policies to improve the quality of intercultural relations. This chapter is structured according to these goals.

18.2 Evaluation of the Three Hypotheses Across 17 Societies

In the 17 country studies, there was a maximum of 44 possible evaluations of the three hypotheses (making a total of 132 evaluations). These studies included samples of both dominant national and non-dominant ethnic groups in all the countries; in some countries, there was more than one study, and more than one dominant and non-dominant sample. In some studies, not all hypotheses were evaluated, reducing the total number of evaluations to 111.

Since each research group examined the three hypotheses, and operationalized the variables, in local and culturally appropriate ways, it is not

Table 18.1. *Summary of evaluations of three hypotheses by country.*

CHAPTER	COUNTRY	SAMPLE	HYPOTHESES		
			Multiculturalism	Contact	Integration
2	Latvia	Latvians	+	0	+
		Russians	0	+	0
	Azerbaijan	Azerbaijanis	+	+	0
		Russians	+	+	+
3	**Russia (1)**	Russians	+	+	+
		Migrants I	+	+	+
		Migrants II	+	0	+
	Russia (2)	Ossetians	+	+	+
		Russians	+	+	+
		Kabardians	+	+	+
		Russia	+	+	0
4	**Estonia**	Estonians	+	+	N
		Russians	+	+	N
5	**Finland**	Finns	+	N	N
		Russians	+	N	N
6	**Norway**	Norwegians	+	+	0
		Russians	+	+	+
7	**Germany**	Germans 1	+	N	N
		Germans 2	+	N	N
		Migrants 1	N	+	+
		Migrants 2	N	+	+
		Migrants 3	N	+	+
8	**Switzerland**	Swiss	N	N	N
		Migrants	N	N	+
9	**Greece**	Greeks	+	+	+
0		Migrants	+	0	+
10	**Italy**	Italians	+	+	+
		Tunisians	+	+	+
11	**Malta**	Maltese	–	+	–
		Migrants	0	–	–
12	**Portugal**	Portuguese	+	+	+
		Migrants	+	0	+
13	**Spain**	Spanish	+	0	+
		Ecuadorians	+	+	0
14	**India**	Hindus	+	+	0
		Muslims	+	+	+
15	**Hong-Kong**	Hong-Kong	+	+	+
		Migrants	+	+	+
16	**Australia**	Australians	+	+	N
		Migrants	+	+	+

Table 18.1. (*cont.*)

			HYPOTHESES		
CHAPTER	COUNTRY	SAMPLE	Multiculturalism	Contact	Integration
17	**Canada**	***Student Study***			
		Canadians I	+	N	+
		International Students	+	0	+
		Worker study			
		Canadians 2	+	N	+
		Migrant workers	+	N	+

Note:
+ Supported
0 No Support
− Contrary result
N Not assessed

possible to adopt the usual standards of comparative research, where there are common conceptual and empirical baselines on which to make strict comparisons.

The distribution of evaluations of the hypotheses is provided in Table 18.1. The + sign indicates that there is some support for the hypothesis in that sample, a O means that there were no significant relationships between the variables, a − sign indicates a finding that is contrary to the hypothesis, and an N means that the hypothesis was not examined in that sample.

Despite the lack of strict comparability, when examining the findings across the 3 hypotheses with the 17 societies, a fairly clear pattern emerges. First for the multiculturalism hypothesis, there were 5 cases where this hypothesis was not evaluated. In 36 of the possible 39, evaluations there was support for the hypothesis; in 3 cases there was no support (in 2 there was no relationship between security and acceptance of others, and in the other there was a contrary finding).

Second, for the contact hypothesis, there were 9 cases where the hypothesis was not evaluated. In 28 of the 35 possible evaluations there was support for the hypothesis. In the 7 cases of no support, there were 6 cases of no relationship between intercultural contact and the acceptance of others, and 1 case of a contrary finding.

Third, for the integration hypothesis, there were 8 cases where the hypothesis was not evaluated. In 28 of the 36 possible evaluations there was support for the hypothesis; there were 8 cases of no support (6 cases of no relationship between preferring integration/multiculturalism and wellbeing, and 2 cases of contrary findings).

This general picture shows that these three hypotheses are supported much more often than not; but the degree of support varies across the three hypotheses. Of particular importance is that there are very few contrary findings.

18.3   Comparing Evaluations in Dominant National and Non-Dominant Ethnic Samples

This general picture varies when we consider the findings in relation to the type of sample (dominant national or non-dominant ethnic). This summary is provided in Table 18.2.

Looking first at the multiculturalism hypothesis, in the dominant group samples, 19 of the 21 possible evaluations provided support for the hypothesis. There were 3 cases of no relationship, and 1 case of a contrary finding. In the non-dominant group samples there were 18 of the 20 possible evaluations that supported it, 2 cases of no relationship, and no case of a contrary finding. This pattern provides a rather high degree of support for security being related to the acceptance of others in both kinds of groups in the study.

Second for the contact hypothesis, in the dominant group samples, 14 of the 15 possible evaluations provided support for the hypothesis; there was one case of no relationship, and no case of a contrary finding. In the non-dominant group samples there were 15 of the possible 19 evaluations that supported it, 3 cases of no relationship, and 1 case of a contrary finding. This pattern also provides a rather high degree of support for the relationship between intercultural contact and the acceptance of others.

Third, for the integration hypothesis, in the dominant group samples, 11 of the possible 16 evaluations provided support for the hypothesis; there were 3 cases of no relationship, and 1 case of a contrary finding. In the non-dominant samples, there were 20 of the 22 possible evaluations that supported it, and one case of no relationship, and one contrary case. This pattern also provides a high degree of support for the relationship between preferring the integration strategy and the multiculturalism expectation and well-being.

This analysis indicates that there is a generally common level of support in these two types of samples across the countries in the study. That is, there is little variation in level of support between dominant national and non-dominant ethnic samples.

Table 18.2. *Summary of evaluations of the three hypotheses by sample type.*

	HYPOTHESES		
SAMPLES	Multiculturalism	Contact	Integration
NATIONAL			
+	19	14	12
0	0	1	2
−	1	0	1
N	1	6	5
ETHNIC			
+	18	15	20
0	2	3	1
−	0	1	1
N	4	3	2

Note:
+ Supported
0 No Support
− Contrary result
N Not assessed

Since the level of support for all three hypotheses was mostly positive, it is useful to consider the cases where there was less support. For the multiculturalism hypothesis, looking first at the dominant national sample findings, there was 1 case of a contrary finding (Malta). In the non-dominant ethnic samples, there were 2 cases of no support (Russians in Latvia, and migrants in Malta) and no case of a contrary finding.

For the contact hypothesis, in the dominant national samples, there was one case of no support for a relationship between contact and positive intercultural relations (Latvians in Latvia) and no cases of a contrary finding. In the non-dominant ethnic samples, there was one case of a negative relationship (migrants in Malta), and 3 cases of no relationship between contact and positive attitude (migrants in Greece and Portugal, and Chinese students in Canada).

For the integration hypothesis, in the dominant national samples, there was 1 case of contrary finding (in Malta), and 2 cases of no relationship (in Norway and among Hindus in India). In the non-dominant ethnic samples, there was 1 case of contrary finding (migrants in Malta) and one case of no relationship (Ecquadoreans in Spain).

18.4   Mutual Relationships

While this overall level of support for the three hypotheses is an important finding, we are interested not only in evidence of support in general, but also in the degree to which there is agreement about these issues between dominant and non-dominant people living in the same society. This is the question of *mutual* intercultural relations, which is paramount in the MIRIPS project. That is, is there support (or not) for the hypotheses in *both* dominant and non-dominant groups within a society?

For the multiculturalism hypothesis, there was agreement in the findings between the two samples in each country in 13 of the 16 societies. In only two societies was there disagreement between the two samples. In all samples but one, this agreement was based on the two samples sharing a positive relationship between security and the acceptance of others. This degree of mutual agreement is substantial, and bodes well for the possibility of a society promoting a common strategy for enhancing feelings of security among all groups or, conversely, of reducing the levels of discrimination.

For the contact hypothesis, there was agreement in the findings between the two samples in 9 societies. There was disagreement in 5 societies. In 3 of these, the disagreement was between no relationship and a positive relationship between intercultural contact and the acceptance of others; in 2 societies, the disagreement was between no relationship and a contrary one. This degree of mutual agreement is relatively high.

For the integration hypothesis, in 7 samples there was agreement in the findings between the two samples that the integration/multiculturalism strategies are positively related to well-being. There was disagreement in 7 samples. In 3 of these samples, the disagreement was between a finding of support and of no relationship; in 2 societies, the disagreement was between support and a contrary finding, and in 2 societies the disagreement was between no support and a contrary one. This level of agreement is only moderate.

As noted in the Chapter 1, the origin of the integration hypothesis was based on the notion that members of non-dominant ethnic groups would achieve greater well-being if they were engaged with more than one cultural group (their own, and others in the larger society). The notion that this relationship may also hold true for members of the dominant national group (who accept the multiculturalism expectation for how to live in the society) has less of a conceptual or theoretical foundation. So, it is not much of a surprise that a lower level of support for the integration hypothesis was found in the dominant national samples.

On the basis of this generally high level of mutuality in the findings overall across the three hypotheses, there is the possibility of developing policies and programmes to improve intercultural relations in those societies. This is most likely to be successful where there is both support for the hypotheses and agreement between groups in their support. However, in those societies where there is a combination of support for an hypothesis and of no relationship, there is still a possibility of developing policies and programmes by working with that sector of society where no support was found. More difficult, of course, is to carry out such work in societies where there are contrary findings.

18.5 Relationships of Support of Hypotheses with Contextual Factors

In Chapter 1, we proposed that contextual factors may provide a basis for understanding variations in the level of support for the three hypotheses. In particular, we outlined three dimensions of variation across societies related to multiculturalism: diversity, integration, and policy. These three dimensions provide the broadest set of contexts within which intercultural relations may be examined. The question in this section is whether there are any relationships across societies between these three dimensions and the way a society deals with these issues? That is, can we discern any relationship between these three dimensions of diversity and the degree of support for the three hypotheses; and if so, does such a relationship exist in both dominant and non-dominant groups?

As noted in Chapter 1, the 17 societies in the project may be classified into three levels on each of the three multiculturalism dimensions: high, medium and low. When this is done, we noted that seven countries are relatively high on the diversity index (Canada, Estonia, Latvia, Switzerland, India, Spain and Australia); five countries are medium (Russia, Germany, Greece, Azerbaijan and Finland); and five countries are relatively low (Italy, Hong Kong, Norway, Portugal and Malta). On the integration index, five countries are relatively high (Portugal, Finland, Norway, Canada and Australia); six countries are medium (Germany, Spain, Italy, India, Switzerland and Estonia); and five countries are relatively low (Greece, Malta, Russia, Azerbaijan and Latvia). Finally for the policy index, seven countries are relatively high (Australia, Canada, India, Finland, Norway, Portugal and Spain); four countries are medium (Russia, Germany, Greece and Azerbaijan); and five countries are relatively low (Italy, Estonia, Latvia, Switzerland and Malta). Note that Hong Kong could not be classified on the last two indexes.

These classifications show only moderate agreement across societies on the three dimensions. For example, among the seven highly diverse countries, only Canada and Australia are also high on the integration and policy indicators. India and Spain are high on diversity and policy, but medium on integration. And Estonia, Latvia and Switzerland are either medium or low on the integration and policy indexes. It thus appears that when there is high diversity in a society, there are no consistent outcomes, in either migrant integration or in multicultural policy. At the other end of the diversity index, in the five low-diversity countries, only Malta is also low on the integration and policy indexes. Italy is medium on the integration and low on policy indexes. Again, at this lower end of the diversity index, there is little consistency with the integration or policy indexes. In general, we may conclude that when diversity is present, countries do not consistently succeed in providing ways for equitable participation, either by integrating migrants, or by responding to their diversity by developing policies to accommodate it.

There was limited support for the hypotheses in Malta, with only the contact hypothesis being supported in the dominant national sample. Malta has a low placement on all three dimensions, which suggests that there should not be a major issue with intercultural relations. That is, it is plausible to think that when there is little diversity, then little migrant integration and little policy support are required. However, immigration has increased in recent years, and at present there is a major issue of migration to and through Malta from North Africa. However, the level of perceived security was relatively high among the Maltese national sample, so the current migration flow appears not to account for the rather negative intercultural findings there.

Can other contextual factors, such as the history of intercultural relations between dominant and non-dominant groups in a society, be related to the degree of support for the three hypotheses? In the studies where there are "Russian" samples, the contact and integration hypotheses were supported less than in the other societies. The history of relationships among cultural groups that existed during the Soviet period may be playing a continuing role here.

In the two Asian societies (India and Hong Kong), which contrast strongly on extant diversity, and where colonization and intercultural conflict have been evident in their histories, both societies provide rather strong support for the hypotheses; 11 of 12 hypotheses were supported in both societies. Hence, extant diversity, a history of colonial occupation nor current conflict seem not to be playing a role.

In the traditional settler societies of Australia and Canada, there is substantial support for the hypotheses (6 of 6 in Australia; 8 of 9 in

Canada). These two societies are high on all three dimensions, and they have multiculturalism policies that provided the basis for the three hypotheses. It may be the case that the concepts that lie at the root of the hypotheses are culturally embedded in these two societies, and hence are biased in favour of finding support there.

However, in the more recent migrant-receiving societies in western and southern Europe, there was also a relatively high degree of support found for the hypotheses. It was highest in Germany and Italy, followed closely by Portugal, Greece and Spain. This suggests that there is a rather positive climate for intercultural relations in these societies, despite the current political debate about immigrants, refugees, and the rise of exclusionary ethnic-based nationalisms.

One general conclusion about the relationship between the placement of a society on the three dimensions and the level of support for the three hypotheses seems to be possible. Where diversity is high, and integration and policy support is present, then there is a higher probability that the hypotheses will find support. In contrast, where diversity is high, and there is a continued presence of non-dominant ethnic populations from the former colonies then less support is found.

18.6   Implications of the Findings: Universals?

The evidence produced by the research teams in these societies on the validity of these three hypotheses, while variable, has provided a large degree of general support for them. Does this level of support provide a basis for claiming that these three hypotheses are likely to be global in their validity? And if so, can they provide a basis for advancing policies and programmes that will improve the quality of intercultural relations in the world?

The studies reported in this book were carried out using a common conceptual framework, and a common empirical instrument. In one sense, these commonalities may have contributed to the observed degree of similarity in the findings, giving rise to the apparent universality of these three principles. However, each research team interpreted and used these in ways that were appropriate to their particular society, and to their specific intercultural arena. So, in another sense, the variability in samples used (migrants, ethnocultural groups, sojourners) and the ways in which the variables were conceptualized and actually measured (sometimes with alternative concepts and instruments) provide a kind of 'multimethod' assessment of the three hypotheses. When research in different societies and samples, and with variations in concepts and measures, generally point to the same conclusions, then we may claim that there is evidence of the existence of phenomena that are independent of the research concepts and methods used. This may be one way of understanding what constitutes a psychological universal.

In my view, while the empirical findings allow us to promote them as candidates for being universal psychological principles of intercultural relations, there are three issues that need to be considered when assessing this claim.

First, it is essential that we take into consideration the contextual factors that have been identified in both the diversity indicators and in the history of intercultural relationships among the dominant national and non-dominant ethnic groups in this project. Clearly, such factors impinge on the degree to which these three principles may operate in plural societies.

Second, while the scope of the MIRIPS project is large, it is neither inclusive nor exhaustive. The plural societies of the UK, the USA and Israel were not included in the project. However, much of the research supporting the three hypotheses that was reviewed in Chapter 1 was drawn from research findings obtained in these three societies. It is clear that parallel studies in other plural societies than those included in the MIRIPS project would have provided more comparative data, and a more comprehensive base on which to base any claim of universality.

As noted in Chapter 1, the three hypotheses have been examined in numerous empirical studies, and have been the subject of meta-analyses. However, most studies in these analyses have been carried out in a limited range of societies. As noted by Whiting (1954), one of the advantage of the cross-cultural method is that it 'extends the range' of social and cultural contexts within which to examine a phenomenon. The MIRIPS project sought to carry out this extension, and thereby to gain a broader picture of whether, where and under what conditions these hypotheses would hold up.

Third, there are other well-established principles of intercultural relations that probably qualify as universals. For example, stereotyping is a universal (and possibly an inevitable) process used in categorizing individuals into groups, and then making attributions of some perceived shared characteristics to all members of the group (Campbell, 1967). Ethnocentrism is also a universal feature of intercultural relations (Levine & Campbell, 1972); this occurs when individuals have a generalized tendency to hold positive ingroup attitudes combined with negative outgroup attitudes. Similarly, social dominance orientation (Sidanius & Pratto, 1999) may qualify as a universal tendency to accept and use hierarchy in social groups relations. Social identity (Tajfel, 1982) processes are also likely to qualify as universal features of intercultural relations. And the burden of historical memory and representations of inter-group conflict (Liu & Hilton, 2005) has been shown to operate widely in many intercultural settings. Although these approaches were implied in many of the country studies, these were not fully included in the MIRIPS project.

18.7 Policy and Programme Implications of the Findings

If the claim for universality is accepted, we can ask the fundamental question: Is there sufficient consistency in the pattern of findings across cultures to serve as a basis for promoting these three principles as a valid basis for developing intercultural policy and programmes in many societies? Although the three principles were drawn from extant intercultural policy (in Canada, Australia and the European Union), they may provide a relevant basis for policy development in other plural societies. In these three cases, there has been a policy transition over the past decades from attempts to assimilate non-dominant (indigenous and migrant) peoples into a homogeneous society, to one that is more integrationist and multicultural. Is it possible to emulate this transition in other plural societies?

In the Canadian case, the questioning of the assimilationist process and goal was questioned early by John Buchan (author and Governor General of Canada from 1935 to 1940). He argued (Buchan, 1937) that immigrant groups "should retain their individuality and each make its contribution to the national character ... each could learn from the other, and ... while they cherish their own special loyalties and traditions, they cherish not less that new loyalty and tradition which springs from their union". This dual sense of belonging has been in evidence in Canada for decades, most recently in a study of immigrants (Berry & Hou, 2016).

Somewhat later, in a position paper presented to an international conference on the integration of post-war migrants (Borrie, 1954) on the appropriate approach to integration, the official position paper of the Canadian delegation stated that Canadian society should be "built on the ideas of individual worth and cultural differences ... The pressure of one dominant group to assimilate, that is to absorb others, is therefore impractical as a general theory" (quoted in Borrie, 1959, p. 51). The lesson here is that change in intercultural policy is possible; if this is so in one society, what conditions may be required in other societies in order to move towards a more pluralist vision?

Is the kind of evidence provided by the MIRIPS project useful and sufficient to persuade other culturally diverse societies to move away from strict assimilation policies that are designed to achieve a culturally homogeneous society, towards a more multicultural one? In my view, policies that are evidence-based are more likely to be successful than those based only on pre-conceptions or political expediency. However, evidence alone (such as that provided in this project) is unlikely to shift public policy towards more pluralist ways of living together. Other factors are also important, particularly public opinion, political ideology, and the availability of resources.

Public education is required in order to bring about any policy change from assimilation towards a multicultural way of living together. The benefits of the multicultural vision (as outlined in Chapter 1) need to be articulated, and advocated widely in ways that the general public can understand and accept; in particular, the claim that life for everyone is enriched culturally and economically. Community mobilisation is also required to push (bottom up) towards achieving a more accepting and inclusive society. In addition, political leadership (top down) is essential. Leaders who could advocate for the pluralist way of living together have clear models to follow: the Canadian and European Union policy statements provide clear examples of these principles, which could be emulated and promoted.

These three principles of intercultural relations (of providing a secure and non-discriminatory social and cultural environment, of opportunities for equitable intercultural contact and participation, and of ways to be engaged in more than one culture) offer a clear basis for moving towards achieving a more harmonious plural society. If this goal of attaining more positive intercultural relations is valued by the general population of the larger society, and by policy makers, then the path forward should be clear to them. Despite obvious difficulties in many contemporary societies, then the three psychological principles of intercultural relations examined in this project would be a good place to start.

18.7   Conclusions

The MIRIPS project is situated in the disciplines of cross-cultural and intercultural psychology. The first main feature of these approaches is that cultural experiences shape the development and expression of human behaviour. The second is that these behaviours are brought to the intercultural arena by both (all) groups and individuals that are in contact. The third main feature is that in order to discern which features of cultural experience shape behaviours in which way, the comparative method is required. And finally, by examining the evidence obtained by empirical research to identify any general patterns across cultures, there is the possibility of discovering some basic pan-cultural (universal or global) psychological principles of intercultural relations. In this project, we have followed the steps on this path. We have sought to articulate these principles, first by conceptually defining some psychological processes that may be theoretically related to intercultural behaviours, and then by empirically examining them across societies.

In a sense, the project is an example of extended replication. Current controversies about the reproducibility of psychological findings, even within the same society, suggest that our knowledge base is not as secure as previously thought. So, it is useful to attempt to repeat the empirical examination of the same three MIRIPS hypotheses in a number of different societies in order to broaden our knowledge base. In this project, despite highly variable conditions (demographic, cultural, historical and policy), there has been a modest degree of replication of psychological findings across contexts. However, more needs to be done to expand the conceptual and empirical basis for appropriate policy development.

References

Berry, J.W., & Hou, F. (2016). Immigrant acculturation and wellbeing in Canada. *Canadian Psychology*, *57*, 254–264.

Borrie, D. (1959). *The Cultural Integration of Immigrants*. Paris: UNESCO.

Buchan, J. (1937). *Address to the Canadian Club of Halifax*.

Campbell, D.T. (1967). Stereotypes and the perception of group differences. *American Psychologist*, *22*, 817–829.

LeVine, R. A., & Campbell, D. T. (1972). *Ethnocentrism: Theories of Conflict, Ethnic Attitudes, and Group Behavior*. New York: Wiley, 1972.

Liu, J. & Hilton, D. (2005). How the past weighs on the present: Social representations of history and their role in identity politics. *British Journal of Social Psychology*, *44*, 537–556.

Sidanius, J., & Pratto, F. (1999). *Social Dominance: An Intergroup Theory of Social Hierarchy and Oppression*. Cambridge: Cambridge University Press.

Tajfel, H. (1982). Social psychology of intergroup relations. *Annual Review of psychology*, *33*, 1–39.

Whiting, J. W. M. (1954). The cross-cultural method. In G. Lindzey (Ed.), *The Handbook of Social Psychology* (Vol. *1*, pp. 523–531). Cambridge, MA: Addison-Wesley.

MIRIPS Questionnaire

This questionnaire draws material from earlier ones, mainly the ISATIS and ICSEY projects.

It is intended for use with dominant (national or regional) samples and with multiple nondominant samples (immigrant or ethnic groups).

These nondominant samples can be newcomers to a country or region (international immigrants, internal migrants), or established populations (ethnic, indigenous or national minority) samples.

In some items, the names of national, regional, immigrant and ethnic groups will need to be inserted. These changes are usually signalled by the use of square brackets, such as [ethnic language] or [national language].

Please see separate "Instructions" sheet for how to use this questionnaire.

1   Age

How old are you? ____ years

2   Sex

What is your sex?
[ ]Female
[ ]Male

3   Education

What is the highest level of schooling that you have obtained?

[ ]   No schooling
[ ]   Some grade/primary school
[ ]   Completed grade/primary school
[ ]   Some high/secondary school
[ ]   Completed high/secondary school
[ ]   Some technical, community college
[ ]   Completed technical, community college
[ ]   Some university
[ ]   Completed university
[ ]   Post-graduate degree
[ ]   Don't know

4   Religion

What is your religion?

[ ]   No religion
[ ]   Christian Protestant
[ ]   Christian Roman Catholic
[ ]   Christian Orthodox
[ ]   Animistic
[ ]   Jewish [expand if needed]
[ ]   Muslim [expand if needed]
[ ]   Buddhist [expand if needed]
[ ]   Hindu
[ ]   Other_____

5   Socioeconomic Status (Work)

What work do you do?

[ ]   Unskilled: such as farm labour, food service, house cleaner
[ ]   Skilled work: such as technician, carpenter, hairdresser, seamstress
[ ]   White collar (office) work: such as clerk, salesperson, secretary, small business
[ ]   Professional: doctor, lawyer, teacher, business executive
[ ]   Not currently working: [ ] unemployed [ ] retired [ ] homemaker [ ] student If not
       currently employed, what is your usual work?_____
[ ]   Other (specify):_____
[ ]   Don't know

6   Socioeconomic Status (Ownership)

Does your family have a telephone? Yes ___ No ___
Does your family have a washing machine or electric stove ?
Yes ___ No ___
Does your family own a car, van or truck? Yes ___ No ___
Does your family own a computer? Yes ___ No ___

7   Ethnic Origin

What is your ethnic background?
    [ ] [xxx]
    [ ] [xxx]
    [ ] Other _____
What is the ethnic background of your (list up to 3 for each parent):
    Father _____
    Mother _____

8   Individual Marriage Preference

Are you currently married? Yes ___ No ___
If not currently married, were you married previously?
Yes ___ No ___
Does/Did your spouse come from the same ethnic group as yourself?
Yes ___ No ___
If not, which ethnic group? _____
If not married, do you prefer to marry someone from the same ethnic group as yourself?
Yes ___ No ___ No preference ___

9   Neighbourhood Ethnic Composition

Which statement is most true about the neighbourhood/village where you live?
    [ ] Almost all people are from a different ethnic group from mine.
    [ ] A majority of the people is from a different ethnic group from mine.
    [ ] There is about an equal mix of people from my ethnic group and other groups.
    [ ] A majority of the people is from my ethnic group.
    [ ] Almost all people are from my ethnic group.

10   Place of Birth/Length of Residence

In what country were you born?

    [ ] [Current country]

    [ ] Another country What country? _____

If born in another country, did you live somewhere else before coming to [current country]? Yes ___ No ___

Which country? _____

If born in another country, how old were you when you came to [current country]? ___ years

11   Languages Known/Used

Here are some questions about languages. Please answer by checking the answer that applies best.

a. What language do you speak at home?

	Not at all	A little	Half the time	A lot	All the time
I speak [ethnic language].	[ ]	[ ]	[ ]	[ ]	[ ]
I speak [national language].	[ ]	[ ]	[ ]	[ ]	[ ]
I speak a regional dialect of the national language.	[ ]	[ ]	[ ]	[ ]	[ ]

b. What language do you speak in your neighbourhood/village (e.g., when shopping)?

	Not at all	A little	Half the time	A lot	All the time
I speak [ethnic language].	[ ]	[ ]	[ ]	[ ]	[ ]
I speak [national language].	[ ]	[ ]	[ ]	[ ]	[ ]
I speak a regional dialect of the national language.	[ ]	[ ]	[ ]	[ ]	[ ]

c. How well do you:

	Not at all	A little	Somewhat	Fairly well	Very well
(a) understand [ethnic language]?	[ ]	[ ]	[ ]	[ ]	[ ]
(b) speak [ethnic language]?	[ ]	[ ]	[ ]	[ ]	[ ]
(c) read [ethnic language]?	[ ]	[ ]	[ ]	[ ]	[ ]
(d) write [ethnic language]?	[ ]	[ ]	[ ]	[ ]	[ ]

d. How well do you:

	Not at all	A little	Somewhat	Fairly well	Very well
(a) understand [national language]?	[ ]	[ ]	[ ]	[ ]	[ ]
(b) speak [national language]?	[ ]	[ ]	[ ]	[ ]	[ ]
(c) read [national language]?	[ ]	[ ]	[ ]	[ ]	[ ]
(d) write [national language]?	[ ]	[ ]	[ ]	[ ]	[ ]

12   Social Contacts

Here are some questions about your friends and people you know. Please indicate the answer that applies best.

a. How many close friends do you have?

	None	Only one	A few	Some	Many
Close [co-ethnic] friends	[ ]	[ ]	[ ]	[ ]	[ ]
Close [national] friends	[ ]	[ ]	[ ]	[ ]	[ ]
Close [other ethnic] friends	[ ]	[ ]	[ ]	[ ]	[ ]

[NB: ask last question for all groups that are relevant to your study.]

b. How often to you meet with?

	Never	Rarely	Sometimes	Often	Daily
Close [co-ethnic] friends	[ ]	[ ]	[ ]	[ ]	[ ]
Close [national] friends	[ ]	[ ]	[ ]	[ ]	[ ]
Close [other ethnic] friends	[ ]	[ ]	[ ]	[ ]	[ ]

[NB: ask last question for all groups that are relevant to your study.]

13   Travel

In the past 5 years, how often have you travelled:

	None	Once	Twice	A few times	Many times
Within your [region]	[ ]	[ ]	[ ]	[ ]	[ ]
Within your country	[ ]	[ ]	[ ]	[ ]	[ ]
Outside your country	[ ]	[ ]	[ ]	[ ]	[ ]

Were these trips for (tick all that apply): [ ] leisure [ ] study [ ] work
In the past 5 years, how many months in total were you away from your neighbourhood/village? ___months

14   Cultural Identity

People can think of themselves in various ways. For example, they may feel that they are members of various ethnic groups, such as Vietnamese (etc.), and that they are part of the larger society, [national society]. These questions are about how you think of yourself in this respect.

a. How do you think of yourself?

	Not at all	A little	Somewhat	Quite a bit	Very much
I think of myself as [ethnic].	[ ]	[ ]	[ ]	[ ]	[ ]
I think of myself as [national].	[ ]	[ ]	[ ]	[ ]	[ ]
I think of myself as part of another ethnic group. What group? _____	[ ]	[ ]	[ ]	[ ]	[ ]

	Strongly disagree	Somewhat disagree	Not sure/ neutral	Somewhat agree	Strongly agree
b. I feel that I am part of [ethnic] culture.	[ ]	[ ]	[ ]	[ ]	[ ]
c. I am proud of being [ethnic].	[ ]	[ ]	[ ]	[ ]	[ ]
d. I am happy to be [ethnic].	[ ]	[ ]	[ ]	[ ]	[ ]
e. I feel that I am part of [national] culture.	[ ]	[ ]	[ ]	[ ]	[ ]
f. I am proud of being [national].	[ ]	[ ]	[ ]	[ ]	[ ]

(*cont.*)

		Strongly disagree	Somewhat disagree	Not sure/ neutral	Somewhat agree	Strongly agree
g.	I am happy to be [national].	[ ]	[ ]	[ ]	[ ]	[ ]
h.	Being [ethnic] is uncomfortable for me.	[ ]	[ ]	[ ]	[ ]	[ ]
i.	Being part of [ethnic] culture is embarrassing to me.	[ ]	[ ]	[ ]	[ ]	[ ]
j.	Being part of [ethnic] culture makes me feel happy.	[ ]	[ ]	[ ]	[ ]	[ ]
k.	Being [ethnic] makes me feel good.	[ ]	[ ]	[ ]	[ ]	[ ]

15   Security

Please indicate the extent to which you agree or disagree with each of the following statements, using a 5-point scale, where 1 means "totally disagree" and 5 means "totally agree". You are free to use all numbers between 1 and 5 to indicate varying degrees of disagreement or agreement.

1.	There is room for a variety of languages and cultures in this country.	1	2	3	4	5
2.	We have to take steps to protect our cultural traditions from outside influences.	1	2	3	4	5
3.	Learning other languages makes us forget our own cultural traditions.	1	2	3	4	5
4.	I am concerned about losing my cultural identity.	1	2	3	4	5
5.	I feel culturally secure as a [national].	1	2	3	4	5
6.	The high level of unemployment presents a grave cause for concern.	1	2	3	4	5
7.	This country is prosperous and wealthy enough for everyone to feel secure.	1	2	3	4	5
8.	High taxes make it difficult to have enough money for essentials.	1	2	3	4	5
9.	People spend too much time fretting about economic matters.	1	2	3	4	5
10.	A person's chances of living a safe, untroubled life are better today than ever before.	1	2	3	4	5

(*cont.*)

		Strongly disagree	Somewhat disagree	Not sure/ neutral	Somewhat agree	Strongly agree
11.	Our society is degenerating and likely to collapse into chaos.	1	2	3	4	5
12.	The reports of immoral and degenerate people in our society are grossly exaggerated.	1	2	3	4	5
13.	People's chances of being robbed, assaulted and even murdered are getting higher and higher.	1	2	3	4	5

16   Acculturation Attitudes and Expectations

A. Nondominant Group Version: Acculturation Attitudes

		Strongly disagree	Somewhat disagree	Not sure/ neutral	Somewhat agree	Strongly agree
1.	I feel that [ethnic group] should maintain our own cultural traditions and not adapt to those of [national].	[ ]	[ ]	[ ]	[ ]	[ ]
2.	It is not important to me to be fluent either in [ethnic language] or [national language].	[ ]	[ ]	[ ]	[ ]	[ ]
3.	I don't want to attend either [national] or [ethnic] social activities.	[ ]	[ ]	[ ]	[ ]	[ ]
4.	I prefer social activities which involve [ethnic group] members only.	[ ]	[ ]	[ ]	[ ]	[ ]
5.	It is important to me to be fluent in both [national language] and in [ethnic language].	[ ]	[ ]	[ ]	[ ]	[ ]
6.	I prefer social activities which involve [nationals] only.	[ ]	[ ]	[ ]	[ ]	[ ]
7.	I feel that it is not important for [ethnic group] either to maintain their own cultural traditions or to adopt those of [national].	[ ]	[ ]	[ ]	[ ]	[ ]

(cont.)

		Strongly disagree	Somewhat disagree	Not sure/ neutral	Somewhat agree	Strongly agree
8.	It is more important to me to be fluent in [ethnic] than in [national language].	[ ]	[ ]	[ ]	[ ]	[ ]
9.	I feel that [ethnic group] should maintain our own cultural traditions but also adopt those of [national].	[ ]	[ ]	[ ]	[ ]	[ ]
10.	I feel that [ethnic group] should adopt the [national] cultural traditions and not maintain those of our own.	[ ]	[ ]	[ ]	[ ]	[ ]
11.	I prefer to have only [national] friends.	[ ]	[ ]	[ ]	[ ]	[ ]
12.	It is more important to me to be fluent in [national language] than in [ethnic language].	[ ]	[ ]	[ ]	[ ]	[ ]
13.	I don't want to have either [national] or [ethnic] friends.	[ ]	[ ]	[ ]	[ ]	[ ]
14.	I prefer to have only [ethnic] friends.	[ ]	[ ]	[ ]	[ ]	[ ]
15.	I prefer social activities which involve both [national] members and [ethnic] members.	[ ]	[ ]	[ ]	[ ]	[ ]
16.	I prefer to have both [ethnic] and [national] friends.	[ ]	[ ]	[ ]	[ ]	[ ]

B Dominant Group Version : Acculturation Expectations

	Strongly disagree	Somewhat disagree	Not sure/ neutral	Somewh-at agree	Strongly agree
1. I feel that [immigrant/ ethnic group] should maintain their own cultural traditions and not adapt to those of [national].	[ ]	[ ]	[ ]	[ ]	[ ]
2. It is not important for immigrants/ethnics to be fluent either in their own language or [national] language.	[ ]	[ ]	[ ]	[ ]	[ ]
3. Immigrants/ethnics should not engage in either [national] or their own group's social activities.	[ ]	[ ]	[ ]	[ ]	[ ]
4. Immigrants/ethnics should engage in social activities that involve their own group members only.	[ ]	[ ]	[ ]	[ ]	[ ]
5. Immigrants/ethnics should be fluent in both [national language] and in [ethnic language].	[ ]	[ ]	[ ]	[ ]	[ ]
6. Immigrants/ethnics should engage in social activities that involve [nationals] only.	[ ]	[ ]	[ ]	[ ]	[ ]
7. I feel that it is not important for immigrants/ethnics either to maintain their own cultural traditions or to adopt those of [national].	[ ]	[ ]	[ ]	[ ]	[ ]
8. It is more important for immigrants/ethnics to be fluent in their own language than in the national language.	[ ]	[ ]	[ ]	[ ]	[ ]
9. I feel that immigrants/ ethnics should maintain their own cultural traditions but also adopt those of [national].	[ ]	[ ]	[ ]	[ ]	[ ]

(*cont.*)

	Strongly disagree	Somewhat disagree	Not sure/ neutral	Somewh- at agree	Strongly agree
10. I feel that immigrants/ethnics should adopt [national] cultural traditions and not maintain those of their own.	[ ]	[ ]	[ ]	[ ]	[ ]
11. Immigrants/ethnics should have only [national] friends.	[ ]	[ ]	[ ]	[ ]	[ ]
12. It is more important for immigrants/ethnics to be fluent in[national language] than in their own language.	[ ]	[ ]	[ ]	[ ]	[ ]
13. I don't want to have either [national] or [ethnic] friends.	[ ]	[ ]	[ ]	[ ]	[ ]
14. Immigrants/ethnics should have only [ethnic] friends.	[ ]	[ ]	[ ]	[ ]	[ ]
15. Immigrants/ethnics should engage in social activities that involve both [national members] and their own group.	[ ]	[ ]	[ ]	[ ]	[ ]
16. Immigrants/ethnics should have both [ethnic] and [national] friends.	[ ]	[ ]	[ ]	[ ]	[ ]

17   Perceived Discrimination

When people with different backgrounds are together, one may some-times feel unfairly treated. The following questions are about these kinds of experiences.

	Strongly disagree	Somewhat disagree	Not sure/ neutral	Somewh- at agree	Strongly agree
I think that others have behaved in an unfair or negative way towards my [ethnic/national] group.	[ ]	[ ]	[ ]	[ ]	[ ]
I don't feel accepted by [ethnic/ national] group.	[ ]	[ ]	[ ]	[ ]	[ ]
I feel [ethnic/national] group has something against me.	[ ]	[ ]	[ ]	[ ]	[ ]

(*cont.*)

	Strongly disagree	Somewhat disagree	Not sure/ neutral	Somewh- at agree	Strongly agree
I have been teased or insulted because of my [ethnic/national] background.	[ ]	[ ]	[ ]	[ ]	[ ]
I have been threatened or attacked because of my [ethnic/national] background.	[ ]	[ ]	[ ]	[ ]	[ ]

18   Multicultural Ideology

Please indicate the extent to which you agree or disagree with each of the following statements, using the following 5-point scale where 1 means "totally disagree" and 5 means "totally agree".

1.	We should recognize that cultural and racial diversity is a fundamental characteristic of [national] society.	1	2	3	4	5
2.	We should help ethnic and racial minorities preserve their cultural heritages in [country].	1	2	3	4	5
3.	It is best for [country] if all people forget their different ethnic and cultural backgrounds as soon as possible.	1	2	3	4	5
4.	A society that has a variety of ethnic and cultural groups is more able to tackle new problems as they occur.	1	2	3	4	5
5.	The unity of this country is weakened by people of different ethnic and cultural backgrounds sticking to their old ways.	1	2	3	4	5
6.	If people of different ethnic and cultural origins want to keep their own culture, they should keep it to themselves.	1	2	3	4	5
7.	A society that has a variety of ethnic or cultural groups has more problems with national unity than societies with one or two basic cultural groups.	1	2	3	4	5
8.	We should do more to learn about the customs and heritage of different ethnic and cultural groups in this country.	1	2	3	4	5

(cont.)

9.	Immigrant/ethnic parents must encourage their children to retain the culture and traditions of their homeland.	1	2	3	4	5
10.	People who come to [country/region] should change their behaviour to be more like us.	1	2	3	4	5

19   Tolerance/Prejudice

Please indicate the extent to which you agree or disagree with each of the following statements, using the following 5-point scale, where 1 means "totally disagree" and 5 means "totally agree".

1.	It is a bad idea for people of different races/ethnicities to marry one another.	1	2	3	4	5
2.	Immigrants/ethnics living here should not push themselves where they are not wanted.	1	2	3	4	5
3.	If employers only want to hire certain groups of people, that's their business.	1	2	3	4	5
4.	It makes me angry when I hear immigrants/ethnics demanding the same rights as [national] citizens.	1	2	3	4	5
5.	Immigrants/ethnics should have as much say about the future of [country] as people who were born and raised here.	1	2	3	4	5
6.	It is good to have people from different ethnic and racial groups living in the same country.	1	2	3	4	5
7.	We should promote equality among all groups, regardless of racial or ethnic origin.	1	2	3	4	5
8.	Some people are just inferior to others.	1	2	3	4	5
9.	To get ahead in life, it is sometimes necessary to step on others.	1	2	3	4	5
10.	If people were treated more equally, we would have fewer problems in this country.	2	2	3	4	5
11.	It is important that we treat other countries as equals.	1	2	3	4	5

20   Attitudes Towards Immigration

A   Perceived Consequences of Immigration

Please indicate the extent to which you agree or disagree with each of the following statements, using the following 5-point scale, where 1 means "totally disagree" and 5 means "totally agree".

1.	[National/regional] children growing up surrounded by people of different ethnic backgrounds will be left without a solid cultural base.	1	2	3	4	5
2.	I feel secure when I am with people of different ethnic backgrounds.	1	2	3	4	5
3.	Immigration tends to threaten [national/regional] culture.	1	2	3	4	5
4.	With more immigration [national/regional] people would lose their identity.	1	2	3	4	5
5.	If more immigrants come to [country/region], there would be more unemployment.	1	2	3	4	5
6.	We will all benefit from the increased economic activity created by immigrants.	1	2	3	4	5
7.	Immigrants take jobs away from other [national/regional] people.	1	2	3	4	5
8.	The presence of immigrants will not make wages lower.	1	2	3	4	5
9.	There is no reason to think that our country is falling apart because of having a variety of ethnocultural groups.	1	2	3	4	5
10.	Immigration increases the level of crime in [country/region].	1	2	3	4	5
11.	Immigration increases social unrest here.	1	2	3	4	5

B   Number of Immigrants

For the next statement, please use a scale where 1 means "too small", 5 means "too large" and 3 means "about right". You can use any number between 1 and 5.

I think that [country/region]'s current population is:	1	2	3	4	5

For the next statement, please use a scale where 1 means "smaller" and 5 means "larger".

In future, I would like to see [country/region] have a ___ population:	1	2	3	4	5

For the next statement, please use a scale where 1 means "strongly disagree" and 5 means "strongly agree".

Overall, there is too much immigration in [country/region]:	1	2	3	4	5

21   Attitudes Towards Ethnocultural (Dominant and Nondominant) Groups

Now I would like to find out about your attitudes towards several social groups. I am going to ask you to use a scale like a thermometer to express your attitude. This attitude thermometer has numbers from 0 degrees to 100 degrees. Here's how it works. If you have a favourable attitude towards members of a group, you would give the group a score somewhere between 50° and 100°, depending on how favourable your evaluation is of that group. On the other hand, if you have an unfavourable attitude towards members of a group, you would give them a score somewhere between 0° and 50°, depending on how unfavourable your evaluation is of that group. The labels provided will help you to locate your ratings on the thermometer. However, you are not restricted to the numbers indicated – feel free to use any number between 0° and 100°.

The social groups I would like you to rate are people from various ethno-cultural origins, who are now living in [country/region]

FAVOURABLE	100°	Extremely favourable
	90°	
	80°	
	70°	
	60°	
	50°	Neither favourable nor unfavourable
	40°	
	30°	
	20°	
	10°	
UNFAVOURABLE	0°	Extremely unfavourable

Please provide a number between 0° and 100° to indicate your attitude towards:

	Degrees
Insert up to 10 groups, starting with own group, national/regional/ethnic, others . . .	_____
	_____
	_____
	_____
	_____
	_____
	_____
	_____

22   Self Esteem

How do the following statements apply to how you think about yourself and your life?

		Strongly disagree	Somewhat disagree	Not sure/ neutral	Somewhat agree	Strongly agree
1.	On the whole, I am satisfied with myself.	[ ]	[ ]	[ ]	[ ]	[ ]
2.	At times I think I am no good at all.	[ ]	[ ]	[ ]	[ ]	[ ]
3.	I feel that I have a number of good qualities.	[ ]	[ ]	[ ]	[ ]	[ ]
4.	I am able to do things as well as most other people.	[ ]	[ ]	[ ]	[ ]	[ ]
5.	I feel I have not much to be proud of.	[ ]	[ ]	[ ]	[ ]	[ ]
6.	I certainly feel useless at times.	[ ]	[ ]	[ ]	[ ]	[ ]
7.	I feel that I am a person of worth, at least on an equal plane with others.	[ ]	[ ]	[ ]	[ ]	[ ]
8.	I wish I could have more respect for myself.	[ ]	[ ]	[ ]	[ ]	[ ]
9.	All in all, I am inclined to feel that I am a failure.	[ ]	[ ]	[ ]	[ ]	[ ]
10.	I take a positive attitude to myself.	[ ]	[ ]	[ ]	[ ]	[ ]

23   Life Satisfaction

How do the following statements apply to how you think about yourself and your life?

	Strongly disagree	Somewhat disagree	Not sure/ neutral	Somewhat agree	Strongly agree
1. In most ways my life is close to my ideal.	[ ]	[ ]	[ ]	[ ]	[ ]
2. The conditions of my life are excellent.	[ ]	[ ]	[ ]	[ ]	[ ]
3. I am satisfied with my life.	[ ]	[ ]	[ ]	[ ]	[ ]
4. So far I have got the important things I want in life.	[ ]	[ ]	[ ]	[ ]	[ ]
5. If I could live my life over, I would change almost nothing.	[ ]	[ ]	[ ]	[ ]	[ ]

24   Psychological Problems

How often do you experience the following?

	Never	Rarely	Sometimes	Frequently	All the time
1. I feel tired.	[ ]	[ ]	[ ]	[ ]	[ ]
2. I feel sick in the stomach.	[ ]	[ ]	[ ]	[ ]	[ ]
3. I feel dizzy and faint.	[ ]	[ ]	[ ]	[ ]	[ ]
4. I feel short of breath even when not exerting myself.	[ ]	[ ]	[ ]	[ ]	[ ]
5. I feel weak all over.	[ ]	[ ]	[ ]	[ ]	[ ]
6. I feel tense or keyed up.	[ ]	[ ]	[ ]	[ ]	[ ]
7. I feel nervous and shaky inside.	[ ]	[ ]	[ ]	[ ]	[ ]
8. I feel restless.	[ ]	[ ]	[ ]	[ ]	[ ]
9. I feel annoyed or irritated.	[ ]	[ ]	[ ]	[ ]	[ ]
10. I am worried about something bad happening to me.	[ ]	[ ]	[ ]	[ ]	[ ]
11. I feel unhappy and sad.	[ ]	[ ]	[ ]	[ ]	[ ]
12. My thoughts seem to be mixed up.	[ ]	[ ]	[ ]	[ ]	[ ]
13. I worry a lot of the time.	[ ]	[ ]	[ ]	[ ]	[ ]

(*cont.*)

		Never	Rarely	Sometimes	Frequently	All the time
14.	I feel lonely even with other people.	[ ]	[ ]	[ ]	[ ]	[ ]
15.	I lose interest and pleasure in things which I usually enjoy.	[ ]	[ ]	[ ]	[ ]	[ ]

25   Sociocultural Competence

Please indicate how much difficulty you experience living here in ___ (country/region) in each of these areas.

Use the following 1 to 5 scale.

1 = no difficulty
2 = slight difficulty
3 = moderate difficulty
4 = great difficulty
5 = extreme difficulty

1.	Making friends	1	2	3	4	5
2.	Finding food that you enjoy	1	2	3	4	5
3.	Following rules and regulations	1	2	3	4	5
4.	Dealing with people in authority	1	2	3	4	5
5.	Using the transport system	1	2	3	4	5
6.	Dealing with bureaucracy	1	2	3	4	5
7.	Making yourself understood	1	2	3	4	5
8.	Going shopping	1	2	3	4	5
9.	Understanding jokes and humour	1	2	3	4	5
10.	Obtaining accommodation	1	2	3	4	5
11.	Going to social gatherings	1	2	3	4	5
12.	Communicating with people of a different ethnic group	1	2	3	4	5
13.	Understanding ethnic or cultural differences	1	2	3	4	5
14.	Worshipping	1	2	3	4	5
15.	Relating to members of the opposite sex	1	2	3	4	5
16.	Finding your way around	1	2	3	4	5
17.	Talking about yourself with others	1	2	3	4	5
18.	Dealing with the climate	1	2	3	4	5
19.	Family relationships	1	2	3	4	5
20.	The pace of life	1	2	3	4	5

26 Social Desirability Scale

Read each statement, and circle the number that best describes you, where 1 means "not true" and 5 means "very true" about you.

1.	I sometimes tell lies if I have to.	1	2	3	4	5
2.	I never cover up my mistakes.	1	2	3	4	5
3.	There have been occasions when I have taken advantage of someone.	1	2	3	4	5
4.	I never swear.	1	2	3	4	5
5.	I always obey laws, even if I'm unlikely to get caught.	1	2	3	4	5
6.	I have said something bad about a friend behind his or her back.	1	2	3	4	5
7.	When I hear people talking privately, I avoid listening.	1	2	3	4	5
8.	When I was young, I sometimes stole things.	1	2	3	4	5
9.	I have never dropped litter on the street.	1	2	3	4	5
10.	I have done things that I don't tell other people about.	1	2	3	4	5
11.	I never take things that don't belong to me.	1	2	3	4	5
12.	I don't gossip about other people's business.	1	2	3	4	5

Author Index

Abbasov, A., 64
Aberson, C. L., 118
Abs, H. J., 173
Abu-Rayya, H., 141, 347
Adam, Z., 170
Adamczyk, A., 190
Alden, L., 16
Alesina, A., 3, 4
Allison, R., 107
Allport, G. W., 26, 52, 141, 205, 227, 253, 314
Ambrosini M., 212
Amoyaw, B., 354, 365
Anagnostaki, L., 191
Andrich, D., 174
Andriessen, I., 170, 182
Ang, I., 348
Annis, R., vi, xii, xv, 353, 354, 364, 365
Apine, I., 60
Arbuckle, J. L., 37, 65
Arends-Tóth, J., 223
Armenta, B. E., 215, 224
Arnaud, D., 3
Arnold, L., 118
Asbrock, F., 148, 149, 161
Asendorpf, J., 191, 224
Ata, A., 337
Atie, R., 341
Australian Bureau of Statistics, 334
Auswärtiges Amt, 146
Aydogan, A. F., 341

Badurashvili, I., 36
Bano, S., vi, xii, xv, 291, 296, 306
Barlow, F. K., 117, 338
Barth, F., 125
Bastian, B., 337
Baumeister, R., 158
Baysu, 170, 182
Belozerov, V. S., 42
Benet-Martínez, V., 182, 227, 311
Ben-Shalom, U., 16

Ben-Yehoyada, N., 217
Bergman, L. R., 221
Berno, T., 356, 371
Berry, J. W., i, iii, v, vi, xii, xvi, xxx, xxxiii, 1, 2, 3, 7, 8, 9, 11, 13, 14, 15, 16, 17, 19, 20, 22, 23, 24, 25, 26, 27, 28, 38, 50, 51, 52, 63, 75, 85, 96, 111, 121, 131, 132, 142, 147, 148, 149, 160, 171, 173, 182, 192, 205, 206, 211, 214, 215, 216, 223, 224, 227, 233, 254, 256, 257, 264, 293, 307, 312, 313, 328, 330, 336, 338, 341, 347, 353, 354, 355, 362, 370, 371, 375, 385
Besevegis, E., 190
Beshiri, R., 365
Bezzina, F., 233, 243
Bilodeau, A., 337
Birman, D., 169, 170, 182
Bizman, A., 109
Bizumic, B., 110
Bjertnæs. M. K., 126
Bloom, S., 63
Bobo, L. D., 51
Boehnke, K., 147
Boekarts, M., 183
Boen, F., 131
Bollen, K. A., 65
Bolzmann, C., 168
Bond, M. H., xviii, 311
Borgmann, C. H., 149
Bornstein, M. H., 10
Borrie, D., 385
Böttinger, H., 147
Bottura, B., 211
Boucher, H., 292
Bourhis, R. Y., 18, 20, 53, 85, 96, 108, 111, 121, 192, 206, 263, 275
Bozatzis, N., 191
Brand, E., 348
Branscombe, N., 25, 27, 371
Breugelsmans, S. M., 7
Brewer, M. B., 141
Brochmann, G., 126

407

Subject Index

Made in the USA
Middletown, DE
13 February 2022

61058907R00255